葡萄酒导购

WINE BUYING GUIDE

富隆葡萄酒文化中心　编著
Aussino Wine Education & Publication Centre

廣東省出版集團
广东科技出版社
·广　州·

图书在版编目（CIP）数据

葡萄酒导购 / 富隆葡萄酒文化中心编著. —广州：广东科技出版社，2011. 1
ISBN 978-7-5359-5451-0

Ⅰ. ①葡… Ⅱ. ①富… Ⅲ. ①葡萄酒—基本知识 Ⅳ. ①TS262. 6

中国版本图书馆CIP数据核字（2011）第000880号

策划编辑：区碧茹
责任编辑：杨柳青 曾燕璇 林雁
装帧设计：温玉芳 司徒碧琼
责任校对：蒋鸣亚 罗美玲 杨崚松 陈杰锋 陈静 陈素华 吴丽霞 黄慧怡
责任印制：严建伟
出版发行：广东科技出版社
（广州市环市东路水荫路11号 邮编：510075）
E-mail: gdkjzbb@21cn.com
http: //www.gdstp.com.cn
经　　销：广东省出版集团图书发行有限公司
印　　刷：广州市东扬彩色印刷有限公司
（广州市天河区棠东广棠西路12号 邮编：510665）
规　　格：787mm×1 092mm 1/16 印张22.5 字数450千
版　　次：2011年1月第1版
2011年1月第1次印刷
印　　数：1～36 000册
定　　价：88.00元

序

Preface

本书的创作灵感来源于富隆酒业的总裁沈宇辉先生。不久以前，一直以创新观念引领中国葡萄酒教育的沈总提出了要做一本关于葡萄酒购买指南的设想，利用富隆酒业本身拥有的专业团队和优势，把葡萄酒的文化知识融入每一款在中国市场上销售的葡萄酒中。

在葡萄酒教育正方兴未艾的中国市场，越来越多的进口葡萄酒呈现在消费者面前。面对琳琅满目的酒品，花花绿绿的酒标、各式各样的广告，如何快速、准确地找到自己需要的那瓶葡萄酒，消费者们需要专业的指引。

在编写本书之前，我们几乎参考了市场上所有的同类书籍，“知己知彼，百战百胜”，要从书海中脱颖而出就必须要给读者选择本书的充分理由。总结之后，我们认为本书的主要特色有：

{产品丰富} 本书共收录了近600款在中国市场有售的国际精品葡萄酒。种类涵盖红葡萄酒、白葡萄酒、起泡葡萄酒、波特酒和干邑等加烈葡萄酒，跨越12个优质葡萄酒出产国，产品价格有高、中、低档，充分满足各地区不同的口感，各种购买预算的需求。

{描述专业} 所有文字的编写来自富隆葡萄酒文化中心——法国波尔多葡萄酒学院的官方授权培训机构。这是一支拥有丰富从业经验的本土专业团队，对酒品的描述和建议均非常统一、专业和准确，而且所有的观点角度从中国人出发，糅合了中西方的饮食文化，更贴近消费者的口感。

{实用性强} 除了开篇的葡萄酒基础入门介绍，还有快捷简便的选酒贴士。每个国家的葡萄酒介绍前都有产区、葡萄品种和法律分级的详细介绍，帮助读者了解每个国家葡萄酒的主要特征。每款葡萄酒均列明所属产区、口感特点、价格范围、适饮温度、适饮场合和建议配餐等极具实用性的信息，帮助读者迅速了解酒品并引导他们正确享用每一款葡萄酒。

{中英双语} 书中的酒品描述特别增加了英文描述部分，方便国内外人士阅读相关的信息和指引。

{指引清晰} 本书的目标读者是那些想从市场上挑选到称心如意酒款的喜爱葡萄酒人士。因此，在附录部分我们列出了能买到书上酒品的230多家全国店铺，为国内消费者提供最清晰便捷的购买指引。

自2006年以来，由富隆文化中心编写的书籍已成为了专业和实用的代名词，所有富隆葡萄酒的系列丛书均在市场上热销。此书是我们的一个新的开端，也凝聚了所有编辑人员和设计人员的心血。在此特别感谢他们的默默付出，并真心地希望这本书能为消费者提供准确、专业和实在的引导，成为读者心目中最喜欢的葡萄酒书籍之一。

富隆葡萄酒文化中心总经理 蔡颖姬
2011年1月

阅读指南
Reading Guide

{价格指数} 本书在介绍葡萄酒时设立了价格指数作为参考，用星级表示如下：

¥	0～100元
¥¥	100～300元
¥¥¥	300～1 000元
¥¥¥¥	1 000～3 000元
¥¥¥¥¥	3 000元以上

{小图标} 为了方便阅读，本书在介绍葡萄酒时使用了小图标，图标示例如下：

- 法定等级/Appellation
- 适饮温度/Serving Temperature
- 适饮场合/Occasion
- 建议配餐/Food Matching
- 推荐理由/Favor

- **中英双语**：本书中对酒的中英双语描述分别针对中文读者和英文读者，两类读者对葡萄酒关注的特点不一样，因此两种语言的描述没有完全一致对应。
- **单词缩写**：Château在本书中采用缩写形式Ch.。
- **页脚说明**：由于法国波尔多的葡萄酒产区众多，两岸各村中名庄林立，本书关于法国波尔多葡萄酒的部分特别选取了知名酒庄最为集中的几条村庄加以介绍，并在各酒庄页脚注明其所在的村庄。

{译名对照表} 目前，国内暂无统一的葡萄品种译名，本书综合各葡萄品种的特点和读音，将常见的葡萄品种名称翻译如下：

酿造红葡萄酒的常用品种	酿造白葡萄酒的常用品种
巴比拉 Barbera	阿巴利纽 Albariño
嘉本纳弗朗 Cabernet Franc	阿内斯 Arneis
嘉本纳沙威浓 Cabernet Sauvignon	雪当利 Chardonnay
加文拿 Carmenère	白翠柠 Chenin Blanc
神索 Cinsault	富美宝 Fume Blanc
多姿桃 Dolcetto	福敏 Furmint
丹菲特 Dornfelder	琼瑶浆 Gewürztraminer
佳美 Gamay	银卓娅 Inzolia
歌海娜 Grenache	美莎丽 Marsanne
玛碧 Malbac	蜜丝佳桃(粉红) Moscato / Muscat
玛佐罗 Mazuelo	密思卡岱 Muscadelle
梅乐 Merlot	碧宝(粉红) Picpoul
梦特普西露 Montepulciano	白贝露 Pinot Blanc
慕合怀德 Mourvedre	灰贝露(粉红) Pinot Gris
纳比奥罗 Nebbiolo	宝雪歌 Prosecco
黑达沃拉 Nero d'Avola	威士莲 Riesling
小华帝 Petit Verdot	白沙威浓 Sauvignon Blanc
贝露曼尼雅 Pinot Meunier	诗故蕾葡 Scheurebe
贝露娃 Pinot Noir	沙美龙 Semillon
贝露特 Pinotage	扎比安奴 Trebbiano
丽福斯科 Refosco	华的龙 Verdelho
圣祖维斯 Sangiovese	维杜索 Verduzzo
穗乐仙 Shiraz / Syrah	维奥妮雅 Viognier
添帕尼优 Tempranillo	维奥娜 Viura
仙粉黛 Zinfandel	

Wine

目录

CONTENTS

第一章 葡萄酒知识
CHAPTER 1 WINE KNOWLEDGE

第二章 新世界葡萄酒
CHAPTER 2 NEW WORLD WINES

第三章 旧世界葡萄酒
CHAPTER 3 OLD WORLD WINES

注：由于智利和法国布根地产区经常出现一家酒庄跨越多个产区的情况，为了清晰地介绍这两个地区的酒款，本书将智利和法国布根地部分按酒庄品牌的顺序排列，其他部分则按产区排列。

MONOPOLE
1996
ROMANÉE-CONTI
Marcarini
BAROLO
WARRE'S
1985
VINTAGE
PORT
2000
HÉTSZŐLŐ
TOKAJI ASZÚ
GRAN RESERVA
1998

[认识葡萄酒，就像去学习一种世界性的语言，它能拉近人与人之间的距离，即使不喝酒的人也会对它的价值表示认同赞赏；认识葡萄酒，又像去解读一个人的一生——幼龄时的青涩羞赧，发展时的初露锋芒，成熟时的意气风发，衰老时的柔弱绵软——从而去感怀它不同时期的不同魅力。]

第一章 葡萄酒知识

CHAPTER 1 WINE KNOWLEDGE

葡萄酒分类

Wine Categories

进入葡萄酒的大千世界，我们会发现葡萄酒的品种复杂繁多，绝对不仅仅是我们日常所说的“红酒”那么简单。想要选购一瓶称心如意的葡萄酒，首先要了解一下，葡萄酒都有哪些类型，什么种类的葡萄酒会是你喜欢的。

按颜色分类

红葡萄酒　绝大部分由红葡萄酿制而成（也有少数红葡萄酒混入少量白葡萄酿制）。红葡萄酒的颜色主要来自于黑、红葡萄的果皮。

白葡萄酒　由白葡萄或红葡萄酿制而成。虽然原料中有白葡萄也有红葡萄，但红、白葡萄均需榨汁后再进行发酵，只有白葡萄在酿制过程中会进行低温浸皮，果皮里的色素没有释放到酒液中去，所以白葡萄酒不呈现红颜色，而是葡萄汁的原色。

玫瑰红葡萄酒（也称粉红葡萄酒）

玫瑰红葡萄酒一般是用红葡萄（如贝露娃Pinot Nior、仙粉黛Zinfandel）酿制而成。在发酵前经过短时间的浸皮，因此在酿制完成后有粉红色的色泽留下。

按酒液中糖分含量分类

干型　平常所说的干红、干白都是属于干型葡萄酒，酒中的糖分含量不超过4克/升。

半干型　介于干型和甜型之间，糖分的含量为4~12克/升，品尝时能辨别出微弱的甜味。

半甜型　甜型的葡萄酒可分为半甜型和特甜型，半甜型葡萄酒中一般糖分含量为12~45克/升。

甜型　糖分含量在45克/升以上的葡萄酒属于名副其实的甜型葡萄酒，许多年轻女性或者刚尝试葡萄酒的人偏爱甜型葡萄酒。冰酒、贵腐葡萄酒都属于甜型葡萄酒。

按酿造工艺分类

冰酒　起源于德国，早在1765年，德国下了一场大的早雪，加上天气冷得很早，雪变成了冰积在葡萄串上，酒农们以为该年的收成都全完了，结果到了11月，葡萄串还好好地挂在树上。因为晚了收割，葡萄比正常情况成熟了好多，糖分增高了。在寒冷的气候影响下，葡萄里的水分大部分结成了冰，而糖分却不容易结冰，所以榨汁后，葡萄汁的甜度很高，因此意外地酿出了举世闻名的冰酒。

贵腐葡萄酒　是用受到贵腐霉菌侵蚀的白葡萄酿成的。由于贵腐霉菌附着在成熟的葡萄上，吸取了葡萄颗粒里的水分，留下很浓的糖分和香味，就像葡萄干一样，用这样的葡萄酿成的酒糖分很高，而且有贵腐霉菌的“参与”，为酒液添加了一些神秘的香味。因为贵腐霉菌的生长受气候的制约，采摘时需按粒挑选，所以这种葡萄酒也变得十分珍贵。

静态酒　我们日常饮用的葡萄酒大部分是静态葡萄酒，也就是指在葡萄酒发酵的过程中，放走二氧化碳，从而得到静态的葡萄酒。

起泡酒　又称为气泡酒，是在酿制过程中保留了发酵时的二氧化碳，也称为汽酒。酒精含量在8%~14%，有红（极少）、白、粉红色3 种。旧世界的起泡酒一般是将不同品种、不同年份、不同产区的酒加以混合而成，目的是使酒的品质保持一定的水准，所以标签也没有标示年份与葡萄品种。除非遇到特别好的年份，才会全部使用当年的葡萄酿酒并在酒标上打上年份。新世界的起泡酒则显得比较简单，一般都会打上年份。

香槟　最著名的起泡酒产于法国香槟区，香槟区位于巴黎东北方约150千米处，是法国位置最北的葡萄园，独特的土壤结构和气候造就了葡萄成熟的得天独厚的条件。为保护香槟的美名，他们注册了香槟的商标。只有按法国法令规定、用香槟区的葡萄、用法定传统的工艺、在香槟区酿造的汽泡酒，才能称之为香槟。酒标上会打上Champagne的标记。如果有其中一个条件不符合，就只能称为Sparkling Wine（汽泡酒）。其他地方生产的起泡酒就算再好，也不能冠以“香槟”的桂冠。

加度酒　加强型葡萄酒是在发酵过程中加入酒精，终止酵母的运作，使其酒精含量提高到了15%~22%，同时也保留了较高的糖分。如西班牙的雪莉酒（Sherry）、葡萄牙的波特酒（Porto）。

雪莉酒　产于西班牙，用晒干的葡萄酿制，在酿造的过程中加入白兰地。在雪莉酒的酿造过程中，要将它装于橡木桶中，暴晒在艳阳之下，3个月后，收起来冷冻贮存。这种特殊的酿制方式，使雪莉酒有一种特殊的风味，因此不仅酒精度高，并且口味也偏甜。雪莉酒有两种不同的种类，一种是不甜的Fino雪莉酒，味道比较鲜美，另一种比较甜的Oloroso雪莉酒，味道比较浓郁。

波特酒　产于葡萄牙，虽然和雪莉酒一样属于加强型葡萄酒，但波特酒是在葡萄汁发酵的过程中便加入了酒精，葡萄汁还没来得及发酵完全便因为高温酒精的加入而停止了发酵，酒液中的糖分被保留了下来，所以波特酒也是甜的。

加味葡萄酒　是在葡萄酒里添加药草、香料等酿制而成的，最常见的是苦艾酒（Vermouth），它的做法是先把艾草浸在酒精里，再和葡萄酒混合而成。其他常见的还有奎宁酒（Quinine）和开胃酒（Aperitif）等等。几乎所有的加味葡萄酒都经过酒精强化，因此它们的酒精度比静态葡萄酒高。

如何选酒

How to Select Wine

挑选葡萄酒，可以从预算、口感、场合和用途等方面考虑。

按预算挑选葡萄酒

300元以下 可以选择阿根廷、智利、澳大利亚、南非等新世界国家的酒。因为新世界国家大多采用现代化的生产设备，生产成本较低，他们出产的葡萄酒可谓价廉物美，而用这个价格在旧世界国家葡萄酒寻找一款同样品质的酒可以说是“不可能的任务”。

300～600元 可以选一些新世界国家较有名气的品牌属下的中端产品，或少部分法国和意大利等旧世界国家一般品牌的葡萄酒。

600～1 000元 可以选择新世界国家名产区的名品牌的高端产品，而旧世界国家则可以选意大利、西班牙、葡萄牙等部分名产区较有名气的产品。法国波尔多部分列级酒庄和家族精品酒庄，布根地和香槟的中等酒庄及法国其他产区的名庄属下产品。

1 000元以下 这样的预算通常是特别的纪念日或者是送礼的用途，所以第一选择肯定是以产区的名气为先——法国波尔多先行，然后是其他国家的著名产区著名酒庄的旗舰产品。

按口感喜好挑选葡萄酒

果香浓郁、酒体丰满 一般初入门的饮家或是喝惯高度白酒、烈酒的人都会喜欢这类型的酒。来自新世界的多个国家所出产的酒都具有这样的特点。

酒质细腻优雅 某些喜欢清淡口感或资深的饮家会特别喜欢一些香气层次丰富但并不喷薄而出、酒体结构细腻而优雅的酒。一般这种类型的酒多产自旧世界国家。

甜美明快 初入门者或女性饮家特别偏爱口感甜美的酒。可以选择出产甜酒的著名国家如：德国、奥地利、加拿大等国家的甜型葡萄酒或冰酒，匈牙利的陶家宜或者是葡萄牙的波特酒。

按用途场合选择葡萄酒

送礼 一般都会选一些来自著名产区的酒，毕竟名气大的产区更能体现送礼人对收礼人的重视和尊敬。无论预算高低，法国酒是个不错的选择。

朋友聚会 如果买葡萄酒是为了朋友聚会或比较热闹场合饮用，建议选用新世界国家果香浓郁甜美的葡萄酒。除非是一帮酒迷的宁静约会，普通的朋友聚会重点在于气氛而非品酒，酒精可为聚会增添气氛，新世界的美酒完全可以独当一面。

烛光晚餐 与爱人约会或求爱、求婚场合一定需要一瓶来自旧世界国家的红葡萄酒或者是一瓶香槟。因为这些场合肯定是事前精心策划和准备的，在表达爱慕的同时，品尝丰富的美酒层次，静静感受她在不同时间散发的动人芳香，在微醺的状态下加速爱情的发展。

按产区或名气挑选葡萄酒

当我们对葡萄酒有了一定的了解之后，就可以直接找对应的产区或品牌了。因为某些产区会以盛产某些葡萄品种的酒而出名，如法国的香槟出产高品质的起泡酒，澳大利亚的巴罗莎谷盛产浓郁甜美的穗乐仙葡萄酒等。如果非常清楚一些著名的酿酒家族则更直接准确了，我们可以直接选取这些家族的出品，如拉菲罗富齐家族、JPM柏图斯家族、天鹏家族等等。大型的酿酒家族除了顶级的名酒以外，往往还会做副牌酒、三牌酒及一些中低价位的优质好酒。这些酒都是在名家的酿酒哲学下所做的，酒质肯定有保障。

其他方法

要挑选葡萄酒还有很多很多的方法，每个人都可以有自己的一套方法。比如说，人的性格跟喜欢的葡萄酒也大有关联。性格文静的人喜欢喝旧世界国家出品的酒，比较温柔细腻型的；性格开朗的人喜欢新世界国家出品的酒，它们热情奔放。某种程度上不同星座或属相的人都有不同的适饮葡萄酒相对应。

如何存酒

How to Store Wine

请记住，葡萄酒是有生命的。从被你带回家直到怦然开启的那一刻，葡萄酒一直在瓶中不断地发展和成熟。主人是否保存得当、细心呵护，会在很大程度上影响葡萄酒的风味和存放的年限。特别是对于未到适饮期的名贵葡萄酒，我们更应该把它好好安置，让它静静地安睡直至成熟再打开尝之。

开启前的保存：6大原则

温度恒定 适合的储酒温度在12℃左右。过高的温度会加剧葡萄酒内部的物理化学变化，而过低的温度则使必要的物理化学变化停滞。这个温度必须是恒定的，剧烈的温差变化会促使软木塞发生热胀冷缩的现象，在这个变化过程中会让空气和细菌进入瓶中，加速葡萄酒的氧化速度，使得葡萄酒迅速老化或酒质受损。

湿度适中 适当的湿度范围是在65%~75%。湿度过低，软木塞会发生收缩干裂现象，加速空气进入瓶中；湿度过高，软木塞容易受潮而发生腐败现象，使得葡萄酒出现大煞风景的坏木塞味道。

光线微弱 光线是葡萄酒陈年的天敌，很多带色的酒瓶都有防紫外线的功能，但是对于强光的照射是起不了保护作用的。如果葡萄酒持续处于强光之下，酒瓶周边的温度就会上升，这样就会使得其发展过快而迅速老化。白葡萄酒对于光线尤其敏感。因此，存放葡萄酒的理想条件应该是漆黑或灯光昏暗的地窖。

空气清新 无论是软木塞封装的葡萄酒还是拧盖的葡萄酒，都需要空气清新的环境来储存，因为葡萄酒在瓶中还是会不停和外界空气发生交换。如果周边空气污浊，气味难闻，这些气体和细菌难免会通过瓶口进入瓶中，使得葡萄酒近朱者赤，近墨者黑。保持良好的通风可以祛除异味。

安静稳定 葡萄酒是需要安睡的，振动和噪音都是必须避免的。只有在安静稳定的环境中，酒体才得到完好地发展。在任何物理振动中，葡萄酒内部的分子结构会发生急剧变化，使葡萄酒尝起来非常粗糙。

打横存放 对于采用木塞封装的葡萄酒，建议把酒瓶打横摆放。主要是保持酒液与软木塞的接触，保持着木塞的湿润，防止木塞干缩而感染细菌。

只要做到了上述的6大要求，你的葡萄酒就可以在一个它最喜欢的环境中安睡。只有在优良的储存环境下陈放的美酒才能发展出它全部的风韵和陈年潜力。如果是在适饮期打开，更能让名贵葡萄酒们充分绽放最美丽的一面。

开启后的保存：2个步骤

一瓶葡萄酒在打开后应尽量喝完，一般红葡萄酒在8小时内，白葡萄酒则在3小时内就要喝完。因为葡萄酒开瓶后和氧气接触，酒精会迅速地氧化成醋酸，结果是葡萄酒香味尽失，味道变得和醋一样酸。但确实无法在规定时间内喝完一瓶葡萄酒怎么办？

抽真空瓶塞

抽真空的瓶塞是利用机械的原理，把瓶子里的空气抽出来，使瓶子里面呈现真空状态，以防止葡萄酒氧化。借用抽真空瓶塞的帮助，葡萄酒可以多延长两天的保质期。但这个时间也是因不同的葡萄酒而异。因为一般酒里都含有少量的二氧化硫，起着消毒和抗氧化的作用，但越名贵的酒加入的二氧化硫数量越少，因此保鲜的能力越差。而普通的酒因为二氧化硫的含量高一点，保鲜能力就会比较好。一般按杯卖葡萄酒的餐厅或者酒吧，都是靠抽真空瓶塞来延长开瓶后葡萄酒的保鲜期。

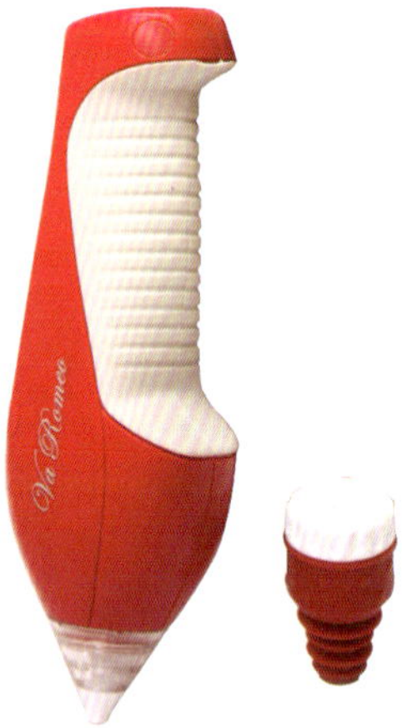

冰箱或恒温酒柜

抽真空后的葡萄酒可以直接放进冰箱或恒温酒柜进行保存，但切记要打竖存放，以减少氧化的面积。但是，无论是采用什么方法来保鲜，隔夜葡萄酒的风味是无法与新鲜葡萄酒相提并论的。所以，我们建议大家还是尽量把一瓶葡萄酒一次性喝完，这样才是最完美的品酒方式。

存酒的地方

恒温酒柜

如果家里有超过10瓶的藏酒，并且过了一年都没舍得喝完，那么该为它们找一个恒温酒柜了。恒温酒柜是按葡萄酒的存放温度设计的，一般的恒温酒柜有两个温区，最上面是高温区，最高可达22℃，最低是12℃；最下面是低温区，最低是5℃，最高是12℃。恒温酒柜的原理和冰箱类似，不过在它顶部加了一个发热的机器，把温度控制在10~18℃，这是适合葡萄酒存放的专业温度。最上层适合放名贵的红葡萄酒，最下层适合放白葡萄酒和汽酒。

市面上在售的恒温酒柜，全进口的价格大概在3万元或以上，而采用进口零件组装的酒柜则相对便宜好多，可存放150瓶酒的酒柜才不到1万元。进口的酒柜相对来说温控精确、噪音小、工艺精细。不过从性价比来说，国内组装的酒柜更优胜一点。消费者可根据自己的预算寻找一些有保障的供应商选购。

私人酒窖 对于热衷于收藏葡萄酒的朋友来说，他们更喜欢在家中打造私人酒窖。如果要做私人酒窖的话，需要注意以下几点：

（1）选址：首先应该参照上文所提及的“存酒6大原则”，在你的家中寻找能符合上述要求的地方。适合改造成私家酒窖的地方有地下室、车库、阁楼（但要避免阳光直射）、大橱柜、储藏室或者餐具室。在上述地方选择一个出入最少但是方便进出的地方作为改造对象，这样招待朋友在家中品酒的时候，你可以畅通无阻地进出酒窖。

（2）装备：私人酒窖应该有灯光、温控、加湿器、酒架这4种装备。灯光不宜强烈，只在进出酒窖的时候方便查看酒而使用；空调可以起到温控的作用，甚至还有加湿功能，还可以购买一个加湿器，使酒窖的空气达到良好的湿度；选择自己喜好的质地、形状、高矮的酒架，可以因地制宜地在家中制作，也可以从市面上购买，价格从500元到上万元不等。

（3）分类：所拥有的葡萄酒可根据葡萄品种、产区、价格、年份等进行分类摆放，方便自己取放寻找。

新的私人酒窖就这样大功告成了，不过请记住最好先使用各种措施消除因装修施工带来的不良气体。等到通风一段时间之后，才可以正式投入使用。

专业酒窖 一些信誉良好的大型专业酒窖会为熟客提供存酒的服务，把美酒托付给专业的人士来照料，这是最快捷方便的方法了。

葡萄酒的陈年潜力

葡萄酒的陈年潜力基本上可以与它的售价画上等号，并非所有的葡萄酒都适合长期存放，只有名贵的葡萄酒才有长年存放的必要。对于短期存放的葡萄酒而言，放到冰箱里是一个更人性化的选择。但如果自己开始经常喝葡萄酒或有一批名贵葡萄酒，最好还是给它们一个更安逸的家吧。酒柜和酒窖，就好比解困房和别墅，大家可以量力而为。

如何品酒

How to Taste Wine

葡萄酒是独具特色的酒精饮品，它蕴含着丰富的历史文化及酿酒人的心血。一款优质的葡萄酒可以比喻为一个独一无二的艺术品。因此，对于葡萄酒来说，无论是在保存或饮用方面都非常讲究。葡萄酒不是可口可乐，不是随便一口吞下去就能领悟到其中的精髓。我们需要在引导下慢慢地学习，以一种崇敬和谦逊的心态去了解它。

开 酒

开酒温度

和储存葡萄酒一样，打开葡萄酒之前先要了解室内的温度是否达标。

不同类型的葡萄酒，适合饮用的温度也不一样。单宁越强、口味越浓的酒，适饮的温度可以相对高一点，而口味清淡的，或者是甜度较高的酒则需要较低的温度。假如温度过高，酒精味会变重，并可能使香味发生不良反应；温度过低，则酒的香味会被锁紧在酒里无法释放，亦影响到酒的口感。

我们常听到某款酒最适合“在室温下饮用”，千万别以为室温就是你当下室内的温度。其实室温是指原产地的温度，而不是中国的室温。以法国葡萄酒而言，“室温”通常是指16~18℃。

各种葡萄酒的一般适饮温度可见下表：

葡萄酒种类	适饮温度
名贵干红酒	18~20℃
中价位干红酒、高品质干白酒	14~17℃
入门级干红酒、中价位干白酒	10~14℃
入门级干型白葡萄酒、玫瑰红酒	7~10℃
普通起泡酒、香槟、半干型白葡萄酒	7~8℃
甜白葡萄酒	4~6℃

开酒环境

开启葡萄酒需要在自然光下进行。只有在充足的自然光下，我们开启葡萄酒后才能在杯中观察到酒的颜色和光泽，便于我们对酒龄、品种等的判断。

品酒必须静静地进行，尤其是品尝优雅的高级葡萄酒，决不能在喧闹嘈杂的夜场、闹市中去进行，否则便无法品尝到它真正的气息。当然，听着轻音乐的环境，更能让品酒者心旷神怡。

不能在有异味或者气味浓重的地方开启葡萄酒，也不能搽着浓味香水，或者边抽烟（除雪茄外）边喝酒，因为这些气息都会影响对葡萄酒气味的判断。在开启葡萄酒的时候，要选择一个空气清新、通风良好的地方去进行。

开酒时机

葡萄酒跟人一样会经历生长、成熟和衰老等阶段。进入衰老期的葡萄酒并不等于变质不能喝，只是这酒已经失去了原有的风采，变成平庸的液体，没有人愿意将它倒进口里了。所以，要喝到一瓶花样年华的美酒，开酒的时机非常重要。

一般的低价餐酒适合在出厂后2~3年内饮用，稍微好一些的葡萄酒的适饮期大概是5~10年，上好的葡萄酒需要储藏8~10年才能有成熟的魅力。而大部分的白葡萄酒、汽酒、玫瑰红酒因为单宁含量少，因此越新鲜饮用越好。

我们经常会碰到有些人要喝一些未到适饮期的名贵葡萄酒的情况，这时就需要醒酒，让酒液迅速氧化。因为葡萄酒根本没有发育成熟，所以只能提前把它“弄醒”，以尽量窥视它的美态。但醒酒时间要根据不同的酒庄不同的年份状况而决定，基本上年份越好，酒的状态越“年轻”，醒酒的时间则越长，反之则越短。如果时间充裕的话，也有一些人喜欢直接把酒倒在酒杯中慢品，感受不同时间散发的香气，这样的感觉更妙一些。

开酒技巧

· 开启软木塞葡萄酒

第一，先用开瓶器的小刀沿着瓶口的圆圈状突出部位，切开封瓶口的胶帽，注意是手转而不是瓶转，否则容易泛起酒渣。

第二，用螺丝钻尖端插入软木塞的正中心，然后直立螺旋钻，顺时针方向缓缓旋转钻入软木塞中，直到留存一环在木塞上方，否则容易钻穿塞子。

第三，将第一个活动关节扣住瓶口，用左手紧紧握住，再用右手将手把直直地提起来。

第四，在木塞拔出一半的时候，再用第二个活动关节扣住瓶口，重复之前的动作，直到完全拔出木塞。

· 开启钵酒和拧盖葡萄酒

除了年份钵酒是用软木塞封瓶之外，其他钵酒都是使用威士忌的盖子，只需用小刀去除锡箔，用手轻轻一拧瓶盖便可以打开，非常方便。

拧盖的葡萄酒更为简单，只需要旋开即可，比软木塞的葡萄酒更省时、省力。

· 开启汽酒

汽酒瓶中的气压较大，如香槟瓶子里就有6个气压，是外面气压的两倍，瓶塞飞出来的时速是200千米/时，在香槟区每年都有人因飞出的瓶塞而受伤，因此开汽酒的时候需要特别小心。

（1）左手握住瓶颈，右手将瓶口的锡纸揭开，将铁丝网套锁松开的同时，左手的拇指紧按住瓶帽。

（2）左手的拇指保持按住瓶帽，食指握住木塞边缘部分，确保你的手握住整个木塞部分。右手握住瓶身，慢慢转动，关键在于转动的是瓶身，而非瓶塞，这个过程要花力气，但一定要令脸部肌肉放松，呈微笑状。

（3）当瓶塞呼之欲出之时，左手迅速揭开它，发出的声音不是响亮的亲吻声，而且一丝轻轻的叹息声，瓶口飘出一缕淡淡的轻雾，仿佛一个公主刚刚从瓶口经过。此时，便已功成名就！

品酒

当葡萄酒伴随着悦耳的声音倾入你的杯中时，你终于可以开始品味了。怎样才能充分品味出一杯美酒的滋味呢？

观色 色、香、味是葡萄酒的3大要素，一杯酒，首先从观色开始。

举起酒杯并将之倾斜45°，在自然光的环境下以白色背景作酒杯的映衬，观察酒的颜色。一般可在酒杯后放一张白纸，为了方便观色，专业的品酒桌会选择白色大理石当桌面。

由于葡萄酒内的黄色素和微量单宁逐渐氧化的关系，酒色会随酒龄变化而改变。通过观色能初步判定葡萄酒成熟度/酒龄的作用。红葡萄酒随着酒龄的增加，酒色一般从紫色到紫红色、棕红色、褐色、淡褐色逐渐转淡；白葡萄酒会随着酒龄的增加从浅绿色、黄色、金黄色、深黄、金色、琥珀色逐渐加深。

摇杯 为了让酒液在杯中加速氧化以散发出更多的香气，我们需摇晃酒杯以增加酒液与空气的接触面积。

顺时针或逆时针晃动酒杯，使酒在杯中打旋。初学者通常总是转动手腕令酒液只能在杯中左右摆动而不是打旋，此时可以将酒杯放在桌子上，以食指和中指夹住杯子并压着杯座，在桌子上转动，这种摇法可以很简易地稳住酒杯的重心，不易于把酒摇出杯子。

白葡萄酒无需剧烈摇动，以避免酒的香气过分散失；汽酒和香槟更不需摇杯，只要凝神倾听她们独有的“私语”即可。

挂杯 摇杯后可以观察“挂杯”的情况。所谓挂杯，就是摇杯停止后葡萄酒从杯壁流下来的酒柱。德国人又把挂杯称为“教堂的窗口”。通过挂杯的持久度，我们可以粗略判断该酒的酒精度和含糖度的高低。酒精度越高的酒，挂杯越粗，流下来的时间越慢；同时也说明此酒的酒体比较丰厚，反之则是酒精度较低、酒体较轻，但挂杯与酒质好坏无直接联系。

闻香 摇杯后，把鼻子伸到杯口并用力吸气。

闻香时首先要判断酒的品质是否正常，确保没有二氧化硫味、烂木塞味或其他难闻的异味。

随后就可以运用你的嗅觉和联想去发掘葡萄酒散发出的美妙香气了。尝试去分辨一下，并联想你所熟知的香味，比如草莓、苹果、奶油、蜂蜜等等。这种品鉴过程是仁者见仁、智者见智的，不必担心你闻错了。假如一次不能确定，就重复摇杯和吸气的步骤。

入口 以上的欣赏过程结束后，举杯尝一口葡萄酒，分量大致在能够漱口的程度，让酒同你口腔与舌头的不同味觉感应区域充分接触，去感受酒的酸、甜、苦、咸、涩、平衡、厚薄等感觉。人的甜味味蕾在舌尖，咸味味蕾在舌缘，酸味味蕾在舌头后缘两侧，苦味味蕾则在舌根。

不胜酒力者也请不要只浅抿一口，因为当酒的分量不够浸润整个舌头时，是无法充分感受酒的香味的。也不要急于咽下，因为口腔中的酒香会进入你的鼻腔，味觉和嗅觉的综合感觉才是判断酒的依据。

当酒在口腔中时，我们可以注意以下几个方面的口感：

是否平衡：品味葡萄酒大致可以区分为4个方向，酸度、甜度、酒精度与单宁。品味时可以感受一下葡萄酒在这4个方向中哪一个最为突出，整体是否平均。

酒体是否饱满：当酒液从舌尖抵达喉咙，在味蕾上是否留下了持久浓稠的感受。假如感受转瞬即逝，则表明酒体很轻，比较淡薄；假如感受持久，口感久久徘徊不去，留下明显的质感，则表明酒体饱满厚重。

单宁质感：单宁细腻时，酒在口中的感受犹如天鹅绒摩擦着味蕾，或者像丝巾一般柔滑。粗糙的单宁则如砂纸一般摩擦着口腔，往往令人感觉生涩干苦。

回味 喝过葡萄酒残留在口腔中的味道，我们也称之为余味。细细品味葡萄酒在口中和喉咙间停留时间的长短——它也是评判一款葡萄酒好坏的其中一个因素。看其余味散发的香气，并感受其持久度。

评酒

任何专业酒商和业余爱好者都不可能喝遍所有葡萄酒，任何新年份的酒是好是坏，在亲自品尝以前都只能猜测，于是业界就诞生了酒评家这个行业。这些酒评家的工作就是替葡萄酒爱好者判断酒的好坏。

然而，每个人都有自己的口味喜好，酒评家中意的口味未必就能代表我们的喜好，反之亦然。所以对于每一款酒，只有亲自尝过才是检验其品质的唯一真理。只要你喜欢，就是好酒，不必对酒评家的评论太过在意。

如何配餐

Food Matching

餐酒搭配是个永恒的话题。首要原则是希望能产生相得益彰的效果，务求两者和谐——既不要令酒的味道过重盖过食物，也不要使食物的味道太突出令酒失去了风情，无论是哪一方想占支配地位，都是不理想的搭配。

理想的搭配可简单地归纳为“平行式”和“抗衡式”两种，即根据餐与酒的味道相似或者相抗进行搭配。掌握了这两个要诀，餐跟酒的配对就不难掌握。当然了，掌握着最终的“话语权”是个人的味蕾，多做尝试才是硬道理。

平行式

即味道相接近的搭配。清淡型的菜肴配清淡型葡萄酒，浓烈型的菜肴配单宁较强、酒体丰满的葡萄酒。另外，“白肉配白酒，红肉配红酒”是每一个初涉葡萄酒之人都会接触到的金科玉律，我们先来理清这两个概念：

“白肉配白酒”受到追捧，是由于白酒中的酸可增加口感的清爽，并有助于去除海鲜的腥味。“红肉配红酒”得到大家的认可，是因为红酒含有的单宁与肉中的蛋白质会发生化学作用，可使肉质更加细嫩和甜美。

需要注意的是，中餐食物的烹调方式和配料会改变食材原本的个性，因此左右了葡萄酒的搭配。例如加入了酱料烧烤的海鲜或者带辣味的白肉和穗乐仙更合适的搭配，由此可见，搭配什么样的葡萄酒，更取决于食物烹煮之后的味道而并非食材原本的味道。

抗衡式

即味道相对抗的搭配。可以利用一些味道的互相抗衡来进行菜肴的搭配。咸的菜式要用酒体较轻的红葡萄酒，避免高单宁葡萄酒；辣的菜式要用带辛辣香味的红葡萄酒或甜白葡萄酒；咖喱菜式可以搭配清淡芬芳的白葡萄酒。

根据食物味道和烹饪方式来搭配葡萄酒，以下几个小窍门可作参考：

偏酸的菜肴	配比食物酸度更高的葡萄酒
偏甜的菜肴	配比食物更甜的葡萄酒
偏咸的菜肴	配轻身餐酒，避免高单宁葡萄酒
偏辣的菜肴	配辛辣或者甜味葡萄酒

新世界葡萄酒，来自新发现的大陆与蓝天之间。她们是清新宜人、活力四射的摩登娇娃。不断探索的现代科技使葡萄与美酒风格时时出现新的变化，各种措施保证酒的品质始终恒久如一，产业化生产令葡萄酒能够被更多的人享用——灵魂中充满自由的开拓精神，新世界的美酒属于每一个人。

第二章 新世界葡萄酒
CHAPTER 2 NEW WORLD WINES

澳大利亚
AUSTRALIA

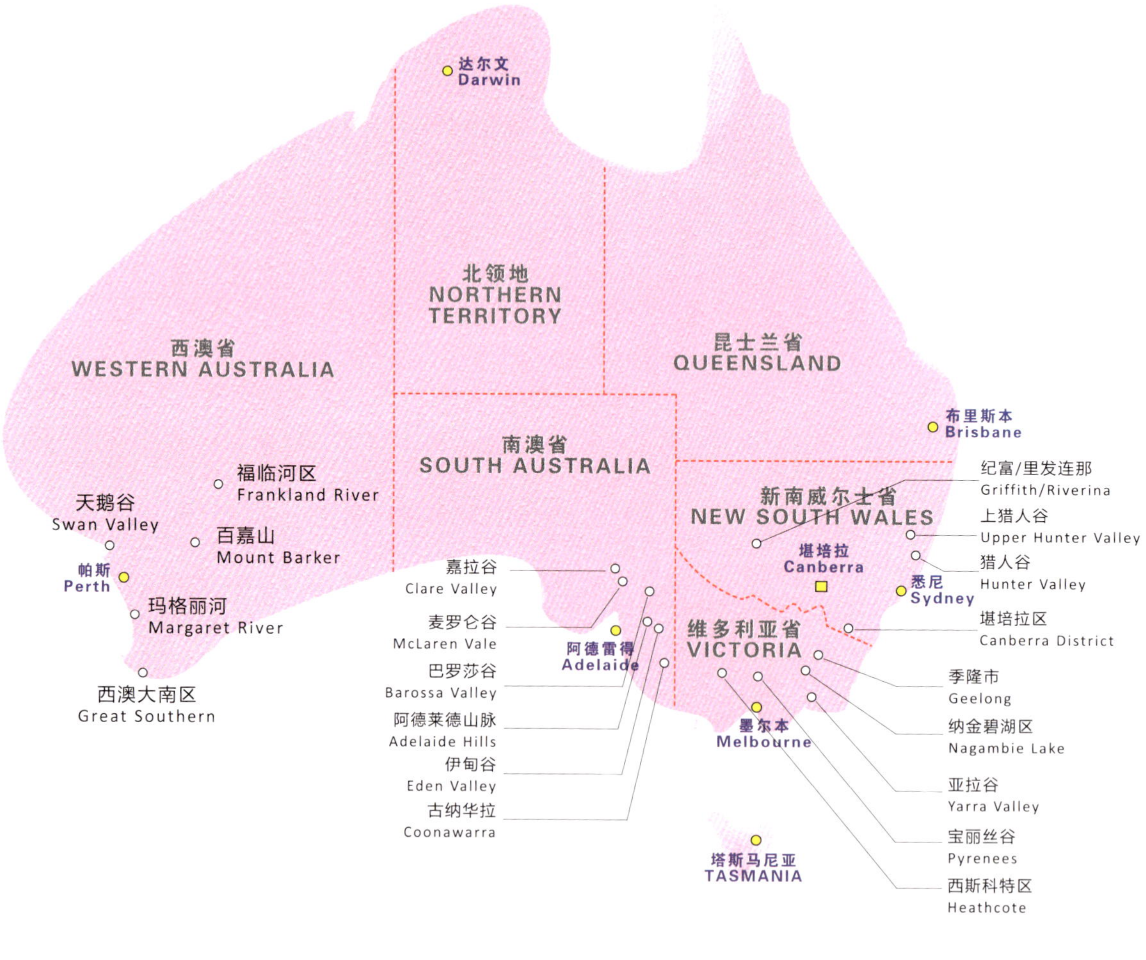

澳大利亚葡萄酒产区示意图

澳大利亚 作为葡萄酒的产地，有着得天独厚的条件。阳光充足，气候优良且稳定，土地矿物质丰富，且地广人稀，环境保留了较多的原始状态，不受污染，因此是十分理想的葡萄种植地。

澳大利亚具有锐意创新、出类拔萃的酿酒技术和多元文化背景的酿酒经验，无疑是世界上最优质葡萄酒出产国之一。澳大利亚的同业们有个不成文的默契：不酿制价格低廉的低级酒，他们把注意力放在质量上而不是数量上。因此在这近20年间澳大利亚冒出不少媲美法国列级名庄的超优质名酒，同时也涌现出一大批价格便宜但质量出众的名牌葡萄酒，是目前很多酒评家认可的最好的新世界葡萄酒出产国。

由于澳大利亚地处南半球，每年5月左右便可以喝到该年份的葡萄酒，可以说是全世界最早上市的葡萄酒。

{葡萄品种}

几乎所有流行的葡萄品种在澳大利亚都有种植。最重要的品种当属穗乐仙，是让澳大利亚葡萄酒成名的关键品种。红葡萄嘉本纳沙威浓、梅乐，白葡萄雪当利、白沙威浓、沙美龙和威士莲等皆在澳大利亚有非常突出的表现。

澳大利亚还有一种特殊的葡萄品种组合叫GSM，即歌海娜、穗乐仙和慕维德3种葡萄。用GSM酿造的葡萄酒是具有澳大利亚特色的葡萄酒之一。

穗乐仙 Shiraz

嘉本纳沙威浓 Cabernet Sauvignon

白沙威浓 Sauvignon Blanc

沙美龙 Semillon

{葡萄酒产区}

从西到东，澳大利亚的优质产酒区主要分布在西澳（Western Australia）、南澳（South Australia）、新南威尔士(New South Wales)、维多利亚（Victoria）和塔斯马尼亚（Tasmania）5个州。

西澳

西澳 是澳大利亚面积最大的州，葡萄产区集中在该州西南部，气候阴凉。这里的葡萄酒产量只占了全澳的5%，但论酒质，全澳约75%的优质葡萄酒都出自这里，这里的酒量少但质优。主要来自3个著名产区：

玛格丽河区 Margaret River

是近年葡萄质量飞跃的产区，有研究指出其土壤、气候与法国右岸相似，出产高雅的嘉本纳沙威浓和丰厚香浓的雪当利。

天鹅谷 Swan Valley

以产丰满醇厚的法国布根地型白葡萄酒闻名，白翠柠、雪当利等白葡萄在此区均有突出表现。

大南区 Great Southern

是西澳最冷的地区，葡萄种植面积也最大，多种红白葡萄都在此区得到发展。

维多利亚

维多利亚 气候较清凉，因此酒的风格较为细致，这里出产优质的起泡酒，其内陆的产区以甜型的加烈葡萄酒闻名，东北部除了甜型酒外，也产酒色深浓、酒精度高、口味重的红葡萄酒。主要有3个产区：

亚拉谷 Yarra Valley

是维多利亚最古老的产酒区，被誉为世界上寒冷气候的最佳葡萄酒产区之一。白葡萄雪当利在该区种植最广泛，口感类型多样，同时也出产优雅细腻的贝露娃。

西斯科特 Heathcote

以产典雅复杂的穗乐仙而出名，维多利亚酒王爵士山庄（Jasper Hill）便位于此区。

宝丽丝 Pyrennees

该区多以精品中小庄园为主，群山环绕，属于典型的干冷气候，出产丰盈馥郁的红葡萄酒，也产爽脆清雅的起泡酒。

南澳

南澳 产量最大，是澳大利亚最重要的葡萄酒产区，气候较炎热，其大部分的葡萄园集中在南谷、河地及阿德莱德山脉（Adelaide Hills）附近区域。著名产区有4个：

巴罗莎谷 Barossa Valley

以产全澳最出名的穗乐仙而闻名于世。它的穗乐仙丰厚、辛辣，可久存。澳大利亚的两大酒王奔富（Penfolds）和汉斯基－神恩山（Henschke-Hill of Grace）都产于此区。

麦罗仑谷 McLaren Vale

同样是以产穗乐仙闻名。该区的穗乐仙新鲜、复杂而且果味甜美，与巴罗莎风格不同，从而满足不同饮家的喜好，近年来每年都与巴罗莎争夺最佳穗乐仙称号。

古纳华拉 Coonawarra

以产丰厚浓郁、略带泥土香味的嘉本纳沙威浓著称，是最早成名的澳大利亚嘉本纳沙威浓产区，同时也产柔顺平和的穗乐仙。

嘉拉谷 Clare Valley

以产有力而高雅的嘉本纳沙威浓和干爽怡人的威士莲著名，被称为澳大利亚的威士莲之乡。著名酒厂泰来斯（Taylors）便位于此区。

新南威尔士

新南威尔士 是澳大利亚最早的葡萄栽种地区，澳大利亚主要知名酒厂都集中在这里，其中澳大利亚最广为人知的葡萄酒产区猎人谷（Hunter Valley）便位于新南威尔士省。

猎人谷离悉尼只有100多千米的路程，开车2小时就到，风景秀丽，吸引很多国内外游人。猎人谷的知名度很高，其沙美龙白葡萄酒最为出名，酒精度通常低于10%，带有富有层次感的芳香，有些还可陈年长达20年。另外白葡萄品种雪当利也有不错的表现。该区传统的红葡萄品种是穗乐仙，嘉本纳沙威浓由福林湖庄园（Lake's Folly）于1963年引进获得成功而一炮而红。

南澳省
South Australia

泰来斯酒庄
Taylors

泰来斯酒庄创建于1969年，在开拓庄园时发现海马化石，因此酒标以海马为标志，每一个海马代表一代经营者。旗下包括泰来斯酒王、泰来斯、海马园、宝美丝4个针对不同市场的品牌，是非常有代表性的新世界葡萄酒的中坚力量。

The tale of Taylors goes back to 1969, when during the initial excavation of the vineyard dam, the founder discovered the fossilized remains of tiny seahorses. Today those seahorses are found on Taylors wine labels all over the world. As the premium brand of exceptional and comparable-quality wines in Australia, it has four series of products, including St. Andrews, Taylors, Jaraman and Promised Land.

泰来斯珍藏
St. Andrews

建园于1896年，于1995年由泰来斯家族购得，是泰来斯的旗舰产品，自从第一个年份1999年上市以来，泰来斯珍藏系列就凭其卓越的品质在国内外获奖无数。

St. Andrews is the flagship range from Taylors. Since the first vintage 1999 released, it has consistently accumulated an impressive number of awards for the outstanding quality.

泰来斯珍藏穗乐仙（红）
Taylors St. Andrews Shiraz

¥¥¥

酒色深浓，散发出肉桂、黑橄榄、巧克力和腰果的香味。酒体丰满，带有中度口感，有香草和烟草香。Intense deep color. Considerable aromas of cinnamon, black olive, chocolate and cashew nuts. A rich wine with a mid palate of vanilla and tobacco characters.

18～20℃

商务宴请，酒友交流 business dinner, wine appreciation

浓味红肉，黑橄榄，蘑菇馅煎饼 rich, red meat dishes, black olive and mushroom frittata

泰来斯酒庄的一大经典力作，在世界权威葡萄酒大赛中荣获众多奖项。An enormously flavorsome wine from Taylors, it has been winning international recognition.

泰来斯珍藏（红）
Taylors St. Andrews Cab. Sauv.

¥ ¥ ¥

酒色深浓，果香复杂，并带有薄荷和巧克力的香气。酒体丰满，口感强劲，甘美而余韵悠长。Intense deep color. Lifted varietals aromas of fruit, mint and oak elements of chocolate. A rich wine, strong and long on the palate.

18～20℃

商务宴请，酒友交流 business dinner, wine appreciation

野味，牛肉类，芝士 rich game or beef dishes, cheese platter

泰来斯酒庄的招牌之作，被人称为澳大利亚的拉菲，是每年产量非常有限的精品庄园酒。Being the flagship of Clare Valley Cabernet, known as the Lafite of Australia, the wine is a limited production of Taylors.

泰来斯珍藏雪当利（白）
Taylors St. Andrews Chardonnay

¥ ¥ ¥

酒色浅黄透亮，散发腰果、甜杏仁、肉豆蔻和肉桂的香味，酒香浓郁，口感丰富。Light yellow color. Rich aromas of cashews, honeyed almonds, nutmeg and cinnamon. A generous and abundant palate, rich and long in flavor.

12～14℃

情侣约会，商务宴请 dating, business dinner

淡味的白肉，意粉，海鲜，浓味芝士，中味型中式菜肴 light white meat dishes, pasta, seafood or rich creamy cheese, light Chinese dishes

这款典雅时尚的雪当利每年的产量非常有限，是精品庄园酒。A demonstration of the region's ability to produce world-class, premium wines.

泰来斯
Taylors

自1973年推出第一批葡萄酒以来，泰来斯酒每年都在澳大利亚国内的葡萄酒大赛中获得殊荣，被澳大利亚业内誉为质量最稳定的庄园酒，是我们全力推荐的超级物超所值酒。

The first ever release of Taylors-Cabernet Sauvignon 1973 won gold medals at every national wine show. The reputation was forged then and continues today, and the range continued to grow over time and now includes many varieties. It is regarded as the wine with most consistent quality and competitive price.

泰来斯贝露娃（红）
Taylors Pinot Noir

¥¥

酒色深红，散发精致的肉桂、烟草和皮革香气，口感温和饱满，呈现出肉桂、香料和泥土味。Deep red color. Subtle bouquet of cinnamon, tobacco and leather. A rich and warming palate with cinnamon, spice and earthy characters.

14~17℃

友人相聚，温馨家宴 friend gathering, family gathering

鹌鹑，鸭肉 quail, duck

物超所值的南澳名酿，此酒结构好，香味极佳，后味持久。Being an affordable wine made in South Australia, it is well structured and has excellent length.

泰来斯穗乐仙（红）
Taylors Shiraz

¥¥

带紫色光泽的宝石红色，入口有几分巧克力和咖啡的香味，酒体饱满柔软。Vivid ruby with purple hues. With dark chocolate and black coffee characters. The mid palate shows softness and generosity.

14~17℃

友人相聚，温馨家宴
friends gathering, family gathering

红肉类菜肴，特别是野味 rich red meat dishes or game, especially venison

由澳大利亚最具特色的葡萄品种——穗乐仙酿造，价格实惠，是日常饮用的极佳选择。Made from the Australian shiraz, the wine is affordable and your first choice for daily wine.

泰来斯梅乐（红）
Taylors Merlot

¥¥

黑樱桃红色，带有甘草、薄荷、巧克力味，雪松和法国香草橡木的香味。酒体柔顺，后味平滑。Dark cherry red, the wine has varietal aromas of licorice, peppermint, cedar chocolate and faint vanilla. A wine of elegant suppleness with a flowing balance and a seamless finish.

14~17℃

友人相聚，商务宴请 friends gathering, business dinner

鸭肉，野鸡，鹌鹑和火鸡，小羊排类菜肴 duck, pheasant, quail or even turkey, rich lamb dish or venison

曾斩获多项国际葡萄酒大奖荣誉，例如国际葡萄酒挑战赛2010铜奖。Awarded in many international wine competitions like Bronze of International Wine Challenge 2010.

泰来斯雪当利（白）
Taylors Chardonnay

¥¥

稻草黄色，带有肉桂、腰果、杏仁味的橡木辛香，口感舒适，有烤果仁面包和酵母味。Straw yellow color. Rich aroma offering enjoyable oak notes of cinnamon, spice, cashews and almonds. A mouth-filling, voluptuous wine with nutty baked bread and creamy yeast.

14～17℃

情侣约会，活力派对 dating party

家禽类及海鲜，素食 most poultry and seafood dishes, vegetarian food

澳大利亚著名葡萄酒杂志*Winestate*称之为四星级葡萄酒。4 star very attractive barrel ferment and Malo aromas-all peaches and cream. Flavorsome nutty and buttery palate with great acid structure. *Winestate Magazine* (AUS)

泰来斯威士连（白）
Taylors Riesling

¥¥

酒色浅黄，带有浓郁的酸橙味。结构平衡，入口带有柠檬香味。酒体优雅，后味持久清醇。Pale straw color. Lifted lime bouquet. The palate balanced with lime. Elegant but still generous ensure a long, pure finish.

7～12℃

友人相聚，浪漫婚宴 friends gathering, wedding

普遍的辛辣食物和海鲜，特别是贝壳类 most spicy dishes and fresh seafood, particularly oysters

产自澳大利亚最佳的威士莲产区，是一款世界级的威士莲。Arguably Australia's premium Riesling growing area, this Clare Valley Riesling is world-class.

泰来斯嘉本纳沙威浓（红）
Taylors Cabernet Sauvignon

¥¥

黑樱桃红色，带有成熟浆果、黑加仑子、黑橄榄和丁香的香气，入口芳香浓郁持久，酒体优雅柔顺，后味平滑完美。Dark cherry red color. Varietal aromas of ripe berry fruit, cassis, black olives and cloves. A wine of elegant suppleness with persistent rounded tannins, a flowing balance and a seamless finish.

14～17℃

友人相聚，商务宴请 friends gathering, business dinner

牛扒，羊扒，芝士 beef steak, lamb, cheese

澳大利亚本土销量第一的嘉本纳沙威浓，是日常饮用的最佳选择，陈年天赋好，窖藏后更佳。This is one of the most popular Cabernet Sauvignon in Australia, displaying considerable richness and length with finesse and complexity.

海马园
Jaraman

海马园系列：澳大利亚土著语里Jaraman是“海马”的意思，因此意译。海马园采用两个产区的葡萄混酿，风格独特，是价格在泰来斯珍藏系列和普通系列之间的精品葡萄酒。

Jaraman is the aboriginal word for seahorse and are found on all of the Taylors wine labels. Jaraman wines are created from the fusion of two exceptional parcels of fruit from icon wine regions in Australia. The result is a single variety wine which is multi-dimensional, highlighting and enhancing the nuances of both terroirs.

海马园嘉本纳沙威浓（红）
Jaraman Cabernet Sauvignon

¥¥¥

复合型果香并带有烤花生面包的香味，后味悠长并带有烟熏味。单宁柔和，入口有烟草叶味和薄荷味。Complex fruit flavours, nutty baked bread and savoury nuances of cedar and butterscotch to the palate and a toasty persistent length. Soft tannins. Varietal characters including tobacco leaf and mint palate.

14~17℃

温馨家宴，商务宴请 family gathering, business dinner

羊排或硬芝士　with Dukka crust or mature, hard cheeses

秉承泰来斯的优秀酿造工艺，获得澳大利亚最著名酒评家之一的詹姆斯·哈立德94分的澳大利亚佳酿。Carrying the outstanding vintage technology of Taylors, the wine is scored 94 points by one of the most famous wine critics James Halliday.

海马园穗乐仙（红）
Jaraman Shiraz

¥ ¥ ¥

樱桃黑，带有甘草、紫罗兰和香草的芬芳。高雅悠长的单宁赋予此酒复杂的后味。Cherry black color. Aromas of licorice, violets and vanilla. Elegant fine and long tannins, and the oak offers a savory complexity to the finish.

14~17℃

情侣约会，温馨家宴 dating, family gathering

鸭肉，鹅肝酱，酿茄子，奶油芝士 duck, liver pate or a stuffed egg plant dish, the creamier cheeses

选用嘉拉谷和麦罗仑谷两地葡萄混酿，值得一提的是，2005年份横扫了2008年各大葡萄酒大赛穗乐仙金奖。Grapes are from Clare Valley and McLaren Vale, the 2005 vintage outstood the peers and got the gold medals in several Wine Competitions in 2008.

海马园雪当利（白）
Jaraman Chardonnay

¥ ¥ ¥

浅金黄色，散发着肉豆蔻香和因橡木桶酿制而产生的腰果、杏仁和雪松味道。酒体平衡丰满，中度酒身。Straw color. Varietal aromas of nutmeg, stylish oak nuances of cashew, almond and cedar. A well balanced and rich wine.

12~14℃

情侣约会，浪漫婚宴 dating, wedding

英国切达干酪，意大利干酪，烤吞拿鱼伴豆沙律，奶油意大利面 rich aged Cheddar and Parmesan, char-grilled Tuna with bean salad or creamy pasta dishes

选用嘉拉谷和阿德莱德山脉两地葡萄混酿，在世界雪当利葡萄酒大赛、上海国际葡萄酒挑战赛等摘得金牌、银牌。Grapes are from Clare Valley and Adelaide Hills, awarded at Chardonnay du Monde, Shanghai International Wine Challenge, etc.

宝美丝
Promised Land

宝美丝系列：泰来斯庄园的入门系列，字面意思为“福地”，定位为以果香讨好，容易欣赏的日常餐酒。

Entrance series of Taylors, which is easy to drink and designed to be fun, fruit-driven and offer tremendous value.

宝美丝穗乐仙嘉本纳（红）
Promised Land Shiraz Cabernet

¥ ¥

带有成熟的浆果的香味特征，交织有烟熏味、雪茄味、橡木味。口感伴有巧克力、奶油、雪茄味和橡木感觉。Varietal bouquet characters of plummy berry fruits, interwoven with smoky, cigar, toasty oak nuances.

14~17℃

友人相聚，浪漫婚宴 friends gathering, wedding

意大利比萨，意式前菜，芝士拼盘，浓味型中式菜肴 pizza, antipasto, a cheese platter, strong Chinese dishes

该酒曾荣获2006年度国际葡萄酒和烈酒评比大赛金奖，是一款性价比高的日常餐酒。As an affordable table wine, it is awarded the Golden Medal of International Wine and Spirit Competition 2006.

宝美丝雪当利（白）
Promised Land Unwooded Chardonnay

¥ ¥

浅黄色，鲜明的热带水果香味，清新可人。入口时结构平实，后味复杂。Bright straw yellow color. Intense aromas of tropical fruits. A balanced wine which initially strikes as firm and austere, but develops to exhibit underlying malolactic fermentation complexities.

12~14℃

情侣约会，友人相聚 dating, friends gathering

普遍的开胃头盘，海鲜 most antipasto, fresh seafood dishes

这款雪当利没有经过橡木桶发酵，为的是保持清新爽脆的原味。适合即开即饮，随时随地享受。This wine shows the pure lifted fruit characters of chardonnay without the influence of oak. Ideal for immediate enjoyment.

宝美丝嘉本纳沙威浓（红）
Promised Land Cabernet Sauvignon

¥ ¥

此酒有辛辣的香料、红醋栗、梅子的香气。口感带有黑醋栗、咖啡以及橡木的香气，余味柔顺而醇厚。Vibrant spicy aromas of red currant, plum and a touch of spice. Juicy blackcurrant fruits along with subtle coffee and savory cedar flavours and a smooth gentle finish.

14~17℃

温馨家宴，友人相聚 family gathering, friends gathering

野味或牛肉类等浓味型菜肴，芝士 rich game or beef dishes, ideally suited to a cheese platter of mature vintage or pungent blue vein

在2010年国际葡萄酒竞赛上，该酒获得铜奖。In 2010, this wine won Bronze of International Wine Challenge.

宝云庄
Bowen Estate

澳大利亚知名度极高的精品小庄园，每年都入选澳大利亚最大葡萄酒拍卖行朗格顿的“澳大利亚89款最受欢迎名酒”之列。由于每年的产品都供不应求，对世界各地代理商采取配额制。

Located on prime Coonawarra terra rossa soil, it is one of the best known names among the small Coonawarra wineries, producing a small quintessential range of classic Coonawarra wines.

宝云庄嘉本纳沙威浓（红）
Bowen Estate Cabernet Sauvignon

酒色深红，入口带有成熟桑果、土壤、矿物、橡木等复杂香味。Intense garnet color. Earthy and mineral tastes with flavours of ripe berries, and oak characters.

18～20℃

商务宴请，酒友交流 business dinner, wine appreciation

牛扒，羊扒，野味，芝士拼盘 beef steak, lamb, game, cheese platter

每年均能入选澳大利亚50大名酒之列。价格则偏低，是葡萄酒爱好者的超值之选。Ranked as the top 50 wines of Australia every year. With a relatively low price, it is the perfect choice for wine enthusiasts.

宝云庄穗乐仙（红）
Bowen Estate Shiraz

宝石红色，有果仁、咖啡和黑巧克力的芳香混合在一起。入口有肉桂、咖啡以及香草味，口感丰富。Rich ruby red color, aromas of nutmeg, coffee and dark chocolate. Flavours intermingle with characters of coffee, mocha and vanillin to give a full palate.

18～20℃

温馨家宴，商务宴请 family gathering, business dinner

红肉，芝士 rich red meat dishes, cheese

该款红酒已成为衡量古纳华拉穗乐仙的基准，同样是葡萄酒爱好者的超级之选。A perennial benchmark in Coonawarra's Shiraz. With a relatively low price, it is the perfect choice for wine enthusiasts.

奔富
Penfolds

澳大利亚知名度极高的精品小庄园，每年都入选澳大利亚最大葡萄酒拍卖行朗格顿的“澳大利亚89款最受欢迎名酒”之列。由于每年的产品都供不应求，对世界各地代理商采取配额制。

One of the most renowned boutique wineries in Australia, which wines are listed as "89 Most Popular Wines" by the biggest Australian Aution House Langtons. Since its limited production, Penfolds adopts quota system to distributors around the world.

奔富之父（红）
Penfolds Bin 95 Grange

¥¥¥¥¥

酒色深红，香浓的洋李和黑莓的芳香，夹杂皮革和黑巧克力香味。酒体丰厚，体现完美的橡木味及耐嚼的单宁。Deep red color. Raspberry and blackberry fruit aromas and leather, dark chocolate and spice. A full-bodied wine with oak and chewy tannins.

18~20℃

商务宴请，酒友交流 business dinner, wine appreciation

牛肉，芝士 beef, cheese

自20世纪50年代开始，该酒一直在澳大利亚最佳葡萄酒的王位上屹立不倒，是国际葡萄酒收藏者追求的顶级佳酿。 From humble beginnings in the 1950s, Grange has maintained its place as Australia's most prestigious red wine. It is eagerly awaited by collectors both in Australia and overseas every year.

奔富707（红）
Penfolds Bin 707 Cabernet Sauvignon

¥¥¥¥

酒色深红，带有复杂的浆果香气，雪松与紫罗兰的味道。酒体饱满，单宁结实细致。Deep garnet color. complex bouquet of cassis fruit with cedary oak and violet nuances. Rich and expansive mid-palate with finely grained tannins.

18~20℃

商务宴请，酒友交流 business dinner, wine appreciation

牛肉，奶酪食品，羊肉 beef, cheese, lamb

澳大利亚顶级嘉本纳沙威浓葡萄酒经典之作。Bin 707 is justifiably regarded as one of Australia's most important cabernets.

奔富407（红）
Penfolds Bin 407
Cabernet Sauvignon

¥¥¥

酒色深红，带有黑醋栗、薄荷香气，略有肉豆蔻与雪松的味道。此酒活泼且极具风味，单宁结实，后味持久。Deep red color. Varietal aromas with blackcurrant and cassis and discernable nutmeg and cedar nuances. Lively palate of great length, facilitated by chunky tannins.

18~20℃

商务宴请，温馨家宴 business dinner, family gathering

牛肉，鸡肉，羊肉 beef, chicken, lamb

从奔富707中获得灵感的407， 是代表澳大利亚多元化的嘉本纳沙威浓葡萄酒的新生代。Inspired by Penfolds-Bin 707, it is the younger generation of versatile Australian Cabernet Sauvignon red wine.

奔富389（红）
Penfolds Bin 389
Cabernet Shiraz

¥¥¥

酒色深红，无须旋转酒杯即可闻到扑鼻的酒香，酒体平衡，入口有巧克力、摩卡咖啡与橡木的雪松味道。 Dark crimson color, vibrant, lively aromas are immediately apparent without any need to swirl the glass. Full-bodied wine with chocolate, mocha flavours and cedary oak.

18~20℃

情侣约会，商务宴请 dating, business dinner

牛肉，鸭肉，野味，羊肉 beef, duck, game, lamb

此经典之作具备陈年的天赋，约12年间为最佳时期。A classic Bin 389, right up there with the best, with long term cellaring potential of over twelve years.

奔富138（红）
Penfolds Bin 138
Shiraz Grenache Mourvedre

¥¥¥

深洋李红色，成熟的歌海娜葡萄香，穗乐仙的肉桂和麝香味，黑甘草的香味交织一起的复杂香气，单宁完美融合于一体。Deep plum red color. Grenache aromas with some Shiraz spices (cinnamon and musk). Full flavoured, rich and generous with ripe chewy tannins.

18~20℃

情侣约会，友人相聚 dating, friends gathering

烤羊腿，奶酪蛋奶酥，红烩牛膝 braised lamb shanks, twice cooked cheese soufflé, osso bucco

获得国际葡萄酒挑战赛2009年推介大赏评价。International Wine Challenge 2009 Commended Award winner.

奔富128（红）
Penfolds Bin 128
Coonawarra Shiraz

¥¥¥

酒色深红，浓郁的黑莓与蓝莓的果香中带有香料与烟草的味道。结构紧密，带有肉豆蔻与丁香的味道，余韵悠长持久。Dense red color, dark spices and tobacco with generous blackberry and blueberry fruits. Defined and tight with nutmeg and clove spices. A long, persistent finish.

18~20℃

商务宴请，温馨家宴 business dinner, family gathering

牛肉，意大利面，羊扒 beef, pasta, lamb

保留奔富128红葡萄酒的一贯作风，性格突出，此经典之作还具有陈年的天分。Keeping with the Bin 128 style, a 'warm vintage' interpretation of this classic wine style, allowing extended cellaring potential, if desired.

奔富28（红）
Penfolds Bin 28
Kalimna Shiraz

¥¥¥

深洋李红色，浓郁的蓝莓水果香气，还带有肉桂、甘草与八角的味道。带有像水果蛋糕般的余韵，酒体醇和且单宁结实。Deep plum red color. Intense aroma of blueberry fruits with cinnamon, liquorice and aniseed. With rich fruitcake flavour, the mid palate has youthful chunky tannins and an alert acidity

14~17℃

情侣约会，浪漫婚宴 dating, wedding

半熟肉眼扒，羊排 rare rib eye steak, lamb

该酒斩获国际葡萄酒挑战赛2009年金奖。It is the winner of Gold Award of International Wine Challenge 2009.

奔富高兰山（红）
Penfolds Koonunga Hill
Shiraz Cabernet

¥¥

深紫红色，带有穗乐仙葡萄特有的黑胡椒味，果味丰富，单宁圆润，陈年2~4年饮用更佳。Deep purple crimson color, with black pepper bouquet from the shiraz. Palate with plenty of fruit, well-formed tannins. Suggesting it will develop nicely over 2~4 years.

14~17℃

情侣约会，商务宴请 dating, business dinner

高脂奶酪 sharp cheese

该酒荣获《品醇客》杂志“2010世界葡萄酒大奖赛”推荐葡萄酒荣誉。It is the winner of Commended Award of *Decanter* World Wine Awards 2010.

奔富高兰山（白）
Penfolds Koonunga Hill
Semillon Sauvignon Blanc

¥¥

酒色淡黄，散发出新鲜采摘的雪豌豆与西番莲的芳香，中等酒体，平衡良好。Pale straw color. Intense, vibrant and lifted aromas show an array of fruits. A medium-bodied wine, showing great balance.

7~12℃

情侣约会， 友人相聚 dating, friends gathering

沙律，海鲜，大部分亚洲菜肴 salads, seafood, many Asian dishes

高兰山最受欢迎的混合勾兑型白葡萄酒，是澳大利亚能出产优秀白葡萄酒的有力佐证。The most popular blended white wine of Koonunga Hill. It is a convincing, well-made wine that shows what Australia is able to do well.

奔富洛神山庄（红）
Penfolds Rawson's Retreat Shiraz Cabernet Sauvignon

¥¥

深红色酒体,有成熟的夏日浆果香和黑色香料的辛香，中度的酒体,柔滑的单宁使浆果味和酒香达到一种有趣的平衡。Bright crimson color. Open bouquet of ripe summer berries and dark spices. The medium bodied wine has a balance of summer berries and light spices.

- 18～20℃
- 情侣约会，温馨家宴 dating, family gathering
- 羊扒，意大利面，比萨，普遍中浓味中式菜肴 lamb, pasta, pizza, strong Chinese dishes
- 由洛神山庄酿酒团队亲自在葡萄园挑选葡萄酿制的超值葡萄酒。The winemaking team spends time in the vineyards prior to vintage to ensure the right style of grapes is picked.

奔富洛神山庄（白）
Penfolds Rawson's Retreat Semillon Chardonnay

¥¥

浅黄色酒体，带有热带水果的香味，橡木带来的复杂感和烤面包香气。热带果香与自然的酸度平衡。Pale yellow color. Expressive bouquet of tropical fruits with oak and toast. Balanced by tropical fruit flavours and natural acidity.

- 12～14℃
- 友人相聚，温馨家宴 friend gathering, family gathering
- 海鲜，鸡，意大利面，淡味中式菜肴配食 seafood, chicken, pasta, light Chinese dishes
- 酿酒的葡萄来源横跨澳大利亚东南部，是洛神山庄混合勾兑型白葡萄酒的心血之作。Sourced from select grape growing regions across Southeast Australia, this wine is an excellent example of the sum of the parts equaling greater than the whole.

克拉斯
Kalleske

以“奔富酒王系列的葡萄供应商”一鸣惊人，克拉斯于2002年创立自己的品牌，被澳大利亚最著名酒评家詹姆斯·哈立德评为“五星级酒庄”。

As the grape supplier for Penfolds Grange for years, Kalleske established its own brand in 2002. It was rated "five-star winery" by James Halliday.

克拉斯特选穗乐仙（红）
Kalleske Greenock Shiraz

¥¥¥

深绛红色，浓郁的可可、咖啡和丁香气味，入口浓郁丰富，酒体丰满，平衡有致，有很好的陈年天赋。Deep red-black color. Concentrated aromas of cocoa, coffee, blackberry and clove spice. A wine with a strong backbone and a long finish that will cellar for a long time.

18~20℃

商务宴请，酒友交流 business dinner, wine appreciation

牛扒，烤羊肉，野味 beef steak, roasted lamb, game

荣获2009年德国BioFach国际葡萄酒大赛金奖，是巴罗莎谷典型的红葡萄酒。The Golden Award winner of BioFach International Organic Wine Awards 2009, it is the masterpiece of the Barossa red wine.

克拉斯（巴罗莎）（红）
Kalleske Clarry's Barossa Red

¥ ¥

中红色调，蕴含土耳其软糖的甜蜜，丁香等各种香草的独特香气，单宁柔顺，酒体结实。Medium red color. Aromas of Turkish delight, spice, cloves, and a hint of dried herbs. Tannins are silky with a solid structure.

- 14～17℃
- 浪漫婚宴，温馨家宴 wedding, family gathering
- 牛扒，烤羊肉，浓味芝士 beef steak, roasted lamb, strong cheese
- 这个系列以酿酒师祖父的名字命名，获得澳大利亚最著名酒评家詹姆斯·哈立德94分评分的澳大利亚佳酿。"Clarry's" is named after winemaker Troy Kalleske's grandfather. The wine is scored 94 points by one of the most famous wine critics James Halliday.

克拉斯（巴罗莎）（白）
Kalleske Florentine Chenin Blanc

¥ ¥

淡麦杆色，充满新鲜的苹果、白桃、梨、醋栗和鲜花香气。单宁柔顺，酒体结实。Bright straw color. Aroma of apple, white peach, pear, gooseberry with floral notes. Tannins are silky with a solid structure.

- 7～12℃
- 情侣约会，友人相聚 dating, friend gathering
- 海鲜，鹅肝，中味芝士 seafood, goose liver, light cheese
- 这是一款没有经过橡木桶，口感愉悦的白葡萄酒，十分适合浅龄饮用。Without receiving any oak, the wine is extremely fresh and vibrant. Best enjoyed while young.

双掌
Two Hands

双掌是澳大利亚新兴的酒业品牌，被著名酒评家罗拔帕克称为“南半球最杰出的酒商”。以南澳著名产区巴罗莎谷为酿酒基地，以酿成澳大利亚最好的穗乐仙为目标，是唯一一个连续6次获得权威葡萄酒杂志《葡萄酒观察家》“全球百佳葡萄酒”称号的酒庄。

It is pronounced as "the finest negociant operation south of the equator" by Robert Parker. The heart of the operation is based in the Barossa Valley, Two Hands has a clear objective of making the best possible shiraz based wines from prized shiraz producing regions within Australia. It is the only winery who has been selected as the TOP 100 WINES in the word for the continuous 6 years by *Wine Spectator*.

双掌（巴罗莎穗乐仙）红酒王（红）
Two Hands Ares Barossa Valley Shiraz

¥¥¥¥

酒色浓黑，散发焦油、泥土、雪松、巧克力的复杂香气，入口即能感受浓稠的酒液，平衡的结构和力道。Deep black color. Complex bouquet of licorice, tar, earth, cedar chocolate. A vicious and powerful wine with excellent poise and balance.

18~20℃

商务宴请，酒友交流 business dinner, wine appreciation

烤肉，鸭肉 grilled meat, duck

这是双掌酒庄的穗乐仙酒王，在100%全新的法国橡木桶中进行陈年。Ares represents the very best selection of Shiraz from Two Hands Wines. This wine matures in 100% new French oak.

双掌（花园系列）巴罗莎穗乐仙（红）
Two Hands Bella's Garden Barossa Valley Shiraz

¥¥¥

酒色深浓至黑，散发成熟的樱桃、焦油、薄荷丁香和苦巧克力味道，酒体有力丰满，口感紧密，单宁干身。Impenetrable red color, a lifted bouquet of ripe cherry, tar, mint, clove and bitter chocolate. The wine is robust and rich with drying and mouth filling tannins.

18~20℃

浪漫婚宴，商务宴请 wedding, business dinner

羊扒 lamb

此酒精选巴罗莎谷多地的穗乐仙进行混酿，多次入选《葡萄酒观察家》"全球百佳葡萄酒"。A blend of the finest Shiraz barrels from across the Barossa Valley region. It is rated in "The Top 100 Wines" by *Wine Spectator*.

双掌（花园系列）龙吟溪穗乐仙（红）
Two Hands Harry & Edward's Garden Langhorne Creek Shiraz

¥¥¥

酒色深紫，蓝莓和桑葚果味突出，夹杂桉树、烤胡椒和雪松气味。中度酒体，有矿物的风味，单宁柔和又平衡。Inky purple color. Outstanding bouquet of blueberry and mulberry with eucalypt, roasted peppers and cedar notes. Medium bodied wine with mineral tones and soft and balancing tannins.

18~20℃

商务宴请，酒友交流 business dinner, wine appreciation

野味，牛扒，羊扒 games, beef steak, lamb

此酒产自澳大利亚最好的葡萄酒产区之一龙吟溪，获得澳大利亚最著名酒评家詹姆斯·哈立德93分高分的双掌佳酿。A very attractive wine that clearly demonstrates why Langhorne Creek is one of Australia's great wine regions, rated 93 by James Halliday.

双掌（花园系列）麦罗仑谷穗乐仙（红）
Two Hands Lily's Garden McLaren Vale Shiraz

¥¥¥

墨紫色，散发着强烈的洋李香味，还有摩卡咖啡和茴香的味道，单宁平衡柔滑，有香浓的香甜水果味道。Inky purple color. Intense bouquet of plum, mocha and aniseed. With well balanced and velvety tannins, the palate has strong fruit flavor.

18~20℃

酒友交流，温馨家宴 wine appreciation, family gathering

铁板牛肉，野味，浓味芝士 grilled beef, games, strong cheese

此酒精选麦罗仑谷葡萄进行酿制，获得《葡萄酒鉴赏家》评分93分的优秀成绩。The pick of the bunch from McLaren Vale vineyards of Two Hands. The wine is rated 93 points by *Wine Spectator*.

双掌（画廊系列）巴罗莎穗乐仙（红）
Two Hands Gnarly Dudes Barossa Valley Shiraz

¥¥¥

酒色深紫至黑，散发出莓果、香料、茴香、浓咖啡和牛奶巧克力的味道。中度酒体，单宁结构良好，酸度平衡。Deep purple to black. Lifted aromas of raspberries, spice, fennel, espresso and milk chocolate. Medium bodied wine with firm but textured tannins and balanced acid.

18~20℃

情侣约会，温馨家宴 dating, family gathering

羊扒 lamb

秉承双掌庄园清澈、清醇、味道丰富的穗乐仙佳酿。An Australian Shiraz wine with the clean, pure, and flavorsome properties of the Two Hands.

双掌（画廊系列）巴罗莎穗乐仙嘉本纳（红）
Two Hands The Bull & The Bear Barossa Valley Shiraz Cabernet Sauvignon

¥¥¥

黑巧克力色，有芳香扑鼻的烟叶、木炭、茴香和黑醋栗的味道。中度的酒体，单宁宜人。Deep dark chocolate color. A powerful bouquet of tobacco leaf, charcoal, aniseed and cassis. A mid-bodied wine with savoury tannins.

18~20℃

商务宴请，温馨家宴 family gathering, business dinner

牛扒，羊扒 beef steak, lamb

此酒中的穗乐仙和嘉本纳沙威浓分别放在美国和法国橡木桶陈年后再进行勾兑，风味独特，适合陈年后饮用。The wine is a blend of Shiraz and Cabernet Sauvignon aging in American and French oak respectively. It will develop better after aging.

双掌（画廊系列）麦罗仑谷穗乐仙（红）
Two Hands Angel's Share McLaren Vale Shiraz

¥¥¥

酒色深黑，有香料、新鲜浓咖啡、巧克力、黑樱桃和烤杏仁的芳香。入口便能感受到甘草、摩卡咖啡、香料气息。Deep black color, open bouquet of spice, fresh espresso, rich chocolate, dark cherries and roasted almonds. The palate is long, dense and coating with liquorice, mocha, and spice flavours.

14~17℃

浪漫婚宴，商务宴请 wedding, business dinner

牛扒，羊扒 beef steak, lamb

真实反映麦罗伦谷穗乐仙优秀的品质。A true reflection of the outstanding quality of Shiraz in the McLaren Vale.

威拿庄
Wirra Wirra

麦罗仑谷的酒王，澳大利亚葡萄酒业中一块亮丽的蓝宝石。澳大利亚最著名的酒评家詹姆斯·哈立德将其视为澳大利亚葡萄酒的典范之作。

The winery produces a stunning array of red wines. James Halliday describes it as follows: "Where do you begin to talk about a winery asstunning as Wirra Wirra? Its vision exemplary, its winemakers some of the best on the planet and its wines… mind blowing! In recent years, this winery has gone from strength to strength, producing what we believe to be some to the best Australian wines ever assembled."

威拿促博园（红）
Wirra Wirra Chook Block Shiraz

酒色紫红，散发着浓烈醇香的黑醋栗果香。单宁结构良好，酒香甘美醇和，入口如天鹅绒般丝滑。Full red-purple color. A dense bouquet of cassis-blackcurrant fruit. It is long and velvet soft smooth with fine tannins.

18~20℃

商务宴请，酒友交流 business dinner, wine appreciation

牛扒，羊排，野味，芝士 beef steak, lamb, game, cheese

只在最好的年份才出产，产量约3 000瓶，是澳大利亚珍稀的极品好酒，广受葡萄酒收藏家的喜爱。Only 250 dozen bottles were made per excellent vintage. It is one of the best and rare Australian fine wines that very popular in the wine collectors.

威拿珍藏穗乐仙（红）
Wirra Wirra R.S.W. Shiraz

酒色深紫，散发肉桂的辛香，甜甘草味，酒体丰厚，有极好的结构和优质的单宁。Dark purple color. Intense bouquet of spices, cinnamon with liquorice sweetness. A full-bodied wine with excellent structure, fine integrated tannins.

14~17℃

酒友交流，温馨家宴 wine appreciation, family gathering

意大利面，浓味芝士，铁板或烧烤的红肉 pastas, cheeses, grilled red meats

该酒以庄园创始人的名字命名，是威拿的旗舰产品，澳大利亚最好的几个穗乐仙酒王之一。其品质完全可挑战奔富之父，但价格只是它的十分之一，非常超值。This wine (one of two Wirra Wirra flagships) is named after the winery's founder Robert Strangways Wigley. He produced a much acclaimed Shiraz. With a similar quality with Penfolds Bin 95 Grange, the price is only one tenth of it.

威拿麦罗仑谷穗乐仙（红）
Wirra Wirra Woodhenge
McLaren Vale Shiraz

¥¥¥

酒色深紫，有典型的黑巧克力香味和麦罗仑谷甘草的特征，酒体丰满，后味悠长。Crimson plum hues. Typical aroma of the dark chocolate and licorice from the McLaren Vale region. Full-bodied wine with a long persistent finish.

14~17℃

友人相聚，浪漫婚宴 friends gathering, wedding

意大利面，浓味芝士，铁板或烧烤的红肉 pastas, cheeses, grilled red meats

该酒是麦罗仑谷的代表作，更在国内外屡获大奖。The reds that are produced in McLaren Valley consistently head the list of winners at Australian and International wine shows.

威拿教堂庄园（红）
Wirra Wirra Church Block Red
(Cab. Sau. Shiraz Merlot)

¥¥

酒色深紫，有紫罗兰、黑莓、八角茴香和肉桂的辛香，酒体丰满，单宁优质。Deep purple color. Open bouquet of violets, blackberries with spicy star aniseed and cinnamon. A full-bodied wine with fine tannins.

14~17℃

友人相聚，活力派对 friends gathering, party

意大利面，铁板或烧烤的牛羊，浓味芝士 pastas, roasted or grilled meat dishes, strong cheese

该酒名是向庄园酒窖附近教堂的致敬。这款酒被视为麦罗仑谷最高性价比的佳酿之一。The name came from the small Bethany Church across the road from Wirra Wirra's century old ironstone cellars. Over the decades, it has been among the best-value reds of Mclaren Vale.

威拿（红）
Wirra Wirra Scrubby Rise
(Shiraz Cab. Sau. Petit Verdot)

¥¥

酒色棕红，散发着浓郁的黑醋栗、洋李和水果蛋糕的香味，单宁柔软细滑。Rich crimson color. Aromas of bright cassis, plum, and fruit cake with fine soft tannins.

14~17℃

活力派对，温馨家宴 party, family gathering

牛扒，羊扒 beef steak, lamb

该酒是威拿庄的入门系列，价格较为相宜。A Wirra Wirra Wine for beginners with a much affordable price.

威拿（白）
Wirra Wirra Scrubby Rise
(Sau. Blanc Semillon Viognier)

¥¥

浅淡黄色，有热带水果、新鲜的青草香，以及轻微的金银花和橙子的香味，口感新鲜丰富。Pale straw color. Aromas of tropical fruits along with fresh green herbaceous characters and slight honeysuckle and orange peel. Rich and fresh palate.

7~12℃

情侣约会，活力派对 dating, party

海鲜，辛香或微辣的菜肴，鱼，贝壳类，沙律 seafood, spicy or slightly hot dishes, fish, shellfish, salads

威拿庄获得无数好评的混酿型白葡萄酒。A Wirra Wirra blend winning numerous reputation.

威拿威士连（白）
Wirra Wirra The Lost Watch Riesling

¥ ¥

酒色浅绿，带有特别明显的橙子和无花果的芳香，美味像果汁，口感比一般年轻的威士莲更容易接受。Lime green color. Strong lime and fig aromas. A juicy palate, more approachable than many young Rieslings.

7～12℃

友人相聚，活力派对 friends gathering, party

海鲜，辛香或微辣的菜肴，鱼，贝壳类，沙律 seafood, spicy or slightly hot dishes, fish, shellfish, salads

此酒葡萄全以手工采摘，将人为因素降到最低，为该酒添加独特的大自然风韵。By 100% hand-picked grapes, the human factors in the wine is greatly reduced, which adds natural quality to it.

威拿蜜丝佳桃（粉红）
Wirra Wirra Mrs. Wigley

¥ ¥

此酒散发花香、麝香味、新鲜夏日浆果和橙皮的清香，口感新鲜活泼，酸度紧实。Fresh Muscat aromas showing floral notes, summer berry fruits and orange peel. A bright and fresh palate with firm and refreshing acid.

7～12℃

情侣约会，友人相聚 dating, friends gathering

蜜糖的浆果夹心烤薄饼，乳清干酪 berry pancakes with fresh ricotta, a drizzle of honey

该酒是为了纪念威拿庄邻居一只波斯猫威格列夫人（Mrs. Wigley），是威拿庄的新生代产品。Mrs. Wigley is the name of a particular pussycat at the neighboring Petrucci residence. This Moscato is Wirra Wirra's newest range.

South Australia

维多利亚省
Victoria

蓝宝丽丝
Blue Pyrenees

蓝宝丽丝位于维多利亚省宝丽丝区，由于该区的山峰长年被淡蓝色的薄雾笼罩而得名。属典型的干冷气候，土壤丰实，矿物质含量丰富，气候特点与法国的很多酒区相似。它曾是法国人头马集团在澳大利亚创立的酒厂，也是第一间由法国人在澳大利亚投资创办的酒庄。

The Blue Pyrenees Estate vineyards nestle in the foothills of the Pyrenees in western Victoria. She was the first winery to be developed in Australia by French company "The Remy-Cointreau Group". The estate was selected in the early 1960's due to its unique "Terroir": a combination of deep gravelly soils and cool climate conditions. Blue Pyrenees is the realization of a desire to create a unique vineyard of superior quality.

蓝宝丽丝珍藏（红）
Blue Pyrenees Estate Reserve

¥¥¥

宝石红色，有明显的雪松、桉树、薄荷等植物香。单宁结构好，余韵精致悠长。Dense ruby red color. Open bouquet of cedar and briar with hints of eucalypt, mint. A fine tannin structure with a long and balanced finish.

14~17℃

浪漫婚宴，酒友交流 wedding, wine appreciation

香肠，烧烤红色肉类，如牛扒，羊扒等普遍中浓味中餐菜肴 chorizo sausage, whole roast baby lamb, un-pasteurised Stilton

在国内外葡萄酒大赛获得多项殊荣，包括旧金山国际葡萄酒大赛金奖和墨尔本酒展银奖等等。Award winner of numerous international and national wine competitions including Gold at the San Francisco International Wine Show and Silver at the Royal Melbourne Wine Show.

蓝宝丽丝嘉本纳沙威浓（红）
Blue Pyrenees Cabernet Sauvignon

¥ ¥

深宝石红色，有黑莓、香草和很好的橡木香味。酒体中至厚身，单宁结构层次丰富，有持久释放的黑加仑子味。Intense ruby color. Blackberry with the vanillin and savoury aromas of new oak. A medium/full bodied wine with fine grain tannins contribute to a long finish of lingering blackcurrant flavours.

18～20℃

浪漫婚宴，温馨家宴 wedding, family gathering

香肠，烧烤红色肉类，如牛扒，羊扒等普遍中浓味中式菜肴 chorizo sausage, whole roast baby lamb, un-pasteurised Stilton

宝丽丝区以出产富有区域特色的嘉本纳沙威浓闻名，这款酒是该区的代表作。The Victorian Pyrenees region is renowned for producing cabernet sauvignon.

蓝宝丽丝穗乐仙（红）
Blue Pyrenees Shiraz

¥ ¥

酒色深宝石红，有胡椒、紫罗兰、香草和烟熏橡木味。单宁结构紧密，余韵有持续的果香。Deep ruby color. Warm aromas of peppery spice, violet, vanilla and toasted oak. Evident tannin with lingering fruit flavours on the long dry finish.

18～20℃

商务宴请，温馨家宴 business dinner, family gathering

烧牛仔腿，烧羊羔腿，烧乳猪等普遍红色肉类，浓味中式菜肴 whole roast baby lamb, roast suckling pig, chorizo and lentil stew

这款酒的葡萄采自庄园低产量的葡萄田，以酿制单宁柔滑且结构丰厚的穗乐仙。Produced from parcels of fruit grown on low-yielding vines creating a wine of the classic rich shiraz structure.

蓝宝丽丝珍藏雪当利（白）
Blue Pyrenees Estate Reserve Chardonnay

¥ ¥ ¥

酒液浅金色，散发诱人的新鲜柚子、腰果和桃子的香味。口感浓郁、复杂，满口平衡的橡木和成熟果香。Brilliant pale gold color. Attractive aromas of grapefruit, cashews and peaches. A rich and palate showing well integrated oak balanced by ripe fruit definition.

12～14℃

情侣约会，温馨家宴 dating, family gathering

淡味的白肉，意粉，乳猪，海鲜，浓味的奶油芝士 light white meat dishes, pasta, seafood, rich creamy cheese

该酒展示了宝丽丝产区雪当利的优秀品质。This wine is designed to showcase the combination of the estate terroirs, varietal definition.

蓝宝丽丝雪当利（白）
Blue Pyrenees Chardonnay

¥ ¥

酒色浅黄，有橙子、柑橘的香味，还有微妙的橡木香。口感丰满、新鲜、爽脆，香味细致持久，后味清新。A pale straw color. The aroma of lifted limes and other citrus, touches of tropical with very subtle oak. A rich and fresh palate showing great length and finesse.

12～14℃

情侣约会，友人相聚 dating, friends gathering

普遍白肉，海鲜和淡味型中式菜肴 most seafood and white meat dishes and light Chinese food

体现宝丽丝产区雪当利的多变，是一款性价比高的白葡萄酒。An affordable white wine showing the versatile Chardonnay of Pyrenees.

蓝宝丽丝白沙威浓（白）
Blue Pyrenees Sauvignon Blanc

¥ ¥

柠檬黄的酒色，有热情轻快的草药、鲜花的香味，充满热带风情。口感新鲜、清爽，后味持久强烈。Pale lemon color. Lifted herbal, grassy, floral and tropical notes. A mid palate with fresh, crisp and clean mouth-feel and a tangy, lingering finish.

- 12～14℃
- 情侣约会，友人相聚 dating, friends gathering
- 海鲜，普遍白肉，淡味型亚洲菜肴配食 most delicate fish, shellfish, white meat dishes, Asian style cuisine
- 该区的干冷气候令白沙威浓的特性得到更好的展现。The cool climate Pyrenees district of Victoria can produce distinctive sauvignon blanc.

蓝宝丽丝午夜浪漫起泡葡萄酒
Blue Pyrenees Midnight Cuvee Chardonnay

¥ ¥ ¥

酒色浅金，气泡细致。有活泼诱人的鲜花香味，口感美妙、清新爽口，酒香开放而复杂。A pale gold color with constant bead. Attractive lifted and floral notes. The palate is fresh and clean, with an explosion of flavours and complexity.

- 4～7℃
- 情侣约会，浪漫婚宴 dating, wedding
- 鱼子，虾刺身，鱼翅汤 caviar, sashimi, shark fin soup
- 选用的葡萄全部都是在午夜时分人工采摘，沿用香槟酒的传统酿造工艺精制而成，堪称澳大利亚品质一流的起泡葡萄酒。Hand-picked at night, the grapes are of exceptional concentration. Used the winemaking process of Champagne and aimed to become the top quality sparkling wine in Australia.

蓝宝丽丝起泡葡萄酒
Blue Pyrenees Vintage Brut

¥ ¥

酒色浅金，泡沫持久细致。先有贝露娃的精致花香，继而有雪当利优雅的成熟果香，最后有贝露曼尼尔的烤面包香。Beautiful light gold color, fine and persistent mousse. Complex aromas of floral notes of pinot noir, ripe fruity overtones of chardonnay and toastiness of Pinot Meunier.

- 4～7℃
- 浪漫婚宴，商务宴请 wedding, business dinner
- 鱼子，虾刺身，鱼翅汤 caviar, sashimi, shark fin soup
- 仿效香槟的工艺由3种葡萄进行混酿而成。适合作高雅宴会餐前酒或接待酒。Using three traditional grape varieties typically used in the Champagne district of France, this brut is suitable for aperitif.

小提琴
Fiddlers Creek

小提琴是蓝宝丽丝庄园的附属产品，是酿酒师们为酿造出一款货真价实，具有高性价比的日常餐酒而创立的品牌。

Fiddlers Creek is provided by the winemakers at Blue Pyrenees Estate with the inspiration to create a range of wines representing honesty, reliability and quality attributes much admired and aspired to.

小提琴穗乐仙嘉本纳（红）
Fiddlers Creek Shiraz Cabernet

泥土红色，散发成熟的黑色和红色浆果香味，复合的橡木味。辛香可口，后味干爽而有力。Earthy red color. Ripe aromas of black and red berries interlaced with subtle oak. The palate is spicy and savoury with a dry finish.

18~20℃

友人相聚，温馨家宴 friends gathering, family gathering

红肉，意大利面，芝士 red meat, pasta, cheese

一款典型的澳大利亚穗乐仙葡萄酒。A typical Australian Shiraz wine.

小提琴嘉本纳梅乐（红）
Fiddlers Creek Cabernet Merlot

泥土红色，有成熟的红色、黑色浆果香，以及微妙橡木香。入口有薄荷与桉树的香味，橡木味相当完整。Earthy red color. Aromas of ripe, red and black berries combine with subtle oak. The palate shows touches of mint and eucalypt and well integrated oak.

18~20℃

酒友交流，温馨家宴 wine appreciation, family gathering

羊肉，意大利面，芝士及浓味型菜肴配食 lamb, any pasta with a rich sauce as well as fine cheese

嘉本纳的强劲和梅乐的柔滑平衡恰到好处，可陈年，现时也适合饮用。This wine is a perfect balance between the strong cabernet sauvignon and the soft merlot. A style for mid term cellaring, but is very approachable now.

小提琴雪当利（白）
Fiddlers Creek Chardonnay

酒色淡绿，有桃子和一丝橡木的香味。入口有橙、蜜瓜及烤面包的香味，留香持久。Pale straw color. A fresh, lively, peachy style with just a hint of oak. Lovely aromas of fresh citrus, melon and toast. Fresh and crisp palate with a lingering finish.

12~14℃

情侣约会，活力派对 dating, party

鸡肉，海鲜 a variety of chicken, seafood dishes

一款性价比高的雪当利葡萄酒，适合作为日常餐酒饮用。An affordable chardonnay wine designed for daily table wine.

德宝庄
Tahbilk

德宝庄是澳大利亚历史最悠久的名庄之一，庄园风景优美，堪称一绝。当代最著名的酒评家罗拔·派克将之誉为超值的澳大利亚明星酒庄，在世界各地最有分量的葡萄酒大赛获得过1 000枚奖牌和奖杯。
Established in 1860，Tahbilk is one of Australia's most beautiful and historic wineries. Tahbilk has possibly the world's oldest Marsanne vines still bearing, planted in 1927.

德宝庄1860年老树穗乐仙（红）
Tahbilk 1860 Vines Shiraz

¥¥¥¥

深宝石红色，有泥土、皮革、姜的香味，入口有黑水果的美味，口感极为丰满、回味无穷。Deep ruby red color. Glimpses of earth and leather and gingery spice. Wonderfully fleshy, with gorgeously fine, chewy, dark fruit flavours.

18～20℃

商务宴请，酒友交流 business dinner, wine appreciation

羊扒，普遍浓味中式菜肴 lamb, rich Chinese food

此酒采用被认为是世界上最古老的1860年老树穗乐仙葡萄酿制，从第一个年份1979年发行以来，受到各地葡萄酒爱好者和收藏家的追捧，是澳大利亚极品好酒。Since its inaugural release in 1979 this piece of liquid history has become one of the most sought after and collectable wines throughout the world. Tahbilk-1860 Vines Shiraz is listed as "Excellent" in Australian wine auctioneers-Langtons Classification of Australian Wine.

德宝庄珍藏穗乐仙（红）
Tahbilk Reserve Shiraz

¥¥¥

深宝石红色，有洋李、咖啡温和的辛香，香味复杂悠长，单宁平衡。Deep ruby red color. Plum, coffee and warm spices on a dry savoury nose. A complex and very long palate with balanced tannins.

18～20℃

商务宴请，酒友交流 business dinner, wine appreciation

羊扒等普遍浓味中式菜肴 lamb, rich Chinese food

用1933年的老树穗乐仙酿造，被澳大利亚最大的葡萄酒拍卖行朗顿誉为"黑马"，陈年天分极佳。With Langtons describing Tahbilk-Reserve Shiraz as a "Dark horse wine with superb class. Incredibly strong regional provenance and made for long term cellaring".

德宝庄嘉本纳沙威浓（红）
Tahbilk Cabernet Sauvignon

¥¥

宝石红色，有胡椒和草药的香味，酒味香浓，柔滑而温和，单宁干爽。Ruby red color. A developed earthy, peppery and herbal nose. A savoury, smooth and gentle palate with supple but drying tannins.

18~20℃

浪漫婚宴，温馨家宴 wedding, family gathering

牛仔腿，烧羊羔腿，烧乳猪等普遍红色肉类，浓味中式菜肴 whole roast baby lamb, roast suckling pig, chorizo and lentil stew

该酒真实反映纳金碧湖地区嘉本纳沙威浓的个性，是德宝庄嘉沙葡萄酒的代表作。A cabernet sauvignon masterpiece from Tahbilk, reflecting the outstanding quality of cabernet sauvignon in the Nagambie Lakes appellation.

德宝庄穗乐仙（红）
Tahbilk Shiraz

¥¥

深宝石红色，有樱桃香，微辛辣的草药、皮革、田野香。结构紧密而又平衡，单宁柔和丝滑。Deep ruby red color. Floral aromas of cherries with lightly spiced and herbal suggestion of leather and farm floor. The wine is tight knit, balanced with fine-grained powdery tannins.

18~20℃

浪漫婚宴，温馨家宴 wedding, family gathering

牛扒，羊扒 beef steak, lamb

一款可陈放7~15年的德宝庄穗乐仙佳酿。A very pleasant Tahbilk Shiraz with a potential to age 7~15 years.

德宝庄雪当利（白）
Tahbilk Chardonnay

¥¥

浅稻草黄色，有复杂烤面包和坚果香，口感丰厚，有成熟桃子、蜜瓜，奶油等复杂香味。Pale Straw color. Intricate toasty, nutty aromas. A full-bodied palate of developed peach and melon fruit flavours and a subtle creamy complexity.

12~14℃

情侣约会，浪漫婚宴 dating, wedding

海鲜，烤虾 seafood pasta, grilled crayfish

德宝庄园唯一一款经橡木桶陈年的白葡萄酒，法国与美国橡木桶的交叉使用为该款葡萄酒带来别致的风味。The only Tahbilk white to have time in wood, the use of both French and American oak contributes lifted spice and butterscotch flavours.

德宝庄美莎丽（白）
Tahbilk Marsanne

¥¥

酒色浅黄，有复杂水果和坚果香。口感有柠檬、蜂蜜和桃子等复杂香味。Pale straw color. Intricate fruity, nutty aromas. Abundance of lemon, honey and peach fruit flavours.

12~14℃

情侣约会，友人相聚 dating, friends gathering

海鲜意粉，烤虾 seafood pasta, grilled crayfish

尽管美莎丽不是澳大利亚主要种植的葡萄品种，不过该款白葡萄酒却成为澳大利亚最受欢迎的葡萄酒之一。Being one of the most loved wines in the country, Marsanne remains an alternative variety in Australia.

澳大利亚精品酒庄
Australian Boutique Wineries

爵士山庄、宾迪山庄、百发庄园是维多利亚省的3个精品酒庄，它们的葡萄酒都是限量生产，是买家追捧的热门澳洲葡萄酒，根据澳大利亚朗顿拍卖行的统计，以上酒庄皆为拍卖行炙手可热的89个澳大利亚名庄之一。

Jasper Hill, Bindi Composition and By Farr is three of the boutique wineries of Victoria, Australia. With an annual limited production, the wines of these three are the favors of buyers. According to Australian auction house Langton, they are among the top 89 wineries of Langton.

爵士山庄穗乐仙（红）
Jasper Hill Shiraz

¥¥¥¥

酒色深红，伴有香料和巧克力香味，柔顺的单宁，平衡自然的酸度。Deep red color. Delightful bouquet of rich spices and chocolate. Fine supple tannins, balanced by great natural acidity.

18~20℃

商务宴请，酒友交流 business dinner, wine appreciation

浓味红肉 red meat with rich sauce

爵士山庄信奉中国道家的“无为”哲学，是公认的维多利亚酒王，澳大利亚朗顿拍卖行89款炙手可热的名庄之一，产量极少。One of the top 89 wines and rated Outstanding by Langton. Delightful expression of fruit as red and dark berries mixed with rich spices and chocolate.

宾迪贝露娃（红）
Bindi Composition Pinot Noir

¥¥¥

酒色亮红，散发圆润甜美的红莓、樱桃、蜜饯、五香粉、肉桂等香料香气。拥有浓郁的红樱桃、红洋李果汁口感，单宁可人。Bright red color. A rounded bouquet of cranberries and candied cherries, five spice and cinnamon. A full and ripe palate with red cherries, red plums and lovely tannins.

18~20℃

商务宴请，温馨家宴 business dinner, family gathering

烧牛柳，粤式扣肉 roast tenderloin, cantonese double braised pork meat with fat

澳大利亚最优秀的三大贝露娃葡萄酒之一。一款物超所值的葡萄酒。One of the top three pinot noir wine in Australia. An excellent wine and offers great value.

百发庄园贝露娃（红）
By Farr Pinot Noir

¥¥¥

酒色紫红，带有腌制樱桃、矿物、烟肉等香味。入口优雅浓郁，单宁柔滑怡人。Bright red purple color. Cherry notes mingle with plums, mineral, earth and smoked meats. An elegant and focused palate with juicy and crisp finishing.

18~20℃

商务宴请，酒友交流 business dinner, wine appreciation

牛扒，羊扒 beef steak, lamb

百发庄园是澳大利亚拍卖行89款炙手可热的名庄之一，这是其最出色的酒款，极具法国布根地风情。One of the top 89 wines by Langton. This Pinot Noir is its best creation with a Burgundy style.

百发庄园穗乐仙（红）
By Farr Shiraz

¥¥¥

酒色暗红，散发明显的熏肉的味道，带有甘草和紫罗兰的馨香。入口优雅浓郁，单宁柔滑。Dark red color. Explosively aromatic nose shows roasted meat, pungent violets and licorice. Suave and elegant palate with silky tannins.

18~20℃

浪漫婚宴，商务宴请 wedding，business dinner

铁板类红肉 teppenyaki red meat

该酒完美体现在凉爽气候条件下成长的穗乐仙的风味。This wine perfectly showcases the depth and complexity of cool climate Shiraz.

西澳省
Western Australia

山度富
Sandalford

山度富由澳大利亚首位测绘局长约翰·赛墨柔创立于1840年，是西澳历史最悠久也是最大的家族酒业之一，酒庄多次荣获国际殊荣并曾接待多个国家领导人的访问。

Founded in 1840 by the State's first Surveyor General John Septimus Roe, Sandalford is one of the oldest and largest private - owned wineries. It is the frequent award-winner at Wine Competitions and has received government officials from other countries.

山度富家族珍藏（红）
Sandalford
Prendiville Reserve
Cabernet Sauvignon

¥¥¥¥

深樱桃红色，此酒表现出玛格丽河区非一般的香气，几乎以花香和香水紫罗兰的味道为主导，单宁柔滑，酸度平衡。Dark cherry color. In what is a typical for Margaret River this wine has almost a floral nose reminiscent of perfumed violets with silk-like tannins and balancing acidity.

18~20℃

商务宴请，酒友交流 business dinner, wine appreciation

鸭肉，羊排，烤羊肉 duck, lamb chop, roasted lamb

以山度富庄主家族姓氏命名，这款酒是山度富的顶级产品，仅在极佳年份酿制，每次仅出品500箱。Named after the Prendiville family, owners of Sandalford Wines, this ultra-premium wine will only be released in great vintages and only as a limited released 500 case lot.

山度富珍藏嘉本纳沙威浓（红）
Sandalford
Estate Reserve
Cabernet Sauvignon

¥¥¥

深樱桃红色，有复合的水果香和烟熏巧克力橡木香味。酒体中至厚身，单宁柔滑。Dark cherry red color. Complex briary fruit with smoldering chocolate oak. Medium to full bodied wine with velvet-like tannins.

18~20℃

商务宴请，酒友交流 business dinner, wine appreciation

羊架，意大利美食及浓味型中式菜肴 rack of lamb, tomato based Italian dishes

具有波尔多风味的澳大利亚佳酿，勇夺2009年澳大利亚葡萄酒大赛最佳嘉本纳沙威浓葡萄酒大奖。A Bordeaux-like Australian wine, winner of Best Cabernet Sauvignon, Australian Wine Challenge 2009.

山度富珍藏穗乐仙（红）
Sandalford Estate Reserve Shiraz

¥¥

深樱桃红色，橡木桶赋予了此酒独特的朗姆酒、葡萄干、摩卡咖啡还有丝丝巧克力的味道。酒体中度至厚身的，单宁丝滑柔顺。Dark cherry red color. The use of oak gives rise to flavours of rum and raisin, mocha and chocolate. Medium to full-bodied wine with silky smooth tannins.

18~20℃

商务宴请，温馨家宴 business dinner, family gathering

红肉菜式，香辣蔬菜 any red meat, spicy vegetarian dishes

该酒采用玛格丽河区的老树穗乐仙葡萄以橡木桶酿制，让穗乐仙的特点表露无遗。The old-vine fruit from Margaret River really shines in this wine, displaying the traditional hallmarks of great Shiraz.

山度富珍藏雪当利（白）
Sandalford Estate Reserve Chardonnay

¥¥¥

稻草黄色，雪当利散发出细腻的白核果味道和香草及法国橡木味，此酒结构良好，酸度平衡得恰到好处，余味清新有活力。Mid-straw color. Chardonnay shows classic white stone fruit nuances and vanillin French oak. A fine-boned wine with balancing acidity and a clean and austere finish.

12~14℃

情侣约会，浪漫婚宴 dating, wedding

鱼肉，白肉 fish, white meat

一款经法国布根地橡木桶陈年的优秀玛格丽河雪当利。An outstanding Margaret River Chardonnay aging in Burgundian French barriques.

元素
Element

同由西澳名庄山度富主理，来自天鹅谷50年树龄葡萄酿造的元素系列，果香怡人，无需陈年太久即可饮用。是容易欣赏，物超所值的日常佳酿。

Fruit driven, immediately approachable and make for soft, easy and uncomplicated drinking. These everyday wines offer fantastic value for money and over-deliver on quality. Most of the wines within the Element range come from 50 years old vines grown in Swan Valley.

元素穗乐仙嘉本纳（红）
Element Shiraz Cabernet

¥ ¥

深樱桃红色，伴有黑浆果的香味，一丝穗乐仙的芳香和嘉本纳的桉树香。柔软绒滑的单宁使酒体结构更佳。Dark cherry red color. Blend of dark berry flavours with hints of Shiraz spiciness and Cabernet eucalypt. The texture of the wine is weighted by soft tannins.

18~20℃

友人相聚，温馨家宴 friends gathering, family gathering

红色肉类，以西红柿做配汁的意大利餐，广东扣肉，湖南肉等浓味菜肴 myriad of Italian tomato based dishes, the more rich meat dishes or fat pork meat

西澳经典穗乐仙嘉本纳名酿。A classy little red from this good Western Australian vintage.

元素梅乐（红）
Element Merlot

¥ ¥

深樱桃红色，典型的洋李香味，伴有樱桃花香味，口感活跃，果味香浓的中等厚度酒体。Dark cherry red color. Classic fresh plums aroma with fragrant cherry blossom. Plenty of sappy, juicy fruit flavours fill out the medium bodied palate.

18~20℃

情侣约会，友人相聚 dating, friends gathering

红色肉类，以西红柿做配汁的意大利餐，广东扣肉，湖南肉等浓味菜肴 myriad of Italian tomato based dishes, the more rich meat dishes or fat pork meat

来自西澳产区的超值梅乐佳酿。An affordable Merlot vintage from West Australia.

元素雪当利（白）
Element Chardonnay

¥ ¥

酒色浅金，有成熟的桃色水果香和法国香草橡木味，入口柔滑美妙，散发有核水果、瓜或无花果香味。Light gold color. Lovely aroma of ripe peachy fruit with vanillin French oak notes. A lovely and creamy palate with stone fruit, melon or fig fruit flavours.

- 18~20℃
- 情侣约会，友人相聚 dating, friends gathering
- 鱼类，白肉 fish, white meat
- 从这款酒你或多或少可以探得澳大利亚雪当利成功的奥妙。The Element Chardonnay demonstrates why Australia has been so successful in making this style of wine.

元素嘉本纳沙威浓（红）
Element Cabernet Sauvignon

¥ ¥

樱桃红色，散发成熟黑醋栗和橡木香气，中度酒体，结构平衡，单宁柔滑。Cherry red color. Ripe savoury cassis with gunflint oak influence. A medium-bodied and well balanced wine with soft velvety tannins.

- 18~20℃
- 友人相聚，温馨家宴 friends gathering, family gathering
- 鸭肉，鹌鹑，牛肉，羊肉 duck, quail, beef, lamb
- 体现了西澳天鹅谷50年树龄嘉本纳沙威浓葡萄特性的红酒，加上2%的玛碧更显魅力。This wine is a showcase of the 50 years old Cabernet Sauvignon vines, to which the 2% Malbec adds a charming character.

豪园

Howard Park

豪园酒庄是蕴含中国风水的西澳名庄，有西澳酒王之美称，是4个获得澳大利亚最著名酒评家詹姆斯·哈立德五星级最高评分的酒庄之一。

Wines bearing the Howard Park label express the very finest fruit grown in the premier regions of Western Australia's Margaret River and Great Southern. WINES in the word for the continuous 6 years by *Wine Spectator*.

豪园珍藏嘉本纳（红）

Howard Park Cabernet Sauvignon

¥¥¥

酒色深红，以乡土味为基调，配合浓郁的黑加仑子水果香味以及高级的雪松橡木香，单宁成熟。Dense blood red color. Dusty earthy tones with dark blackcurrant fruits and high class cedary oak. Matured ripe tannins.

- 18~20℃
- 商务宴请，酒友交流 business dinner, wine appreciation
- 牛扒，羊扒 beef steak, lamb
- 目前西澳三大红酒王之一，被澳大利亚酒评家雷乔丹视为西澳最好的嘉本纳沙威浓。Judged best West Australian cabernet by Australia's wine critic Ray Jordan, and ranked as being "…the years best Australian wine, bar none".

豪园礼士顿庄园穗乐仙（红）

Howard Park Leston Shiraz

¥¥¥

石榴红色，散发着成熟的洋李和水果蛋糕的芳香。充满甜美的水果口味，单宁成熟。Garnet red color. A demonstration of ripe plum and fruitcake like aromas and flavours. A palate of fruit sweetness with full ripe tannin.

- 18~20℃
- 浪漫婚宴，温馨家宴 wedding, family gathering
- 猪肋排，火鸡，烧烤 spare ribs, turkey with stuffing, barbecues
- 此系列以酒庄老板杰夫博诗的父亲名字命名，100％采用西澳著名产区玛格丽河的葡萄，风格沉稳有力。Named after Jeff Burch's father, the Leston Shiraz is 100% Margaret River Shiraz with strong regional definition.

豪园礼士顿庄园嘉本纳（红）
Howard Park Leston Cabernet Sauvignon

酒色深红，散发成熟黑加仑子、紫罗兰和阔叶林植被的味道，中度酒体，单宁紧实且圆润。Dark red color. Intense bouquet of ripe blackcurrants, violets and leafy forest floor with dusty and savoury undertones. Mid-palate with firm but fine textured tannins.

18～20℃

浪漫婚宴，商务宴请 wedding, family gathering

烧牛柳，粤式扣肉 roast tenderloin, cantonese double braised pork meat with fat

获得英国《品醇客》杂志四星级评分。This wine is awarded four-star wine by *Decanter in Uk*.

豪园白沙威浓（白）
Howard Park Sauvignon Blanc

浅稻草黄色，散发豌豆、鼠尾草干，百香果的香气，有草药以及青草的风味，展现了白沙威浓典型清新的酸度。Pale straw color. A fragrant nose of snow peas, guava, dried sage and passion fruit. The palate has herbal and grassy notes, displaying the typical crisp acidity of Sauvignon Blanc.

7～12℃

浪漫婚宴，温馨家宴 wedding, family gathering

牡蛎，蟹肉，鸡肉 oyster, crab, chicken

此酒入选詹姆斯·哈立德的澳大利亚百佳葡萄酒，近年来均获得著名酒评家92分以上的评分。Listed in Top 100 Wines of James Halliday and won remarks higher than 92 points in recent years.

豪园诗歌庄园穗乐仙（红）
Howard Park Scotsdale Shiraz

酒色深浓，有该区地道红酒特有的丁香、茴芹气息，入口即感浓香馥郁，有胡椒、香料的味道，单宁精致复杂。Dense red color. Aromas of spicy clove and anise so typical of the apellaltion. A rich and opulent palate with licorice spicy and peppery notes. Fine and complex tannins.

18～20℃

情侣约会，温馨家宴 dating, family gathering

铁板类红肉 teppenyaki red meat

斩获各项国际大奖，包括2008年穗乐仙国际葡萄酒大赛银奖。Award winners of various wine competition including Silver Medal of 2008 Syrah du Monde.

豪园诗歌庄园嘉本纳（红）
Howard Park Scotsdale Cabernet Sauvignon

¥¥¥

酒色黑红，散发浓郁丰富的浆果香和烤黑巧克力味。单宁结实。Dark blood red color. Intense bouquet of ripe, rich berry fruits and dark cooking chocolate with firm tannin.

- 18~20℃
- 商务宴请，温馨家宴 business dinner, family gathering
- 意大利面，铁板或烧烤的牛羊，浓味芝士 pastas, roasted & grilled meat, dishes and strong cheese
- 在1999年推出第一个年份，在短时间内就取得了巨大的成功，是西澳嘉本纳沙威浓的优秀代表作。First produced in 1999, this wine has already in its short life span proved how good the cool climate Great Southern can be, defining Great Southern Cabernet Sauvignon.

豪园威士莲（白）
Howard Park Riesling

¥¥¥

浅稻草黄色，散发酸橙、苹果花蕾、茉莉花的味道。纯净浓郁的果香，搭配矿物的味道，酸甜的口感平衡极好。Very pale straw color. Lime juice, floral notes of apple blossom and jasmine. Great focused palate with purity of fruit and a mineral texture balanced by clean acidity.

- 12~14℃
- 情侣约会，温馨家宴 dating, family gathering
- 蔬菜类菜肴，烤三文鱼，蟹肉 vegetable dishes, grilled Salmon, crab
- 澳大利亚本土好评如潮，曾获四星级及以上评分。A four-star rating wine enjoying an outpouring of favorable comments in Australia.

豪园雪当利（白）
Howard Park Chardonnay

¥¥¥

浅稻草黄色，此酒香气优雅圆润，散发香瓜、腰果、矿物和柑橘的水果气息，入口能感其以果香为主导，配有淡淡的橡木香。Very pale straw color. This is an elegant wine with melon, cashew, mineral and citrus aromas. Subtle oak supports the fruit and barrel fermentation characters.

- 12~14℃
- 情侣约会，浪漫婚宴 dating, wedding
- 龙虾，鸡肉，海鲈鱼 lobster, chicken, sea bass
- 豪园白葡萄酒佳作，斩获多项国际大奖如国际雪当利葡萄酒大赛金奖等荣誉。A master piece of Howard Park white wine, awards winner of various international wine challenges such as Gold at Chardonnay du Monde.

狂鱼
Mad Fish

狂鱼是由豪园酒庄老板拥有的新一代明星酒庄，其酒容易欣赏，主要是面向热爱生活、家庭、朋友、美食与美酒的葡萄酒爱好者。

Mad Fish was produced with an emphasis on enjoyment and drinkability. These wines are great for those who enjoy the pleasures of life, family, friends, food and wine.

狂鱼贝露娃（红）
Mad Fish Pinot Noir

¥¥

酒色亮红，散发诱人的红樱桃、草莓和泥土的气息，单宁结构紧密但不失精致。Bright crimson red color. Attractive aromas of red cherry, strawberry and earth. The palate exhibits a firm yet subtle backbone of tannin.

14~17℃

情侣约会，友人相聚 dating, friends gathering

三文鱼，意大利香肠，猪肉 salmon, Italian sausage, pork

是备受英国《品醇客》杂志推崇的贝露娃佳酿。A pinot noir vintage highly recommended by *Decanter in UK*.

狂鱼穗乐仙（红）
Mad Fish Shiraz

¥¥

酒色亮红，有芬芳的黑果、巧克力和新鲜黑胡椒的味道，口感丰富且轻柔，高雅。良好的单宁和橡木香。Vibrant red color. Fragrant aromas of black fruits, chocolate and fresh black pepper. Rich and elegant palate with fine tannin and elegant background oak.

14~17℃

浪漫婚宴，温馨家宴 wedding, family gathering

烧烤类菜肴，牛扒 barbecues, beef steak

此酒表现出突出的西澳穗乐仙特色，备受年轻人欢迎。A wine reflects classic Shiraz characters from the southwest of Western Australia, popular with the younger generation.

狂鱼嘉本纳梅乐（红）
Mad Fish Cabernet Sauvignon Merlot, Cabernet Franc

¥¥

酒色深红，散发黑樱桃、蓝莓和巧克力香味，口感丰富，带有烤咖啡豆、桑葚口味，单宁紧密，酸度平衡。Dark crimson red color. Aromas of black cherry, blueberry and chocolate. A complex palate with flavors of roasted coffee beans, mulberries, dusty tannins and well balanced acidity.

14~17℃

友人相聚，温馨家宴 friends gathering, family gathering

牛扒，羊扒 beef steak, lamb

一款优雅，易饮易明的葡萄酒，在澳大利亚与欧美市场都大受欢迎。An elegant wine,easy to understand.It is popular in Australian,U.S.A.and European market.

狂鱼清纯雪当利（白）
Mad Fish Chardonnay

¥¥

淡稻草黄色，复合的熟白桃、蜜瓜香，优质的柚子和柑橘香气，层次丰富的口感展示出柑橘味之间的平衡。Pale straw color. A combination of riper white peach, melon aromas, finer grapefruit and citrus nose. Complex palate with layers of fruit flavours balanced against the citrus flavours.

12~14℃

情侣约会，友人相聚 dating, friends gathering

鸡肉，火鸡 chicken, turkey

受到美国葡萄酒杂志《葡萄酒观察家》和著名酒评家罗拔•派克的推崇。This wine is highly recommended by *Wine Spectator* Magazine and the world-renowned wine critic Mr. Robert Parker.

狂鱼白沙威浓（白）
Mad Fish Sauvignon Blanc Semillon

¥¥

柠檬金色，带有类似香槟的气味，以及稀有白垩土矿物质的独特气息。复杂而多层次的风味，酒体平衡柔软。Crisp golden yellow color. Almost like you find in champagne, with a wonderful chalky mineral character. A platter with complex array of flavors, a balance and soft body wine.

7~12℃

情侣约会，友人相聚 dating, friends gathering

龙虾，蟹肉 lobster, crab

荣获2005年国际葡萄酒与烈酒大赛英国站铜奖的佳酿。Winner of Bronze of 2005 International Wine and Spirits Competition – UK.

新南威尔士省
New South Wales

福林湖
Lake's Folly

福林湖是由麦斯雷克于1963年创立的澳大利亚首个商铺式酒园。庄主大胆在原本种植穗乐仙和沙美龙的葡萄园上改种嘉本纳沙威浓，并戏谑地把酒庄取名为Lake's Folly(意为雷克的愚蠢所为)。结果却酿出猎人谷的头号名酒。
Established by Dr. Max Lake in 1963, Lake's Folly was one of Australia's first boutique wineries. The vineyard is regarded as one of the best sites in the Hunter Valley yet it began by planting Cabernet Sauvignon and Chardonnay in a region better known for Shiraz and Semillon. It is no doubt that Lake's Folly is the No.1 winery in the valley since its success benefit the whole Hunter Valley.

福林湖庄园嘉本纳（红）
Lake's Folly Cabernets

¥¥¥

酒色砖红，散发黑樱桃、桑葚以及黑森林巧克力蛋糕香味，中度酒体，口感丰富，带有柔顺的单宁。Vibrant brick red color. Aromas of black cherry, mulberry and black forest cake. A medium-bodied wine with rich palate and soft tannins.

18~20℃

商务宴请，酒友交流 business dinner, wine appreciation

红烧翅，扣辽参，羊肉，鲍鱼 shark's fin, braised sea cucumber, lamb, abalone

猎人谷酒王。它非凡的酒质无疑在爱酒之人的追求行列中！ Lake's Folly is a small and iconic Hunter winery and vineyard whose followers are doubtless rejoicing in the remarkable consistency and quality.

麦威廉酒厂
McWilliam's

由麦威廉酒业集团创建于1877年，是澳大利亚最老牌的葡萄酒企业之一。金河、珍品、吧王系列是集澳大利亚著名葡萄产区的优质葡萄，以精湛工艺酿造而成。该产品产量及品质稳定，是物美价廉的畅销葡萄酒系列。
For 120 years since Samuel McWilliam planted his first vines in 1877 successive generations of the McWilliam family have been making fine wines bearing the McWilliam's name. McWilliam's Inheritance, River Gum ranges are made to a consistent style, are well priced for their quality.

金河穗乐仙嘉本纳（红）
River Gum Shiraz Cabernet

¥ ¥

酒色砖红，芳香扑鼻，带有森林浆果和黑加仑子的香气。入口微辛辣，充满黑加仑子味及橡木味，后味柔顺持久。Brick red color. Fragrant spicy, forest berry, blackcurrant aromas. The palate is spicy with blackcurrant fruit flavours accompanied by vanilla oak. The finish is long and soft.

18~22℃

友人相聚，活力派对 friends gathering, party

牛扒，烤羊肉，意大利餐 beef steak, lamb roast, Italian cuisine

金河获得无数好评的混酿型红葡萄酒。A River Gum blend winning numerous reputation.

金河雪当利（白）
River Gum Chardonnay

¥ ¥

酒色浅黄，散发有核果实和蜜瓜香气，口感带浓郁的成熟水蜜桃香味。酸度紧致，结构平衡，后味悠长。Pale yellow color. Stone fruits and melon aromas with rich peach characters in the palate. Tight acid and lingering finish.

12~14℃

情侣约会，友人相聚 dating, friends gathering

海鲜类如虾蟹，龙虾等 seafood dishes like shrimp, crab, and lobster

麦威廉旗下一款性价比好的日常餐酒。An affordable McWilliam table wine with good quality.

珍品穗乐仙嘉本纳（红）
Inheritance Shiraz Cabernet

¥ ¥

深棕红色，气味芳香，有森林浆果、丁香橡木的香味。口感有成熟洋李味，新鲜活跃，余韵柔软而持久。Brick red color. Fragrant spicy, forest berry aromas combined with clove oak characters. The palate is vibrant and fresh with ripe plum. The finish is quite long and soft.

- 18~22℃
- 友人相聚，温馨家宴 friends gathering, family gathering
- 牛肉，烤羊肉，意大利菜 beef casseroles, lamb roast, and Italian cuisine
- 价钱实惠，品质稳定的澳大利亚优质餐酒。An affordable Australian table wine with stable quality.

珍品梅乐穗乐仙（红）
Inheritance Shiraz Merlot

¥ ¥

酒色深红，既有穗乐仙辛辣和浆果的香味，也有梅乐带有的柔和洋李香气。伴有辛辣水果和香草及雪松的味道。Bright crimson color. Perfectly combines the spicy, berry flavours of Shiraz with the soft, plum characters of Merlot. Spicy fruit flavours combined with a touch of vanilla and cedar oak.

- 18~22℃
- 友人相聚，温馨家宴 friends gathering, family gathering
- 牛扒，羊扒 beef steak, lamb
- 性价比高的新南威尔士穗乐仙佳酿。An affordable Shiraz of New South Wales.

珍品哥伦巴雪当利（白）
Inheritance Chardonnay

¥ ¥

酒色浅黄，带有成熟的蜜瓜和有核果实特有的香气。入口有清爽的、成熟的雪当利葡萄果香，酸度平衡恰到好处。Pale yellow color. The nose shows buttery melon and stone fruit characters. A palate with clean ripe Chardonnay fruity flavours balanced with crisp acidity.

- 7~12℃
- 情侣约会，活力派对 dating, party
- 亚洲美食，海鲜 asian cuisine, seafood
- 雪当利与哥仑巴葡萄搭配的完美例子，一款酸度平衡恰到好处的白葡萄酒。A perfect match of Chardonnay and Colombard grapes.

吧王嘉本纳沙威浓（红）
Barwang Hilltops Cabernet Sauvignon

¥ ¥ ¥

宝石红色，散发黑加仑、甘草和微妙的薄荷香气。该酒有黑加仑、甘草和黑巧克力口味，单宁柔顺，后味绵延。Ruby Red color. Aromas of blackcurrant, licorice and subtle mint notes. Dominant flavours of cassis, licorice and dark chocolate. Savoury tannins with lingering finish.

- 18~22℃
- 商务宴请，温馨家宴 business dinner, family gathering
- 浓味红肉 red meats with a rich sauce
- 从1996年起，此酒每年在国内外均有获奖，且最少一枚金牌入囊。Since 1996, this wine has been wining numerous international challenges.

吧王穗乐仙（红）
Barwang Hilltops Shiraz

¥¥¥

宝石红色，充满辛辣的成熟黑莓、李子、香草和豆蔻的香气，该酒口感丰富，单宁柔顺，酒体紧密。Ruby Red color. Spicy blackberry, ripe plum, vanilla and nutmeg oak. A rich palate with soft and fine tannins binds the wine together.

- 18～22℃
- 浪漫婚宴，商务宴请 wedding, business dinner
- 牛扒，羊扒 beef steak, lamb
- 澳大利亚著名酒评家詹姆斯·哈立德称赞其兼具上乘且稳定的质量。James Halliday comments that its each vintage has been extremely good, with very clear varietal character.

吧王雪当利（白）
Barwang Tumbarumba Chardonnay

¥¥¥

稻草黄色，雪当利赋予该酒浓郁桃仁香。蜜瓜、香草酥饼和橡木刨花香味浓厚，余味散发可口橙子皮清香。Straw yellow color. Intense peach kernel Chardonnay aromas with honeydew melon, shortcake and pencil shaving oak notes. A finish with orange peel acid.

- 12～14℃
- 情侣约会，友人相聚 dating, friends gathering
- 鸡肉，鸭肉 chicken, duck
- 一款十分讨好的新南威尔士白葡萄酒。A charming New South Wales white wine.

美 国
AMERICA

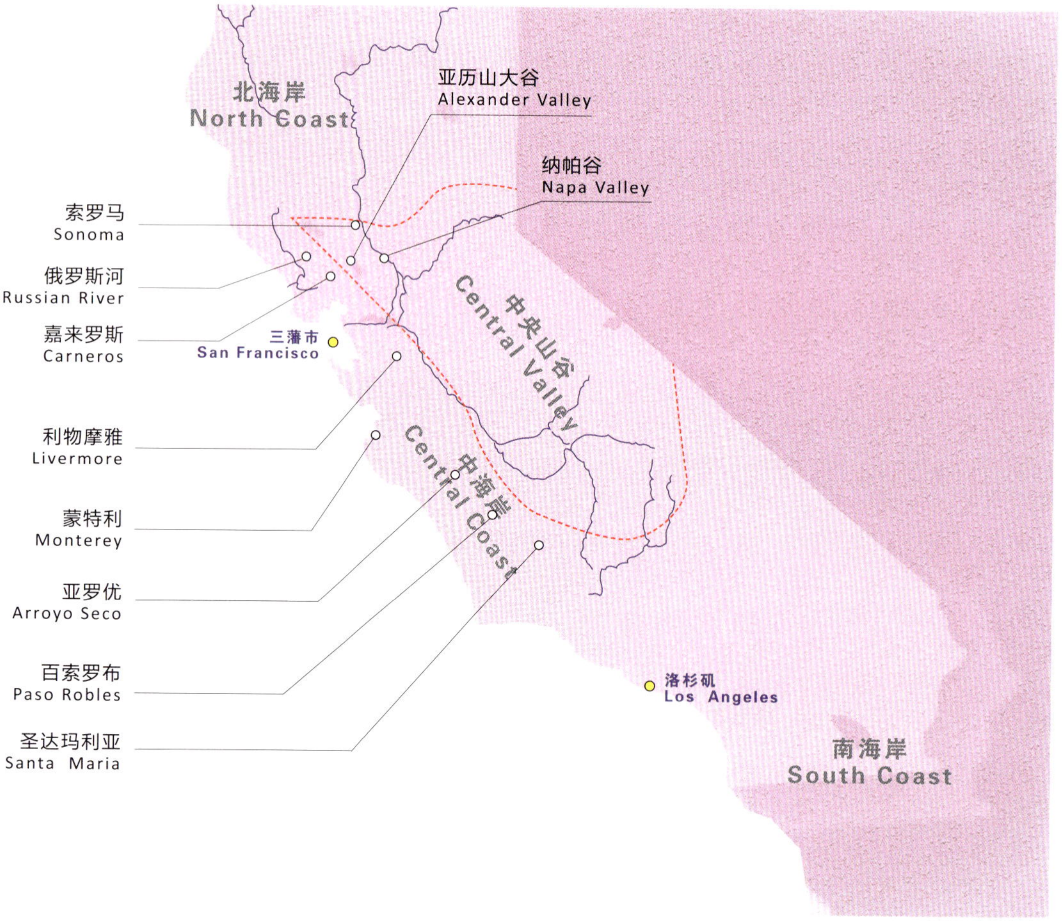

美国葡萄酒产区示意图

美 国 与澳大利亚一起被誉为最成功的两大新世界葡萄酒生产国。其产区主要集中在加利福尼亚州（以下简称“加州”）、华盛顿州和俄勒冈州，无论是在美国国内还是国际市场上，目前加州的葡萄酒产量和知名度在美国酒中占绝对的优势，以至于有人说它将会追赶上法国，并且在不久的将来与法国葡萄酒并驾齐驱。

美国葡萄酒业在品牌、包装策略及酿酒技术方面有不少特长，甚至对消费者喜好的口味都有深入的研究。虽然气候炎热，但因为有海洋的调节，加州葡萄酒保留了优雅细致的风味。大部分的加州葡萄酒都是单一葡萄品种。加州酿酒葡萄是一个开放的市场，透过供需之间的平衡，葡萄种植者可依据市场需求作出弹性调整。相对于欧洲的传统方式及严格的法定管制，这简直是难以置信的美国神话。

{葡萄品种}

仙粉黛在美国成名，是美国最具代表性的葡萄品种，在加州的种植仅次于嘉本纳沙威浓。此外，各大流行品种在美国均有种植，如红葡萄品种穗乐仙、梅乐、贝露娃；白葡萄品种雪当利等。

仙粉黛 Zinfandel

嘉本纳沙威浓 Cabernet Sauvignon

梅乐 Merlot

雪当利 Chardonnay

{美国葡萄种植区制度}

美国政府没有效仿欧洲国家采取葡萄酒分级制度，而是根据本国葡萄酒发展的实际情况，于1983年由美国酒类、烟草和武器局（BATF）开始实施美国葡萄种植区制度（American Viticulture Areas，简称AVA），成功保护和规范了葡萄酒生产。

AVA是一个类似于法国的AOC制度的法规，主要根据地理和气候的特点来划分全国的葡萄酒产区，不像法国的AOC还对葡萄品种和酿造方法等有具体要求。

根据BATF规定，在酒标上标明内容需达到2个要求：

1. 85%的葡萄必须来自标明的产区。

2. 只有采用了75%以上的某葡萄品种，才允许在酒标上标明该品种名称，85%的葡萄必须来自标明的产区。

此外，生产商可以根据自身需要种植任何葡萄品种，采用任何种植技术。实际上，美国政府并不希望通过AVA来评判某个产区的葡萄酒质量，也算是美国人一贯崇尚的自由精神的一种体现。

葡萄酒产区

加州 美国的葡萄酒产区基本集中在加利福尼亚州，根据品种区域化和土壤气候条件，加州划分为五个各具特色的葡萄产区，从南往北为：考施拉（Coachella）、蒙特利（Monterey）、弗瑞斯诺（Fresno）、洛蒂（Lodi）和纳帕（Napa）。这5个区只有弗瑞斯诺和纳帕区是酿酒区，其中最经典的是纳帕谷（Napa Valley）。

纳帕谷 Napa Valley

纳帕谷的酒因在1976年巴黎评酒会击败包括法国在内诸多国家的葡萄酒摘得桂冠而成名，是第一个跻身世界级的葡萄酒产区。近年又有许多国际酒界巨头到此开辟疆土，如法国武当王家族的作品一号（Opus One）和柏图斯家族的杜美尼斯（Dominus）等等。2005年在奥斯卡奖中大出风头的电影《杯酒人生》，更是把纳帕谷的迷人风光和葡萄酒魅力展示在全世界面前；2009年好莱坞又开拍了《酒瓶惊世》等与纳帕谷有关的电影。来自各方面的种种关注让纳帕谷从未离开过酒迷的视线。

纳帕谷主要种植的红葡萄为嘉本纳沙威浓，是在巴黎评酒会成名的葡萄品种，可酿出波尔多风格且高雅浓郁的红葡萄酒；白葡萄为雪当利，是典型的布根地白葡萄酒风格，丰厚醇和。另外，纳帕谷还出产老龄葡萄树的仙粉黛葡萄酒，树龄一般超过40年甚至100年，辛香明显，口感复杂富有层次。

目前，纳帕谷的酒庄已经成为加州的观光重点。200来家大小酒庄几乎都提供葡萄酒试饮服务，旅馆、餐厅林立，各式配套设施齐全，被称为葡萄酒爱好者的迪斯尼乐园。

加州其他产区

- 索罗马谷（Sonoma Valley）：靠近纳帕谷，是加州第二大重要产区，生产大量的中端至精品葡萄酒。
- 亚历山大谷（Alexander Valley）：以浑厚有力的嘉本纳沙威浓出名。
- 利物摩雅（Livermore）和蒙特利（Monterey）：中端酒产量较大，也不缺少精品酒。
- 百索罗布（Paso Robles）：新星产区，以仙粉黛葡萄酒出名。
- 俄罗斯河谷（Russian River Valley）：气候凉爽，以果香浓郁、口感饱满的雪当利和柔顺香醇的贝露娃出名。

华盛顿 华盛顿州位于加州北海岸的正上方，与波尔多地区处于同一纬度，气候跟新西兰十分相似。华盛顿州大部分的葡萄园都是坐落在哥伦比亚谷（Columbia Valley）。夏季日照时间比纳帕谷还要长，可使葡萄充分成熟，而夜晚气温却比加州低，可使葡萄保留较高的酸度。华盛顿的葡萄酒特点是有芳香的水果口感，其白葡萄酒十分出色。此外，嘉本纳沙威浓、梅乐、雪当利、白沙威浓以及威士莲都非常不俗。

俄勒冈 俄勒冈州的酒庄规模普遍不大，该区最大最出名的产区是威廉美特山谷（Willamette Valley），俄勒冈大约70%的酒庄都位于此，以与法国布根地风格相似的贝露娃葡萄酒出名，品质极高，非常值得一试。

纳帕谷
Napa Valley

作品一号
Opus One

此酒由法国酒王菲力溥男爵和美国酒王罗拔·蒙大卫联手打造的加州顶级品牌，创下了无数个加州葡萄酒的第一，拥有无数酒评家的好评，以出产美国最好的葡萄酒而闻名世界。
Joint venture between Robert Mondavi from USA and Baron Philippe de Rothschild from France producing a proprietary Bordeaux-style blend. Winner of numerous awards and highly recommended by the wine critics.

作品一号庄园（红）
Opus One

¥¥¥¥¥

深宝石红色，此酒带有干草莓、香草豆和摩卡咖啡的香气，后味带有甘甜的黑巧克力味和一丝烟草余韵。 Deep ruby-red color. Aromas of dried strawberry, vanilla bean and mocha. The wine finishes with bittersweet chocolate and a hint of smoke.

- 18~20℃
- 商务宴请，酒友交流 business dinner, wine appreciation
- 牛扒，羊扒 beef steak, lamb
- 美、法两国酒王联手打造的顶级佳酿，获得的奖项和赞誉无数，受到爱酒之人的追捧。Joint venture between Robert Mondavi from USA and Baron Philippe de Rothschild from France.One of the top Napa wineries.

乔丹酒园
Jordan

自第一个年份1976年上市以来，乔丹一直是加州葡萄酒的佼佼者，在国际上声誉良好，是法国传统酿酒艺术与美国创新酿制科技的完美结合。

The first vintage 1976 craved out its way to the top winery in California. Jordan combines the French traditional winemaking and American way of innovation, standing reputably in the wine world.

乔丹酒园嘉本纳沙威浓（红）
Jordan Cabernet Sauvignon

¥¥¥

宝石红色，有复合的水果香和烟熏橡木香，酒体复杂而多层次，悠长的后味带出雪茄和矿物的味道。Ruby color, Rich berry and full fruit capped with a toasty oak nose. The wine very rich in texture, a lingering finish of subtle earth, cigar tobacco and is cedar.

- 18~20℃
- 商务宴请，酒友交流 business dinner, wine appreciation
- 烤肉或烧肉类 roasted and grilled meats
- 美国白宫的御用葡萄酒。是加州上等葡萄酒的典范之作，被美国《酒》杂志评为2007年50款最受欢迎的红葡萄酒之一，位于消费者最喜爱的嘉本纳沙威浓第二名。The wine was selected by White House with strong Bordeaux style. An exemplary wine in California, it is ranged No. 2 by the 2007 *Wine & Spirit* magazine's 50 most popular red wines.

乔丹酒园雪当利（白）
Jordan Chardonnay

¥¥¥

酒色金黄，带有青苹果、奇异果、蜂蜜的味道，并渗透出轻微的橡木桶烟熏味道。酒体清爽，带有黄油般的圆润口感。Golden yellow color, a citrus and mineral bouquet includes delicate aromas of crisp green apple, kiwi, honey and lightly toasted oak. A light-bodied wine with creamy palate.

- 7~12℃
- 浪漫婚宴，商务宴请 wedding, business dinner
- 虾蟹类海鲜 seafood dishes like shrimps, pawns and crabs
- 美国白宫的御用葡萄酒。被美国《酒》杂志评为2007年50款最受欢迎的白葡萄酒之一，位于消费者最喜爱的雪当利第五名。The wine selected by White House. It is ranged No. 5 by the 2007 *Wine & Spirit* magazine's 50 most popular white wines

嘉威逊
Cuvaison

享誉世界的纳帕谷名庄，嘉威逊的酿酒哲学是“保持其原有的风味，又不失庄园特色”，建园于1969年，嘉威逊的美酒现已进入多家航空公司和豪华邮轮，在40多个国家和地区都有销售。

Cuvaison believes that "Our wines must be the unique expression of the singular sites from which they come, and it' s our wonderful vineyards that shape the style of each wine." Now it is distributed in all 50 states and are presented in over 40 international markets, first class airlines and on the top rated cruise lines.

嘉威逊嘉本纳沙威浓（红）
Cuvaison Cabernet Sauvignon

¥ ¥ ¥

此酒酒香以红色水果味为基调，带有摩卡咖啡，可可豆和香兰素的芬芳。口感带有浓厚的果核芳香，单宁结实。Vibrant red fruit tones, layered with mocha, cocoa, vanillin notes with a sweet, dense core and solid tannins, finely hewed for long cellaring.

18~20℃

商务宴请，温馨家宴 business dinner, family gathering

黑椒牛扒，烤肉，熏肉 black pepper steak, roast meat, bacon meat

一款嘉威逊酒庄典型的混酿红酒佳酿，极具陈年天分。A typical Cuvasion blended red wine with great potential in cellar.

嘉威逊贝露娃（红）
Cuvaison Pinot Noir

¥¥¥

酒色深红，散发着红色覆盆子、黑樱桃、烟熏皮革还有百香果的芬芳。口感浓郁，单宁完整且精致，余韵悠长。Deep crimson red color. Aromas of red raspberry, black cherry, smoky leather and allspice. A rich palate with integrated tannins and a long finish.

18~20℃

浪漫婚宴，温馨家宴 wedding, family gathering

烧牛柳，粤式扣肉 roast tenderloin, Cantonese double braised pork meat with fat

这是一款非常典雅的贝露娃葡萄酒，是庄园的代表之作。This is a classic example of Pinot Noir grown in the Estate Vineyard.

嘉威逊雪当利（白）
Cuvaison Chardonnay

¥¥¥

稻草黄色，该酒带有甜蜜醉人的花香和当地特有的气息。有白桃、香料、热带水果的香味，如丝柔滑的口感更让人一试难忘。Light straw color. This handcrafted Chardonnay is rich with white peach, spice, tropical fruit and has a lush velvety texture.

12~14℃

情侣约会，酒友交流 dating, wine appreciation

鸡肉，火鸡，龙虾，海鲈 chicken, turkey, lobster, sea bass

该区凉爽的气候有利于雪当利葡萄的生长，加上酒园工人的悉心照料，造就了这款顶级葡萄酒。The cool climate vineyard allows the Carneros Estate nearly perfect conditions year after year to produce world class Chardonnay.

杜美尼斯
Dominus

杜美尼斯位于历史悠久的纳帕谷，由享誉世界的法国酒王之王柏图斯老板JPM家族创于1983年，致力于酿造反映当地风土特色的葡萄酒，是美国葡萄酒新生代领军品牌之一。
Dominus is the proprietary red wine produced in the heart of Napa Valley by Christian Moueix and his team. Since 1983, our goal has been express the unique terroir found at the historic Napanook Vineyard.

杜美尼斯（红）
Dominus

¥¥¥¥

酒色深红，带有浓烈的黑色浆果、烟草、可可的香气，入口感觉刚柔并济，单宁结实，口感圆润优雅。Dark red color. The nose is dense with dark berry, blond tobacco and cacao. The entry is both powerful and supple with firm tannins, round and elegant.

18~20℃

商务宴请，酒友交流 business dinner, wine appreciation,

牛扒，羊扒 beef steak, lamb

由法国酒王之王柏图斯老板JPM家族创于1983年，以酒体的复杂性和迷人的泥土气息在众多加州酒中脱颖而出。Produced by Moueix family in 1983, it has become known since its first release for its complexity and earthy character.

小常识
Q & A

问：进口葡萄酒为什么会有中文背标?

答：根据中国法律，所有的进口食品都要加中文背标，如果没有中文背标，有可能是走私进口，质量不能保证。按照国家进出口商品、国家卫生部和国家商标法的规定，进口酒的中文标签主要包括：葡萄品种、葡萄酒中文名、收成年份、质量等级（按出产国法规而定）、产区、产酒国名、净含量、酒精浓度、灌装日期、国内经销商或代理商的公司名及联系方式等项。

利物摩雅和蒙特利
Livermore & Monterey

威迪酒园
Wente

威迪酒园建园于1883年，现在已经传到第五代人，是加州最古老的酿酒家族之一。其代表的不仅是质高价优的中高档葡萄酒，更代表一种高品质的加州葡萄酒乡生活方式。出品绝对是高性价比和风格优雅的加州名酿。
Today, the Wente family remains focused on their enduring winemaking philosophy of creating wines that reflect their vineyard origins and the unique qualities of the San Francisco Bay (Livermore Valley) and Monterey (Arroyo Seco) American viticultural areas.

威迪珍藏嘉本纳沙威浓（红）
Wente Charles Wetmore Cabernet Sauvignon

¥¥¥

宝石红色，该酒带有非常浓郁黑加仑子、巧克力、黄糖、香料的味道，酸味平衡，口感圆润、余味丝滑悠长。
Ruby red color. Flavors of black cherry, chocolate, brown sugar and spice. Balanced acidity and round mouthfeel with a smooth, long-lasting finish.

18~20℃

商务宴请，温馨家宴 business dinner, family gathering

羊肉，红烧翅，扣辽参，鲍鱼 lamb, braised sea cucumber, shark's fin, abalone

该园种植了创始人在19世纪从法国波尔多名村玛歌村带回的嘉本纳沙威浓，是威迪的一个顶级庄园。The cabernet sauvignon in the vineyard which is one of the best in Wente is brought back by the founder from Magaux in France.

威迪酒园珍藏梅乐（红）
Wente Crane Ridge Merlot

¥ ¥ ¥

深宝石红色，入口顺滑、单宁诱人。山莓、草莓、香草橡木和焦糖的味道明显，余味悠长，还充满水果气息。Bright ruby color. With a smooth palate and inviting tannins, this wine has flavors of raspberry, strawberry, vanilla oak, caramel and a long, fruity finish.

- 18~20℃
- 浪漫婚宴，温馨家宴 wedding, family gathering
- 浓味型主菜，芝士拼盘 hearty entrée, a selection of rich cheese
- 美国白宫的指定用酒之一。用法国、美国小橡木桶酿造而成。The wine selected by White House, aging in small French and American oak barrels.

威迪珍藏贝露诺（红）
Wente Reliz Creek Pinot Noir

¥ ¥ ¥

酒色深红，富有樱桃、香草、烟熏橡木、泥土和雪茄盒的味道。该酒回味后感觉到泥土和丁香的味道。Deep ruby-red color. Aromas of cherry, vanilla, toasted oak, earth and cigar box. Undertones of earth and clove.

- 18~20℃
- 酒友交流，温馨家宴 wine appreciation, family gathering
- 三文鱼，吞拿鱼，鸡肉，鸭肉 salmon, tuna, chicken, duck
- 获得2010年罗拔惠特利酒评挑战赛的银牌。Winner of Critics Silver Medal, Robert Whitley's Critics Challenge, June 2010.

威迪珍藏雪当利(白)
Wente Riva Ranch Chardonnay

¥ ¥ ¥

酒色金黄，味道富有蜂蜜、麦子、肉桂和淡淡的花香，入口口感平衡，因在橡木桶内陈年而赋予了精致的橡木、黄油、香草味道。Rich golden color. Aromas of honey, graham, cinnamon and light floral notes. In the palate, it's balanced by subtle oak, butter and vanilla from barrel aging.

- 12~14℃
- 浪漫婚宴，温馨家宴 wedding, family gathering
- 虾，蟹，海鲈 lobster, crab, sea bass
- 在2010年斩获多项世界大奖，是威迪的精品雪当利。A premium chardonnay of Wente. Winners of several wine challenges around the world in 2010.

威迪酒园雪当利(白)
Wente Morning Fog Chardonnay

¥ ¥

酒色浅黄，带有因陈年而产生的青苹果、热带水果、肉桂、香草和精致的橡木香气。入口可感饱满的酒体，酸度平衡。Pale yellow color. Aromas and flavors of green apple, tropical fruits, subtle oak, cinnamon and vanilla from barrel aging. The wine is with a mouth-filling body and balanced acidity.

7~12℃

情侣约会，浪漫婚宴 dating, wedding

海鲜，淡味型中式菜肴 seafood, light Chinese dishes

为保证特有的风味与品质，所有的葡萄都由威迪家族葡萄精心培育。To ensure the quality and flavor of the chardonnay wine, all grapes are carefully selected and grown by the Wente Family.

威迪酒园白仙芬黛(粉红)
Wente Summerset White Zinfandel

¥ ¥

呈现三文鱼色调，是一款新鲜、清爽风格的粉红酒。香气和口感都带草莓、西瓜的味道。其果味突出但甜度并不彰显。This salmon-colored White Zinfandel is made in a light bodied. Delicate and refreshing with strawberry and watermelon aromas and finishing with a good, crisp balance.

7~12℃

情侣约会，友人相聚 dating, friends gathering

海鲜，鸡肉，淡味型中式菜肴 seafood, chicken, light Chinese food

一款呈现美国特色的粉红葡萄酒佳酿。With white Zinfandel, it is a typical American rose.

威迪酒园嘉本纳沙威浓（红）
Wente Southern Hill's Cabernet Sauvignon

¥¥

酒色深红，此酒散发着丰富的樱桃和洋李的香味。单宁柔滑、容易入口。余味丝滑悠长。Deep red color, This Cabernet Sauvignon is with mouth-filling flavors of black cherry and plum. Rich, yet approachable tannins provide a long, smooth finish.

18~20℃

友人相聚，温馨家宴 friends gathering, family gathering

烤肉或烧肉类，浓味型的鱼类菜肴 roasted and grilled meats, fuller flavored fish

此酒葡萄来自由庄园创始人在19世纪从法国波尔多名村引进的优秀品种，当地的土壤和微型气候为其提供了非常适合的生长环境。Carefully age and blend this wine to produce a Cabernet Sauvignon that is supple and smooth with lush flavours of cherry and cassis, and hints of cedar and floral violets in the nose.

威迪酒园仙芬黛（红）
Wente Beyer Ranch Zinfandel

¥¥

宝石红色，带有仙粉黛经典又独有的洋李、山莓和蓝莓的味道，酒体厚身、结构良好，酸味与烤橡木味平衡得恰到好处。Ruby Red color. Classically fruity Zinfandel with aromas of plums with hints of rasberry and blueberry. It is well-balanced on the palate with good acidity and delicious toasty oak.

18~20℃

友人相聚，浪漫婚宴 friends gathering, wedding

铁板烤肉，辛辣的意大利面，水果，芝士 grilled meats, spicy pasta sauces, fruits, cheese

此酒具有典型的仙粉黛香气，是加州葡萄酒中的优秀之作。A masterpiece of Californian wine with typical Zinfandel aroma.

百索罗布
Paso Robles

海狸庄园
Castoro Cellars

海狸是创始人尼尔在意大利工作时朋友对他的昵称，尼尔很喜欢此名，用它来命名自己的酒庄，并用可爱的小海狸作为酒标。海狸庄园是美国新生代酒庄的代表，注重创新，每个年份都有新惊喜。

The founder Niels' long-time nickname "Beaver," evolved further when he was working in Italy and his friends soon took to calling him "Il Castoro," which is beaver in Italian.Castoro Cellars' "dam fine wines" sport a picture of a beaver on each label. Each vintage presents a new challenge and Niels is more than willing to constantly and creatively experiment.

海狸庄园嘉本纳沙威浓（红）
Castoro Cellars Cabernet Sauvignon

¥¥

矿石红色，闻之有复合的水果香和烟熏橡木香。入口有成熟的浆果和水果味以及烤橡木香，单宁感较强，适合陈年饮用。Deep red brick color. This wine is packed with rich berry and full fruit capped with a toasty oak nose. A finish with lush flavors that are not blown away with excessive.

18～20℃

浪漫婚宴，温馨家宴 wedding, family gathering

牛扒，羊扒 beef steak, lamb

经橡木桶23个月培养的嘉本纳沙威浓佳酿，从庄园旗下数个葡萄园精选葡萄混酿而成。The is made from a blend of several outstanding vineyards. Aged for 23 months in select French and American oak barrels.

海狸庄园梅乐（红）
Castoro Cellars Merlot

¥¥

此酒有热情的果香。酸度与糖度相当平衡，入口有精细而丰富的果味和橡木香。The wine reaches full maturity with great balance in acid and sugar. This Merlot has a subtle but full nose of fruit and oak.

- 18~20℃
- 情侣约会，浪漫婚宴 dating, wedding
- 烤肉，烟熏肉 roasted meat, barbecued steaks
- 荣获圣地亚哥葡萄酒挑战赛金奖的梅乐佳酿。Winner of Gold Medal at San Diego Wine Competition.

海狸庄园仙粉黛（红）
Castoro Cellars Zinfandel

¥¥

深矿石红色，有典型的仙粉黛香味，伴有葡萄干、巧克力、咖啡和烟熏的味道。入口有强烈的浆果、肉桂的香味。Deep red brick color. Typical Zinfandel fruit with slight raisin and spice notes. The aroma has intense berry interspersed with a touch of cinnamon.

- 18~20℃
- 友人相聚，商务宴请 friends gathering, business dinner
- 红肉，芝士，烤鸭，乳鸽 light red meat dishes, roast goose, roast pigeon or a cheese platter
- 此酒是海狸庄园的旗舰产品。所用葡萄选自庄园最顶级的葡萄园。Zinfandel has emerged as the flagship varietal of Castoro Cellars. Created primarily from vineyards in the Templeton Gap.

海狸庄园雪当利（白）
Castoro Cellars Chardonnay

¥¥

浅稻草黄色，有复杂的柑橘和苹果香。口感丰富，有橡木香，爽脆持久。Straw yellow color. A complex wine full of citrus and apple notes with oak aromas, a lush mouth feel and a lingering crisp finish.

- 7~12℃
- 情侣约会，活力派对 dating, party
- 海鲜，芝士意粉，鸡肉 seafood dishes, rich cream sauces on pasta, chicken
- 此酒用加州百索罗布几个葡萄园的葡萄混合酿造。This wine is rich in every sense. Castoro Cellars have blended several local vineyards; Hog Canyon, Blind Faith and Abernathy.

海狸庄园富美宝（白）
Castoro Cellars Fume Blanc

¥¥

酒色浅黄，酒香新鲜清爽，有很好白沙威浓果香。入口清新，有持久的柑橘味。Bright straw yellow color. This is a fresh and crisp vintage, with classic Sauvignon Blanc aromas. The mouth is clean and has lingering citrus notes.

- 7~12℃
- 活力派对，浪漫婚宴 party, wedding
- 贝壳类海鲜头盘，普遍淡味型鱼类 shellfish appetizers, most light fish entrees
- 旧金山市和中央海岸葡萄酒挑战赛银奖得主。Winner of Silver Medal at San Francisco & Central Coast Wine Competitions.

中海岸

Central Coast

喜事园

Hayes Ranch

喜事园是美国葡萄酒市场的传统中坚品牌之一，这里的酿酒师尊崇传统的酿酒工艺，采用的葡萄均精选自加州优质的葡萄园，所产的佳酿自然也有别具一格的风土特色。其产品品质优物美且价格合理，是加州优质葡萄酒的典范之一。

The Hayes family was a true California ranching family whose livelihood depended on the land. Their winemaker carries on the Hayes tradition by crafting bright, delicious wines from premier California vineyards.

喜事园嘉本纳沙威浓（红）

Hayes Ranch Cabernet Sauvignon

¥ ¥

酒色亮红，微微的烟熏味道加上浓郁的水果香味，构成了该款酒的主骨架。口感平衡，单宁圆润细滑，丰厚优美。Bright red color, fruity flavors and light oak hints are the backbone of this wine, bringing good balance and tannins with a smooth finish.

18～20℃

友人相聚，活力派对 friends gathering, party

烧烤类食物，意大利面 grilled foods, pasta dishes

喜事园的极品酒之一。One of the top wines of the Hayes Family.

喜事园雪当利(白)

Hayes Ranch Chardonnay

¥ ¥

酒色金黄，充满成熟的苹果和香草的味道，还有香草和黄油的清香。酒体丰富复杂的果香和油香，圆润且后味持久。Golden yellow color, aromas of ripe apple, vanilla and hints of butter. With subtle flavors are a very smooth wine has a soft fruity finish.

7～12℃

情侣约会，活力派对 dating, party

海鲜，浓味家禽菜肴 seafood dishes, rich cream sauces on chicken

是典型的雪当利葡萄品种所酿出的精品酒。A fine wine made by typical chardonnay varietal.

California

阿根廷
ARGENTINA

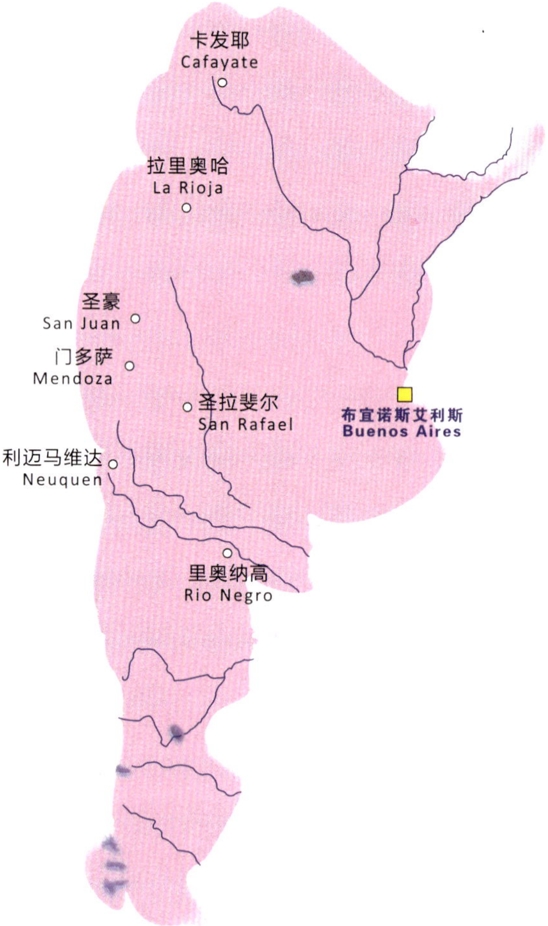

阿根廷葡萄酒产区示意图

阿根廷 的葡萄酒受到欧洲特别是西班牙酿酒技术的影响。在16世纪，阿根廷成为西班牙殖民地的时期，葡萄藤嫁接的技术传到阿根廷，从此葡萄的种植和葡萄酒生产技术迅速在阿根廷境内传播。

在阿根廷葡萄酒业的发展初期，当地的酒庄是重量不重质，90%的产量都被国内的市场消化。到了20世纪90年代，阿根廷已成为欧洲外最大的葡萄酒产国，随着本土市场的对外开放，阿根廷的酒庄开始狠抓质量，葡萄酒的品质一日千里，并逐渐成为南美洲第二大葡萄酒出口国。

葡萄品种

玛碧虽然源于法国，但目前却在阿根廷表现最好，是阿根廷最出名、最具特色且最广泛种植的葡萄品种。其他品种也在一批批的欧洲移民热潮中逐一引进，如法国的嘉本纳沙威浓、梅乐、穗乐仙、雪当利，西班牙的添帕尼优，意大利的圣祖维斯、多姿桃和巴比拉等。也有一部分历史悠久的本土葡萄品种，不过大部分不外销，因此不太为人所知。

玛碧 Malbec

嘉本纳沙威浓 Cabernet Sauvignon

梅乐 Merlot

雪当利 Chardonnay

{法定产区标准法令}

为有效控制葡萄酒生产质量，阿根廷国家农业技术研究院（Instituto Nacional de Tecnologia Agropecuaria）于1999年提出了一系列方案，经政府核定而成为阿根廷法定产区标准（D.O.C.）的法令，唯有符合资格的葡萄酒标签上可以注明D.O.C.法定产区的字样。施行至今，已核定4个法定产区，分别是位于门多萨（Mendoza）的卢冉德库祖（Lujan de Cuyo）、圣拉斐尔（San Rafae）与迈普（Maipu）和位于拉里奥哈（La Rioja）的法马汀娜谷（Valle de Famatina）。

法定产区的内容包括4个重点：

（1）必须全部使用划定的法定产区内生产的葡萄。

（2）每公顷不得种植超过550株葡萄藤。

（3）每公顷葡萄产量不得超过1万千克。

（4）葡萄酒必须在橡木桶中培养至少1年，并且必须在瓶中熟成至少1年。

这样的法定产区标准限制了葡萄的种植不至于滥产，也同时保障了葡萄酒的基本质量。但实际上，许多有分量的酒庄仍然没有实行D.O.C.标准，依旧沿袭传统方式栽种、照顾和酿造，继续坚持自我风格。

{葡萄酒产区}

门多萨 位于安第斯山脉（Andes）脚下的门多萨产区，由于天然融雪的自然灌溉系统，非常适合各种葡萄的生长，是最优秀、最出名的产区，占全国葡萄酒产量的一半以上。

圣豪 是阿根廷的第二大葡萄酒产区，气候比门多萨更干更热，以产穗乐仙出名，也产类似雪利的加强型葡萄酒。

拉里奥哈 是阿根廷历史最悠久的葡萄酒产区，面积小，以本土葡萄品种Torrontes Riojano出名。

里奥纳高 位于阿根廷最南端的葡萄酒产区，所产葡萄酒口感平衡。

门多萨
Mendoza

美贝园
Finca EL Origen

美贝园是由智利享有盛誉的老牌家族酒厂圣卡罗在阿根廷投资兴建的贵族酒园。该园位于阿根廷优质葡萄产区的黄金地带，拥有得天独厚的自然条件，加上圣卡罗首席酿酒师的精心打理，这里的美酒品质出众，性价比甚高。
Finca el Origen is a noble winery invested by Santa Carolina, one of the well-known brands in Chile. Thanks to favorable conditions in the exceptional vineyards, head winemaker of Santa Carolina is able to produce the best quality wines at reasonable prices.

美贝园至尊珍藏玛碧（红）
Finca EL Origen Gran Reserva Malbec

¥¥

酒色亮红，散发甜甜的浆果和洋李酱香味还有丝丝香料味道，单宁圆滑，口感浓郁，酒体结构良好。Exceptional bright red color. Sweet aromas of berries, plum jam and the soft spice notes. Very concentrated palate with round tannins and great structure.

18~20℃

酒友交流，温馨家宴 wine appreciation, family gathering

烧鹅，烧乳鸽，酱鸭，羊扒，牛仔扒，芝士 red meats, any pasta with a rich sauce as well as fine cheeses

经全新法国橡木桶12个月的培养，是该园的极品酒。Ageing in French oak for 12 months, this wine is the top in Finca el Origen

美贝园珍藏玛碧（红）
Finca EL Origen Reserva Malbec

¥ ¥

宝石红色，成熟洋李、蓝莓、草莓和肉桂的味道非常突出。单宁柔顺丝滑，余韵怡人。Ruby red colors. Intense aromas of ripe plums, blue berries and strawberries accompanied with cinnamon notes. Soft tannins with a pleasant finish.

- 18～20℃
- 浪漫婚宴，温馨家宴 wedding, family gathering
- 烧鹅，烧乳鸽，酱鸭，羊扒，牛仔扒，芝士 red meats, any pasta with a rich sauce as well as fine cheeses
- 获得《葡萄酒观察家》和《品醇客》杂志推崇的阿根廷佳酿。Highly recommended by *Wine Spectator* and *Decanter*.

美贝园珍藏嘉本纳沙威浓（红）
Finca EL Origen Reserva Cabernet Sauvignon

¥ ¥

石榴红色，覆盆子的味道在烟草的香味下衬托得更明显。有成熟水果的浓郁味道，余味悠长。Intense deep dark garnet color. Aromas of raspberries enhanced by tobacco notes. Good concentration with ripe fruit flavours and a persistent finish.

- 18～20℃
- 商务宴请，酒友交流 business dinner, wine appreciation
- 牛扒，烤羊 beef steak, roast lamb
- 世界酿酒大师米切尔罗兰也是其顾问，此酒是物美价廉之选。With consultation from Michel Rolland, the world's top winemaker. A good wine bears reasonable price.

美贝园珍藏维奥娜(白)
Finca EL Origen Reserva Viognier

¥ ¥

酒色金黄，此酒散发着成熟的热带水果和杏子芳香。口感轻身爽脆，结构良好，且带有美妙的柠檬香味冲击着味蕾。 Greenish-yellow color. This wine offers ripe tropical fruits and apricot aromas. The mouth-feel is light, crisp and well-balanced with great citric notes.

- 7～12℃
- 情侣约会，友人相聚 dating, friends gathering
- 沙拉，白肉，豆类，鳟鱼，三文鱼 salads, white meats, pulse, trout, salmon
- 一款非常讨好的白葡萄酒，是海鲜餐馆的最爱。An adorable white wine, the perfect partner of seafood restaurants.

美贝园嘉本纳沙威浓（红）
Finca EL Origen Cabernet Sauvignon

宝石红色，复杂的成熟水果香混合上甜甜的香料气息。酒体结构良好，口感丝滑，黑色水果和黑醋栗味道持久。Bright ruby red color. With complex aromas that blend ripe fruit and sweet spices. This well-structured wine has velvety texture with a palate of black fruits and cassis.

18～20℃

活力派对，浪漫婚宴 party, wedding

辣味肉食，家禽 spicy meat, game birds

美贝园经典的嘉沙葡萄酒，获得市场的欢迎。As a typical Cabernet Sauvignon red wine of Finca el Origen, it is highly demanded by the market.

美贝园玛碧（红）
Finca EL Origen Malbec

酒色深紫色，有黑色水果香，伴随着紫罗兰和烤面包的味道。酒体丰满，入口即能感受到它浓郁，成熟的黑醋栗以及甜甜香料味道。Dark purple color. This wine offers bright black fruit aromas with light violet notes and a touch of toast. Full and rich palate with ripe cassis and sweet spice.

18～20℃

活力派对，浪漫婚宴 party, wedding

红肉，意粉 red meats, pasta

该酒庄入门级的玛碧红葡萄酒，却能充分展示玛碧的魅力。A starter Malbec wine of Finca EL Origen but clearly displaying the charisma of Malbec.

美贝园雪当利（白）
Finca EL Origen Chardonnay

酒色黄绿色，此酒散发着热带水果的味道，宜人的烤面包香和榛果味道。酒体口感浓稠，有柠檬清香和矿物的味道。Greenish-yellow color. Aromas of tropical fruits with pleasant toast bread notes and toasted hazelnuts. Fresh, generous in volume and concentration, citric, mineral; elegant.

7～12℃

情侣约会，浪漫婚宴 dating, wedding

蔬菜沙拉，白肉类菜肴 green salads, white meat dishes

该酒展示了门多萨地区雪当利的优秀品质。This wine shows the outstanding quality of Chardonnay in Mendoza.

安第雄狮（红）
Andes Leopardo Malbec

¥

酒色亮红，散发活泼的黑色水果甜香、微妙的甘草味，口感香甜，单宁柔顺，适合浅龄饮用。Bright crimson color. Open bouquet of sweet black fruit and subtle licorice. A sweet palate with supple tannins. Easy to drink.

14～17℃

友人相聚，活力派对 friends gathering, party

烤肉，意大利面，中至辣味菜式，中硬度芝士 grilled meat, pasta, mild to spicy cuisine, semi-hard cheeses

阿根廷雪当利与白翠柠绝妙搭配的完美体现。A perfect showcase of Chardonnay and Chenin Blanc blend in Argentina.

安第雄狮（白）
Andes Leopardo Torrontes

¥

酒色亮黄，散发白玫瑰、柑橘的香气，口感清新柔和，后味带有橡木桶的烟熏气息。Bright yellow color. Aromas of white roses and citrus. Fresh, crispy and smooth, with an oaky touch balanced finish.

7～12℃

情侣约会，活力派对 dating, party

意大利烟熏火腿，鸡肉，布尔辛芝士 prosciutto, chicken, Boursin

圣安纳酒厂为中国饮家量身订造的白葡萄酒，价廉物美，适合入门饮家。A white wine tailor-made by Santa Ana for Chinese beginner with a reasonable price.

圣安纳
Santa Ana

圣安纳创建于1891年，是阿根廷历史悠久且一直处于领先地位的极少数品牌之一，近年来在国际重大葡萄酒大赛屡获殊荣，品质受到越来越多人的关注与赞赏。

Santa Ana was founded in 1891 by one of the pioneers in the development of wine-making in Argentina. It is one of the very few wineries founded in the 19th century that have been able of adapt itself to the constant changes in the markets and consumers to maintain its leadership and have received an important number of awards in recent years.

酒王
Unanime

酒名意为“共同的理念”，指的是圣安纳团队达成的共识：国内外的认可给予酒庄推出圣安纳酒王的信心，2005年是其第一个年份，是圣安纳的标杆之作。

It refers to a group of people sharing the same views, summarizing the agreement of Santa Ana's winemakers and agronomists: to craft a superior red blend since 2005.

圣安纳至尊酒王（红）
Santa Ana Unanime

¥ ¥ ¥

樱桃红色，酒香优雅，果味、巧克力、烟草的味道，又混合了黑椒和肉汁的香味。圆润的单宁与新鲜的酸度平衡恰到好处。Cherry-red color. An elegant aromas of chocolate and tobacco, with black pepper and some fleshy notes. Round tannins that blend nicely with its fresh, juicy acidity.

18~20℃

商务宴请，酒友交流 business dinner, wine appreciation

烤红肉，炖肉，砂锅菜 grilled red meat, stews, casseroles

此酒采用平均树龄为50年的葡萄酿制。The grapes of this wine were grown in selected old vineyards and the vines average 50 years old.

玛诗歌园
La Mascota

采用玛诗歌园的葡萄酿制而成，在橡木桶陈年9~15个月，特点是口感复杂、平衡。
specially cared from its origin in "La Mascota" vineyard and aged from 9 to 15 months in oak barrels. Complex, balanced, sophisticated.

玛诗歌园玛碧（红）
La Mascota Malbec

¥¥

酒色紫红，散发浓郁的黑色水果味道，混合了香草、果酱还有甘草的淡香，口感香甜，单宁结构丰满。Purple red color, aromas of black fruits, jam and vanilla, with a subtle licorice touch. Sweet attack and full bodied tannins.

18~20℃

浪漫婚宴，商务宴请 wedding, business dinner

烤肉，浓味芝士 grilled meats, strong cheeses

获得罗拔派克85分评分的玛碧佳酿。A Malbec wine winning 85 points made by Robert Parker.

玛诗歌园嘉本纳沙威浓（红）
La Mascota Cabernet Sauvignon

¥¥

酒色深红，有甘草、醋栗和覆盆子果酱的混合香气，入口有烤胡椒和巧克力香味，酒体丰满，后味悠长。Deep red color, aromas of licorice, cassis and warm raspberry jam. Elegant touch of roasted pepper and chocolate. Full-bodied, very long aftertaste.

18~20℃

商务宴请，温馨家宴 business dinner, family gathering

意大利面，红肉，成熟的软芝士 pastas, red meats, mature soft cheeses

该酒真实反映纳门多萨地区嘉本纳沙威浓特色。A cabernet sauvignon masterpiece from Mendoza.

玛诗歌园雪当利（白）
La Mascota Chardonnay

¥¥

酒色浅黄，梨子、菠萝芳香四溢，经橡木桶陈年所赋予的甜美香草气息更增添了其可人之处。Light yellow color. Aromas of pears and pineapples are enhanced with a subtle layer of sweet vanilla from barrel ageing.

7~12℃

情侣约会，友人相聚 dating, friends gathering

烤鸡肉，新鲜三文鱼，龙虾等白肉，淡味意大利面 grilled chicken, fresh salmon, lobster, light pasta dishes

该酒采用优质橡木桶陈年，展示了玛诗歌园雪当利的优秀品质。Aging in the highest quality oak, this wine shows the outstanding quality of La Mascota Chardonnay.

珍藏
Reserve

白葡萄酒和红葡萄酒在橡木桶分别陈年9个月和12个月，酒液在橡木桶的作用下更加顺滑芳香。

The best of the fruit together with the smooth complexity of the oak. Aged between 9 and 12 months in oak barrels.

圣安纳珍藏玛碧穗乐仙（红）
Santa Ana Reserve Malbec Shiraz

¥¥

酒色亮红，散发甜美的黑莓、橡木、洋李，还有丝丝入扣的香草味道，酒体结构良好，单宁绵软。Intense red color. Sweet aromas of blackberries, oak and plums, combined with a subtle vanilla notes. Good structure and velvety texture, with soft tannins.

18~20℃

浪漫婚宴，温馨家宴 wedding, family gathering

火鸡，意大利面，烧烤，炖肉 turkey, pastas, barbecue, stews

获得多项国际大奖，如国际葡萄酒和烈酒大奖的铜奖。An international awards winner such as the bronze medal at International Wine & Spirits Competition.

圣安纳珍藏嘉本纳沙威浓（红）
Santa Ana Reserve Cabernet Sauvignon

¥¥

宝石红色，黑加仑子和黑醋栗的果香四溢，还有胡椒和香料的味道构成了更复杂的香气。酒体平衡，单宁成熟。Deep ruby red color. Blackcurrant and cassis fruit aromas layered with green peppercorns and spicy complexity. Well balanced mouth-filling wine textured with ripe tannins.

18~20℃

友人相聚，温馨家宴 friends gathering, family gathering

调味的红肉，羊肉，发酵成熟的芝士 seasoned red meats, lamb, ripe cheeses

获得罗拔派克87分评分的嘉沙佳酿。A Cabernet Sauvignon wine winning 87 points made by Robert Parker.

圣安纳珍藏多伦提斯（白）
Santa Ana Reserve Torrontes

¥¥

酒色浅黄，散发白色玫瑰的香气，伴有酸橙的甜味。口感酸爽柔顺。Pale yellow color. Very typical and elegant aromas of white flowers and roses on the nose layered with citric notes. Crispy and smooth mouth filling.

7~12℃

友人相聚，浪漫婚宴 friends gathering, Wedding

海鲜，中味至辣味菜式 seafood dishes, mild to spicy cuisine

获得阿根廷国内多项大奖，深受当地人民喜爱的一款白葡萄酒。Winners of numerous Argentinean competitions, popular with the local market.

单品
Varietals

采用多个葡萄园的单一葡萄品种酿制而成，体现的是单一品种的特色。

Grapes are from selected vineyards in the High Area of Mendoza River, to show you a 100% varietal wines.

圣安纳玛碧（红）
Santa Ana Malbec

¥

酒色亮红，散发浓郁紧密的果香，如李子和樱桃的味道。酒体结构平衡，口感绵软，余味优雅。Lively red color, intense aromas of fruits such as plums and cherries. Well balanced in the mouth with soft and nice finish.

18~20℃

友人相聚，活力派对
friends gathering, party

烤肉，意大利面，中至辣味菜式，中硬度芝士 grilled meat, pasta, mild to spicy cuisine, semi-hard cheeses

此酒在亚洲市场大获成功，曾获得日本国际葡萄酒挑战赛最受欢迎葡萄酒奖项。This wine enjoys a great success in Asian market, a winner of Japan International Wine Challenge Seal of Approval.

圣安纳嘉本纳沙威浓（红）
Santa Ana Cabernet Sauvignon

¥

酒色深红，入口有香浓的果味，酒体结构平衡，单宁甜美。Deep red color. Fruity and well-balanced in the mouth, with presence of black fruits and sweet tannins.

18~20℃

友人相聚，活力派对
friends gathering, party

烤肉，水煮蔬菜，中硬度芝士 grilled red meat with vapour-cooked vegetables, semi-hard cheeses

此酒在亚洲市场大获成功，曾获得日本国际葡萄酒挑战赛最受欢迎葡萄酒奖项。This wine enjoys a great success in Asian market, a winner of Japan International Wine Challenge Seal of Approval.

圣安纳多伦提斯（白）
Santa Ana Torrontes

¥

亮丽的黄绿色，散发着白花、玫瑰花的香气。更有柑橘酸橙味道。口感新鲜爽脆，余味香气平衡，有橡木气息。Yellow greenish color. White flowers, roses and citric aromas. Fresh, crispy palate, with an oaky touch balanced finish.

7~12℃

友人相聚，活力派对 friends gathering, party

海鲜，中味至辣味菜式 seafood dishes, mild to spicy cuisine

荣获2008年国际葡萄酒挑战赛银奖。Winners of Silver Medal at International Wine Challenge 2008.

佳品
Caracter

由各占一半的两种葡萄品种混酿而成，口感清新活跃、属果香型葡萄酒。

Products of a defined personality that reflect the best of each grape. Young, fruity wines, ideal for every moment.

佳品（红）
Caracter Cabernet Merlot

亮丽的宝石红色，浓郁的红色水果味香气四溢。入口能感酒体平衡，单宁成熟圆润，果香甜美。Ruby red color. Intense aromas of red fruits in the nose. Well-balanced in the mouth, with sweet and round tannins.

- 14~17℃
- 活力派对，浪漫婚宴 party, wedding
- 红肉，意大利面 red meats, pasta dishes
- 阿根廷嘉本纳与梅乐绝妙搭配的完美体现。A perfect showcase of Cabernet and Merlot blend in Argentina.

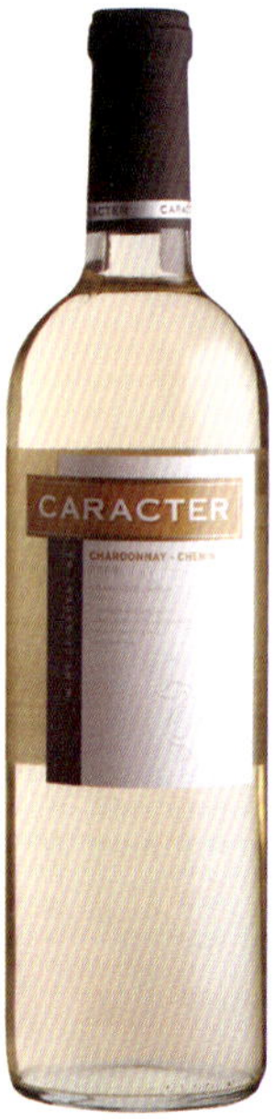

佳品（白）
Caracter Chardonnay Chenin

明亮的黄色，雪当利葡萄贡献了此酒热带水果的热情芳香口感，加之白翠柠赋予的无花果香甜让此酒入口即有平衡宜人的感觉。Bright yellow color. Good balance between the tropical aromas of Chardonnay and the fig fruits found in Chenin Blanc.

- 7~12℃
- 情侣约会，活力派对 dating, party
- 清淡味道菜肴 light food
- 阿根廷雪当利与白翠柠绝妙搭配的完美体现。A perfect showcase of Chardonnay and Chenin Blanc blend in Argentina.

小常识
Q & A

问：喝葡萄酒为什么舌头会变黑?

答：很多人都有喝酒后嘴唇和舌头会变黑的情况，其实，这是非常正常的，并不是人工添加了色素所致。一般来说，葡萄酒能够着色于人的嘴唇和舌头上，说明酒的年份好，酿酒葡萄的成色好，来自温暖地带。像法国南部、澳大利亚南部等地区出产的葡萄酒，酒质丰厚，色泽深浓，口感醇厚。残留在嘴唇和舌头上的色素，是通过发酵过程提取出来的。如果要区别它与人工添加的色素，可将此酒滴一滴在白布上，如果是葡萄酒中的天然色素，一般很难洗掉，但人工添加的色素则可轻易洗去。

智 利
CHILE

智利葡萄酒产区示意图

智 利 地域狭长，东倚安第斯山脉（Andes），西濒太平洋，南接南极洲。智利属于典型的地中海气候，日照充足，夜晚温度低，夏季漫长且干燥，冬季寒冷多雨，很少会受到葡萄病毒的入侵。此外，智利还有来自安第斯山脉积雪融化的天然水源，这么优越的葡萄种植环境，在全球都很少见。

智利的葡萄酒酿制历史非常长，可以说是新世界里的旧世界。早在公元4世纪，智利就已经有酿酒的记录，不过当时只是用于宗教仪式，并没有普及，直到19世纪，智利的葡萄酒才开始真正的发展。

智利的葡萄品种大都在19世纪引进于法国，不久后，欧洲就爆发一场几乎摧毁整个葡萄酒业的根瘤蚜虫病害，智利是少数几个未受影响的产酒国之一。

20世纪80年代后，几个世界顶级的葡萄酒巨人如法国的拉菲（Ch. Lafite Rothschild）、武当王（Ch. Mouton Rothschild）和西班牙的桃乐丝（Torres）等，投资于智利葡萄种植和酿酒业，对智利原有的酒庄也是一种激励，在葡萄酒业的现代化进程中奋起直追。如今，智利已涌现了不少让世界刮目相看的酒庄。

{葡萄品种}

几乎所有流行的葡萄品种在智利均有种植。红葡萄以嘉本纳沙威浓最为闻名，是助智利成名的功臣；加文拿是智利最具代表性的葡萄品种；另外梅乐与穗乐仙也开始备受关注。白葡萄以雪当利和白沙威浓的表现最出色。

加文拿 Carmenere

嘉本纳沙威浓 Cabernet Sauvignon

雪当利 Chardonnay

{分类}

智利葡萄酒的分级制度并不是那么严格和完善，即使同一级别不同酒庄的酒也不能直接比较，而要根据不同酒庄对品质的要求而论。智利葡萄酒大体上分为4个级别，由低到高如下：

家族珍藏
Reserva de Familia
某酒庄最好的酒，也可能以别的名字来命名，如圣卡罗（Santa Calorina）的顶级系列命名为圣卡罗红酒王（VSC）。

▲

特级珍藏
Gran Reserva
在橡木桶储藏时间较长的酒，品质更佳。

▲

珍藏
Reserva
在橡木桶储存过的酒。

▲

单品
Varietal
使用单一葡萄品种酿造的酒。

{葡萄酒产区}

智利的葡萄酒产区分3个区域，13个产区。第一个区域包括：北部的艾尔基谷（Elqui Valley）和利马里谷(Limari Valley)；第二个区域为中央谷（Central Valley），是酿酒葡萄最为主要的产区，细分为8个产区；第三个区域包括南部的伊塔塔谷（Itata Valley）、比奥比奥谷（Bio Bio Valley ）和马勒考谷（Malleco Valley）。

中央谷的8个产区由北到南为：

阿空加瓜谷 位于中央谷的最南端，由1870年开始广泛种植红葡萄。

卡萨布兰卡谷 是智利唯一一个白葡萄种植多于红葡萄的产区，葡萄采摘的时间差不多是整个智利最迟的，出产优质雪当利和世界级的白沙威浓葡萄酒。

圣安东尼奥谷 产区较小，靠近海边，气候寒冷干燥，土壤贫瘠，多产白葡萄酒且带有特殊的矿物味。

美宝谷 可以说是智利最炎热的葡萄酒产区，夏天温度可高达32°C，但夜晚的温度却比其他产区低。这种温差较大的气候与美国纳帕谷的上游河段相似。是智利最佳的嘉本纳沙威浓产区，以成熟的果香、丰厚的酒体享誉世界。

卡查波谷 出产口味优雅的嘉本纳沙威浓葡萄酒。近年种植的加文拿和穗乐仙都有不错的表现。

哥查加谷 是大区兰佩谷（Rapel Valley）的子产区，在10年前仍默默无闻，现在已成为智利最知名的葡萄酒产区之一，几乎是智利好酒的名片。这里的气候干暖，为众多红葡萄品种提供了极佳的生长条件。

库里科谷 风光迷人，是智利白沙威浓葡萄酒产量最大的产区。

摩利谷 是智利葡萄种植面积最大的产区，体现了传统和现代酿酒工艺的结合。

活灵魂
Almaviva

1997年，法国波尔多一级名庄武当王庄主罗富齐女男爵，与智利酒王Viña Concha y Toro的主席Eduardo Guilisasti Tagle签署合作协议，决定合作打造一款品质超卓的佳酿，于是，这款名为“活灵魂”的葡萄酒诞生了。
In 1997, Baroness Philippine de Rothschild, Chairman of the Advisory Board of Baron Philippe de Rothschild, and Eduardo Guilisasti Tagle, Chairman of Viña Concha y Toro S.A., sealed a partnership agreement with a view to create an exceptional Franco-Chilean wine called Almaviva.

活灵魂（红）
Almaviva Cabernet Sauvignon, Cabernet Franc, Merlot

¥¥¥¥

深宝石红色，散发着新鲜的成熟水果香，混合了矿物、香料、烟草和咖啡的味道。酒体有力，口感柔滑，结构平衡。Dark ruby red color. The nose reveals fresh ripe fruits aromas associated with mineral notes, spices, tobacco and coffee. A powerful wine with silky palate, showing a well-balanced structure.

18~20℃

商务宴请，酒友交流 business dinner, wine appreciation

牛扒，羊扒 beef steak, lamb

活灵魂被誉为智利酒王，是法、智两国酿酒文化的奇遇，是令人一喝难忘的智利顶级佳酿。As the king of wine of Chile, it is a wonderful adventure between the wine making of France and Chile, an impressive top Chilean wine.

嘉斯山
MontGras

嘉斯山酒厂——智利葡萄酒行业中一个最具现代化规模并在国际上日誉声隆的名牌，2002年被国际葡萄酒及酒类大赛评为“智利最佳葡萄酒生产商”，旗下品牌包括云顶山、歌颂、伊翠园、海韵园、嘉斯山等，都是倾力打造的高品质佳酿。

MontGras was the first winery in Chile to plant on the plateau of a hill with a project known Ninquen. Each of their wines is a true reflection of MontGras' winemaking abilities, combined with the extraordinary character of the grapes from the Colchagua Valley. In 2002, MontGras was voted as Best Chilean Wine Producer at the International Wine & Spirit Competition.

云顶至尊（红）
Ninquen

¥¥¥

深宝石红色，有新橡木、巧克力、咖啡和黑色浆果等优雅的芳香。单宁细致柔和，余味精致而优雅。Dark ruby in color. This wine has an elegant nose of new oak, chocolate, coffee and dark fruits. With fine supple tannins, the finish is fine and elegant.

- 18~20℃
- 商务宴请，酒友交流 business dinner, wine appreciation
- 辛辣的菜肴，羊排，红酒炆牛排 a big spicy dish, oriental lamb, beef medallions in red wine sauce
- 嘉斯山酒业最顶级的葡萄酒，采用云顶山庄园的特级优质红葡萄酿制。The top wine of MontGras, using the best grade of red grapes of Ninquen Estate.

安图（红）
Antu Cabernet Sauvignon

¥¥

深紫色，有成熟的水果芳香，同时伴有香草味。口感丰满浓郁，圆润平和，余味中能感觉到精致的单宁。Dense purple color. Deliciously ripe fruit dominates the nose, supported with spicy vanilla notes. A full but rounded palate with fine grained tannin on the finish.

- 18~20℃
- 浪漫婚宴，温馨家宴 wedding, family gathering
- 红肉，意大利面 red meat, pasta dishes
- 采用云顶山庄园的特级优质红葡萄酿制。Using the best grade of red grapes of Ninquen Estate.

歌颂珍藏（红）
Quatro

¥¥

深红色，果香浓郁。经过橡木桶陈年，展示了其酒体的良好平衡与成熟水果的风味，还有像天鹅绒般柔滑的单宁。Deep red color. Intense aromas with fruitiness. Aged in oak, leading to the optimum balance between ripe fruit and velvety smooth tannins.

18~20℃

商务宴请，温馨家宴 business dinner, family gathering

浓味型意大利面，鱼类小吃，红肉类菜肴 hearty pasta dishes, flavourful fish entrées, red meats

歌颂珍藏红葡萄酒由4种葡萄的绝妙混合酿制而成。Quatro is the outcome of a judicious blend.

伊翠园（红）
Intriga Cabernet Sauvignon

¥¥

深宝石红色，散发成熟的黑色水果、黑醋栗味，还有摩卡咖啡、薄荷、香料、香草的味道，口感成熟浓郁。Deep ruby red color. The core is loaded with ripe black fruit and cassis, mocha and mint, surrounded by elegant spice and vanilla notes. Rich and concentrated palate.

14~17℃

友人相聚，商务宴请 friends gathering, business dinner

牛扒，羊扒 beef steak, lamb

被酒庄称为“不可思议”的杰作，获得智利第六届葡萄酒金奖，受到多家权威媒体和杂志的推崇和高度评价。Regarded as "Enigma" by the winery. Gold medal winner at 6th Annual Wines of Chile Awards, high score gainer of several media and wine magazines.

海韵园白沙威浓（白）
Amaral Sauvignon Blanc

浅黄色，香气浓郁，橘子、酸橙和白花的香气突出，口感干爽，专属于利达谷葡萄的酸度跃然味蕾之上。Pale yellow color. Medium to high intensity, appearing then some citric aromas like tangerine, lime and white flowers. Dry wine that fills the mouth. Natural acidity typical of that valley.

- 7~12℃
- 友人相聚，活力派对 friends gathering, party
- 鳟鱼，龙虾，鸡肉 trout, lobster, chicken
- 在2006年才推出第一个年份，却在伦敦葡萄酒大赛、《品醇客》葡萄酒大赛摘得银奖，在智利酒中少之又少。Silver medal winner at International Wine Competition UK and *Decanter* World Wine Competition since its first appearance in the market in 2006.

海韵园雪当利（白）
Amaral Chardonnay

深稻草黄色，散发强烈的矿物、石墨味道，同时伴有丝丝凤梨、桃子和白花香味作点缀，酸度恰到好处。Deep straw yellow. Intense, with mineral notes, some graphite. You can also find hints of pineapple, peach and white flower. Fresh with an attractive combination of acidity.

- 7~12℃
- 情侣约会，浪漫婚宴 dating, wedding
- 蘑菇汁三文鱼，大虾沙律 salmon with mushroom sauce, shrimp salad
- 酒庄位于太平洋沿岸，气候湿冷，绝佳的天然条件赋予这款雪当利独特的矿物味和清新感。This along with a semi and climate given by the maritime influence, gives this Chardonnay elegance and personality attainable only by coming from the Pacific Oceans edge.

嘉斯山珍藏嘉本纳沙威浓（红）
Mont Gras Cabernet Sauvignon Reserva

¥¥

深红色，带有黑醋栗水果和香草的香味。果香浓郁，单宁柔滑，酒体优雅且后味持久。Brilliant red color. With noses of blackcurrant fruit and vanilla. Smooth tannins with ripe fruit flavors and a soft elegant finish.

- 18~20℃
- 浪漫婚宴，商务宴请 wedding, business dinner
- 东坡肉，牛肉干 fat pork meat, dry beef
- 2009年国际葡萄酒与烈酒大赛银奖得主。Winner of Silver Medal at International Wine & Spirit Competition 2009.

嘉斯山珍藏加文拿（红）
Mont Gras Carmenere Reserva

¥¥

深紫红色，有成熟的黑莓和李子味道，并伴有烤面包、香草和胡桃韵味。单宁成熟甜美又不失优雅，赐予此酒良好的结构。Deep purple red color. Ripe blackberries and plums, pepper, tobacco toast, vanilla and walnut. Loaded with ripe, sweet and elegant tannins that give structure to this wine.

- 14~17℃
- 浪漫婚宴，商务宴请 wedding, business dinner
- 味道酸甜的餐前小吃，家常炖菜，以孜然调味的菜肴 sweet and sour preparations, home style stews dishes, seasoned with cumin
- 被《纽约时报》评选为"顶级&最佳价值"葡萄酒。Regarded as Top Rated & Best Value Wine by *THE NEW YORK TIMES*.

嘉斯山珍藏雪当利（白）
Mont Gras Chardonnay Reserva

¥¥

深稻草黄色，有热带水果的香气，还伴有杏子和蜂蜜的味道，入口时桃子和奶油香充满整个口腔，余味优雅悠长。Deep straw yellow color. Tropical fruits combined with apricot and honey. Peach and creamy flavours that linger into an elegant finish.

- 7~12℃
- 情侣约会，活力派对 dating, party
- 淡味的白肉，意粉，海鲜，浓味芝士，中味型中餐菜肴 light white meat dishes, pasta, seafood or rich creamy cheese, light Chinese dishes
- 2008年国际葡萄酒与烈酒大赛银奖得主。Winner of Silver Medal at International Wine & Spirit Competition 2008.

嘉斯山嘉本纳沙威浓（红）
De Gras Cabernet Sauvignon

¥

深宝石红色，极具嘉沙的风格，带有黑醋栗与雪松的香味。口感丰富圆润，单宁柔滑，果香浓郁持久，容易入口。Deep ruby color. With the classic Cabernet nose of blackcurrants and cedar. Rich and smooth palate with soft tannins and lingering spicy fruit make for easy drinking.

- 18~20℃
- 活力派对，商务宴请 party, business dinner
- 黑椒牛扒，烤肉，熏肉 black pepper steak, roast meat, bacon meat
- 一款很容易让人联想到智利热带风情的佳酿。A wine associated with Chilean tropical style.

嘉斯山梅乐红葡萄酒
De Gras Merlot

¥

深宝石红色，带有温和的成熟梅子与洋李的香味。入口有成熟的山莓与黑醋栗的味道，果味丰富，单宁柔滑。Deep ruby color. With soft, ripe fruit flavours of plums and damsons. Ripe raspberries and black currants on the palate. Fruitful with good depth and soft tannins.

- 18~20℃
- 活力派对，商务宴请 party, business dinner
- 意大利面，烧烤肉类菜肴，浓味型的奶酪 pasta dishes, grilled meats, hard cheeses
- 一款独特的智利红葡萄酒。A red wine with distinctly Chilean character.

嘉斯山白沙威浓（白）
De Gras Sauvignon Blanc

¥

浅黄色，带有青椒、醋栗与热带水果的香气。浓郁的水果风味，酸甜干爽，鲜果味余韵悠长。Straw with tones of green. Green bell pepper, gooseberry and notes of the tropical fruit maracuya. Explosive fruit flavors, crisp acid and lingering fresh fruit.

- 7~12℃
- 情侣约会，浪漫婚宴 dating, wedding
- 鱼类和贝壳类菜肴，干果食品，沙律，清淡的夏日菜肴 fish and shellfish, starters, salads, light summer dishes
- 此酒充分反映了酒标上安第斯山脉以及南智利热带雨林的主题。A wine reflecting the theme of the Andes and South American Tropical Rainforest.

圣卡罗
Santa Carolina

圣卡罗酒厂始创于1875年，以创始人爱妻的名字命名，是智利四大酒王之一，在国内外屡获奖项。其酒窖现已被列为智利国家博物馆。

Established in 1875, Santa Carolina is named after the name of the founder's wife. Now it is one of the four wine kings in Chile and the regular medal winners at home and abroad. Moreover, its wine cellar is rated as the National Museum by the government.

圣卡罗世纪传承（红）
Santa Carolina Herencia Carmenere

¥¥¥¥

口感柔滑丰满、充满香浓醋栗和欧亚甘草的芬芳酒香。单宁甜美圆润，余味持久，果香浓烈。Ripe aromas of plums and cherries mixed with hints of tobacco and clove. Smooth palate with flavors of cassis and liquorice. Sweet and round tannins and juicy and persistent finish.

18~20℃

商务宴请，酒友交流 business dinner, wine appreciation

牛扒，羊扒 beef steak, lamb

圣卡罗系列顶级加文拿佳酿，陈年能力达10年乃至更长，是目前圣卡罗系列最顶级的产品。A premium Carmenere wine of Santa Carolina which can be aged for at least ten years. It is the topmost product of Santa Carolina.

圣卡罗红酒王（红）
Santa Carolina VSC

¥¥¥

深宝石红色，散发松露和可可豆的芳香，与甘甜的香料味道平衡得恰到好处。单宁成熟，酒体丰厚。Deep ruby red color. Aromas reminiscent of truffles and cocoa, balanced with the sweet spices. A velvety texture and a great body.

18~20℃

商务宴请，酒友交流 business dinnor, wine appreciation

牛扒，羊扒 beef steak, lamb

该酒是酒厂顶级的出品，是智利高品质和高性价比葡萄酒的代表作。It is the premium wine by Santa Carolina. With such high quality and value-for-money characteristics, it is the representative of Chilean fine wines.

圣卡罗家族珍藏嘉本纳沙威浓（红）

Santa Carolina Reserva de Familia Cabernet Sauvignon

¥ ¥

深宝石红色，李子和果酱的香味尤其突出，伴有香料的味道和果香。口感柔滑，有肉桂和胡椒的辛香，单宁柔滑。
Deep red-ruby color. Spicy and fruity aromas with intense flavors of plum and jam. Round palate with smooth and velvety tannins, rich with cinnamon and pepper notes.

- 18~20℃
- 浪漫婚宴，温馨家宴 wedding, family gathering
- 牛扒，羊扒，芝士 beef steak, lamb, cheese
- 1875年开始酿制，初时只供家族饮用，是圣卡罗最传统和经典的系列。The first line of fine wines produced in 1875 for their private consumption and special occasions.

圣卡罗家族珍藏雪当利（白）

Santa Carolina Reserva de Familia Chardonnay

¥ ¥

金黄色，凤梨和番木瓜的味道，还伴有烤橡木的香味。酸度良好，结构精致，入口有椰子和香蕉等热带水果香味。
Golden-yellow color. Intense fruit aromas of pineapple and papaya, with toasted oak notes. Good acidity, supple texture and plenty of tropical fruit flavors such as coconut and banana.

- 7~12℃
- 情侣约会，浪漫婚宴 dating, wedding
- 英国切达干酪，意大利干酪，烤吞拿鱼伴豆沙律，奶油意大利面 rich aged cheddar, parmesan, char-grilled Tuna with bean salad, creamy pasta dishes
- 来自智利最优秀的雪当利葡萄产区卡萨布兰卡谷。The grapes of this wine are from Casablanca Valley, the best Chilean Chardonnay appellation.

圣卡罗橡木桶特别珍藏（红）

Santa Carolina
Barrica Selection
Cabernet Savignon
Carmenere Syrah

宝石红色，散发李子、黑醋栗和森林果实的味道，随后是丝丝肉豆蔻、烟草、雪松和香料的香味，单宁结构紧实，酸度良好。Ruby red color. Aromas of plum, black currant, and forest fruits, followed by a touch of nutmeg, tobacco, cedar, and spices. Firm but silky tannins, nice acidity.

18~20℃

友人相聚，温馨家宴 friends gathering, family gathering

意大利面，红肉，白肉，芝士 pasta dishes, red meat, white meat, mature cheese

采用各区最优质的葡萄酿造的特级佳酿。A special vintage wine blended by the best grapes from different vineyards and appellations.

圣卡罗橡木桶精选加文拿（红）

Santa Carolina
Barrica Selection Carmenere

亮红色，散发出莓果、黑莓和蓝莓的香味，随后有黑色水果和香料的味道，单宁成熟，入口有精致的橡木味。Bright red color. Initial aromas of raspberries, blackberries, and blueberries and then black fruit and spice. Very ripe tannins with subtle oak on the palate.

18~20℃

酒友交流，温馨家宴 wine appreciation, family gathering

意大利比萨，意式前菜，芝士拼盘，浓味型中式菜肴 pizza, antipasto, a cheese platter, strong Chinese dishes

该酒采用最具智利特色的加文拿葡萄酿制。It is made by the most Chilean Carmenere grapes.

圣卡罗橡木桶精选穗乐仙（红）

Santa Carolina
Barrica Selection Syrah

石榴红色，带有莓果、蓝莓、紫罗兰和紫丁香的香味。口感大气，带有丝丝肉香，单宁成熟，结构良好。Deep garnet red color. Fruit-forward aromas of raspberries and blueberries, with notes of violets and lilacs. The palate is big and meaty with very ripe tannins.

18~20℃

商务宴请，温馨家宴 business dinner, family gathering

红肉，芝士拼盘，浓味型中式菜肴 red meat, a cheese platter, strong Chinese dishes

限量出产，是橡木桶精选系列的佼佼者。With a limited production, the wine is outstanding in the Barrica Selection.

圣卡罗珍藏嘉本纳沙威浓（红）
Santa Carolina Reserva Cabernet Savignon

¥ ¥

宝石红色，成熟的樱桃味香气醉人，同时伴有黑加仑子、巧克力还有胡椒的辛香味道，酒体丰满，果香味和橡木味完美平衡。Vivid ruby red color. It features ripe cherry and black currant with chocolate and pepper aromas. The dry and full-bodied wine offers a perfect balance between fruit and oak.

- 18~20℃
- 浪漫婚宴，温馨家宴 wedding, family gathering
- 牛肉，芝士，羊肉 beef, cheese, lamb
- 一款体现圣卡罗高超酿造工艺的嘉本纳沙威浓佳酿。 A Cabernet Sauvignon fine wine reflecting the superb winemaking technology.

圣卡罗珍藏加文拿（红）
Santa Carolina Reserva Carmenere

¥ ¥

深宝石红，散发出丰郁的水果香，还有紫罗兰花香与柔顺的香料味道。酒体丰满，香气浓郁又复杂，结构严谨，单宁结构良好。Intense and deep red color. Fruity aromas with floral hints of violets and soft spicy notes. Highly concentrated and complex palate with a firm structure, fine tannins.

- 18~20℃
- 浪漫婚宴，温馨家宴 wedding, family gathering
- 牛肉，鸡肉，羊肉 beef, chicken, lamb
- 一款不可多得的体现智利兰佩谷风味的加文拿佳酿。A Carmenere wine reflecting the Rapel Valley style.

圣卡罗珍藏雪当利（白）
Santa Carolina Reserva Chardonnay

¥ ¥

金黄色，混合了梨、无花果、菠萝和香蕉等多种水果的香味。一旦入口，该酒将带你领略成熟的热带果香和隐隐约约的香草及太妃糖的味道。Golden color. Intense aromas of pear, figs, pineapple and bananas. Fruity, fresh and well-balanced palate with ripe tropical fruit and a soft, mild buttery texture, hints of vanilla and toffee.

- 7~12℃
- 情侣约会，友人相聚 dating, friends gathering
- 沙律，海鲜，大部分亚洲菜肴 salads, seafood, many Asian dishes
- 荣获加拿大渥太华食品与葡萄酒展览银奖。Winner of Silver Medal at Ottawa Food & Wine Show, Canada.

圣卡罗嘉本纳沙威浓（红）
Santa Carolina Cabernet Sauvignon

明亮的宝石红色，带有浆果香、甜甜的香料味道和橡木的香味。酒体丰满，结构良好。Bright ruby red color. Rich berry aromas with soft layers of sweet spices and a strong prevalence of fruit over a touch of oak. This is a full-bodied wine with a good structure.

- 18～20℃
- 活力派对，浪漫婚宴 party, wedding
- 牛扒，羊扒 beef steak, lamb
- 一款性价比高的智利嘉本纳沙威浓红酒。An affordable Chilean Cabernet Sauvignon red wine.

圣卡罗加文拿（红）
Santa Carolina Carmenere

有浓郁的成熟红色水果香味、梅子味和肉桂味。酒体中度，有丝滑柔顺的结构，圆润成熟的单宁。Intense aromas of ripe red fruit, raspberries and notes of cinnamon. On the palate, this medium-bodied wine has a velvety texture and round ripe tannins.

- 18～20℃
- 活力派对，浪漫婚宴 party, wedding
- 东坡肉，牛肉干 fat pork meat, dry beef
- 一款物超所值的日常餐酒。An affordable daily table wine.

圣卡罗白沙威浓（白）
Santa Carolina Sauvignon Blanc

此酒的果香味非常突出，伴有李子、桃子和丝丝酸橙类水果的味道。入口新鲜爽脆，结构良好。This wine has the outstanding fruitiness with pear, peach and delicious hints of citrus aromas. On the palate it is fresh and crispy with an excellent structure.

- 14～17℃
- 情侣约会，活力派对 dating, party
- 海鲜，白肉菜肴，淡味型亚洲菜肴 most delicate fish, shellfish, white meat dishes, Asian style cuisine
- 一款香气浓郁的葡萄酒，具有智利典型的白沙威浓葡萄品种特色。An aromatic wine with typical Sauvignon Blanc varietal characters.

圣卡罗雪当利（白）
Santa Carolina Chardonnay

这款雪当利葡萄酒口感新鲜，有热带水果，如菠萝、香瓜和香蕉的味道。浓郁的果香与丝丝薄荷和茴芹味道协调得恰到好处。This Chardonnay is fresh and fruity, with white and tropical fruit flavours like pineapple, melon and bananas. It features intense fruit aromas in harmony with slight mint and anise notes.

- 7～12℃
- 情侣约会，活力派对 dating, party
- 家禽类，海鲜，素食 most poultry, seafood dishes, vegetarian food
- 这款雪当利没有经过橡木桶发酵，适合日常饮用。Without the influence of oak this Chardonnay is ideal for immediate enjoyment.

圣卡罗尊荣（红）
Santa Carolina Premio Red

清新而多汁，口感饱满，突显出成熟浆果的芳香，拥有丝般柔滑的结构和典型智利酒的特点。Fresh and juicy, this full-flavored red wine features ripe berries aromas, typical from Chile and a delicious silky texture.

- 18~20℃
- 友人相聚，活力派对 friends gathering, party
- 牛扒，羊扒 beef steak, lamb
- 一款典型的智利日常餐酒。A typical Chilean daily table wine.

圣卡罗尊荣（白）
Santa Carolina Premio White

清新柔和且果味丰富，口感浓郁，富含热带水果及柑橘的香味。Fresh, soft and fruity, this excellent white blend features intense flavours and aromas of tropical fruits and citrus.

- 14~17℃
- 友人相聚，活力派对 friends gathering, party
- 海鲜，鸡，意大利面 seafood, chicken, pasta
- 圣卡罗开胃酒之选。A perfect aperitif of Santa Carolina.

圣卡罗美景（红）
Santa Carolina Vistana Red

口感清新且果味丰富，个性独特，带有黑莓和黑樱桃的芳香，后味愉悦。Fresh and fruity, this red wine shows incredible character with aromas and flavours of blackberries and black cherry, as well as offering a pleasant finish.

- 14~17℃
- 活力派对，浪漫婚宴 party, wedding
- 黑椒牛扒，烤肉，熏肉 black pepper steak, roast meat, bacon meat
- 一款适合年轻时饮用的日常餐酒。A daily table wine ideal for drinking when it is young.

圣卡罗美景（白）
Santa Carolina Vistana White

热带水果气息明显，有酸橙、柠檬等香味。酸度宜人，带来美味口感。This white wine has lots of tropical flavours and aromas as well as lime, citric notes. On the palate it has a delicious texture with pleasant acidity

- 14~17℃
- 活力派对，浪漫婚宴 party, wedding
- 沙律，海鲜，大部分亚洲菜肴 salads, seafood, many Asian dishes
- 智利中央谷产区优质白酒的典型代表。A perfect example of a classic white wine from Chile's central valley.

圣卡罗起泡葡萄酒
Santa Carolina Brut Sparkling Wine

¥ ¥

细小的奶油色气泡透露出此酒优秀的品质。带有柠檬的新鲜香气，中度酒体，有奶油般柔滑的口感。Small creamy bubbles show its outstanding quality. Its aromas present citric fruit tones like fresh limes. Medium-full bodied, with creamy texture.

4~7℃

情侣约会，浪漫婚宴 dating, wedding

鱼子，虾刺身，鱼翅汤 caviar, sashimi, shark fin soup

适合作宴会餐前酒或接待酒。This brut is suitable for aperitif in a banquet.

小常识
Q & A

问：请问所有的起泡酒都可以叫香槟吗?

答：只有在法国的香槟区出产的，采用法定的葡萄品种和相关的一系列酿酒法规，经过瓶中二次发酵酿造而成的起泡葡萄酒才能在酒标上标“Champagne”，这种酒才是真正的香槟酒。其他国家出产的起泡葡萄酒，无论是否采用香槟的酿造法，都不能叫香槟，只能叫起泡葡萄酒。

安第神鹰（红）
Andes Condor Red

¥

亮红色，散发黑莓和黑樱桃的甜香，口感清新且果味丰富，后味愉悦。Bright red color. Fresh and fruity, this red wine shows incredible character with aromas and flavours of blackberries and black cherry, as well as offering a pleasant finish.

- 14~17℃
- 友人相聚，浪漫婚宴 friends gathering, wedding
- 黑椒牛扒，烤肉，熏肉 black pepper steak, roast meat, bacon meat
- 圣卡罗为中国消费者量身订造的精选红酒，是酒厂精粹的体现。Custom-made by Santa Carolina for Chinese drinkers, it is a selected red wine to reflect the essence of Santa Carolina.

安第神鹰（白）
Andes Condor White

¥

淡黄色，有浓郁的桃子果香和淡淡的柑橘味。口感清脆，平衡同时又不失优雅。Pale yellow color. Outstanding aromas of peach and delicious hints of citrus. Fresh and crispy palate with an well-balanced and elegant structure.

- 12~14℃
- 活力派对，浪漫婚宴 party, wedding
- 淡味的白肉，意大利面，海鲜，浓味芝士，中味型中餐菜肴 light white meat dishes, pasta, seafood, rich creamy cheese, light Chinese dishes
- 圣卡罗为中国消费者量身打造的精选白葡萄酒，是酒厂精粹的体现。Custom-made by Santa Carolina for Chinese drinkers, it is a selected white wine to reflect the essence of Santa Carolina.

南非
SOUTH AFRICA

南非葡萄酒产区示意图

南 非 是一个既现代又富有历史色彩的国家，早在1652年，荷兰人就率先在南非建立了第一个葡萄园。300多年后的今天，南非已经是世界九大葡萄酒出产国之一。南非葡萄酒的特色是既富有旧世界葡萄酒的优雅和高贵，又带有新世界葡萄酒的野性与果香。

位于非洲大陆的南部尖角，印度洋和大西洋在美丽的好望角（Cape of Good Hope）交汇。这里夏天很长，有充足的日照，冬天气候暖和而湿润，是典型的地中海气候，这为葡萄的生长提供了优越的自然条件。同时，由于靠近海洋，云层比较厚，为葡萄起到良好的保温作用。但海洋气候也有不利的一面：葡萄的收成受气候的影响非常大，一旦有风暴来袭，葡萄园将会有颗粒无收的危险。因此，喝南非的葡萄酒跟旧世界的葡萄酒类似，也讲究年份。

葡萄品种

主要的白葡萄品种有白翠柠、哥仑巴、雪当利、威士莲等。贝露特是南非具有代表性的红葡萄品种，由来自法国布根地的贝露娃和法国南部广泛种植的神索异花授粉杂交而成。其他的红葡萄品种包括嘉本纳沙威浓、神索、梅乐、穗乐仙等。

贝露特 Pinotage

葡萄酒原产地制度

1973年，南非政府开始实行葡萄酒原产地制度（Wine of Origins，简称WO），向法国等著名产酒国看齐。南非的WO把全国的产酒区域划分为4个级别，跟法国的AOC相似：

大区域（Geographical Units）

▲

地方区域（Region）

▲

行政区域（Districts）

▲

小区域（Wards）

前3个级别主要按政治意义上的边界划分，最后一个小区域则侧重区分不同的风土特点。

WO对葡萄品种有严格的要求，若采用单一品种命名的葡萄酒，必须至少要含该品种的75％，如要出口，则要达到85％。另外，对产量、灌溉也有相应的控制措施。

{葡萄酒产区}

南非葡萄酒产区主要分布在西开普（Western Cape），集中在港口城市开普敦（Cape Town）周围。主要的优质产区有：康斯坦提亚（Constantia）、斯坦陵布什（Stellenbosch）、帕尔（Paarl）、艾尔金（Elgin）、罗贝尔森（Robertson）、黑地（Swartland）、沃克湾（Walker Bay）和伍斯特（Worcester）等。其中最有名气的要数帕尔、康斯坦提亚和斯坦陵布什3个区域。

帕尔 是开普敦西北部最有名气的葡萄酒产区，传统上以生产白葡萄酒为主，但由于拥有地中海气候和土壤，现在生产的重点已转移到红葡萄酒上。弗兰谷（Franschoek Valley）是帕尔区内的一个小区域，面积虽小，但名气非常大，以芳香馥郁、酸度讨好的白葡萄酒和个性独特的红葡萄酒著称。另外，弗兰谷又素有“南非烹饪之乡”的美誉，是名副其实的美酒和美食天堂，是很多游客来南非必游的胜地。

康斯坦提亚 位于开普敦的南郊，是南非第一个开始种植葡萄的地区。葡萄园沿着康斯坦提亚山脉生长，并且得益于大西洋寒流的影响，生产的葡萄酒品质高雅、清爽怡人。

斯坦陵布什 在开普敦的东部，是南非最出名的葡萄园区，也是世界各国名酒厂在南非设立的葡萄园汇聚之地。这里的地质结构复杂，东部是花岗岩的土质，适合种植红葡萄，而西部则是砂岩土壤，适合种植白葡萄，被细分为几个小的葡萄种植区。

艾尔金 位于斯坦陵布什的东面，海拔比较高，气候比其他地区寒冷，是一个新兴的葡萄酒产区。

罗贝尔森 位于开普敦东面120千米处，是一个以白葡萄酒闻名的区域，雪当利最为出名。

黑地 是开普敦北部的一个葡萄种植大区，出产醇厚的红葡萄酒和一些顶级的加强型葡萄酒。

沃克湾 是一个气候寒冷的葡萄酒产区，到目前为止只有少数几个葡萄酒商，但近年该区出色的贝露娃、雪当利和白沙威浓显示其的潜力。

伍斯特 属于开普敦附近一个比较温暖的葡萄产区，葡萄生产由几个大的合作社酒商操控，同时也是南非最重要的白兰地产区。

弗兰谷
Franschoek Valley

乐梦迪
La Motte

乐梦迪和猎豹庄由南非最有威望的鲁伯家族拥有。鲁伯家族旗下有多个世界顶级奢侈品牌。乐梦迪坐落在著名的弗兰谷，是南非历史最悠久的葡萄园之一，生产的传统南非葡萄酒，具有经典和优雅的风韵。

La Motte and Leopard's Leap belongs to Rupert family, who also poccesses Cartier, Dunhill, Montblanc, etc. Situated in the beautiful Franschhoek Valley in South Africa's Cape winelands, La Motte is home to some of South Africa' s finest wines, recognized internationally for their exceptional quality.

乐梦迪穗乐仙（红）
La Motte Shiraz

¥¥¥

典型的香料味道，结构紧密，有良好的陈年潜质。Spicy, berry and violet flavors. Firm structure, promising a good maturation potential.

14~16℃

商务宴请，酒友交流 business dinner, wine appreciation

烤野味，牛肉，牛扒，肉类炖菜 roast game, beef, beef steak, meaty stews

带有南非穗乐仙特有的典雅和多层次的香料气息。With unique characteristics of South African Shiraz: elegant layers of spice.

乐梦迪加本纳沙威浓（红）
La Motte Cabernet Sauvignon

¥¥¥

有明显的肉桂、丁香、肉豆蔻、松露和黑巧克力的香味。Cinnamon spice, violets, truffle and dark chocolate.

14~16℃

友人相聚，活力派对 friend gathering, party

烧烤，鹿肉，红色肉类 roasts, venison, red meats

南非嘉本纳沙威浓葡萄的优雅风格尤其突出。An elegant, typically South African style Cabernet.

乐梦迪千禧珍藏（红）
La Motte Millennium

¥¥¥

有浓郁的樱桃、烟草和丁香的气味，还带有轻微的泥土与薄荷味。Intense flavors of cherry tobacco and cloves, as well as a hint of earthiness and mint on the nose.

14~16℃

商务宴请，酒友交流 business dinner, wine appreciation

红肉，野味，烧烤 red meats, game, roast

是波尔多风格的调配佳酿。A trusted Bordeaux-style blend made from Cabernet Sauvignon, Merlot, Cabernet Franc and Malbec.

乐梦迪雪当利(白)
La Motte Chardonnay

¥¥

浓郁的柑橘果香，与坚果的香味完美结合。The intense citrus aromas, well balanced with straw and nut and wood flavours.

8~12℃

情侣约会，浪漫婚宴 dating, wedding

沙拉，海鲜，海鲜面食，偏辛辣的亚洲菜式 salads, seafood, seafood pasta, spicy foods

具有崇高品质，多次被评为“南非最佳雪当利”。This wine's premium quality has won it numerous titles of "Best South African Chardonnay".

西开普
Western Cape

猎豹庄
Leopard's Leap

猎豹庄得名于曾在葡萄园出没的开普猎豹，是年青有活力、时尚而又不失高贵气息的新一代南非酒。
Leopard's Leap is named after the Cape Leopards haunted around in the vineyards. This premium range of new South African style wines combines the best of what farms situated in diverse climatic regions have to offer.

猎豹庄家族典藏（红）
Leopard's Leap Family Collection Shiraz Mourvedre Viognier

¥ ¥

有香料的味道，还有花香、红色浆果的香味。中度至丰厚的酒体，单宁成熟且优雅，余味悠长。Spicy floral with red berry undertones. The wine is medium to full-bodied. Ripe but elegant tannin structure with lingering aftertaste.

16~18℃

温馨家宴，活力派对 family gathering, party

烤肉，蔬菜，牛尾，鹿肉，炖菜 roast meat, vegetable, oxtail, venison, goulash.

由穗乐仙、慕尔伟德、维奥娜等3种葡萄混合酿制，具有明显的法国葡萄酒风格。A blend of Shiraz, Mourvèdre and Viognier. A typical example of the French style.

猎豹庄嘉本纳梅乐（红）
Leopard's Leap Cabernet Merlot

¥ ¥

口感极佳，酒体饱满，单宁柔滑，带有咖啡和太妃糖的味道。A smooth and full-bodied Cabernet Merlot, enhanced by coffee and toffee undertones.

14~16℃

友人相聚，温馨家宴 friends gathering, family gathering

肉食主导的菜肴，各种坚果，芝士 hearty meat dishes, nuts, cheeses

采用法国波尔多常用葡萄品种混合酿制，风格经典。A classically styled wine, similar to Bordeaux style wines.

猎豹庄贝露特穗乐仙（红）
Leopard's Leap
Pinotage Shiraz

¥¥

带有洋李、桑椹的味道与一点点香草的气息，中度酒体。Soft, medium-bodied with plum and mulberry flavors, enhanced by vanilla undertones. A spicy character. Perfect!

16~18℃

活力派对，商务宴请 party, business dinner

牛尾，烤猪肉，炖菜 oxtail, roast pork, hearty stews

融合了穗乐仙与南非本土贝露特的风格。A perfect combination of Shiraz and South African native variety Pinotage.

猎豹庄白翠柠（白）
Leopard's Leap
Chenin Blanc

¥¥

充满热带水果的香味，能在葡萄酒和食物间营造出一种浪漫的氛围。This well-balanced Chenin Blanc with hints of tropical fruit and guavas is a dishy complement to seafoods, soups and all sorts of snacks.

10~12℃

情侣约会，温馨家宴 dating, family gathering

海鲜，汤，各种小吃 seafood, soup, assorted snacks

获得2008年《品醇客》世界葡萄酒大赛银奖。Winner of Silver Award of *Decanter* World Wine Conpetition 2008.

猎豹庄（红）
Leopard's Leap
Lookout Red

¥

呈现充满朝气的紫红色，酒体中度，极具辛香的浆果风味，是一款值得畅饮的佳酿。Attractive spicy berry flavors. A medium-bodied, sumptuous wine, also a succulent, quaffable wine.

14~16℃

温馨家宴，活力派对 family gathering, party

肉类，沙拉，芝士 hearty meat, salads, cheeses

由7种红葡萄混合酿制而成，易于欣赏，可以畅饮。On the palate you can experience the unique blend of seven red varieties.

猎豹庄（白）
Leopard's Leap
Lookout White

¥

浓郁的成熟热带水果香味，伴有一丝酸橙香，非常讨人喜欢。Ripe, tropical fruits and a pleasant presence of lime. Such a sunny, happy wine is open to endless experiments.

10~12℃

温馨家宴，活力派对 family gathering, party

海鲜，意大利面，重味芝士 seafood, pasta dishes, heavy-flavored cheese

能反映南非友好、宽容和阳光的风情。This well-balanced wine captures the essence of South Africa-friendly, expansive, bright as sunshine,

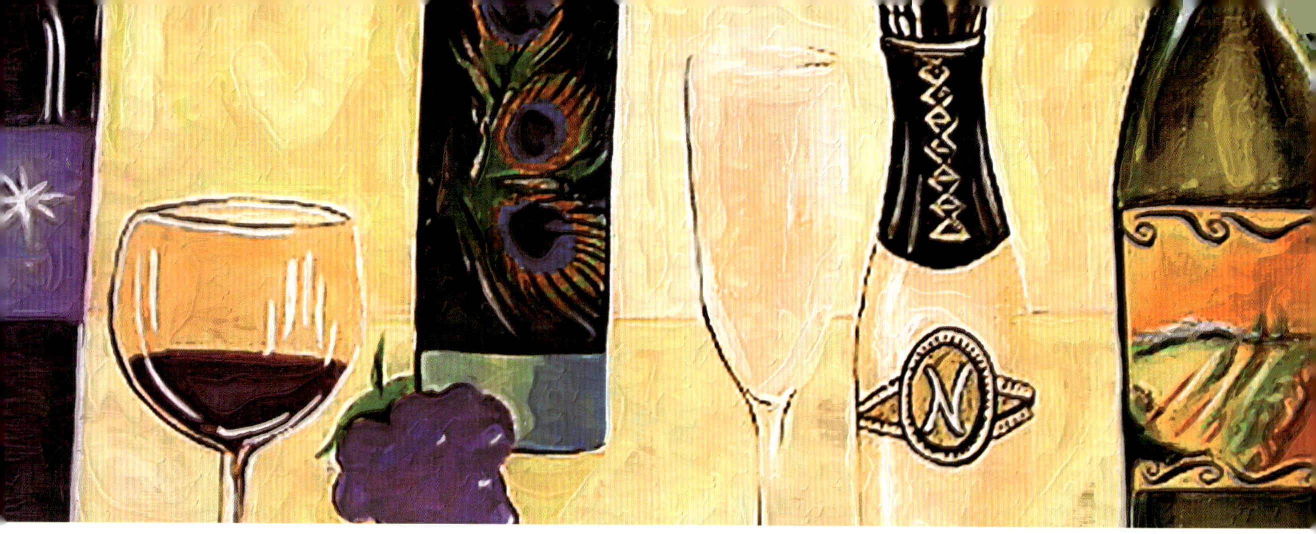

新西兰
NEW ZEALAND

新西兰葡萄酒产区示意图

新西兰 整体气候干爽清凉，分南北两岛，南岛较北岛寒冷，四面环海，日照时间长。白葡萄酒占全国产量的90%，尤以白沙威浓葡萄酒最出名，其有着独特的番石榴等水果芳香，以南岛的万宝龙（Marlborough）最佳；另外新西兰也是贝露娃红葡萄酒的著名产区，酒体柔顺明快，被誉为续法国布根地后的又一贝露娃名产区。

新西兰酿制葡萄酒的历史相对较短，源于19世纪初的英国殖民地时期，然而发展速度却非常惊人。在这片景色秀美、远离污染的土地上，适宜的气候、独特的地形以及注重高品质的酿酒者共同造就了品质杰出、特色鲜明的新西兰葡萄酒。

葡萄品种

白葡萄品种除了被誉为新西兰葡萄酒标志的白沙威浓外，威士莲、雪当利、灰贝露、琼瑶浆等在新西兰也有良好的长势，它们所酿的酒果香浓郁。红葡萄品种除了贝露娃外，梅乐、嘉本纳沙威浓等在新西兰特别是较温暖的北岛地区都可酿制出一流的红葡萄酒。

威士莲 Riesling

梅乐 Merlot

白沙威浓 Sauvignon Blanc

雪当利 Chardonnay

葡萄酒产区

由北到南，新西兰有十大葡萄酒产区，当中以位于北岛的奥克兰（Auckland）、吉士帮（Gisborne）与霍克斯湾（Hawkes Bay）和位于南岛的万宝龙（Marlborough）、中奥塔哥（Central Otago）较为出名。其中，霍克斯湾与万宝龙并称为新西兰两大产区。

万宝龙 是新西兰产量最大和葡萄种植面积最广的产区。充沛的日照，适度的雨量以及满布卵石、排水性佳的河流砂土等条件，让这一个新兴的年轻产区能够出产香味丰富、口味清新的顶级白沙威浓。用雪当利和灰贝露传统制法起泡酒也拥有相当好的潜力。其贝露娃红葡萄酒也在国际上获奖无数。

中奥塔哥 是位于全球最南面的葡萄酒产区，也是新西兰海拔最高的葡萄酒产区。该区是得天独厚的大陆性气候，夏季干热而冬季干冷，土壤特质与法国布根地相似，因此也是以娇贵刁钻著称的贝露娃葡萄的绝佳生长地。

霍克斯湾 是新西兰最具历史而且品质最好的产区之一，产量居新西兰第二。气候比较干燥，阳光充沛。此区雪当利的种植最广，嘉本纳沙威浓是表现最好的红葡萄品种，经常混合梅乐葡萄酿酒，另外也出产不错的威士莲和白沙威浓白葡萄酒。

奥克兰 气候相当潮湿，葡萄的种植逐渐减少，除了本地的葡萄外，区内的酒厂也同时从南部其他产区运来很多葡萄，作为酿酒的材料。

吉士帮 是位于全球最东面的葡萄酒产区，年降雨量颇高，以出产高品质的雪当利和琼瑶浆白葡萄酒而日渐受到重视，吉士帮所生产的葡萄酒特点是口味浓厚且带有浓郁的热带水果香。

万宝龙
Marlborough

胜嘉力
Saint Clair

新西兰的葡萄酒新贵，1994年才推出第一个年份，却是第一个获得重大国际奖项的新西兰酒厂，出品品质优秀，受到众多酒评家的肯定和称赞。

Their first wines were only produced in 1994, but Saint Clair Estate Wine's reputation as one of New Zealand's leading wine companies with an exceptional quality record is growing fast.

胜嘉力梅乐（红）
Saint Clair Merlot

¥¥

单宁细致、典雅，不失果味，风格自成一体。A medium bodied wine showing plum and dark berry fruit characters.

- 12~14℃
- 情侣约会，友人相聚 dating, friends gathering
- 烧烤牛肉，羊肉 barbequed beef or lamb
- 优雅时尚、容易欣赏的新西兰美酒，果香十分迷人。It's an elegant and stylish wine, which is also fruit driven and easy drinking.

胜嘉力贝露娃（红）
Saint Clair Pinot Noir

¥¥

迷人的深宝石红色，散发出黑莓和草莓的香气，口感圆润柔顺，后味持久留香。Flavors of blackberry and boysenberry on a round, a luscious, medium bodied, soft palate leading to a full, lingering finish.

- 12~14℃
- 情侣约会，活力派对 dating, party
- 烤羊肉，浓味鱼类，正宗意大利肉酱面 barbequed lamb, strongly flavoured fish, authentic Italian pasta with meat sauces
- 获得2007年度悉尼国际葡萄酒大赛蓝金奖。Blue-Gold Medal winner of Sydney International Wine Competition 2007.

胜嘉力（白）
Saint Clair Sauvignon Blanc

¥¥

石榴香味非常明显，馥郁而又不失典雅、清香和浪漫。Mouth-watering acidity and an intense minerality is balanced by a full yet elegant palate that leads to a long lingering finish.

- 12~14℃
- 温馨家宴，情侣约会 family gathering, dating
- 餐前菜，焗时蔬，新鲜海鲜 antipasto, grilled seasonal vegetables, fresh seafood
- 获得2006年度新西兰航空主办的新西兰葡萄酒大赛金奖。This wine was the winner of Gold Medal, 2006 Air New Zealand Wine Awards.

中奥塔哥
Central Otago

红石酒园
Rockburn

红石酒园是新西兰的金牌酒庄，土壤特质与法国布根地相似，以生产贝露娃闻名于世。其他葡萄品种的佳酿也在国内外获得众多奖项，旗下有红石酒园、魔梯等品牌。

They share a climate that is similar to Burgundy, the great Pinot Noir producing region of the world. Situated between these extremes are our vineyards that produce not only Pinot Noir of stunning quality, but also medal winning Sauvignon Blanc, Chardonnay, Pinot Gris, Riesling and Gewurztraminer.

红石酒园贝露娃（红）
Rockburn Pinot Noir

¥¥¥

酒体中度，口感柔顺清晰，余味和谐。The palate is medium bodied, very supple and clean with a harmonious finish.

12~14℃

友人相聚，浪漫婚宴 friends gathering, wedding

海鲜，白肉类菜肴，淡味芝士 seafood, white meat, light cheese

2009年份被澳洲中小酿酒商协会评为“年度最佳贝露娃”及“全场最佳葡萄酒”。Rockburn 2009 Pinot Noir has won the Award for Best Pinot Noir and the Trophy for Wine of Show at the Association of Australian Boutique Winemakers Awards.

红石酒园威士莲（白）
Rockburn Riesling

¥¥

产区的干冷气候赋予此酒橙子、杏仁香味以及新鲜的口感。Exhibiting classic cool climate aromas of lime and apricots leading into a palate of ripe yet refreshing stone fruit.

7~10℃

友人小聚，活力派对 friends gathering, party

鸡肉，禽类，味道略重的贝类，龙虾 chicken, fowl, richer-flavored shellfish, lobster

能给人带来十分清新、愉悦的口感。It offers an exceptionally refreshing and pleasant taste.

魔梯贝露娃（红）
Devil's Staircase Pinot Noir

¥ ¥

带有洋李还有烤面包的香气，水果味明显，口感平衡精致。Aromas of black doris plums and toasty oak, very fruity, rich and supple with finely balanced acid and oak on the palate.

- 12~14℃
- 情侣约会，友人相聚 dating, friends gathering
- 贝类，龙虾浓汤，蘑菇，豆类 shellfish, lobster bisque, mushrooms, legumes
- 口味独特，充满黑布林、烤橡木、树莓和焦糖布丁香味，一饮过后自然会想要更多。The flavours are practically immoral,full of black plums,flame-toasted oak and bramble fruit crème brulée,and will leave you with an insatiable desire for more.

魔梯灰贝露（白）
Devil's Staircase Pinot Gris

¥ ¥

桃子、芒果和柠檬的香味明显，口感精致且有持久清新的后味。 Nashi pears, mango and lemon zest. Very fruity and delicately sweet with a long cleansing finish on the palate.

- 7~10℃
- 温馨家宴，情侣约会 family gathering, dating
- 三文鱼，贝类，清淡口味的意式焗饭 salmon, shellfish, light risottos
- 每人心中都有一个魔鬼，这款精致典雅的白葡萄酒就是引诱魔鬼现身的阶梯。There's a little devil in everyone's heart. This elegent, attractive white wine is the stairway for the devil to show up.

旧世界葡萄酒，深具气质的名门闺秀，不断延续的世代传承。她们尊重传统，遵循法规，尊崇葡萄产地的原初“风土”。那些历史悠久的经典佳酿，血统中浓缩的是始于罗马帝国、贯穿文艺复兴、迎向21世纪的欧洲大陆文明。葡萄酒文化源远流长，而旧世界葡萄酒正是葡萄酒魅力的经典传承者。

第三章 旧世界葡萄酒
CHAPTER 3 OLD WORLD WINES

法　国
FRANCE

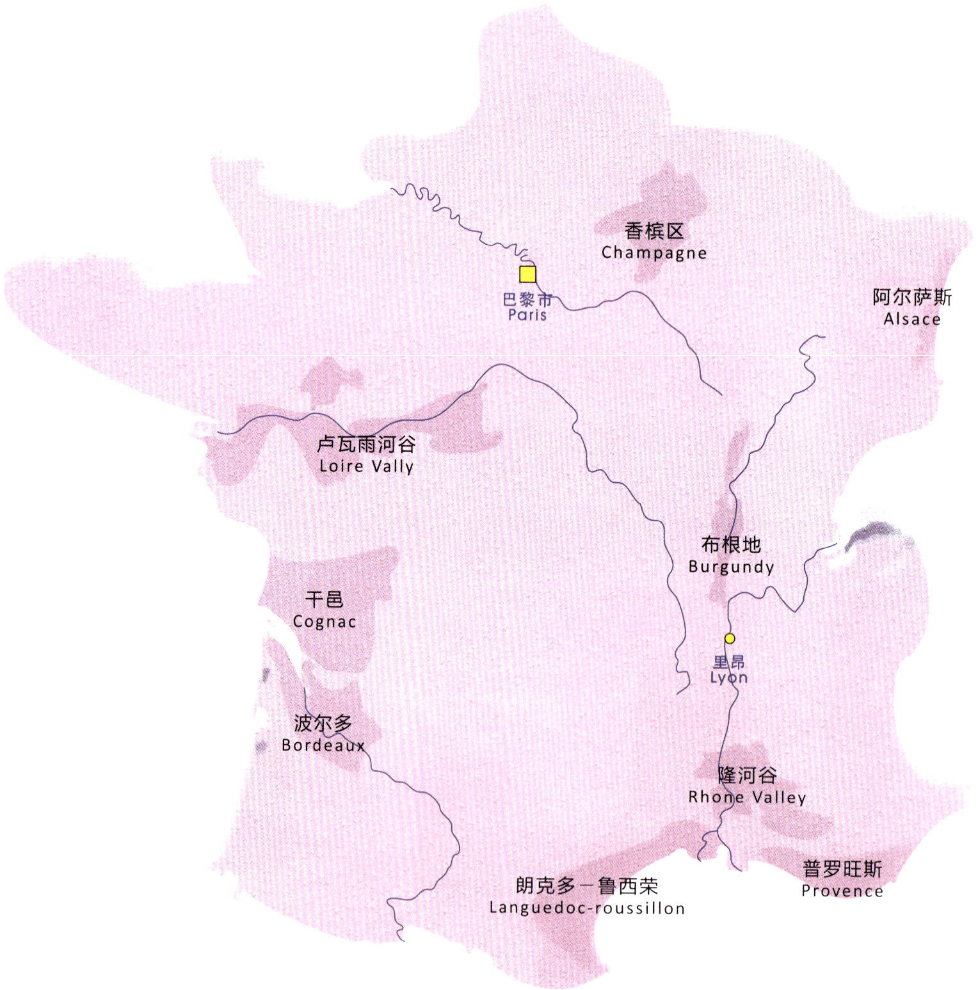

法国葡萄酒产区示意图

法国 是葡萄酒世界的绝对主角，生产着世界上最优秀的葡萄酒。“有法国葡萄酒的风骨”已经成为对葡萄酒的赞美之辞。与其他产酒国相比，无论是葡萄品种、气候、土壤、湿度、酿酒技术还是葡萄酒的管理，法国始终占据着绝对的优势。

{分级制度}

法国的原产地命名管理局（INAO）对葡萄树的种植、葡萄园的管理，葡萄酒的酿造及销售等葡萄酒行业的全部环节都有严格的法律约束，建立的葡萄酒分级制度堪称世界葡萄酒生产国的最佳典范，许多国家都纷纷仿效。

根据产量、品质和法定要求，法国的葡萄酒一共分为4个级别，从低到高分别是：

法定产区
Appellation Original Controlee, 简称 AOC

▲

准法定产区
Vin Delimites de Qualite Superieure, 简称 VDQS

▲

优良餐酒
Vin de Premium, 简称 VDP

▲

日常餐酒
Vin de Table, 简称 VDT

波尔多
Bordeaux

波尔多 是个默念都感觉酒香在唇齿漫溢的地方。位于法国西南部，西临大西洋，一条吉隆河（Gironde）把波尔多分为左岸和右岸，形成特色鲜明的各种风格产区。得天独厚的气候条件，多样性的土壤，令波尔多出产多种不同风味和不同形态的葡萄酒。除了出产占总量88%的红葡萄酒，还出产干白葡萄酒，甜白葡萄酒、粉红葡萄酒、淡红葡萄酒和起泡酒。波尔多的红葡萄酒产量大、品质高，她是法国最大的一个法定产区。几乎所有法国的美酒故事都与波尔多有关，全球顶级的好酒绝大部分都来自波尔多。毫无疑问，波尔多是法国葡萄酒业的一颗明珠。

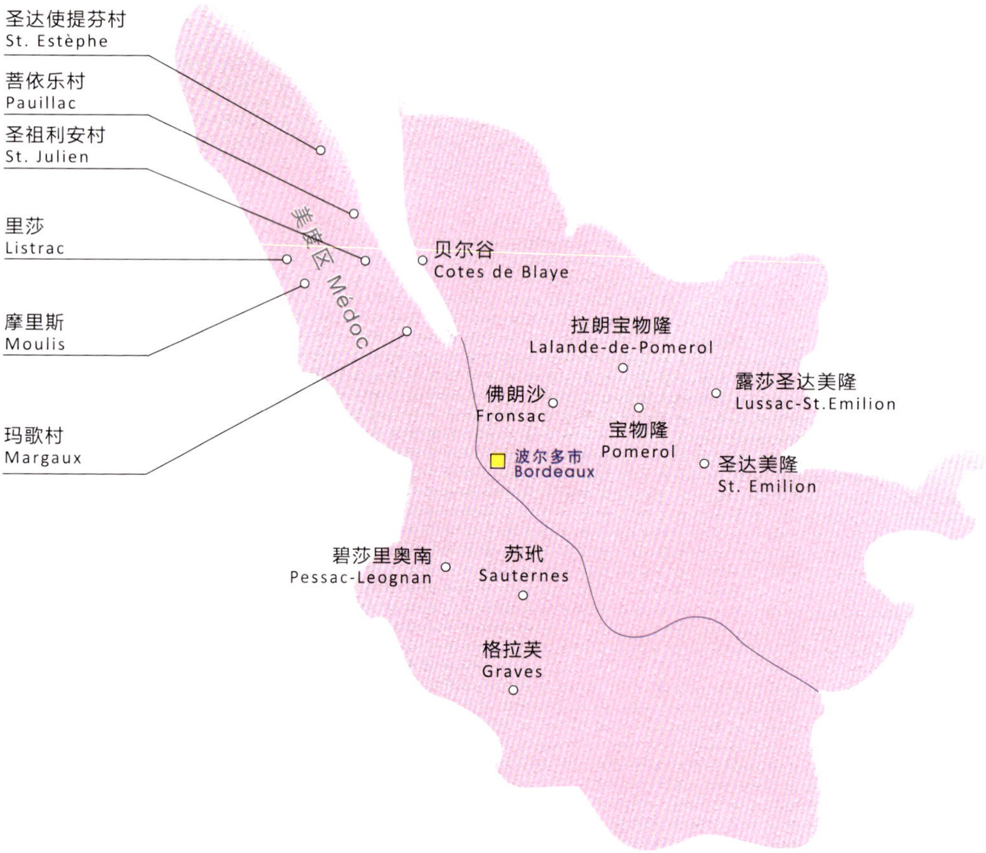

法国波尔多葡萄酒产区示意图

{葡萄品种}

波尔多主要的红葡萄品种包括嘉本纳沙威浓、嘉本纳弗朗、梅乐、小华帝和玛碧。

白葡萄品种主要有白沙威浓、沙美龙和密思卡岱、哥伦巴、琼瑶浆。

嘉本纳沙威浓 Cabernet Sauvignon

梅乐 Merlot

白沙威浓 Sauvignon Blanc

沙美龙 Semillon

酒庄评级

除了原产地命名管理局所制定的法定产区标准，在波尔多的不同法定产区里还存在着一些关于酒庄的评级制度。

1855年波尔多酒庄评级
1855 Bordeaux Classification

产红葡萄酒的美度区和产贵腐甜酒的苏玳—巴萨区酒庄的两个评级。

美度区评级一共选出了61个酒庄，分为5个级别，这些上榜酒庄被称为“列级名庄”。其中最为人熟知的是当时列入第一级的4个顶尖名庄：拉菲庄（Ch. Lafite）、拉图庄（Ch. Latour）、玛歌庄（Ch. Margaux）和红颜容庄（Ch. Haut Brion）。武当王庄（Ch. Mouton Rothschild）当时排在第二级的第一位。1973年，法国政府为表彰武当王对整个葡萄酒行业的伟大贡献，破格把他提升为一级庄，所以一级酒庄的数量增加至5个，这也是该评级迄今为止所作出的唯一一次修改。在61个酒庄中，只有红颜容庄来自格拉芙区，剩下的60个酒庄全部来自于美度半岛。

苏玳—巴萨区的贵腐甜酒评级则选出了一个超一级庄（Premier Cru Supérieur）：滴金庄（Ch. d'Yquem），剩下的分别是一级庄和二级庄。

1953年格拉芙评级
1953 Classification of Graves

为弥补1855年评级中只有干红酒而没有干白酒的遗憾，1953年格拉芙区决定进行一次红白葡萄酒庄园评选，该次评级于1959年曾作过一次修改，共16个酒庄的13款干红酒，10款干白酒获选。

由于入围的16个酒庄都位于碧沙（Pessac）和里奥南村（Leognan），证明这两个村庄的土质优越，所以1987年起碧沙里奥南（Pessac-Leognan）成功通过审批独立成为一个法定产区，该评级又被称为1987年碧沙里奥南评级。

1955年圣达美隆评级
1955 Classification of St. Emillion

来自波尔多右岸的著名产区圣达美隆也有自己的评级，圣达美隆的评级每10年重新评审一次，评级规定酒庄必须每年提交酒样送检，只有10年的样品全都通过盲品测试才有参选资格。

圣达美隆的评级只分两级，而第一级中又分为了A组和B组。自1955年起到现在，一级中的A组酒庄一直都没有改变，他们是白马庄（Château Cheval Blanc）和欧颂庄（Château Ausone）。

最后的一次评级原定于2006年公布，但由于一些降级酒庄向法院起诉某些升级酒庄与评审组织有利益关系，法院决定宣布2006年的评级作废，暂时沿用1996年的评级。最新的评级预计在2011年公布。

明星庄评级
Cru Bourgeois

由于1855年的评级只针对一些高端的酒庄，反映优质中价位葡萄酒的明星庄评级应运而生。早在1934年就进行过一次美度区明星庄的评级，但由于没有得到法国政府的许可，所以一直没有引起重视。经过多年的努力，2003年的明星庄评级重新出炉，247个酒庄上榜，一共分成了3个级别：超级明星庄、优质明星庄和明星庄。但好景不长，该评级也在2007年因故废止了。2009年，明星庄的评级委员会再次修改评级的要求和内容，宣布在2010年重新推出明星庄评级。

罗拔•派克评级
Robert Parker

1855年的评级经过了这么多年的发展，很多庄园的品质都发生了变化。特别是第二次世界大战后崛起的波尔多右岸的宝物隆，虽然因为产区面积太小而一直没有设立评级制度，但却出产像酒王之王柏图斯（Petrus）等天价葡萄酒，优秀的酒质与当年左岸的顶级名庄相比都有过之而无不及。鉴于当年的评级忽略了右岸的名庄，美国著名酒评家罗拔•派克（Robert Parker）根据庄园的现状和个人的专业意见，在1998年也发布一个新的评级标准。

{波尔多葡萄酒}

波尔多拥有得天独厚的气候条件及地理条件，贫瘠的沙砾土、黏土和石灰土构成了复杂多样的地质结构，让波尔多能出产丰富多样的葡萄酒。

>>左岸

波尔多被由南向北流入大西洋的吉隆河一分为二，但他们在习惯上并不以东西岸来划分，而是根据地理位置上人的左右方向来划分。左岸有1855年波尔多评级的五大一级名庄和波尔多最有名气的美度半岛，因此左岸总是充满一种古典贵族的气息，所产葡萄酒也更加严谨复杂，葡萄品种以嘉本纳沙威浓（Cabernet Sauvignon）为主，产区主要由美度半岛和格拉芙两大区域构成。

美度半岛内有4个最著名的村庄，包括圣达使提芬村（St. Estèphe）、菩依乐村（Pauillac）、圣祖利安村（St. Julien）和玛歌村（Margaux）。格拉芙有两个最著名的村庄，包括碧莎（Pessac）和里奥南（Leognan）。

>圣达使提芬村 St. Estèphe

圣达使提芬村是美度四大名村中最靠北面的村。与左岸其他3个名村比，圣达使提芬拥有第二大的酒田面积，但是葡萄酒事业的发展却较其他3个名村晚。因此在1855年的评级中只有5家入围，是四大名村中最少列级名庄的村庄。然而，在近几十年的发展中却涌现出一批品质优秀，性价比甚高的明星庄（Cru Bourgeois）。

圣达使提芬的土质黏土成分大，土质去水不易，因此葡萄比其他村庄成熟得晚。所产的葡萄酒颜色深浓，单宁密集紧实，年轻时果味丰富。相对其他美度区的酒，圣达使提芬村酒属大型酒（Big Wine）。

爱士图尔（红）
Cos d'Estournel

¥¥¥¥

酒色深浓，带有馥郁的果香，单宁柔滑，口感强劲且平衡。Intense deep coulor. Powerful open bouquet of aromatic fruit. A wine with superb balance between power and finesse.

1855年波尔多列级名庄第二级 2eme Cru-1855 Classification

18～20℃

酒友交流，浪漫婚宴 wine appreciation, wedding

烤肉，羊扒 grilled meat, lamb

圣达使提芬村的酒王，位列二级庄之首。此酒相传是恩格斯送给马克思的结婚贺礼，深受前苏联高官的喜爱。The wine king of St.Estèphe. As a gift from Friedrich Engels for Karl Marx's wedding, Cos d'Estournel was also very popular among Soviet officers.

爱士宝塔（红）
Les Pagodes de Cos

¥¥¥

深宝石红色，带有浆果和干花气息，酒体丰满，装瓶后10年饮用最佳。Deep ruby color. Very intense aromas of berries and pressed flowers. Should be drunk within ten years after bottling.

爱士图尔副牌酒 2nd wine of Cos d'Estournel

14～17℃

友人相聚，情侣约会 friends gathering, dating

烧鸭，烟熏肉类 roast duck, bacon dishes

一款口感强劲可陈年的副牌酒，具有正牌酒的风范。 A very well-done muscular second wine.

小常识
Q & A

问：葡萄酒的酒精度为什么会不一样?

答：不同国家地区的气候、葡萄品种、年份等因素都会影响葡萄的糖分导致葡萄酒酒精度的不同。如美国加州和澳大利亚的葡萄酒，通常糖分会多些，因此美国的葡萄酒酒精度大都在13%，澳大利亚的葡萄酒酒精度数在13.5%，甚至14%；像法国、德国等气候相对寒冷的国家则葡萄糖分较少，从而葡萄酒酒精度也相对较低。

凯隆世家（红）
Ch. Calon-Ségur

¥¥¥¥

深红色，富有层次的香气，浆果、紫罗兰、香水的芬芳令人难忘，酒体丰满，单宁丝滑，余韵悠长。Amazing red color, remarkable for its layers of berry, violets and perfume. It's full-bodied and very velvety on palate, with an ultra long finish.

- 1855年波尔多列级名庄第三级 3eme Cru-1855 Classification
- 18～20℃
- 情侣约会，浪漫婚宴 dating, wedding
- 铁板类红肉 teppenyaki red meat
- 示爱、求婚必备佳品！历史上其主人同时拥有拉菲及拉图，但最喜爱的还是此酒庄，更将心形图案印于酒标。 An ideal wine to blurt a confession. The heart on the label signifies the motto of Calon-Ségur, said from Nicolas de Ségur: "I make wine at Lafite and Latour, but my heart is at Calon."

小凯隆（红）
La Chapelle de Calon

¥¥¥

酒体轻身，单宁轻柔，带有樱桃和烟熏气息，后韵烟草味愈浓。Light, somewhat watery, with light tannins and hints of cherries, raison, toasted oak, and tobacco with a stronger tobacco finish.

- 凯龙世家副牌酒 2nd wine of Ch. Calon-Ségur
- 14～17℃
- 友人相聚，温馨家宴 friends gathering, family gathering
- 浓味红肉 red meat with rich sauce
- 一款口感清雅、令人愉悦的副牌酒。 A soft second wine offering great pleasure.

玫瑰山庄（红）
Ch. Montrose

¥¥¥¥

深紫色，带有成熟的黑加仑子、雪松和烟草芳香，是力量型的大酒，后味悠长，适合陈年。The wine is very deep red with blue edges. This is a masculine wine laden with blackcurrant, cedar and tobacco with greater power, depth and length.

- 1855年波尔多列级名庄第二级 2eme Cru-1855 Classification
- 18～20℃
- 酒友交流，浪漫婚宴 wine appreciation, wedding
- 烤肉，羊扒 grilled meat, lamb
- 与爱士图尔齐名的圣达使提芬村名庄，现由红颜容的酿酒师Jean-Bernard Delmas主理。A wine as famous as Cos d'Estournel,now has installed Jean Delmas, onetime winemaker at Haut-Brion, in charge of the chai.

飞龙世家（红）
Ch. Phélan Ségur

¥¥¥

深红酒色，以香料和雪松气息为主，另有鲜肉和浆果香气。酒体丰满，单宁紧密，后味愉悦。Intense red color. Spice and cedar, with hints of meat and berries. Full-bodied, with well-integrated tannins and an exotic finish.

- 2003年美度区超级明星庄 2003 Cru Bourgeois Exceptionnel
- 14～17℃
- 酒友交流，浪漫婚宴 wine appreciation ,wedding
- 牛扒，传统炖菜 beef steak, traditional stew
- 2003年超级明星庄，多次评为全球最超值的葡萄酒之一，品质超群。"Cru Bourgeois Exceptionnel" in 2003 classification, recognized as one of the best value wine in the world.

弗朗飞龙（红）
Frank Phélan

¥¥¥

深宝石红色，带有淡淡的葡萄干及莓子芬芳，酒体丰满，单宁丝滑，后味充满成熟浆果的气息。Deep ruby color. A wine with loads of ripe fruit on the nose, from light raisins to plums. Full-bodied, with well-integrated tannins and a silky, ripe fruit finish.

- 飞龙世家副牌酒 2nd wine of Ch. Phélan Ségur
- 14～17℃
- 友人相聚，情侣约会 friends gathering, dating
- 烤乳鸽，红肉 grilled pigeon, red meat
- 被认为是"一款非常好的副牌酒"，价廉物美。Regarded as "a very good second wine, almost too good". A value-for-money choice.

>菩依乐村
Pauillac

菩依乐村是左岸最出名的葡萄酒名村，占地只有1 000公顷左右，但在1855年的列级名庄评级中却有18个名庄入围，而且1 000公顷的酒田大部分由这18个名庄拥有。其余不属列级名庄的庄园，由于拥有优秀的土壤和区域微型气候，所以一样能出产品质上乘的菩依乐风格酒。菩依乐出名的另一原因是村内拥有最多的一级名庄：拉菲、拉图和武当王，五大一级庄之其三都位于菩依乐。

菩依乐的酒不妥协，不刻意讨好，但大部分饮家都对它情有独钟。它的特点是酒体丰满、浓密，单宁丰富，适合陈年饮用，酒香通常带有黑加仑子、松木和咖啡香。

拉菲家族
Lafite Rothschild Family

拉菲罗富齐家族是法国波尔多最负盛名的三大酒业集团之一。该家族自1868年购的世界最出名的酒庄拉菲庄后一直拥有至今，而且把拉菲庄的质量和声誉也维持至今。除了拉菲，该家族还拥有四级名庄都夏美隆等，并于1984年购得苏玳区贵腐葡萄品牌拉菲丽丝。

Domaines Barons de Rothschild (Lafite) is one of the three most famous wine families in Bordeaux France. Purchasing Château Lafite Rothschild in 1868, the family keeps the ownership and the reputation of Lafite till today. And Ch. Duhart Milon in Pauillac and Ch. Rieussec in Sauternes are under the control of this renowned family as well.

拉菲罗富齐庄园（红）
Ch. Lafite Rothschild

¥ ¥ ¥ ¥ ¥

深黑色，优雅的成熟水果香气，单宁如丝柔滑，层次极其丰富，酒性温柔醇和，是菩依乐村的酒后。Black intense color. Incomparable best, lots of ripe, aromatic fruit, and soft tannins. There is a lot of structure there, but finesse and delicacy prevail. The wine queen of Pauillac.

- 1855年波尔多列级名庄第一级 1er Cru-1855 Classification
- 18～20℃
- 酒友交流，商务宴请 wine appreciation, business dinner
- 羊扒，烧鹅，烩鹅掌 lamb, roast goose, braised duck webs
- 世界上最出名的葡萄酒，位居波尔多八大名庄之首。The most famous wine in the world, the leading château among the top 8 châteaux of Bordeaux .

拉菲庄园副牌（红）
Carruades de Lafite

¥¥¥¥¥

深宝石红色，带有烟草、紫罗兰、浆果芳香以及矿物味，酒体厚身，单宁柔滑，余韵悠长。Dense and dark ruby color. Tobacco, with intense violet, berry and notes of mineral in bouquet. Full-bodied, with silky tannins and a long, succulent and flavourful finish.

- 拉菲副牌酒　2nd wine of Ch. Lafite Rothschild
- 18～20℃
- 酒友交流，商务宴请 wine appreciation, business dinner
- 煎焗海鲜，烧腊 deep fired seafood, roast meat
- 全球最受追捧的副牌酒。The most popular second wine in the world.

都夏美隆（红）
Ch. Duhart-Milon (Lafite)

¥¥¥¥

深宝石红偏紫色，带有黑加仑子、香草和矿物味，入口可感受到甜美的水果味，酒体中度，单宁成熟，后味甘美。Impressively saturated dark ruby/purple-colored. The nose offers up sweet black currant fruit, vanilla, and minerals. With sweet fruit on the attack, medium body, ripe tannin, and a lush finish.

- 1855年波尔多列级名庄第四级 4eme Cru-1855 Classification
- 14～17℃
- 友人相聚，浪漫婚宴 friends gathering, wedding
- 牛扒，羊扒 beef steak, lamb
- 由拥有拉菲庄的罗富齐家族酒业集团主理，酒性与拉菲相似，性价比甚高。Belongs to the Lafite Rothschild family. A good value wine with similar character of Ch.Lafite Rothschild.

都夏美隆副牌（红）
Moulin de Duhart

¥¥¥

明亮的宝石红色，馥郁的黑莓、皮革和烟草香气，酒体中度，后味充满浆果香味。Bright ruby red. Intense aromas of black berry, leather and tobacco. Medium bodied with a lovely berry finish.

- 都夏美隆副牌酒 2nd wine of Ch. Duhart-Milon
- 14～17℃
- 情侣约会，友人相聚 dating, friends gathering
- 黑椒牛扒，烤肉，熏肉 black pepper steak, roast meat, bacon meat
- 出身于拥有拉菲庄的罗富齐家族酒业集团的佳酿。Belongs to the Lafite Rothschild family.

拉菲贵族甜葡萄酒（白）
Ch. Rieussec

¥¥¥¥

色泽金黄，馥郁的新鲜柑橘香气，酸甜度平衡，是一款优雅醇和的贵腐酒。Golden color. The nose offers a lot of freshness with citrus notes dominated by grapefruit. In the mouth, its moderate richness in sugar makes it a wine full of finesse and elegance.

- 1855波尔多苏玳甜白葡萄酒评级一级庄 1er Cru-1855 Sauternes & Barsac Classification
- 4~7℃
- 情侣约会，酒友交流 dating, wine appreciation
- 鹅肝，蓝芝士 goose liver, bule cheese
- 世界上最出名的贵腐甜酒之一，大股东是拉菲酒庄的主人罗富齐家族。 Acquired by Domaines Barons de Rothschild (Lafite) in 1984, it is one of the most famous sweet wine in the world.

拉菲丽丝（白）
R de Rieussec

¥¥

浅金黄色，带有馥郁的热带水果香气，以芒果味为主调，口感新鲜饱满，酒体平衡，余味持久带有柑橘味。A pale gold color. Powerful exotic fruits dominated by mango on nose. The wine is balanced and the length is long. Citrus notes appear at the finish.

- 波尔多法定产区酒 Bordeaux AOC
- 7~12℃
- 情侣约会，友人相聚 dating, friends gathering
- 中淡味海鲜 medium to light seafood
- 由拥有拉菲庄的罗富齐家族酒业集团主理，是苏玳区一级名庄拉菲贵族甜酒庄出品的一款干白葡萄酒。Rothschild family makes this dry white wine. The wine is produced on the Château Rieussec estate, a 1st growth Sauternes wine.

小常识
Q & A

问：法国酒庄在什么情况下出产副牌酒？

答：副牌酒的酿造主要有两种情况，一是由于当年天气不好、橡木桶陈年出现问题；二是庄园里比较年轻或品质稍次的区域出产的葡萄。凡达不到酿制正牌酒标准的葡萄、葡萄汁都不会用于酿造正牌酒，通常会用来酿制质量标准比正牌酒次一等级的副牌酒。由于都是采用同一庄园的葡萄和酿造技术，副牌酒都具有正牌酒的神韵，但浓郁和复杂程度、留香时间就不及正牌酒，自然价格也实惠许多，且年轻时即可饮用。

拉图
Latour

拉图酒庄位于菩依乐村的东南角，与圣祖利安村相邻，在1855年评级中位列一级名庄，是全球最昂贵的酒园。拉图酒性雄浑有力，极具陈年潜力，号称菩依乐村的酒王。除正牌酒外还出产副牌酒小拉图（Les Forts de Latour）和三牌酒拉图菩依乐。

Ch. Latour lies at the very southeastern tip of the commune of Pauillac at its border with Saint-Julien. It was rated as a First Growth under the 1855 Bordeaux Classification. In addition to its Grand vin, Latour has also produced the second wine Les Forts de Latour and a third wine, Pauillac.

拉图庄园（红）
Ch. Latour

¥¥¥¥¥

酒色深浓，带有胡桃木、皮革和黑加仑子芳香，酒体饱满。波尔多最浓郁最耐久存的葡萄酒之一，是菩依乐村的酒王。Dark ruby-colored. Has a wonderful bouquet of fresh walnuts, leather, and black currants. One of Bordeaux's most concentrated rich and full-bodied wines. The wine king of Pauillac.

- 1855年波尔多列级名庄第一级 1er Cru -1855 Classification
- 18～20℃
- 酒友交流，友人相聚 wine appreciation, friends gathering
- 烧牛柳，粤式扣肉 roast tenderloin, cantonese double braised pork meat with fat
- 波尔多八大名庄之一，全球最昂贵的酒园。 One of the top 8 châteaux of Bordeaux, the most expensive vinyard in the world.

拉图庄园副牌（红）
Les Forts de Latour

¥¥¥¥

深宝石红色，带有迷人的果香，单宁柔顺，可用较实惠的价格欣赏到拉图庄的神韵。Dense and dark ruby in color. Deep, long wine, with super fruit and good tannins. Excellent quality and good value.

- 拉图副牌酒 2nd wine of Ch. Latour
- 18～20℃
- 情侣约会，温馨家宴 dating, family gathering
- 东坡肉，牛肉干 fat pork meat, dry beef
- 采用与正牌酒不同的独立葡萄园的葡萄酿造，是波尔多最好的副牌酒之一。 Using the grape from individual vineyard of Ch. Latour. One of Bordeax's best second wines.

武当罗富齐家族
Mouton Rothschild Family

武当罗富齐家族是法国波尔多最负盛名的三大酒业集团之一，被称为备受葡萄酒酿造业崇拜的成功模范，是唯一一个让法国政府对1855年波尔多列级名庄评级作修改的酒庄。除了一级名庄武当王，旗下还拥有美隆修士堡和小丑人庄园等备受推崇的精品酒庄。

Baron Philippe de Rothschild is one of the three most famous wine families in Bordeaux France. It is regarded as the exemplar for the wine industry, and the only winery which convinced French government to make an adjustment for the classification of 1855. Besides the first growth château Mouton, the family also owns several premium wineries such as Ch. Clerc Milon and Ch. d'Armailhac.

武当罗富齐庄园（红）（又称：武当王）
Ch. Mouton Rothschild

¥¥¥¥¥

深宝石红色，有香草、桑果、薄荷和香料等优雅气息，口感有力圆润，骨架感强，单宁柔顺，后味悠长平衡。
Deep ruby color. The elegant nose combines refined vanilla with intense bilberry fruit, and touches of mint and spice as well. Powerful yet silky on the palate, it displays densely-textured, supremely patrician tannins. Very long, complete and balanced finish.

- 波尔多列级名庄第一级（1973年从二级擢升）1er Cru-Classification
- 18～20℃
- 酒友交流，浪漫婚宴 wine appreciation, wedding
- 羊肉，红烧肉 lamb, pork cooked in soya sauce
- 波尔多八大名庄之一，是“酒庄装瓶”的开拓者，每年均请著名艺术家为酒标作画。One of the top 8 châteaux of Bordeaux. The first estate to begin château-bottling and create Museum of Wine and Art.

小武当
Le Petit Mouton de Mouton-Rothschild

¥¥¥¥

深红色，带有红色浆果、黑加仑子以及优雅的烤橡木气息。酒性丰厚且柔和，富有层次，单宁甘美。Intense red color. Nose of lots of bright berry, currant and toasted oak. Full-bodied, with chewy tannins.

- 武当罗富齐副牌酒 2nd wine of Ch. Mouton Rothschild
- 18～20℃
- 酒友交流，友人相聚 wine appreciation, friends gathering
- 扒类，烤肉 steak, roast red meat
- 巧得正牌酒的风骨，虽是副牌酒，但定价甚至超过不少二级名庄。An outstanding second wine with high price, even higher than some 2em Crus.

美隆修士堡（红）
Ch. Clerc Milon

¥¥¥

宝石红酒色，带有香甜的黑色水果和矿物香气，单宁成熟，圆润的奶油口感让人难忘。Beautiful ruby-red color. Nose of classic, minerally sweet black fruits. Ripe tannins, coating the palate. Rich and a touch creamy.

- 1855年波尔多列级名庄第五级 5eme Cru-1855 Classification
- 14～17℃
- 温馨家宴，友人相聚 family gathering, friends gathering
- 烧肉，牛扒 roast meat, beef steak
- 菩依乐酒迷必试葡萄酒，由拥有武当王庄园的罗富齐家族拥有。A property with which all lovers of Pauillac should be familiar. Belongs to the Mouton Rothschild family.

小丑人庄园（红）
Ch. d'Armailhac

¥¥¥

宝石红酒色，带有咖啡、太妃糖和黑加仑子等活跃香气，口感丰盈，单宁成熟且排列紧密，让人爱不释口。Beautiful ruby-red color. Attractive youth on the nose, brimming over with coffee, arry treacle toffee and blackcurrant aromas. Intense and concentrated, with pure black fruits and ripe, firm tannins.

- 1855年波尔多列级名庄第五级 5eme Cru-1855 Classification
- 14～17℃
- 温馨家宴，友人相聚 family gathering, friends gathering
- 中浓味菜肴 medium to heavy dishes
- 历史上曾是拉菲罗富齐家族的物业，现为武当罗富齐家族拥有，是名家之酒。Once owned by Lafite Rothschild family before, now under the direction of Mouton Rothschild family.

碧尚女爵堡（红）
Ch. Pichon Longueville Comtesse de Lalande

¥¥¥¥

深宝石红色，带有紫罗兰、香草和肉桂气息，单宁成熟柔滑，结构强劲而柔韧，酒体平衡，余韵悠长。Dark ruby in color. Aromas of violet, vanilla and cinnamon. A palate with mature and melted tannins. An affirmed structure with perfect harmony and long finish.

- 1855年波尔多列级名庄第二级 2eme Cru-1855 Classification
- 18～20℃
- 酒友交流，浪漫婚宴 wine appreciation, wedding
- 浓味红肉 red meat with rich sauce
- 历史上属于碧尚家族，后庄主在子女间实行了分配，碧尚女爵堡由女儿继承，现由路易王妃集团拥有。The seeds of the creation of the Pichon domaine, which was split to form the two Pichon châteaux. This property belonged to the daughters and now owned by Rouzand family.

碧尚女爵堡副牌（红）
Reserve de la Comtesse

¥¥¥

深宝石红色，伴有巧克力和黑色浆果的气息，容易欣赏，单宁成熟柔滑，结构优雅。Dark ruby color. An easy-to-drink, seductive style with plenty of chocolate-infused black currant fruit. Supple tannin and elegant structure.

- 碧尚女爵堡之副牌酒 2nd wine of Ch. Pichon Lalande, Pauillac AOC
- 14～17℃
- 浪漫婚宴，友人相聚 wedding, friends gathering
- 红烧肉 pork cooked in soya sauce
- 以丰满、奢华的结构和高质量征服众多爱酒之人。A fat, sumptuously-textured, rich, hedonistically-styled wine that will surprise many consumers with its high quality.

碧尚（菩依乐）（红）
Pauillac de Ch. Pichon Lalande

¥¥¥

宝石红酒色，带有紫罗兰、皮革和香草的香气。口感结实，优雅平衡，带有樱桃的味道，余味悠长。A deep crimson color, a nose of red fruit, violets, leather and vanilla. The palate is well structured, with flavours of cherry and excellent length.

- 碧尚女爵堡之三牌酒 3rd wine of Ch. Pichon Lalande, Pauillac AOC
- 14～17℃
- 温馨家宴，友人相聚 family gathering, friends gathering
- 腊肠，烧腊 flavoured sausage, toasted red meat
- 一款性价比甚高的三牌酒。Good for value to enjoy such seductive tribute at a lower price.

碧尚男爵堡（红）
Ch. Baron de Pichon-Longueville

¥¥¥¥

深黑色，有干樱桃和洋李的芳香，并带有烤橡木味道，酒体中度，单宁良好，后味愉悦。Deep dark red. Plenty of dried cherry and plum aromas. Hints of toasted oak. Medium-bodied, with fine tannins and a light finish.

- 1855年波尔多列级名庄第二级 2eme Cru-1855 Classification
- 18～20℃
- 酒友交流，商务宴请 wine appreciation, business dinner
- 红焖野味，浓味红肉 braised game, red meat with medium to heavy sauce
- 历史上属于碧尚家族，后庄主在子女间实行了分配，碧尚男爵堡由儿子继承，现由AXA集团拥有，酒性强健有力。The seeds of the creation of the Pichon domaine, which was split to form the two Pichon châteaux. This property belonged to the sons and now owned by AXA group. A masculine wine.

小村庄（红）
Ch. Petit Village

¥¥¥¥

深红色，带有该区特有的精致且浓郁的香气，单宁柔顺，散发着肉汁香味，结构平衡。Beautiful deep red. It possesses the richness and incomparable finesse of great Pomerol. The tannins are supple, fleshy and powerful. The structure is balanced.

- 宝物隆法定产区酒 Pomerol AOC
- 18～20℃
- 情侣约会，友人相聚 dating, friends gathering
- 牛扒，烧鸭 beef steak, roast duck
- 宝物隆的十大酒庄之一，是产量稀少的精品好酒，现由著名的AXA保险集团拥有。One of the top 10 Pomerol estates today under the control of the AXA Millesimes.

靓茨伯庄园
（又称：林卓贝斯）（红）
Ch. Lynch Bages

¥¥¥¥

深红色，伴有典雅的橡木、薄荷、树脂、摩卡咖啡的香味，单宁成熟，余韵有紫罗兰和黑莓的味道。Intense red color. The nose is powerful with elegant oak background, menthol, resin and moca. Concentration of ripe, round tannin. With a touch of violet, blackberry in finish.

- 1855年波尔多列级名庄第五级 5eme Cru-1855 Classification
- 18～20℃
- 酒友交流，浪漫婚宴 wine appreciation, wedding
- 牛柳，羊鞍 beef, lamb
- 具有挑战一级庄的实力。与粤剧名伶靓茨伯同名，是华人心目中的十大名庄。在香港被誉为亿万富翁的日常餐酒。It was called the daily wine for millionaire in Hong Kong. As the pronunciation Lynch Bages is similar to a well-known Canton Opera singer's name, it is ranked the Top 10 popular imporeed wine of Chinese market.

靓茨伯庄园
（又称：林卓贝斯）（白）
Blanc de Lynch Bages

¥¥¥

浅金黄色，先有柠檬酥，后有菠萝与杏仁的香气。酒体中度，口感平衡，后味带有香草与奶油柠檬派的余韵。A pale golden hue. Initially showing lemon pastry, but later pineapple and marzipan. Medium bodied, it shows a good texture. Plenty of spice and an almost creamy lemon pie note on the finish.

- 波尔多法定产区酒 Bordeaux AOC
- 12～14℃
- 商务宴请，温馨家宴 business dinner, family gathering
- 香煎海鲜，烩鲍鱼 pan-fried seafood, braised abalone
- 产量稀少，质量优秀的白葡萄酒。A small production and good quality white wine.

奥德碧丝（红）
Ch. Les Ormes de Pez

¥¥¥

深红色，在复杂的成熟浆果芬芳中带有一丝木香味。酒体有力，口感平衡，余味悠长。Deep and dark color. Very complex nose of mature fruits with a touch of wood. Long aftertaste. Powerful and well-balanced.

- 2003年美度区超级明星庄 Cru Bourgeois Exceptionnel
- 14～17℃
- 友人相聚，浪漫婚宴 friends gathering, wedding
- 铁板类红肉 teppenyaki red meat
- 是靓茨伯庄园主人Cazes家族的旗下作品，并由靓茨伯庄园精心打造。A fine wine produced by Cazes family，and refined by their excellent team.

宝德嘉纳庄园（红）
Ch. Pontet Canet

￥￥￥

中度红色。气味复杂，带有明显的黑色浆果香。口感圆润，优雅，酒体平衡。A moderate color. An intense, complex medley of blackcurrants and other black fruits.A fat round yet elegant palate, with good balance structure.

- 1855年波尔多列级名庄第五级 5eme Cru-1855 Classification
- 18～20℃
- 酒友交流，商务宴请 wine appreciation, business dinner
- 牛扒，羊扒 beef steak, lamb
- 波尔多第一个采用生物动力学酿酒哲学的列级名庄，近年最能给人惊喜的酒庄之一。The first Grand Cru châteaux to adopt biodynamics in Bordeaux. One of the most promising wineries in recent years.

都卡斯庄园（红）
Ch. Grand-Puy Ducasse

￥￥￥

呈亮丽的红色，带有浆果和烟草气息，酒体中度，单宁集中，余韵清新。A well-crafted red. Nose of berry and tobacco character. Medium-bodied, with medium tannins and a fresh finish.

- 1855年波尔多列级名庄第五级 5eme Cru-1855 Classification
- 18～20℃
- 友人相聚，温馨家宴 friends gathering, family gathering
- 浓味红肉 red meat with rich sauce
- 性价比最高的波尔多名庄酒之一。One of the best buys among Bordeaux Grands Crus Classés.

歌碧（红）
Ch. Croizet Bages

￥￥￥

中至深红色，果香曼妙，有清新的橡木味。入口柔顺有果香，单宁成熟，口感平衡。Medium-dark red color. Good fruit nose, some new wood. Smooth and soft fruit attack, tannins ripe, and nice balance.

- 1855年波尔多列级名庄第五级 5eme Cru-1855 Classification
- 18～20℃
- 情侣约会，商务宴请 dating, business dinner
- 牛扒，羊鞍 beef steak, lamb
- 与大名鼎鼎的林卓贝斯庄园相邻，是轻盈平顺，容易欣赏的菩依乐酒。Sharing the similar micro-climate of Ch.Lynch-Bages. An easy drinking Pauillac wine.

歌碧副牌（红）
La Tourelle de Croizet Bages

￥￥￥

紫红色，带有玫瑰花、山楂果、玫瑰、水果干以及当归香气。口感丝滑，单宁良好，后味有肉桂和甘草的味道。Sparkle red purple. Nose of floral, whitethorn, rose and preserved fruit, angelica. Mellow and smooth. Good tannins and has wonderful aftertaste of cinnamon and liquorice.

- 歌碧庄园副牌酒 2nd wine of Ch. Croizet Bages
- 14～17℃
- 友人相聚，温馨家宴 friends gathering, family gathering
- 红烧鱼，牛扒 pan-fried fish, beef steak
- 性价比极高的副牌酒，具有菩依乐村的优雅风格。Good value second wine expresses the elegance of Pauillac.

宝丽嘉庄园（红）
Ch. Bellegrave

深宝石红色，带有水果和橡木的清香，酒体中度，有力且雅致，余味中等。A dark ruby color. Well extracted, good use of oak and fruit shines through. Medium bodied with a moderate finish. Opulent depth and fullness with elegance.

- 菩依乐法定产区酒 Pauillac AOC
- 14～17℃
- 情侣约会，友人相聚 dating, friends gathering
- 中浓味菜肴 medium to heavy dishes
- 位于拉图庄与靓茨伯庄之间，年产量只有6 000瓶，但物超所值。States near glittery neighbors Ch. Latour and Ch. Lynch-Bages. Very low production every year but acceptable price.

百德诗歌（红）
Ch. Pedesclaux

深紫色，酒香较浓，有成熟的黑色浆果和树木的芳香。单宁柔和，结构良好。Very deep blue. Powerful nose, redolent of ripe black fruit and some wood.Soft tannins, and well structured.

- 1855年波尔多列级名庄第五级 5eme Cru-1855 Classification
- 14～17℃
- 情侣约会，商务宴请 wine appreciation, wedding
- 羊扒，鸭胸 lamb, duck breast
- 酒体结实，回味甘香，价格合理。Powerful nose, redolent of ripe black fruit and some wood. Lots of aromas of good fruits, soft tannins, and well structured.

拉高斯（红）
Ch. Grand-Puy-Lacoste

深紫色，有活跃的黑色水果和香草的香味，还伴有甘草、浆果、铅笔木和花的香气，酒体丰满，单宁恰到好处。Blackish, purple color. Generous, open nose of black fruit and vanilla. Licorice, berry and lead pencil, with flowers. Full-bodied, with fine tannins and a long finish.

- 1855年波尔多列级名庄第五级 5eme Cru-1855 Classification
- 18～20℃
- 温馨家宴，友人相聚 family gathering, friends gathering
- 萝卜牛腩等浓味菜肴 braised beef brisket with radish or spicy meat dishes
- 以稳定的质量和鲜明的菩依乐风格赢得众多饮家的喜爱。Adored by many wine lovers for its stable quality and obvious Pauillac style.

Pauillac

>圣祖利安村
St. Julien

圣祖利安村的面积是四大名村中最小的，酒田面积只有700多公顷。在1855年的评级中，该村共有11家酒庄上榜，全部是二至四级庄。除此以外，其余的酒田基本上被优秀品质的明星酒庄所占领，所以，圣祖利安村的酒可以说是波尔多名村中葡萄酒平均质量最高的，饮家们都认为圣祖利安酒是信心的保证。

宝嘉龙家族
Ducru Beaucaillou Family

宝嘉龙的字面意思为“美丽的鹅卵石”，在1855年评级中名列第二级，是具有挑战一级名庄实力的“超二级”酒庄，被称为圣祖利安村的代表作。除了正牌酒外，宝嘉龙每年都生产副牌酒，另外还酿制拉朗宝怡、都加索等产量小、品质精的佳酿。

Meaning beautiful pebbles in literal, Château Drcru Beaucaillou is the second growth château in the classification of 1855. It is regarded as the super 2 which can be a rival of the first growth châteaux. Besides the Grand Vin, Château Drcru Beaucaillou produces a second wine as well, as long as other limited-yield and high-quality products such as Château Lalande-Borie and Château Ducluzeau.

宝嘉龙庄园（红）
Ch. Ducru Beaucaillou

¥¥¥¥

深宝石红色，带有迷人的花香和烟草、甘草的香味，结构感强，单宁柔顺，余味悠长。Dark ruby color. Fresh aromatic flavour from flower, reveal with tobacco smile and liquorices. Well-structured, smooth tannins with long finish.

- 1855年波尔多列级名庄第二级 2eme Cru-1855 Classification
- 18～20℃
- 酒友交流，商务宴请 wine appreciation, business dinner
- 铁板类红肉 teppenyaki red meat
- 得到世界多位著名酒评家赞赏的波尔多五星级酒庄，因温柔婉约享有“圣祖利安的拉菲”的美誉。The wine imbued with subtlety and femininity is regarded as Lafite of St.Julien. Five star winery praised by many famous wine critics.

宝嘉龙副牌（红）
Croix de Beaucaillou

¥ ¥ ¥

深宝石红色，带有樱桃、泡草莓的香气和极具风味的红浆果味，口感非常好，浑厚有劲，余韵微辛辣。Dark ruby color. Noses of cherry and wild strawberry. Good weight on the palate with some savoury red fruits in the core. Bright and vigorous with a sprightly peppery finish.

- 宝嘉龙庄园副牌酒 2nd wine of Ch. Ducru Beaucaillou
- 14～17℃
- 情侣约会，温馨家宴 dating, family gathering
- 烤肉，羊扒 grilled meat, lamb
- 一款反映圣祖利安村优雅、富有陈年天赋的个性副牌酒。A wine which reveals its assets earlier than the great wine but also the characteristics of a great St Julien: elegance, finesse and its ability to age.

拉朗宝怡（红）
Ch. Lalande-Borie

¥ ¥ ¥

深黑色，有烟熏黑樱桃香和蜜糖烤坚果味道。中度酒体，以柔和的成熟单宁和恰到好处的酸度贯穿品尝过程。Youthful hue, Smoky black cherry nose, with a sweet, honey-roast nut sideline. Medium body, a gentle presence of ripe tannin to give a little backbone, and good acidity. Flows across the palate.

- 圣祖利安法定产区酒 St. Julien AOC
- 14～17℃
- 情侣约会，友人相聚 dating, friends gathering
- 烧鸭，烟熏肉类 roast duck, bacon dishes
- 此庄园由宝嘉龙家族拥有，被酒评家视为明日之星。The same owner as Ch. Ducru Beaucaillou. One of the most promising wines for some critics.

都加索庄园（红）
Ch. Ducluzeau

¥ ¥ ¥

酒红色调，强烈的薄荷和雪松味道，口感柔顺，伴有成熟樱桃清香，单宁感不强，是可以较早饮用的酒。Red color. An intense minty, cedary nose. Soft and ripe with cherry fruit. Not much tannin, fine but early drinking wine.

- 美度丽莎法定产区酒 Listrac-Médoc AOC
- 14～17℃
- 温馨家宴，友人相聚 family gathering, friends gathering
- 中浓味菜肴，炖牛肉 medium to heavey dishes, braised beef
- 一款非常少见的产自波尔多左岸以梅乐为主的葡萄酒，由宝嘉龙家族主理。A simple, unorthodox Merlot based wine made by Ducru Beaucaillou family.

小常识 Q & A

问：葡萄酒瓶的瓶口为什么有层塑料封套?

答：是为了防止虫子咬软木塞。有时封套上留有小孔，是为了葡萄酒能与外界交换呼吸，主要用于浅龄酒。

雄狮庄园（红）
Ch. Léoville Las Cases

¥¥¥¥

明亮的宝石红色，带有浆果、香草和泥土的芳香。中度酒体，单宁柔滑，余韵较淡。Bright ruby color. Berry, vanilla and earth character. Medium body, soft tannins and light finish.

- 1855年波尔多列级名庄第二级 2eme Cru-1855 Classification
- 18～20℃
- 酒友交流，商务宴请 wine appreciation, business dinner
- 烤肉，羊扒 roast meat, lamb
- 是声誉最接近一级庄的波尔多顶尖佳酿。与其他圣祖利安村名庄风格不完全一样，更似菩依乐村拉图庄的雄劲。Undoubtedly a remarkable wine, one that is lauded by critics. A Pauillac-style wine produced in St. Julien.

雄狮侯爵园（红）
Clos Du Marquis

¥¥¥

宝石红色，果香馥郁诱人，单宁成熟，丰富且有质感的口感令人回味，后韵愉悦。Ruby color. An attractive nose, with dense and dark fruits. Weighty, supple fruit on the palate, elegant but with substance. Ripe tannin. Very approachable at the finish.

- 雄狮庄园副牌酒 2nd wine of Ch. Léoville Las Cases
- 14～17℃
- 友人相聚，温馨家宴 friends gathering, family gathering
- 羊扒，烧鸡 lamb, roast chicken
- 一款口感馥郁的经典副牌酒。A classically composed wine.

巴顿庄园（红）
Ch. Léoville Barton

¥¥¥¥

深紫红色，紫罗兰芳香中带有一丝葡萄干的味道。中度至浑厚酒体，单宁结构良好，余韵柔滑。Deep ruby colour Violet with hints of currant on the nose. Medium to full-bodied, with fine, integrated tannins and a long, silky finish.

- 1855年波尔多列级名庄第二级 2eme Cru -1855 Classification
- 18～20℃
- 酒友交流，商务宴请 wine appreciation, business dinner
- 黑椒牛扒，烤肉，熏肉 black pepper steak, roast meat, bacon meat
- 酒质接近一级名庄的二级名酿，是酒评家公认的“物值最高”的波尔多名酿之一。A 2nd growth château which conquers the world for both its quality and integrity.

丽冠巴顿庄园（红）
Ch. Langoa Barton

¥¥¥

酒色亮丽有光泽，富有层次的果香扑鼻而来，还伴有热带水果和橡木香。口感平和，单宁丝滑，酒体浓郁平衡。A glorious, very pure color. Piles of fruit on the nose, with exotic notes and some oak still. Pure, glossy mouth-feel, silky tannin and good concentration.

- 1855年波尔多列级名庄第三级 3eme Cru-1855 Classification
- 18～20℃
- 温馨家宴，商务宴请 family gathering, business dinner
- 中浓味菜肴，烧鹅 medium to heavey dishes, roast goose
- 一款堪称精致的葡萄酒，口感温雅偏女性化。A delicate wine, showing a feminine and approachable face.

龙船
Beychevelle

龙船庄虽在1855年评级中位列第四级，却凭其吉祥的酒名、易认的酒标、卓越的酒质成为除一级庄外在国内名声最响的法国名庄。其副牌酒和附属品牌都与正牌酒出自同一酿酒团队之手，是中国葡萄酒市场最畅销的葡萄酒系列之一。

As a 4th growth château in the 1855 Bordeaux classification, Château Beychevelle is the most reputable French winery after the 1st growth châteaux in China, for its auspicious name, memorable label and outstanding quality. Its second wine and other sub-brands, which are made by the same team and technique, are among the best-sellers in China' s wine market.

龙船庄园（红）
Ch. Beychevelle

¥¥¥¥

深宝石红色，带有蓝莓、红加仑子、矿物质与香料等微妙气息。酒体浑厚，单宁完整，余味新鲜悠长。Dark ruby color. This floral-scented wine offers nose of blueberries, red currants, minerals, and spice. Full-bodied, with well- integrated tannins and a long, fresh finish.

- 1855年波尔多列级名庄第四级 4eme Cru-1855 Classification
- 18～20℃
- 酒友交流，商务宴请 wine appreciation, business dinner
- 卤水鸭掌，烧鹅 brine duckpalm, roast goose
- 拥有被誉为“波尔多凡尔赛宫”的后花园，酒名寓意吉祥，是除一级庄外在中国名声最响最受关注的法国名庄。With a grand building called "Versailles in Bordeaux", it has a musical legend and auspicious name. The most reputable French winery after the 1st growth châteaux in China.

龙船将军（红）
Amiral de Beychevelle

¥ ¥ ¥

深紫红色，带有诱人的玫瑰、浆果和新鲜烟草的香味。中度酒体，单宁良好，余韵中度。Deep purple-red color. Attractive aromas of roses, berries and fresh tobacco. Medium-bodied, with fine tannins and a medium finish.

- 龙船庄园副牌酒 2nd wine of Ch. Beychevelle
- 18～20℃
- 友人相聚，温馨家宴 friends gathering, family gathering
- 羊扒，鸭胸 lamb, duck breast
- 与正牌酒采用相同的酿酒工艺，可以较低的价钱欣赏龙船庄园和圣祖利安名酿的风韵。Made according to the same secular tradition as its glorious elder, it reveals its qualities earlier, giving the wine lover all the vivacity of youth.

龙船美度（红）
Les Brulières de Beychevelle

¥ ¥ ¥

酒色深浓，带有黑色浆果与樱桃的气息。酒体醇和，清新怡人。单宁成熟温和，极具陈年天分。Very dense color. With fruity flavours of black berries and cherry, it is very pleasant and fleshy. The tannins are ripe, mild and nicely-pronounced. It has a lot of aging potential.

- 上美度法定产区酒 Haut-Médoc AOC
- 14～17℃
- 友人相聚，情侣约会 friends gathering, dating
- 烧牛柳，粤式扣肉 roast tenderloin, cantonese double braised pork meat with fat
- 龙船庄的附属产品，由龙船庄原班人马采用先进设备酿制，是质优价廉的名门之秀。Sub-brand of Ch. Beychevelle and with the same equipment and technique as its grand vin. A distinguished wine at reasonable price.

金龙船（红）
Secret de Grand Bateau

¥¥¥

深红色，带有成熟浓郁的果香，还混合有香料、巧克力和烘焙的香味，酒体中浓，入口时黑色水果的香味尤为突出。Dense color. With ripe and intense fruit flavours mixed with spices, chocolate and torrefaction, it is medium-full bodied red wine with concentrated black fruits taste.

- 波尔多法定产区酒 Bordeaux AOC
- 14～17℃
- 情侣约会，友人相聚 dating, friends gathering
- 东坡肉，牛肉干 fat pork meat, dry beef
- 用波尔多最好的红葡萄品种酿制，是波尔多四级名庄龙船庄的荣誉出品。Produced by Château Beychevelle, it is blended with Bordeaux' s best red grape varieties.

金龙船（白）
Secret de Grand Bateau Blanc

¥¥

淡黄色调，入口即可感到其复杂且美妙的柑橘、白花香味。此酒风格优雅，口感温和。Pale yellow hint. An extraordinary wine with wonderfully complex aromas of citrus fruits and white flowers.

- 波尔多法定产区酒 Bordeaux AOC
- 7～12℃
- 情侣约会，友人相聚 dating, friends gathering
- 生蚝，鱼肉，白肉，沙拉 oysters, fish, white meat, salad
- 龙船庄的附属产品，一款酸甜度平衡得恰到好处的白葡萄酒。Sub-brand of Ch. Beychevelle, with lovely and balanced acidity and sweetness.

小龙船（红）
Grand Bateau Rouge

¥¥

酒色深澈有光泽，有明显的成熟红色水果、香料、新橡木香，口感和谐有力，单宁成熟，余味香浓。Deep bright color. Expressive nose of ripe red fruits, spices with an elegant touch of new oak. A harmonious and relatively powerful wine. Ripe tannins and savoury finish.

- 波尔多法定产区酒 Bordeaux AOC
- 14～17℃
- 活力派对，友人相聚 party, friends gathering
- 烤鸭，乳鸽等中浓型红肉 medium red meat dishes, roast goose, roast pigeon
- 龙船庄的附属产品，在中国同价位红葡萄酒中最畅销的一款。Sub-brand of Ch. Beychevelle. One of the most popular wines in China at the similar price range.

小龙船（白）
Grand Bateau Blanc

¥¥

浅黄色，带有黄油、香草、橡木和奇异果的气息。口感丰满洁净，酸度适宜，后味极好。Light yellow color. Nose of buttery-vanillin oak flavours and exotic fruit. The wine is powerful and fleshy. Clean and lively acidity. Excellent finish.

- 波尔多法定产区酒 Bordeaux AOC
- 7～12℃
- 活力派对，友人相聚 party, friends gathering
- 淡味海鲜 light seafood
- 龙船庄的附属产品，一款超值的波尔多白葡萄酒。Sub-brand of Ch. Beychevelle. A good-valued Bordeaux white wine.

小常识
Q & A

问：100元的葡萄酒与1 000元的葡萄酒有什么差别?

答：影响葡萄酒售价的因素有5个：

（1）葡萄酒品质的优劣与知名度；

（2）葡萄酒的酿制成本；

（3）葡萄酒原产地的特色风味以及产量、质量，自然物以稀为贵；

（4）葡萄品种的成本，例如Syrah的成本是Chardonnay的两倍；

（5）供求情况，这是影响售价的关键，如果某个酿酒商的葡萄酒供不应求，只能满足市场需求的10%（如许多上等法国布根地葡萄酒和波尔多宝物隆葡萄酒），其售价就会非常高。

大宝庄园（红）
Ch. Talbot

¥¥¥¥

深紫红色，带有丰富的雪松木、香草、栗子的芳香，口感丰富成熟，单宁柔滑如丝。Claret color. Richly aromatic with a bouquet of cedar wood and vanilla scented cassis fruits. A palate packed with finely integrated tannins.

- 1855年波尔多列级名庄第四级 4eme Cru-1855 Classification
- 18～20℃
- 酒友交流，商务宴请 wine appreciation, business dinner
- 香肠，风干肉类 sausage, dry meat
- 得名于英法百年战争中的大宝将军，传说庄园地底下埋有珠宝，是精心酿造、品质稳定的列级名庄葡萄酒。Named after Talbot, an English warrior. Ch. Talbot has a reputation for consistency and is one of the most carefully made and reliable wines of the Crus Classes.

大宝王子（红）
Connétable Talbot

¥¥¥

深红色，带有波尔多经典的黑色水果、雪松和皮革香，口感有力浓郁，层次丰富，单宁柔顺，后味单宁感不强。Deep red color. Classic Bordeaux scents of black fruit and cedar with pleasant leathery undertones. Powerful and concentrated wine with a rich and supple attack.

- 大宝庄园副牌酒 2nd wine of Ch. Talbot
- 18～20℃
- 温馨家宴，友人相聚 family gathering, friends gathering
- 中浓味菜肴，烧腊 medium to heavy dishes, roast meat
- 列级名庄大宝的副牌酒。除了陈年时间较短外，其他工艺与正牌酒无异。The second wine of Château Talbot. This younger sibling receives the same careful treatment as its elder, the only difference being that its maturation period is just slightly shorter.

大宝庄园（白）
Caillou Blanc du Ch. Talbot

¥¥

金黄色，芳香怡人，透出桃子和白花的浓郁香气。口感洁净且丰富。A golden color. Its very subtle bouquet offers aromas of peaches and white blossom. Clean and fleshy.

- 波尔多法定产区酒 Bordeaux AOC
- 12～14℃
- 浪漫婚宴，友人相聚 wedding, friends gathering
- 蒸虾球，白切鸡，炒蔬菜 braised shrimp, poach chicken, stir-fry vegetable
- 美度区最具历史的白葡萄酒之一，产量稀少，品质超群。It is one of the oldest dry white wines of the Médoc. A rare and exceptional white wine.

歌丽雅庄园（红）
Ch. Gloria & Julien

¥¥¥

深红色，带有浆果、樱桃和黑色水果的芳香。中度酒体，流畅而适中的口感与结实的单宁配合恰到好处。Deep red color. Full of berry, cherry and releases lovely black fruit aroma. Medium-bodied, , chewy tannin, fluid mid palate, and tannic finish.

- 2003年波尔多明星庄 Cru Bourgeois-2003
- 18～20℃
- 友人相聚,情侣约会 friends gathering, dating
- 羊肉，炖海参 lamb, braised sea cucumber
- 曾是圣祖利安市市长的物业，现在在其女婿的管理下蒸蒸日上。Once belonged to the mayor of St.Julien. Now his son-in-law continue his good job.

力关圣祖利安庄园（红）
Ch. Lagrange Saint-Julien

¥¥¥¥

深宝石红色，有黑樱桃和橡木香，还有烤面包的气息。单宁紧密，酒体饱满，带有黄油般的水果味道，深具陈年的天分。Dark, glossy hue. Fat and rich on the nose, with dense black cherry fruit and oak, with a burnt, toasty edge. There is a hint of fat, rich opulence here and buttery fruit.

- 1855年波尔多列级名庄第三级 3eme Cru-1855 Classification
- 18～20℃
- 酒友交流，商务宴请 wine appreciation, business dinner
- 红烧肉 pork cooked in soya sauce
- 源于16世纪的古老庄园，该地曾是法国国王私人秘书的享乐地。Century-old château. In history it was the wonderland of the private secretary of French king.

百利通庄园（红）
Ch. Branaire Ducru

¥¥¥

深紫红色，除了蓝莓、黑莓等果香，还有石墨、铅笔芯的气息，口感饱满多层次，酒体中度，单宁软熟。Deep ruby color. Scents of graphite, lead pencil shavings, blueberries and raspberries. The wine is rich, layered, medium-bodied, a complex St.-Julien with soft tannin.

- 1855年波尔多列级名庄第四级 4eme Cru-1855 Classification
- 18～20℃
- 酒友交流，商务宴请 wine appreciation, bussiness dinner
- 烤肉，野味 grilled meat, game
- 近年进步最快、最受关注的波尔多佳酿之一，被著名酒商BBR称为“波尔多饮家的葡萄酒”。The property has now come into its full stride in terms of quality. Regarded as "the wine of choice for the Bordeaux cognoscenti" by BBR.

百利通上美度（红）
Le Haut Médoc de Branaire-Ducru

¥¥

深红色至黑色，闻有黑皮水果和香料的气息，口感有力度，单宁细致，酒香浓郁。Deep almost black color. The expressive nose exudes aromas of black fruits and spices. This wine has great intensity while remaining smooth through the finesse of its tannins.

- 上美度法定产区酒 Haut-Médoc AOC
- 18～20℃
- 情侣约会，友人相聚 dating, friends gathering
- 牛扒，烤羊 beef steak, roast lamb
- 百利通的三牌酒，由年轻葡萄树的果实酿造，主打的是果香，口感平易近人。The 3rd wine of Ch. Branaire-Ducru. This wine is made from grapes of young vines, making it to be a fruity, acceptable and enjoyable wine.

>玛歌村 Margaux

玛歌村是四大名村中面积最大的一个，共有3 000多公顷的葡萄园。如果说菩依乐村因为拥有最多的一级庄而闻名于世，那玛歌村则是拥有最多列级酒庄的村庄。在1855年的评级中，玛歌村占了21间，从一级至五级都有，大部分是二级和三级，另外还有一批质量优异的明星酒庄。

玛歌村出产美度区最柔顺的葡萄酒，带有雅致的酒香，复杂而有层次，有花香、果香和橡木香。其酒质精致、纤细，酒身较轻。玛歌村的酒一般比较容易欣赏，陈年后将愈发香浓圆润。

玛歌庄园（红）Ch. Margaux

¥¥¥¥¥

酒香富有层次，酒体丰盈，口感有力且优雅，像在舌头味蕾上跳的一曲芭蕾舞。单宁细致，是波尔多罕见的明丽清澈型葡萄酒。The fundamental virtue of a great Château Margaux is poise; the way it tiptoes on the palate like a ballerina, full of strength and grace. Its tannin is a finer, lending the wine a certain transparency and clarity that is rare in Bordeaux.

- 1855年波尔多列级名庄第一级 1er Cru-1855 Classification
- 18～20℃
- 酒友交流，商务宴请 wine appreciation, business dinner
- 牛柳，羊鞍 beef steak, lamb
- 波尔多八大名庄之一，以温柔和顺的口感成为最具女性魅力的葡萄酒。胡锦涛主席访法时，法国政府盛意邀请其参观了该庄。Rhythm of beauty. Certainly the most feminine and most charming of the First Growths. It is the only château visited by Chinese president Hu Jintao when he visited France.

玛歌红亭（红）
Pavillon Rouge du Ch. Margaux

¥¥¥¥

深宝石红色，带有特别的欧亚甘草、浆果及樱桃的芳香，中度酒体，单宁优质，入口十分柔滑且余韵十足。Very deep ruby color. Aromas of red licorice, berry and cherry. Medium-bodied, with fine tannins and a fine, silky finish.

- 玛歌庄园副牌酒 2nd wine of Ch. Margaux
- 18～20℃
- 酒友交流，商务宴请 wine appreciation, business dinner
- 羊肉，红烧肉 lamb, pork cooked in soya sauce
- 是副牌酒中的精品，酒香和酒体均显浓郁、果香集中的个性。The pearl of crown among second wines. A delicate character.

玛歌白亭（白）
Pavillon Blanc du Ch. Margaux

¥¥¥¥

淡稻草黄色，有清新的果香和明显的草药味道，口感圆润宽广，结构感强，是一款精致的白葡萄酒。Pale straw yellow color. Full of refreshing fruit aromas and explicit herbal fragrance. Rich, quite broad and textured on the palate. A lovely polished style.

- 波尔多法定产区酒 Bordeaux AOC
- 7～12℃
- 浪漫婚宴，商务宴请 wedding, business dinner
- 淡至中味芝士，贝类 light to medium cheese, shell seafood
- 被誉为波尔多最卓越白葡萄酒之一，尽显其贵族气派。One of Bordeaux's most sublime and prestigious white wines, Cast in the great, aristocratic Margaux style.

宝马庄园（红）
Ch. Palmer

¥¥¥¥

初时是黑色水果香气，随后有薄荷、香草、烟熏和甘草的气息，层次感极强，单宁雅致，酒体柔滑，余味悠长。Black fruits first, then spearmint, vanilla, smoke and licorice notes appear. With great pleasure the wine continues its soft and serene progression for a long and flavoursome finish.

- 1855年波尔多列级名庄第三级 3eme Cru-1855 Classification
- 18～20℃
- 酒友交流，商务宴请 wine appreciation, business dinner
- 牛扒，羊扒 beef steak, lamb
- 是唯一可挑战一级名庄的三级庄。将军和酒庄夫人的浪漫爱情传说，使她具有风花雪月的气息。With a romantic love story between a general and a winery window. An exceptional third grouth wine peers the first rank.

宝马庄园副牌（红）
Alter Eago Palmer

¥¥¥

富有光泽的深红色，带有可人的浆果、李子和花的香味。中度酒体，单宁柔滑，余韵悠长而带果香。Deep bright red color. Lovely berry, plum and floral character. Medium-bodied, with silky tannins and a long, fruity finish.

- 宝马庄园副牌 2nd wine of Ch. Palmer
- 18～20℃
- 友人相聚，温馨家宴 friends gathering, family gathering
- 扒类，烤红肉 steak, roast red meat
- 价格适中，品质优秀的副牌酒，很好地反映了宝马庄园复杂优美的个性。A high quality second wine which inherits the elegant and feminine style of Palmer.

力士金（红）
Ch. Lascombes

¥¥¥

酒色如墨汁般深浓，有强烈的无花果干香味，柔滑的单宁以及适中的骨架带来甘美的果香口感。Very deep, inky color. Powerful nose of dried figs and dates. A superb, fat mouthful of luscious fruit with soft tannins, and considerable backbone.

- 1855年波尔多列级名庄第二级 2eme Cru -1855 Classification
- 18～20℃
- 酒友交流，商务宴请 wine appreciation, business dinner
- 烤肉，羊扒 grilled meat, lamb
- 由拉菲前任总酿酒师多米尼克·贝夫主理后，酒质得到大幅度的提升，是物超所值的二级名庄。The quality of the wine has been improved a lot after Dominique Befve who had been the chief winemaker of Château Lafite took over the château.

力士金骑士（红）
Chevalier de Lascombes

¥¥¥

酒色深浓，带有甜美的成熟樱桃香气，单宁柔滑，酒体偏轻盈，酸度适中，口感甜美。Deep color. Sweet ripe cherries on a rounded, relatively developed nose. Good depth. Soft tannins and a supple body. Moderate acidity with a sweet palate.

- 力士金副牌酒 2nd wine of Ch. Lascombes
- 18～20℃
- 情侣约会，友人相聚 dating, friends gathering
- 牛扒，羊扒 beef steak, lamb
- 以较实惠的价格就可欣赏玛歌村名庄的神韵。You could appreciate Margaux wine with a pleasant price.

宝爵庄园（红）
Ch. Pouget

￥￥￥

酒色深浓，带有果香和坚果香气，口感圆润，有奶油质感，微辛辣，余韵带有巧克力味。Deep color. Nutty oak aroma over a layer of fruit. It shows a little fat, creamy and rounded through the midpalate, with some peppery character. Chocolate notes on the finish.

- 1855年波尔多列级名庄第四级 4eme Cru-1855 Classification
- 18～20℃
- 酒友交流，商务宴请 wine appreciation, business dinner
- 牛扒，羊扒 beef steak, lamb
- 遵循古老的方法种植葡萄，并坚持人工进行采摘酿造而成的优质葡萄酒。保持原始风味中又有其独特的个性。The general balance is always elegant, more aromatic than powerful, characteristic of the traditional Margaux wines.

宝爵庄园副牌（红）
Antoine Pouget

￥￥￥

色泽浓厚，带有水果与香料的复杂香味。酒体平衡而优雅，具有传统玛歌葡萄酒的特色。成熟的单宁使其具备陈年的天分。In the mouth, the entry often straightforward. Then comes a mouthfilling volume. At the end, the ripe tannins assure excellent aging capability.

- 宝爵庄园副牌酒 2nd wine of Ch. Pouget
- 18～20℃
- 情侣约会，友人相聚 dating, friends gathering
- 铁板类红肉 teppenyaki red meat
- 虽然酒庄很少做宣传，但这是一款性价比甚高的佳酿。Although rare promoted, it's a highly impressed good-valued wine.

迪仙庄园（红）
Ch. d'Issan

￥￥￥￥

深红色，有复杂的红果香，入口单宁柔和，有华美的果香，陈年后饮用更佳。Excellent color. A complex nose with red fruit. On the tongue the tannin is still present, without being at all aggressive. There is really gorgeous fruit behind this stuff.

- 1855年波尔多列级名庄第三级 3eme Cru-1855 Classification
- 18～20℃
- 酒友交流，商务宴请 wine appreciation, business dinner
- 牛扒 beef steak
- 典型的玛歌风格酒，被称为"皇帝的贡品，神的祭品"。Has accolades of tribute for the king and present for god. Classical Margaux style.

康帝庄（红）
Ch. de Candale

￥￥￥

深紫色，带香浓甜蜜的黑加仑子和香料的香味，酒体丰满，口感浓郁，具有雨后森林的气息，令人舒适。Dark purple color. Nose is a spicy with a sweet nose of blackcurrant. Full-bodied, well concentrated without being too muscular. A wine with typical breeze from forest after rain.

- 上美度法定产区酒 Haut-Médoc AOC
- 14～17℃
- 情侣约会，友人相聚 dating, friends gathering
- 东坡肉，羊扒 fat pork meat, lamb
- 与玛歌村三级名庄迪仙属同一庄园，因法定产区的分界而诞生康帝庄。由迪仙酿酒团队倾力酿造，但是价格却不及迪仙的三分之一。Seperated from Château d'Issan by the haut-Médoc appellation. Using the same winemaking team of d'Issan but bearing lower than one third price of Château d'Issan.

肯德布朗庄园（红）
Ch. Cantenac Brown

¥ ¥ ¥

深红色，带有干浆果、樱桃和香草的香味。中度至浑厚的酒体，伴有丝滑的单宁。Very deep ruby color. Dried berry and cherry aromas, with a hint of vanilla. Medium-to full-bodied with silky tannins.

1855年波尔多列级名庄第三级 3eme Cru-1855 Classification

18～20℃

酒友交流，商务宴请 wine appreciation, business dinner

羊肉，炖海参，鱼翅 lamb, braised sea cucumber, shark's fin

1989年后，由AXA保险公司购得，由波尔多酿酒世家Cazes主政，声誉日隆。Has a rising reputation since being acquired by AXA and controlled by the Cazes family in 1989.

露仙歌（红）
Ch. Rauzan-Gassies

¥ ¥ ¥

深红色，酒缘偏蓝。成熟果香开放而柔和。单宁成熟，余味平衡持久。Deep red, with blue at edges. Open and soft nose of ripe fruit. Good ripe tannin, well balanced with good length.

1855年波尔多列级名庄第二级 2eme Cru-1855 Classification

18～20℃

酒友交流，商务宴请 wine appreciation, business dinner

东坡肉，牛肉干 fat pork meat, dry beef

近年来，在《葡萄酒观察家》、《品醇客》等众多权威葡萄酒杂志中获得极高的评价。It has been obtained high rating in authoritative wine magazines such as *Wine Spectator* and *Decanter*.

麒麟庄园（红）
Ch. Kirwan

¥ ¥ ¥

呈亮丽的红色，带有复杂的李子、烟草和咖啡的香气。酒体中度至浑厚，单宁柔滑，口感极佳。Brilliant red color. Complex aromas of plums, tobacco and coffee. Medium to full in body, with soft, excellent tannins.

1855年波尔多列级名庄第三级 3eme Cru-1855 Classification

18～20℃

酒友交流，商务宴请 wine appreciation, business dinner

牛扒，羊扒 beef steak, lamb

传说美国第三任总统托马斯·杰弗逊是喝着此酒起草《美国独立宣言》的。It is said that the Declaration of Independence was written by Tomas Jefferson while he was drinking this wine.

豆莎庄园（红）
Ch. Dauzac

¥¥¥

宝石红色，明显的巧克力香中伴有烤肉和黑醋栗的香气，还有泥土气息。酒体圆润不失强劲，单宁结实而细滑。Ruby-red color. Aromas of chocolate along with roasted meat, black currants, and damp earthy scents. Sleek and powerful. Full-bodied, with compacted fruit and silky tannins.

- 1855年波尔多列级名庄第五级 5eme Cru-1855 Classification
- 18～20℃
- 友人相聚，温馨家宴 friends gathering, family gathering
- 中浓味菜肴，烧肉 medium to heavy dishes, roast pork
- 由波尔多著名的酿酒家族安德烈•吕东主理后，酒庄重新焕发了光彩。The old château with high reputation has engaged the services of Andre Lurton, the famous winemaking family in Bordeaux.

柏菲露丝庄园（红）
Ch. Paveil de Luze

¥¥¥

丰厚的深红色，带有黑色浆果和香料气息，成熟的水果口感中透出愉悦的酸度。单宁顺滑，回味无穷。Beautiful garnet color. Supple nose of black fruit and herbs. Ripe, juicy fruit across the palate with good underlying acidity. Velvety tannins and a long, smooth finish.

- 2003美度区优质明星庄 Cru Bourgeois Superieur
- 18～20℃
- 温馨家宴，浪漫婚宴 family gathering, wedding
- 小牛肉，蘑菇，家禽肉，红肉 veal, mushrooms, fowl, red meat
- 以拥有香水般馥郁的香气著称，是一款外柔内刚的葡萄酒。A fragrant, feminine Bordeaux wine with great power and suppleness from a well-situated and historic château.

美乐诗歌庄园（红）
Ch. Malescot St. Exupery

¥¥¥

酒色深浓，带有茴香豆、月桂树叶和黑加仑子的芳香。单宁诱人，入口有黑橄榄的香味，余味悠长。Dark hue. Good depth to the nose, offering a little aniseed and bay leaf to the spiced, macerated blackcurrant fruit. A good grippe core of tannin, wrapped in black olive fruit. A fine persistence.

- 1855年波尔多列级名庄第三级 3eme Cru-1855 Classification
- 18～20℃
- 酒友交流，商务宴请 wine appreciation, business dinner
- 烧鸭，烟熏肉类 roast duck, bacon dishes
- 曾是法王路易十四幕僚的物业，地窖曾是宝马庄地窖的一部分，近年声誉渐隆。Once owned by King's Counsel to Louis XIV for decades and shared the same cellar with Ch. Palmer until 18th Century, it is the rising fame in recent years.

百康亭庄园（红）
Ch. Brane-Cantenac

¥¥¥

以黑色水果香气为主，口感舒适圆熟，有奶油质感。单宁微辛辣，结构平衡且有少许强劲。Dark and spicy fruit profile. Soft, rounded, creamy quality on the palate. Spicy tannins and a well balanced character, but still with a little masculine structure underneath.

- 1855年波尔多列级名庄第二级 2eme Cru-1855 Classification
- 18～20℃
- 酒友交流，温馨家宴 wine appreciation, family gathering
- 烧牛柳，粤式扣肉 roast tenderloin, cantonese double braised pork meat with fat
- 价格平实的玛歌村列级名庄酒，由波尔多著名酿酒家族Henri Lurton拥有。A notable Margaux Grand Cru Classé at affordable price, owned by Henri Lurton, the famous winemaking family in Bordeaux.

>格拉芙
Graves

格拉芙是位于波尔多市的南部的产酒区。Graves相当于英文单词Gravel，是砂石的意思。格拉芙的酒田主要以砂石为主，所以酒性自成一格。

格拉芙可算是波尔多最早的红葡萄酒产区，早在11世纪已有酒田，并开始了酿酒，当时的美度区还是沼泽地，交通极不便利，但由于格拉芙靠近波尔多市，产品的销售有地理优势。但是，随着波尔多市的不断扩展，近郊的酒田也不断受到侵蚀而转变为民居和商业楼，再加上在其他产区大产红酒之际，格拉芙区却有不少酒田以种植白葡萄为主，至使近代格拉芙在名气上落后于美度、圣达美隆和宝物隆。幸好格拉芙有一位超级巨星红颜容（Château Haut-Brion）。在1855年的评级中几乎是美度酒的天下，唯一一个在美度区以外的酒庄就是红颜容，而且还是第一级，这令格拉芙保持着一定的知名度。

格拉芙区的优秀名庄绝大部分都汇聚于碧沙（Pessa）和里奥南村（Leognan），其所产的红葡萄酒酒身轻盈、洁静典雅，陈年后有明显的烟草气息，同时又洋溢着坚果气息。格拉芙区出产了不少名贵白葡萄酒，它们主要是用白沙威浓和沙美龙两种葡萄勾兑而成。

红颜容
Ch. Haut-Brion

魅力无法挡的美女酒王红颜容位于格拉芙区，是唯一一个位于美度区外的1855年评级列级名庄，与格拉芙十大名庄之一的修道院红颜容同为法国酿酒世家迪龙家族所有，是葡萄酒爱好者不可错过的波尔多名酿。
Château Haut-Brion is located in Graves, the only château beyond Médoc listed in the classification of 1855. It belongs to Domaine Clarence Dillon, which also the owner of Château La Mission Haut-Brion, one of the top ten châteaux in Graves. Both of them are the must-drink wines for the serious wine lovers.

红颜容庄园（红）
Ch. Haut-Brion Rouge

¥¥¥¥¥

亮丽的宝石红色，带有独特的烟熏、烟草、咖啡、雪松木的气息，口感浓郁复杂，单宁结构精致，非常适合陈年。Brilliant ruby color. Elegant, complex and powerful nose, with smoke, tobacco, coffee and cedar. Concentration and complexity, excellent tannins and structure enough for long life.

- 1855年波尔多列级名庄第一级 1er Cru-1855 Classification
- 18～20℃
- 酒友交流，商务宴请 wine appreciation, business dinner
- 扒类，烤红肉 steak, roast red meat
- 波尔多八大名庄之一，是美国总统托马斯·杰弗逊最喜爱的法国酒。红颜容的酒性无比柔美，有“美女酒王”之称。The favourite of former American President Thomas Jefferson. It is a very feminine and delicate wine, with a good name of "the queen wine".

红颜容庄园（白）
Ch. Haut-Brion Blanc

¥¥¥¥¥

金黄色，带有麝香的气息，有烤蜂蜜杏仁和果仁糖的口感，是一款可深度陈年的白葡萄酒，令人难忘。Golden color. You can taste the musk, that unctuous Muscat. You also find the flavour of finely roasted, honey-coated almonds suggesting delicious praline. With age all these impressions combine and relate to those evoked by the aromas of a liquorous wine.

- 碧莎里奥南法定产区酒 Pessac-Leognan AOC
- 12～14℃
- 酒友交流，商务宴请 wine appreciation, business dinner
- 香煎海鲜，烩鲍鱼 pan-fried seafood, braised abalone
- 产量稀少的珍品，公认为波尔多最顶尖的白葡萄酒。With unique style and small production, it is called the best white wine in Bordeaux.

百安红颜容庄园（红）
Ch. Bahans Haut-Brion

¥¥¥¥

明亮的宝石红色，香气优雅而浓郁，有成熟的浆果香。口感充满可人的果香，单宁细腻，结构精致。Brilliant ruby color. Elegant and powerful nose, with lots of berry aroma. With a mass of lovely fruit, good tannins and fine structure.

- 红颜容副牌酒 2nd wine of Ch. Haut-Brion
- 18～20℃
- 酒友交流，商务宴请 wine appreciation, business dinner
- 牛扒，羊扒 beef steak, lamb
- 与红颜容的酿造工艺如出一辙，酒质稳定，物有所值。Although a second wine, it receives the same treatment as Ch. Haut-Brion. A great wine on its own merits.

修道院红颜容（红）
Ch. La Mission Haut-Brion

¥¥¥¥

色泽深浓，初时有甜椒的香气，随后是李子和核类水果的香气。入口丝滑，酒体优雅且复杂，后味舒适。A striking color. The first whiff of sweet pepper disappears when ripe plum takes over, and above all stone fruits abound. In the mouth the wine is silky, delicious and complex. The finale is soft.

- 格拉芙区列级名庄 Graves Cru Classe
- 18～20℃
- 酒友交流，商务宴请 wine appreciation, business dinner
- 牛柳，羊鞍 beef, lamb
- 被认为是最有能力挑战一级名庄的超二级产品。Regarded as the Super Second which can be on a par with the first growth châteaux.

修道院红颜容副牌（红）
La Chapelle de La Mission Haut-Brion

¥¥¥

酒色深浓，带有迷人的成熟水果芬芳，单宁充足且柔和，口感浓郁，酒体圆润，余味悠长。A superb color both dense and deep. The nose encompasses the assortment of all the fruits at the peak of their maturity. Abundant and irrevocably soft tannin. This succession of fullness, of concentration offers a palate with a length and finale that is matchless.

- 碧莎里奥南法定产区酒 Pessac-Leognan AOC
- 18～20℃
- 温馨家宴，友人相聚 family gathering, friends gathering
- 中浓味菜肴 medium to heavy dishes
- 行家们非常欣赏的极品葡萄酒之一。A wonderful wine appreciated by the connoisseurs.

拉图红颜容庄园（红）
Ch. La Tour Haut-Brion

¥¥¥

紫红色，优雅的红莓芳香，有平衡的酒体和结构。Purple red color. Characterized by an elegant bouquet of red berries followed by a harmonious, structured balance of sensation in the mouth.

- 格拉芙区列级名庄 Graves Cru Classe
- 18～20℃
- 酒友交流，友人相聚 wine appreciation, friends gathering
- 浓味红肉 red meat with rich sauce
- 与红颜容庄同一主人，从2006年开始并入酿造修道院红颜容副牌酒。The same property owned by Dillon family, the wine is combined into La Chapelle de La Mission Haut-Brion in 2006.

小常识
Q & A

问：酒签的漂亮程度和酒有关系吗？

答：每一个庄主都有自己的审美观，有的喜欢简约的酒签设计，有的庄主热爱绘画艺术，会请艺术家设计酒签，例如波尔多名庄武当王。酒标只能体现庄主的审美情趣，漂亮的酒签并不代表漂亮的酒。但是，酒签越详细，标示的产地范围越小，葡萄园位置越具体的酒，品质也越优良。

骑士庄园（红）
(又称：舒威利亚)
Domaine de Chevalier

¥¥¥

拥有成熟的浆果、樱桃和烘橡木的香味。酒体丰厚，口感浓郁，适合陈年饮用。Aromas of ripe berry, cherry with roasted oak character on the nose. Full-bodied wine and high concentrated, good for aging.

- 格拉芙区列级名庄 Graves Cru Classe
- 18～20℃
- 酒友交流，商务宴请 wine appreciation, wedding
- 红烧肉 pork cooked in soya sauce
- 被誉为格拉芙地区最有名的三大酒庄之一，是酒评家的至爱，被称为“真正鉴赏家的葡萄酒”。One of the best three châteaux in Graves. A wine with the accolade as "wine for real connoisseur" because of its subtle flavour.

骑士庄园（白）
Domaine de Chevalier Blanc

¥¥¥

香气十分优雅，果香丰富且有层次感。口感舒适，余韵迷人，酸度适中。This has an elegant nose with plenty of fine aromatics and bright fruit, but there is a suggestion of depth also. A good substance and a nice grip on the finish, with rather gentle acidity.

- 格拉芙区列级名庄 Graves Cru Classe
- 12～14℃
- 友人相聚，情侣约会 friends gathering, dating
- 焖鱼类，白肉 braised fish, white meat
- 格拉芙区顶级白葡萄酒之一。One of the top white wines in Graves.

黑教皇城堡庄园（红）
Ch. Pape Clément

¥¥¥¥

有李子、浆果和泥土的气息，还有烤肉与烘烤过的橡木味道，酒体丰满，单宁柔滑。Aromas of plum, berry and earth, with a grilled meat and roasted oak character on the nose and palate. Full-bodied, with a velvety tannin structure.

- 格拉芙区列级名庄 Graves Cru Classe
- 18～20℃
- 酒友交流，商务宴请 wine appreciation, business dinner
- 牛扒，羊扒 beef steak, lamb
- 格拉芙区最有声望的特级名庄之一，历史上曾为罗马教皇所拥有，被众多酒评家评为波尔多最优雅和香味最复杂的酒。Owns its name to the most illustrious owner, Archbishop of Bordeaux. Many famous wine critcs praised it as "the most complicated and most elegant wine".

黑教皇城堡副牌（红）
Les Clés de Pape Clément

¥¥¥

紫红色，带有迷人的花香和果香，还有橡木桶赋予的香草气息，口感圆润，单宁紧密，后味宜人。Purplish red in color. The floral and fruity notes harmonize completely with a vanilla touch coming from the oak. The tasting then develops into a rich but mellow combination, a firm clothed tannin giving a lot of pleasantness to the finish on the palate.

- 碧莎里奥南法定产区酒 Pessac-Leognan AOC
- 18～20℃
- 情侣约会，友人相聚 dating, friends gathering
- 牛扒，烧鸭 beef steak, roast duck
- 一款堪称精品的名庄副牌酒。An excellent second wine.

丽嘉红颜容庄园（红）
Ch. Les Carmes Haut-Brion

¥¥¥

宝石红色，带有烟熏、草药以及黑加仑子的香气，酒体中度，口感微甜，单宁成熟。Ruby red color. Smoky, grilled herb, and black currant-scented fruit. Medium-bodied, with excellent to outstanding concentration as well as purity, a sweet mid-palate, and ripe tannin.

碧莎里奥南法定法区酒 Pessac-Leognan AOC

18~20℃

酒友交流，商务宴请 wine appreciation, business dinner

铁板类红肉，腊肠 teppenyaki red meat, flavoured sausage

与一级名庄红颜容为邻，历史上与红颜容同宗，是非常超值的酒。This little treasure of a vineyard near Haut-Brion consistently produces fine wines. This beauty wine is well-worth searching out.

使密拉菲庄园（红）
Ch. Smith Haut Lafite

¥¥¥¥

明亮的宝石红中带有蓝色，新鲜的柚子、丁香、蜂蜜和成熟橘子的芳香，酒体中度，口感平衡，余味伴有少许烘烤味。Bright ruby with little blue. Lively and fresh, with well-defined grapefruit, lilac, and honey and orange peel flavours. Medium-bodied and wonderfully harmonious, showing depth and length on the lightly toasty finish.

格拉芙区列级名庄 Graves Cru Classe

18 ~ 20℃

酒友交流，商务宴请 wine appreciation, business dinner

牛扒，羊鞍 beef steak, lamb

1990年换主人后大肆改革，酒质有革命性的进步，甚受饮家青睐。Began to shine after the revolution by the new château owner in 90's and become well-known.

>上美度
Haut-Médoc

位于波尔多左岸环绕美度四大名村附近的区域。此地有5家1855年的列级名庄：三级庄乐拉宫（La Lagune），四级庄拉图嘉利（La Tour Carnet）和3个五级庄百家富（Belgrave）、佳德美（Cantemerle）和金美莎（Camensac）。另外还有100多家明星酒庄。

除了上述村庄出产名贵红葡萄酒以外，下列的左岸酒区都是不可忽视的新兴物值型葡萄酒产区：位于美度半岛最北端的美度法定产区（Médoc）、中部的莫丽丝（Moulis）和丽莎（Listrac）等等。

拉图嘉利（红）
Ch. La Tour Carnet

¥¥¥

酒性浓郁，新鲜，多果香，可早饮用。This is a big wine, with masses of ripe fruit, fine soft tannins, and enough structure to make it a real vin de garde.

1855年波尔多列级名庄第四级 4eme Cru-1855 Classification

18～20℃

商务宴请，友人相聚 business dinner, friends gathering

红肉，中浓味菜肴 red meat, strongly flavoured dishes

物超所值的四级名庄。Acclaimed to be a good-for-value 4eme Cru in Haut-Médoc.

拉图嘉利副牌（红）
Cuvée Légende de Ch. La Tour Carnet

¥¥¥

新鲜，多果香，可早饮用。Enjoy its aromatic flavours and fine tannins even in an early vintage.

拉图嘉利之副牌酒 2nd wine of Ch. La Tour Carnet

18～20℃

友人相聚，情侣约会 friends gathering, dating

椒盐虾，中浓味菜肴 pepper-salt shrimp, medium to heavy dishes

虽为副牌酒但所获奖项，从波尔多大赛金奖到葡萄酒国际挑战赛银奖，数不胜数。Though just being a second wine, it is entitled enormously from Bordeaux Wine Competition's Gold medal to International Wine Challenge's Silver medal.

佳得美庄园（红）
Ch. Cantemerle

¥¥¥

入口柔顺圆滑，单宁良好，回味有水果、香料、木材的清香。Rich and round middle of mouth, fine tannic, with aromatic finish of wood and of mature fruits.

- 1855年波尔多列级名庄第五级 5eme Cru-1855 Classification
- 18～20℃
- 商务宴请，友人相聚 business dinner, friends gathering
- 牛扒，烧鸭 beef steak, roast duck
- 是一款既可年轻饮用又具陈年潜质的名庄酒。A combination of good quality, in keeping with a fifth growth château, and a good price.

佳得美庄园副牌（红）
Les Allées de Cantemerle

¥¥¥

果香浓郁、覆盆子的味道扑鼻而来，花香满溢。Its expressive aromas open up to show very fruity, raspberry notes.

- 佳得美庄园之副牌酒 2nd wine of Ch. Cantemerle
- 18～20℃
- 温馨家宴，情侣约会 family gathering, dating
- 椒盐虾 pepper-salt shrimp
- 充分承载着美度区特色的美酒；口感宜人、柔顺精致。It is a wine made for pleasure, both supple and refined; an ideal lunchtime Médoc that wine lovers can begin enjoying now.

百家富（红）
Ch. Belgrave

¥¥¥

果香浓郁，有层次丰富的单宁与结构；在瓶中陈酿一定时间后将会有更好表现。Fruit, tannins and structure all there in abundance; will be a very fine bottle in time.

- 1855年波尔多列级名庄第五级 5eme Cru-1855 Classification
- 18～20℃
- 商务宴请，酒友交流 business dinner, wine appreciation
- 牛扒，烤羊 beef steak, roast lamb
- 世界酿酒大师米切尔罗兰也是其顾问，物美价廉。With consultation from Michel Rolland, the world's top winemaker. A good wine bears reasonable price.

德拉曼庄园（红）
Ch. de Lamarque

¥¥¥

入口有肉汁的味道，结构良好，酒香浓郁，单宁的精致更增添了口感的风味。Fleshy, well structured, and with rich, flavoursome tannins.

- 2003年波尔多明星庄 Cru Bourgeois
- 18～20℃
- 浪漫婚宴，情侣约会 wedding, dating
- 牛扒，羊扒 beef steak, lamb
- 该庄园位于旧时法国行军地，是将士们行军打仗时饮用的葡萄酒，在法国历史上有着极高的地位。The château is unquestionably, not only one of the foremost in Guyenne, but also one of the most illustrious in France.

宝爵龙庄园（红）
Ch. Lamothe Bergeron

¥¥¥

入口有绝佳的平衡感，酒质醇厚，又有淡淡的樱桃和香草味道。A great Cru Bourgeois with pure cassis and blackcurrant on the nose, backed by a hint of a cedar on the palate.

2003美度区优质明星庄
Cru Bourgeois Supérieur

18～20℃

酒友交流，商务宴请 wine appreciation, business dinner

烧鸡，烤三文鱼片 griddled chicken, roasted salmon fillets

庄主暨著名农学家宝爵龙先生发明了"应用于波尔多地区的葡萄接枝法"，影响了法国葡萄种植几个世纪。酒质有保证。Named after its historical owners Bergeron, the famous theorist and of whom first to use acacia wood to make stakes and achieved deep influence around Bordeaux.

宝梦庄园（红）
Ch. Beaumont

¥¥

单宁细滑，如丝般轻抚过味蕾。余味更有水果的芳香。Its first impression in the mouth caresses your taste bud very pleasantly, gently, growing on tannins and some very fruity notes in the finish.

2003年美度区优质明星庄
Cru Bourgeois Supérieur

18～20℃

情侣约会，酒友交流 dating, wine appreciation

浓味红肉 red meat with rich sauce

由掌控圣祖利安名庄龙船庄的法国GMF集团和日本三得利集团合资拥有。同样优越的管理哲学，赋予该酒系出名门的优异品质。Château Beaumont started its new life with the arrival of the Group GMF, which joined together with the Japanese group Suntory created a wine company, also the owner of Château Beychevelle.

嘉士顿庄（红）
Ch. Gaston-Réna

¥¥¥

该酒是优质的村庄级葡萄酒。酒体结构良好，酒香醇美，散发着红色水果的味道。On the palate, a lively, spirited attack is followed by an attractive, supple structure and red fruit aromas.

上美度法定产区酒 Haut-Médoc AOC

18～20℃

情侣约会，温馨家宴 dating, family gathering

烧牛仔腿 roast beef lack

创始人是波尔多葡萄酒大学的酒类专家，酒标设计灵感来源于沙滩上一对抢着葡萄嬉戏的情侣。Created in 1991 by Daniel Gaston, oenologist at the University of Oenology of Bordeaux. A couple playing a game of snatching the grapes give the inspiration to the wine label.

红磨坊庄园（红）
Ch. du Moulin Rouge

¥¥¥

带有红樱桃，香草和橡木的香味。单宁柔和，果味与酸度平衡佳，余韵果味持久。With fruity flavours of red berries, vanilla and oak. Medium-bodied with soft tannins. Long fruity finish.

2003年美度区明星庄 Cru Bourgeois

18～20℃

友人相聚，酒友交流 friends gathering, wine appreciation

烤羊鞍，牛柳，牛仔骨 grilled lamb rack, steak, beef rib

《葡萄酒观察家》杂志将之评为"2005年度最物有所值的明星酒庄"，酒评家也频频对它打出高分。*Wine Spectator* rank it among the most appreciated of the Haut-Médoc Crus Bourgeois. Most of the critics mark it nearly 90/100.

Haut-Médoc

>>右岸

右岸的著名产区主要有圣达美隆、宝物隆及弗朗沙。与左岸的城堡庄园相比，右岸的酒庄名气多是在第二次世界大战之后才发展起来。大部分是一些乡间别墅型的小酒庄，规模远不及左岸，但充满了个性和人情。右岸所产的葡萄酒比较温柔优雅，葡萄品种以梅乐为主，因为优秀的品质和稀少的产量，右岸冒升出很多超级贵价的酒庄。

>宝物隆 Pomerol

宝物隆位于波尔多的右岸，只有约800公顷的酒田（相当于一个中大型澳洲酒园的面积）。小区内有100多个酒庄，每个酒庄都不是很大，最小的只有2公顷。独特的黏土土质和梅乐葡萄酒，是成就宝物隆的两大重要原因。

宝物隆没有列级名庄分级制度，但却是波尔多乃至当今世界上出产名贵珍酿最多的小区。只要是打着宝物隆产区的酒，基本都不会便宜。

宝物隆的酒王柏图斯（Petrus）也是波尔多的酒王。酒王柏图斯的对手是1979年才崛起的里鹏（Le Pin）。另外有一批质量和价格都可与传统五大名庄媲美的家族精品酒庄，如：花庄（Lafleur）、卓龙（Trotanoy）、柏图斯小酒王（Lafleur Petrus）、拉图宝物隆（Latour A Pomerol）、迪美庄（Certan de May）、威登庄（Vieux Château Certan）、伊云卓（L'Evangile）、嘉纳庄（Clinet）等。

宝物隆的红葡萄酒通常带有松露的气息，酒体圆润，入口柔顺，陈年后更加优雅平衡，相对美度区酒，宝物隆酒更加细致，需早些饮用。

JPM家族
JPM Family

JPM酒商集团由波尔多葡萄酒教父Jean-Pierre Moueix先生于1913年创立，当右岸葡萄酒还籍籍无名时，是他先知了梅乐葡萄的潜在魅力并将其发扬光大。其集团产业包括了出产世界上最昂贵的葡萄酒之一的柏图斯，还独家代理了右岸十几个杰出庄园的葡萄酒，其影响力非常大。JPM集团和左岸的两个罗富齐家族一起，被合称为“波尔多三霸”。

Mr. Jean-Pierre Moueix founded JPM wine merchant bussiness in 1931. At that time the wines of Libourne were little known, Moueix was astute to foresee the Merlot grape's ability to seduce. JPM's estate include Petrus, who produces one of the world's most expensive wines. JPM also distributes the famous right bank château wine exclusively, with a status similar to mouton family in the left bank.

柏图斯庄园（红）
Petrus

¥¥¥¥¥

令人惊叹的饱满浓稠度，优越地展现出水果、黑莓和巧克力的特质。单宁坚实，后味格外持久。Astounding. This is wonderfully concentrated with fabulous fruit, chocolate and berry character. Full-bodied, with chewy tannins and a long, long finish.

- 宝物隆法定产区酒 Pomerol AOC
- 14～17℃
- 商务宴请，酒友交流 business dinner, wine appreciation
- 熊掌，海参 bear's paw, sea cucumber
- 位列波尔产区八大名庄之首，是目前波尔多质量最好、价格最贵的酒王之王。是英女皇伊丽莎白的婚宴用酒，曾是白宫主人肯尼迪总统的最爱。It's the best of best. A king wine shining at the wedding of the queen of Britain. A wine beloved by owners of American White House.

柏图斯小酒王（红）
Ch. La Fleur-Pétrus

¥¥¥¥¥

有甜果子和橡木赋予的野肉气息。口味微妙，是甜西梅和密实的单宁。余韵中感觉平和。Sweet nose on the nose, touched with gamey richness and oak. Sweet plummy fruit with a firm and attactive character. Towards the finish it shows an attactive, flattering body.

- 宝物隆法定产区酒 Pomerol AOC
- 14～17℃
- 友人相聚，友人相聚 wine appreciation, friends gathering
- 牛扒，鹿肉 beef steak, venison
- 由JPM家族拥有的宝物隆名庄，某些年份的分数可与柏图斯媲美。Belong to the JPM family. In some exceptional vintages its marks peers Petrus.

凯歌庄园（红）
Ch. Hosanna

¥¥¥¥

酒体圆熟，有肉汁、香油的味道，单宁紧密，酸度活跃，结构良好。The wine has a dense and meaty character on the nose, with a little trace of high-toned balsamic. Very ripe in style, dense tannins, but there is good acidity too.

- 宝物隆法定产区酒 Pomerol AOC
- 14～17℃
- 温馨家宴，友人相聚 family gathering, friends gathering
- 酱牛肉，煎羊扒 sauced beef, frying lamb chops
- 曾经和老牌顶级名庄威登庄园同宗，于1999年归JPM家族拥有，100%梅乐风情，年产稀少。The estate was once part of the original Certan property. Belong to JPM since 1999. The annual production is typically limited bottles with 100% Merlot.

卓龙（红）
Ch. Trotanoy

¥¥¥¥

色浓，闻香有萃取的果味，比很多酒显得洁净，单宁细密，酒体紧致。Dark, pure and defined fruit on the nose, cleaner than some other wines. On the nose a very structred and upright of Pomerol, with tightly packed and polished fruit, and a mildly stony, reserved texture.

- 宝物隆法定产区酒 Pomerol AOC
- 14～17℃
- 商务宴请，友人相聚 business dinner, friends gathering
- 烤乳猪，叉烧 roast suckling pig, barbeque pork
- 曾是宝物隆村最顶尖名庄，声誉超过柏图斯。后由柏图斯老板JPM收购成旗下名庄之一，此酒是饮家级的佳酿。It was once the top in The wines are vinified and handled in exactly the same way as Petrus.

花庄宝物隆（红）
Ch. Lafleur Pomerol

¥¥¥¥¥

酒体浓郁，有奶油质感，富有层次，甜香水果包裹着坚实又细滑的单宁，陈年天赋极好。Dense, creamy, textured, sweet fruit coating the tannins which are firm. Full of potential.

- 宝物隆法定产区酒 Pomerol AOC
- 14～17℃
- 酒友交流，友人相聚 wine appreciation, friends gathering
- 煎牛扒，海参 frying steak, sea cucumber
- 被酒评家称为“宝物隆的珠宝”，“贵得有道理”的葡萄酒，年产仅1 000箱。Wine critics called it "the jewel of Pomerol" and "the wine amply deserves its high prices." Only 1 000 cases are made every year.

花庄副牌（红）
Pensees de Lafleur

¥¥¥¥

带有新鲜肉汁味，酒体强健有力，是优秀的副牌酒。It was fresh, meaty with strong backbone, powerful and firm finish. Well-knitted. Terrific second wine.

- 宝物隆法定产区酒 Pomerol AOC
- 14～17℃
- 商务宴请，情侣约会 business dinner, dating
- 酱牛肉，酱猪脚 sauced beef, pig's knuckle
- 是花庄宝物隆的副牌酒，年产仅400箱。It is a second wine of Ch. Lafleur Pomerol.Only 400 cases are made.

拉图宝物隆庄园（红）
Ch. Latour A Pomerol

¥¥¥¥

美妙的李子、莓果香味在中度酒体中慢慢伸展开来，单宁强劲。Beautiful aromas of plums, berries and raspberries follow through to a medium-bodied palate, with fine tannins and a medium finish. Slightly austere finish.

- 宝物隆法定产区酒 Pomerol AOC
- 12～14℃
- 温馨家宴，友人相聚 family gathering, friends gathering
- 烤乳猪，炖牛肉 roast suckling pig, braised beef
- JPM出品的备受酒评家关注的宝物隆佳酿。A famed wine from JPM, recommended by wine critics.

力关（红）
Ch. Lagrange

¥ ¥ ¥

深紫色，有香草、薄荷和黑果的香气。酒体饱满，结构平衡，余味悠长且柔和。Deep purple colour. Complex nose with lots of vanilla, blackcurrant and mint. A full structured body, well balanced, long and smooth.

- 宝物隆法定产区酒 Pomerol AOC
- 12～14℃
- 温馨家宴，商务宴请 family gathering, business dinner
- 腊肉，香肠 preserved meat, sausage
- 是JPM最早购入的4个酒庄之一，近年来在罗拔·派克评分都在89～91，质量稳定。It was one of the first four wineries JPM purchased. In recent years Rober Parker's mark for this wine is no less than 81. Very stable quality.

力富歌仙（红）
Ch. Lafleur-Gazin

¥ ¥ ¥

中度酒体，有成熟洋李、剪草和浆果的香味，中度酒体，单宁强实，结构丰富，余味中有新橡木气息。La Fleur-Gazin reveals chalky tannin in the finish. It is accompanied by ripe plum, prune, and berry fruit, medium body, and plenty of structure as well as tough tannin.

- 宝物隆法定产区酒 Pomerol AOC
- 14～17℃
- 浪漫婚宴，商务宴请 wedding,business dinner
- 野味，荤菜 game, meat diet
- 近年来在JPM的监护下，声誉日隆。It gets a rising fame under JPM's monitor.

威登玛莎庄园（红）
Ch. Certan Marzelle

¥¥¥¥

灵动的花香和水果气息。入口便能感受到和谐、平衡、新鲜的单宁，余味中有怡人的花香。On the nose, one finds a vivid bouquet with floral and fruits scents. On the palate, a good harmony and balance with fresh tannins ending on an aromatic and very pleasant finale.

宝物隆法定产区酒 Pomerol AOC

14～17℃

温馨家宴，酒友交流 family gathering, wine appreciation

牛扒，羊肉 beef steak, lamb

由酒王之王柏图斯老板Moueix拥有。庄园占地仅5公顷，只种植梅乐，目前平均树龄为25岁，酿出的酒口感柔顺雅致，清新诱人。Property of Jean-Pierre Moueix. The vineyard is just 5 acres and 100% Merlot planted with vines of average 25 year-old. The wine is supple and generous and from its youngest age, very seductive.

泰勒庄园
Ch.du Tailhas

¥¥¥

香气复杂，有新鲜的薄荷、巧克力和雪松的香味。中度口感，酸度适中，单宁精致且伴有烤杏仁的香。Complex nose which reveals fresh notes of mint as well as warm aromas of chocolate and cedar. Tender, followed by a well-melted acidity balancing the mid-palate. Fine Tannins with notes of roasted almond.

宝物隆法定产区酒 Pomerol AOC

14～17℃

商务宴请，情侣约会 business, dinner dating

煎牛扒，羊腿 frying steak, lamb leg

是13世纪由英格兰国王爱德华一世创立的贵族酒庄，工艺传统，以老树葡萄而闻名。Created in 1289 by the sovran in English. Old vines. Featured Pomerol.

佳露庄园（红）
Ch. Guillot

¥¥¥

散发出迷人的黑莓和草莓香气，还略带一丝巧克力香。酒体中度，单宁柔滑，后味持久。Enticing aromas of blackberries and cherries, with a hint of chocolate. Medium-bodied, with fine tannins and a long finish.

宝物隆法定产区酒 Pomerol AOC

14～17℃

温馨家宴，商务宴请 family gathering,wine appreciation

牛扒，羊扒 beef steak, lamb

以合适的价格就能品尝到右岸的风情，物有所值。Fine wine from Pomerol with good value.

迪美庄园（红）
Ch. Certan De May de Certan

¥ ¥ ¥ ¥

深红色，浓郁的黑树莓和泥土芳香，单宁丰富，酒体丰腴。This rustic, opaque garnet-colored wine offers plenty of sweet, black raspberry, earthy fruit, full body, and plenty of tannin.

- 宝物隆法定产区酒 Pomerol AOC
- 14～17℃
- 酒友交流，友人相聚 wine appreciation, friends gathering
- 肘子，腱子肉 pork joint, tendon
- 和老牌威登庄园同宗，被称之为“右岸酒后”，历史悠久且产量稀少。An outstanding wine named Queen of Wine on The Right Bank, was sibling of Vieux Ch. Certan.

美特朗庄园（红）
Ch. Magdelaine

¥ ¥ ¥ ¥

有黑色浆果的香甜丰满气息和少许橡木味。单宁强壮，酒体复杂，入口后有紫罗兰和甘草的香气。Sweet, plump, black fruits and some oak. Sweet, plump, black fruits and some oak.Fresh acidity. Concentrated, with violet and liquorice flavour.

- 圣达美隆名庄 St. Emilion Grand Crand Cru.
- 12～14℃
- 酒友交流，温馨家宴 wine appreciation, family gathering
- 牛扒，野肉 beef steak, game
- 曾经被誉为“圣达美隆区的柏图斯”。1952年由酒王之王柏图斯老板木艾家族购得。It once was called "Petrus in St. Emilion" in history. Acquired by Ets. Jean-Pierre Moueix in 1952.

JPM柏图斯家族波尔多（红）
Jean Pierre Moueix Bordeaux

¥ ¥ ¥

有诱人的橡木桶气息和优雅的口感，是微妙的葡萄酒。With seductive bouquet and elegant palate, it is a superb wine.

- 波尔多法定产区酒 Bordeaux AOC
- 12～14℃
- 温馨家宴，情侣约会 family gathering, dating
- 牛扒，荤菜 beef steak, meat diet
- 专为中国顾客打造的佳酿，采用波尔多上好葡萄酿造而成，是波尔多风味的集中体现。Exclusively made for Chinese wine lover. A typical Bordeaux style, made with the best grapes in Bordeaux.

JPM柏图斯家族圣达美隆（红）
Jean Pierre Moueix St. Emilion

¥ ¥ ¥

传统的圣达美隆风味，柔顺易饮。A typical St. Emilion wine, with smooth palate and easy to drink.

- 圣达美隆法定产区酒 St. Emilion AOC
- 12～14℃
- 温馨家宴，情侣约会 family gathering, dating
- 家禽，猪手 poultry, pork joint
- 专为中国顾客打造的佳酿，是性价比甚高的信心之选。Exclusively made for Chinese wine lover. A choice based on confidence for its reputable owner.

JPM柏图斯家族宝物隆（红）
Jean Pierre Moueix Pomerol

¥ ¥ ¥

一款鲜香宜人，口感轻柔的葡萄酒。A wine with fresh fragrance and soft and comfortable palate.

- 宝物隆法定产区酒 Pomerol AOC
- 12～14℃
- 温馨家宴，情侣约会 family gathering, dating
- 家禽，牛肉 poultry, beef
- 专为中国顾客打造的佳酿，是精工细作的家族经典之作。Exclusively made for Chinese wine lover. A classic work of Pomerol and A well-crafted family wine.

天鹏家族
Thienpont Family

比利时的天鹏家族是波尔多最具传奇色彩的酿酒家族。旗下有世界上最贵的葡萄酒“里鹏”，老牌名庄威登庄园，近年来声名鹊起的碧嘉露庄园，适合年轻时尚群体的天鹏系列等，人称“魔法酿酒师”。旗下以“翅膀”为名的酒商公司，行销世界，为消费者提供系列雅俗共赏的葡萄酒。

Belgian Thienpont family is the legend in Bordeaux. Vieux Château Certan, Château Puygueraud or Le Pin are some of the famous properties belonging to the Thienpont family. François Thiepont created his own company called WINGS in 1995. This well-known and innovative wine merchant has been trading throughout the world, offering the most prestigious châteaux as well as less renowned estates, to buyers who are often wine experts.

里鹏庄园（红）
Le Pin

¥ ¥ ¥ ¥ ¥

迷人的香水气息，有西洋李子、香草、胡椒和香料的味道，酒体极端复杂。The nose offers a beautiful perfume, with fine damson and plum fruit purity with notes of vanilla, pepper and spice. Complexity.

- 宝物隆法定产区酒 Pomerol AOC
- 14～17℃
- 酒友交流，商务宴请 wine appreciation, business dinner
- 熊掌，鲍鱼 bear's paws, abalone
- 由人称“魔法酿酒师”的天鹏家族拥有，2公顷的土地，年产仅500箱，是世界上公认的天价葡萄酒。A mythical wine produced by the Thienpont family. Only 500 cases are made from the two hektares annually. The most expensive wine in the world.

威登庄园（红）
Vieux Ch. Certan

¥¥¥¥

有黑莓、樱桃、巧克力、薄荷和香草的味道。酒体厚身，天鹅绒的单宁，余味可口而悠长。Sweet, plump, black fruits and some oak. Full-bodied, with very velvety tannins and a long, flavourful finish.

- 宝物隆法定产区酒 Pomerol AOC
- 12～14℃
- 酒友交流，情侣约会 wine appreciation, dating
- 小牛肉，羔羊肉 veal, lamb
- 是宝物隆历史最悠久的名庄，现为天鹏家族拥有，由天价葡萄酒里鹏的酿酒团队酿制。A famous château with long history in Pomerol and owned by Thienpont family currently. It is managed by the same winemaking group of Le Pin.

小威登（红）
La Gravette de Certan

¥¥¥

气味开放、有力，入口果香集中，酒体结构硬朗，单宁柔滑，渗透着薄荷香。Enormous, powerful nose of ripe black fruits. Medium-bodied, with good fruit and a silky tannin structure with hints of mint.

- 宝物隆法定产区酒 Pomerol AOC
- 14～17℃
- 温馨家宴，情侣约会 family gathering, dating
- 烧鹅，烤鸭 grilled goose, roast duck
- 采用威登传统的酿酒方法酿造的副牌酒，酒体浑厚，单宁精致，有正牌酒的风范。Vinified according to the traditional methods from which the old Certan castle, remaining the style of Certan with rich and delicate body.

碧嘉露庄园（红）
Ch. Puygueraud

¥¥¥

以优雅的单宁著称，结构良好，个性突出。黏土香气赋予此酒有力的酒体。Château Puygueraud produces wines which are elegantly tannic, structured and have great personality. The clay soils give them power and body.

- 弗朗谷法定产区酒 Cotes de Francs AOC
- 14～17℃
- 温馨家宴，友人相聚 family gathering, friends gathering
- 咸猪肉，腌肉 bacon, brawn
- 由拥有天价里鹏的天鹏家族主理。是该区唯一入选法国“葡萄酒米其林指南”、日本葡萄酒漫画《神之水滴》和《品醇客》杂志2005年波尔多新酒推荐名单的葡萄酒。Owned by the legendary wine family Thienpont. Featured in Wine Michelin Guide of France and Japanese comics *God's Drops*. Recommended in *Decanter*'s 2005 Best Wine List.

天鹏家族（圣达美隆）（红）
Terra Burdigala St. Emilion Grand Cru

入口能感受到其无尽优雅又浓郁的酒体，酒香平衡，单宁丝滑柔顺。It is a powerful wine with individuality and typicality. Enormously concentrated much elegance, compact and balanced. Strong reverberation with mild, silky tannins.

圣达美隆特等园法定产区 St. Emilion Grand Cru AOC

14～17℃

温馨家宴，友人相聚 family gathering, friends gathering

小牛肉，火鸡 veal, turkey

由酿造天价葡萄酒里鹏的天鹏家族精心主理，酒质优秀，富陈年潜力。It is a high quality wine made by the well-known Thienpont family who is the owner of Le Pin. Good potential.

天鹏家族（波尔多）（红）
Terra Burdigala Bordeaux Rouge

散发出浓郁的森林水果，洋李子和黑加仑子的香味。结构圆润，单宁细致紧密。A rich aromas such as forest fruits, plum and black currant.It is with a velvety red wine structure and fine, fine tannis.

波尔多法定产区酒 Bordeaux AOC

14～17℃

温馨家宴，活力派对 family gathering, party

火腿，里脊肉 ham, fillet

由酿造天价葡萄酒里鹏的天鹏家族精心主理，性价比超高的波尔多酒。It is a high quality wine made by the well-known Thienpont family who is the owner of Le Pin.Good value Bordeaux wine.

天鹏家族（波尔多）（白）
Terra Burdigala Bordeaux Blanc

水果的鲜香怡人，有醋栗、柚子的味道。此酒轻身，但香气紧密，是款口感非常优雅的波尔多白酒。Characterized by a fruity nose, freshness, gooseberry and grapefruit flavours.It is a light, dense and very elegant white wine.

波尔多法定产区酒 Bordeaux AOC

7～12℃

温馨家宴，活力派对 family gathering, party

清蒸鱼，水饺 steamed fish, boiled dumpling

由酿造天价葡萄酒里鹏的天鹏家族精心主理，性价比超高的波尔多白葡萄酒。It is a high quality wine made by the well-known Thienpont family who is the owner of Le Pin.

Pomerol

依云卓庄园（红）
Ch. L'Evangile

¥ ¥ ¥ ¥

有紫罗兰、黑醋栗和树莓的香气。入口则散发出浓郁的莓子、黑莓和矿物的味道。It has a bouquet of violets, rasberries and cassis.The flavours are lush and rich with a mixture of rasberry, blackberry and mineral notes.

宝物隆法定产区酒 Pomerol AOC

14～17℃

酒友交流，商务宴请 wine appreciation, business dinner

鲍鱼，烧鹅 abalone, grilled goose

位于柏图斯和白马庄之间，有两大名庄之风。庄园名为“福音”之意。1990年后武当王酒庄的罗富齐男爵入股。Château L'Evangile is located between Ch. Petrus and Ch. Cheval Blanc. Its name means evangel.The Rothschild group purchased a controlling interest in the property in 1990.

嘉仙庄园（红）
Ch. Gazin

¥ ¥ ¥ ¥

含有优美而浓郁的烤橡木香味，并散发着洋李子、黑莓和葡萄干的幽香，入口柔滑、美味。An excellent sweet nose of lavish toasty oak intertwined with plums, black cherries, and currants dominates the olfactory senses. In the mouth, this wine is elegant and lush.

宝物隆法定产区酒 Pomerol AOC

14～17℃

酒友交流，商务宴请 wine appreciation, business dinner

菌类菜肴，猪脚 dish with mushroom, pig's knuckle

由法国历史最悠久的贵族世家拥有，迄今已到了第26代传人。It is owned by the oldest nobel family, with 26 generations.

嘉仙庄园副牌（红）
L'Hospitalet de Gazin

¥ ¥ ¥

果香比其他宝物隆酒更加微妙，并带有橡木和坚果味道。It has more subtle fruit on the nose than some of the other Pomerols, with more nutty oak evident.

嘉仙庄园副牌酒 2nd wine of Ch. Gazin

14～17℃

情侣约会，温馨家宴 dating, family gathering

炖牛肉，烤肉 braised beef, roast meat

是酒王之王柏图斯的邻居嘉仙庄的副牌酒。于1986年推出，年产量仅2 000箱，典型的宝物隆风格。Second wine of Château Gazin neighboring Petrus. The first wine produced in 1986 and the total output is 2000 cases. A typical Pomerol style.

嘉纳庄园（红）
Ch. Clinet

¥ ¥ ¥ ¥

有湿润泥土的气息和辛香料的味道，隐隐透出奶糖、黑莓、洋李子的香气。酒体醇厚，单宁柔滑而不失强劲。With coaxing, notes of damp earth, spicy new oak, truffles, blackberry and plum fruit emerge. Dense, Full-bodied, with velvety tannins, considerable power.

- 宝物隆法定产区酒 Pomerol AOC
- 14～17℃
- 酒友交流，温馨家宴 wine appreciation, family gathering
- 菌类菜肴，小牛肉 dish with mushroom, veal
- 以世界级的酿酒大师米切尔罗兰为智囊酿得的嘉纳庄园，深得酒评家的赞赏。With the consultation from world's top wine maker Michel Rolland. Received full adimitration in the world.

格兰治庄园
Ch.Grange-Neuve

¥ ¥ ¥

如奶油般的质感，丝丝入口的巧克力香，让人忘情于典型的梅乐风格中，是别具特色的宝物隆佳酿。A typical good wine of Pomerol with silky and intense body which is made by the high quaity of merlot.

- 宝物隆法定产区酒 Pomerol AOC
- 14～17℃
- 活力派对，情侣约会 party, dating
- 火鸡，烤鸭 turkey, roast duck
- 性价比超高，受众多年轻人热捧的波尔多佳酿。A wine popular with the young thanks to good value.

康赛隆庄园（红）
Ch. La Conseillante

¥ ¥ ¥ ¥

从香气、入口到余味，都能持续感受到淡淡的红桑果芬芳，同时还混合着一丝甜甜的木质香。Clean sheets of red silk of raspberry, touches of red cherry and the slightest hint of sweet woodiness.

- 宝物隆法定产区酒 Pomerol AOC
- 12～14℃
- 酒友交流，商务宴请 wine appreciation, business dinner
- 野味，鹿肉 game, venison
- 拥有300年历史的康赛隆酒庄是"列级名庄联合会"以及"波尔多葡萄酒学会"的成员。300-year-old Ch. La Conseillante is member of the Union des Grands Crus and of the Bordeaux Wine Academy.

大炮庄园（红）
Ch. Canon

¥¥¥¥

浓郁有力，中度单宁，鲜甜的果味足，陈年饮用更佳。The wines from Canon exhibits expansive, sweet fruit that more than compensates for the moderate tannin level.

圣达美隆列级名庄第一级 1er Grand Cru Classe

14～17℃

商务宴请，酒友交流 business dinner, wine appreciation

羊扒，牛扒 lamb, beef steak

现为香奈尔集团拥有，由原拉图庄大总管主理，是讲究经典和时尚的艺术酒庄。It belongs to Chanel Group，fashionable while classical, and it is managed by the former director of Ch.Latour.

卓龙梦特庄园（红）
Ch. Troplong Mondot

¥¥¥¥

充满高雅的黑浆果香气，酒体相当浑厚有力，单宁非常结实密集。The wine exhibits a powerful nose of licorice, black currants, and spicy new oak. There is sweet fruit on the attack and medium body, but the firm tannin gives the wine grip and delineation, as well as a certain austerity.

圣达美隆列级名庄第一级 1er Grand Cru Classe

14～17℃

商务宴请，酒友交流 business dinner, wine appreciation

羊扒，牛扒 lamb, beef steak

品质在近年不断提升的圣达美隆列级名庄，在2006年的评级中被提升为一级酒庄。This grand cru class wine has been improved in recent years after Alexandre Valette family took over. It was awarded 1er Grand Cru Classe status in 2006.

雷曼庄园（红）
Ch. Larmande

¥¥¥

有黑果和莓子的香味。入口后酒液留给你味蕾无限的温软和清新口感，余味精致诱人。The nose displays hints of raspberries and blackcurrants. On the palate there is an impression of softness and freshness. The palate is also long with great finesse.

圣达美隆列级名庄 Grand Cru Classe

14～17℃

浪漫婚宴，情侣约会 wedding, dating

烧鹅，烤鸭 grilled goose, roast duck

圣达美隆历史最悠久和葡萄园面积最大的酒庄之一，同时是女性酿酒师主理的庄园，源自老藤的葡萄酒，格外温柔优雅。One of the oldest and largest estates in Saint Emilion. The wine are from old vines. The Château is managed by a woman winemaker.

拉图飞卓（红）
Ch. La Tour Figeac

¥¥¥

富含成熟的水果香味和丰富的浆果芳香。中度酒体，有结实的单宁及中度的余味。With plenty of ripe fruit. Good intensity of berry, aromas.

圣达美隆列级名庄 Grand Cru Classe

14～17℃

友人相聚，温馨家宴 friends gathering, family gathering

火腿，里脊肉 ham, fillet

是生物动力学酒庄。庄园原为飞卓庄的一部分，现位于白马庄和飞卓庄中间，是典型的圣达美隆葡萄酒。A biodynamically operated winery.In 1879 Château La Tour Figeac was devided from Château Figeac. A typical St. Emilion wine.

德事雅（红）
Ch. Teyssier

¥¥¥

酒体中度，柔滑。在中段呈现出紧密肉汁味道。有圆熟单宁和酸度搭建起的骨架，后味良好。Nice weight on the palate, creamy. It shows a denser, more meaty side through the midpalate. This has a fine, firm style with a good backbone of acidity and ripe tannins at the finish.

圣达美隆名庄 St. Emilion Grand Cru

14～17℃

温馨家宴，友人相聚 family gathering, friends gathering

酱牛肉，叉烧 sauced beef, barbeque pork

酒庄坐落在圣达美隆的核心地带，建立于18世纪初期，是物超所值的右岸酒。This Grand Cru estate, dated back to 1714, situates in the heart of St. Emilion. Good value right bank wine.

乐士高庄园（红）
Ch. de Lescours

¥¥¥

酒体非常柔和，有浆果和香草的芳香，单宁很细，典型的右岸风格。Excellent concentration. Berry nose with vanilla flavours and complex oakiness.

圣达美隆特名庄 St. Emilion Grand Cru

14～17℃

温馨家宴，友人相聚 family gathering, friends gathering

烧鹅，火鸡 grilled goose, turkey

是圣达美隆区历史最悠久的酒庄之一，于14世纪为国王骑士所建造，具有典雅的贵族气质。As one of the oldest and most renowned properities in the Saint-Emilion district, the classical Ch. De Lescours was built in 1341 by a knight of King Edward I.

巨石庄园（红）
Ch. Gros Caillou

¥¥¥

香味浓郁，红浆果和樱桃的味道柔顺平和，入口有胡椒，烟熏气息。单宁圆熟，余味微木香。A large and generous nose, with aromatic notes of mature Merlot and aromatic attack.Peppery and smoky. Mellow tannins without excess. A slightly woody finish.

圣达美隆名庄 St. Emilion Grand Cru

14～17℃

温馨家宴，友人相聚 family gathering, friends gathering

火腿，腊肉 ham, preserved meat

该酒庄是迪皮耶家族五代人精心管理的精品酒庄，葡萄园面积仅为6公顷，走质高量少的路线。A 5-generation wine-making family, Dupuy family's Ch. Gros Caillou (6 hectares) produces excellent wines with a low production and high quality.

>苏玳
Sauternes

位于波尔多市区南部40千米处，该产区以甜白葡萄酒闻名，尤其是香浓甜美的贵腐霉葡萄酒，产区内的滴金庄园（Ch. d'Yquem）在1855年评级时被评为超一级庄园。苏玳甜白葡萄酒通常采用沙美龙、白沙威浓和密思卡岱葡萄混酿而成，芳香浓郁，风格独特。产区内的巴萨克村（Barsac）所产葡萄酒既可以打上巴萨克法定产区的标记，又可以打上苏玳法定产区的标记。

迪甘甜酒王（白）
Ch. d'Yquem

¥ ¥ ¥ ¥ ¥

浓郁雅致的花果香，经橡木桶发酵后有微妙的香草和烤面包的味道。入口圆润柔顺，酒体平衡。While gifted tasters can identify some of the aromas and flavours of it in an effort to define its complexity, they never really succeed in communicating its essence or explaining its mystery.

- 1855波尔多甜白葡萄酒分级特一级庄 Grand Premier Cru-1855 Sauternes & Barsac Classification
- 4～7℃
- 情侣约会，浪漫婚宴 dating, wedding
- 牛白汁生蚝，鱼类，龙虾 oysters, lobster, fish
- 与法国皇室一直有着千丝万缕的关联，曾被美国第三任总统杰弗逊所拥有，也是华盛顿总统的心头好。昂贵的价格屡次刷新世界白葡萄酒拍卖的记录。The only Sauternes given such designation in 1855 Sauternes & Barsac Classification and was a wine loved by American president Thomas Jefferson and Washington. People sigh that every drop of this wine is as rare and shining as gold.

滴金（白）

Y d'Yquem

¥¥¥¥

有蜂蜜，蜂胶及浓郁的果味。新鲜爽脆又花香四溢的口感强劲冲击着味蕾，非常讨好。This wine starts out very crisp and aromatic before filling out on the palate. The aroma of honey, propolis and fruits can be found in this wine.

- 波尔多高级法定产区酒 Bordeaux Supérieur AOC
- 7～10℃
- 浪漫婚宴，酒友交流 wedding, wine appreciation
- 鲜贝，生蚝 scallop, oyster
- 年产量约5 000瓶，只有在特定年份才会酿造，每10年中约只有3个年份生产，是一款稀有的佳酿。A special vintage comes every other 2 years on average which let it low the annual yeild to about 5 000 bottles.

小华轩庄园（甜白）

Ch. Petit Vedrines

¥¥¥

桔子柠檬果酱的香味浓郁诱人。有足够的酸度来平衡甜味，余味清新怡人。It is absolutely a beauty. Full of concentrated marmalade jam characters.

- 苏玳法定产区酒 Sauternes AOC
- 4～7℃
- 温馨家宴，情侣约会 family gathering, dating
- 鹅肝，芦笋 foie gras, asparagus
- 综合香气、观感、结构以及价格等因素来衡量，该酒无疑是苏玳酒中的赢家。Château Petit Vedrines definitely gets the nod; great flavours, intensity and texture, at a very reasonable price. A winner.

小常识 Q & A

问：甜白葡萄酒的最佳饮用温度是多少？

答：葡萄酒的饮用温度对于酒的口感和芳香有非常大的影响。较低的温度会突出酒的酸度与单宁，同时减弱芳香；较高的饮用温度会弱化酒的酸度和单宁的表现，同时增加香气。白葡萄酒通常需要冰镇后饮用，但温度太低会导致酒的轻盈香气无法散发出来。对于甜白葡萄酒来说，最佳饮用温度为6~10℃，我们可以在饮用前1小时将酒放入冰箱冷藏室，拿出来饮用时酒的温度基本上就是理想的饮用温度了。

>波尔多法定产区
Bordeaux AOC

歌迪雅
Cordier

歌迪雅集团是拥有11个列级名庄的大酒商，旗下曾包括了大宝庄在内的杰出庄园。其酒都非常突出自己所在产区的个性和特点。目前集团历史已经超过了120年，信誉有保证。

Cordier started its expertise in marketing classified growth wines, with its experience forged by purchasing and running over 11 prestigious Grand Crus– Ch. Lafaurie Peyraguey, Ch. Meyney, Ch. Talbot, etc. Cordier is skillful in explaining every different terroir through their wines. Now it has a history over 120 years, with the reputed and canonica brand.

歌迪雅圣达美隆（红）
Desire Cordier Rouge

¥¥¥

有肉桂、甘草混合胡椒烧烤的味道，还有玫瑰、樱桃等花果香。口感舒适，力量之余展示新鲜，单宁柔顺紧密。

Cinnamon, liquorice mingling with roasted and slightly peppered notes.Scents of roses are subtly blending with stewed cherry and red fruits aromas.On the palate, it is ample and powerful becoming then crispy and fresh thanks to soft and tight tannins.

- 圣达美隆特等园法定产区酒 St. Emilion Grand Cru AOC
- 14～17℃
- 温馨家宴，情侣约会 family gathering, dating
- 烧烤，烤乳猪 barbecue, roast suckling pig
- 该款2006年份葡萄酒是为了纪念集团成立120周年而特别发行的，酒标上用人手装饰上昂贵的施华洛世奇水晶，凸现该酒的高贵气质，具有收藏意义。The 2006 vintage wine is the 120th anniversary wine of the maison. This emblematic character's remarkable collection of wines deserved a masterpiece:The neckpin is set in Swarovski crystal, delicately mounted by hand.It is a wine good for commemoration.

歌迪雅至尊（红）
Cordier Prestige Rouge

¥¥¥

有香草、胡椒、樱桃果碎和熏面包的味道，特别之处在于后味持久、辛辣。It offers a long lasting and spicy finish with notes of vanilla, pepper and cedar and a smashing ending on cherry and toasted aromas.

波尔多法定产区酒 Bordeaux AOC

12～14℃

活力派对，情侣约会 party, dating

微辣肉，熏肉 light spicy meat, bacon

歌迪雅的荣誉出品，精选波尔多优质的葡萄，使用法国橡木桶进行陈酿，散发更复杂而有层次的酒香。The wine is the representative of Cordier group, the good quality comes from winegrower's carefully selection, French oak aging which makes the aromas more complex and elegant.

歌迪雅至尊（白）
Cordier Prestige Blanc

¥¥

有白桃、柑橘、梨子、香草和矿物的味道。口感圆润饱满、新鲜，还带有奇异果、柚子和糖柠檬的后味。On the nose it exhibits aromas of white peach, citrus and pear as well as hints of vanilla and mineral notes. In the mouth the wine is full and round, with a spicy freshness and an attractive aftertaste of exotic fruits, candied lime and grapefruit.

波尔多法定产区酒 Bordeaux AOC

7～12℃

活力派对，情侣约会 party, dating

咖喱鸡饭，清蒸鱼 chicken curry, steamed fish

来自低产的老树白沙威浓和沙美龙，与亚洲菜是天作之合。From old and low yield Semillon and Sauvignon. A beautiful white will be a winner with Asian food.

歌迪雅（红）
Cordier Rouge

¥¥

有怡人的酸樱桃和黑莓果香气。良好的单宁，平衡的酒香，圆润迷人。This wine is with a fruity bouquet revealing aromas of morello cherry and blackberry. It has a charming qualities, good tannic structure and harmonious balance. Enjoyable young for its fresh fruit.

波尔多法定产区酒 Bordeaux AOC

14～17℃

活力派对，情侣约会 party, dating

猪脚，炖牛肉 pig's knuckle, braised beef

风格清新、明快富有活力，融入了首席美女酿酒师佩丝•伊兹帕卓对于葡萄酒灵魂的理解，非常适合年轻人饮用。This is a good choice for young people with its passion from the chief wine maker，angelical lady Paz Espajo.

歌迪雅（白）
Cordier Blanc

¥¥

酒色清澈，有浓烈的柚子、无花果、矿物和花的味道，是一款很好的开胃酒。A brilliant, clear colour with green hints, and an intense, well-developed bouquet of fruity (grapefruit and fig) mineral and floral (acacia blossom) notes. Good aperitif wine.

波尔多法定产区酒 Bordeaux AOC

7～12℃

活力派对，情侣约会 party, dating

鸡肉沙律，生蚝 chicken salad, oyster

主要针对时尚潮人，明快富有活力，体现出歌迪雅葡萄酒口感讨好的风格。This is a good white wine choice for young people. Cordier is good at making the pleasant wine for the young.

花骑士（红）
Lafleur Chevalier Rouge

¥ ¥

有薄荷浆果香味，口感活跃，酒体和谐柔顺。Lafleur Chevalier is a wine with a lively taste, a harmonious and supple body. A combination of minty berry aroma.

- 波尔多法定产区酒 Bordeaux AOC
- 14～17℃
- 活力派对，情侣约会 party, dating
- 肉类食品，芝士 hearty meat dishes, cheese
- 优质的法定产区酒，四平八稳的酒风，非常容易欣赏。The red is easily enjoyed when it is young.

德嘉斯（红）
Ch. Des Graves

¥ ¥

酒体，圆润柔滑，带有一丝樱桃的果味，橡木味平和，结构可人。This is a delicious, rounded, soft wine possessing light cherry fruits. Beautifully balanced oak and a lovely structure.

- 波尔多高级法定产区酒 Bordeaux Supérieur AOC
- 18～20℃
- 情侣约会，活力派对 dating, party
- 红肉类菜肴 light red meat dishes
- 想要尝试左手鲜香水果，右手优雅雪茄的味道吗？让它们在你的口中彼此交融吧。Enjoy the exquisite experience bewteen sweet fruits and elegant cigar by this wine.

花骑士（白）
Lafleur Chevalier Blanc

¥ ¥

口感新鲜，有活跃的果香和花香，酸度和果味平衡，令人愉快。The white is fresh, dry and clean with a pleasing balance between the acidity and the fruit.

- 波尔多法定产区酒 Bordeaux AOC
- 7～10℃
- 活力派对，情侣约会 party, dating
- 海鲜，清淡菜肴 seafood, light-seasoned dishes
- 声誉不衰，多年来一直受欢迎的波尔多白葡萄酒。A Bordeaux favourite for years, now you can enjoy it on your table too.

玛迪奥庄园（红）
Ch. Mathiot

¥¥

如德国巴腾堡蛋糕般的杏仁蛋白香甜，还带有黑醋栗的气息。Deep ruby colour, with Marzipan (Battenberg cake) and some cassis in the nose.

- 波尔多法定产区酒 Bordeaux AOC
- 14～17℃
- 温馨家宴，情侣约会 family gathering, dating
- 烧肉，熏肉，北京烤鸭，芝士 grilled meat, bacon, peking duck, cheese
- 对于一款入门级别的波尔多红酒来说，这款葡萄酒拥有令人惊喜的复杂、丰富口感。Surprisingly complex on the palate for "entry level" Bordeaux.

百利安（红）
Ch. Haut-Belian Rouge

¥¥

有明显的红色水果香和优雅的橡木香。中度酒体，口感平衡。Expressive nose of red fruits, spices and with an elegant touch of oak. Medium body wine, the tannins is soft and well balance.

- 波尔多法定产区酒 Bordeaux AOC
- 18～20℃
- 温馨家宴，友人相聚 family gathering, friends gathering
- 羊扒，干烧鱼类 lamb, barbeque fish
- 适合每日饮用，容易欣赏。Easy to drink. A typical everyday wine.

百利安（白）
Ch. Haut-Belian Blanc

¥¥

气味芬芳，有活跃的果香和花香，香味优雅。口感新鲜、不甜而爽，酸度和果味平衡，令人愉快。The white is fresh, dry and clean with a pleasing balance between the acidity and the fruit.

- 安德牧斯法定产区酒 Entre-Deux-Mers AOC
- 7～10℃
- 活力派对，温馨家宴 party, family gathering
- 海鲜，清淡型菜肴 seafood, light-seasoned dishes
- 波尔多多年来一直受欢迎的好酒。A Bordeaux favourite for years.

宝来湖庄园（红）
Ch. Bellevue Rouge

¥ ¥

酒香层次丰富而成熟，单宁适中，酒体复杂。Nose opulent and ripe, complex body, fine tannic and comfortable palate.

- 波尔多高级法定产区酒 Bordeaux Supérieur AOC
- 18～20℃
- 温馨家宴，情侣约会 family gathering, dating
- 牛扒，鸡肉 beef steak, chicken
- 源于17世纪的古老庄园，口感舒服，适合配餐。A château originated from 17th century and a good wine for food matching.

宝来湖庄园（白）
Ch. Bellevue Blanc

¥ ¥

非常优雅，热带水果的清香中带有青草的异香气味。The wines produced are extremely elegant, with a fresh nose.

- 安德牧斯法定产区酒 Entre-Deux-Mers AOC
- 7～10℃
- 友人相聚，情侣约会 friends gathering, dating
- 烤猪肉 roast poultry
- 适合出现在充满水果，烤鱼、生蚝的餐桌上。A table around a plate of fruit seas, grilled fish and oysters.

花悦波尔多（红）
Lafleur Gloria Bordeaux

¥ ¥

淡淡的烟草清香，酒体柔顺丰厚，带有成熟樱桃的果味，芳香可人。Delivers loads of fruity aromas with the notes of tobacco, rounded and moderate body, boasting a fabulous cherry and smokey flavour.

- 波尔多法定产区酒 Bordeaux AOC
- 14～17℃
- 活力派对，友人相聚 party, friends gathering
- 淡味红肉，烟熏肉类 light red meat, smokey meat
- 在中国市场上耳熟能详的日常餐酒，性价比高。A famous, easy-drinking daily wine in China market.

小宝庄园（红）
Le Petit Bois

¥ ¥

有浓郁的黑色水果的香味和香草橡木味。单宁结构紧密，余韵悠长、干爽，有持续的果香。Intense black fruit flavours give way to a rich, mid-pallet of vanilla oak. A firm structure with evident tannin compliments lingering fruit flavours on the long dry finish.

- 波尔多法定产区酒 Bordeaux AOC
- 14～17℃
- 活力派对，友人相聚 party, friends gathering
- 红烧肉 pork cooked in soya sauce
- 波尔多传统庄园酒，容易欣赏。Traditional Bordeaux AOC wine with easy-access.

梦露庄园（红）
Ch. Monroze

¥ ¥

明显的红色水果香味。酒体优雅，单宁柔滑，容易欣赏。Expressive nose of red fruits, spices and reveals of an elegant touch of oak. Medium body wine, the tannins is soft and well-balanced. Easy to drink.

- 波尔多高级法定产区酒 Bordeaux Supérieur AOC
- 18～20℃
- 情侣约会，活力派对 dating, party
- 铁板类红肉 teppenyaki red meat
- 有跟酒名一样性感的酒体，是送给佳人的佳品。This is a fine wine bearing the sexy name and the equivalent sexy body. A wine gift for beauties.

白马亭园（红）
Clos du Cheval Blanc

¥¥

有成熟的红色水果香味，单宁成熟，余味香浓可口。Expressive nose of ripe red fruits. Ripe tannins and savoury finish.

- 迪宝谷法定产区酒 Côtes de Bourg AOC
- 18～20℃
- 温馨家宴，友人相聚 family gathering, friends gathering
- 东坡肉，牛肉干 fat pork meat, dry beef
- 上市后无需陈酿便可欣赏的日常波尔多酒。Perfect for drinking at the moment and can match food easily.

玛丽庄园（红）
Ch. Sainte-Marie

¥¥

酒香浓郁，有山莓、香料、香草和一丝丁香的味道。Raspberries, spices, vanilla and a hint of clove in the nose. Strong structure with well-blended tannins.

- 波尔多高级法定产区酒 Bordeaux Supérieur AOC
- 18～20℃
- 友人相聚，情侣约会 friends gathering, dating
- 黑椒牛扒，烤肉 black pepper steak, roast meat
- 新派庄园酒，有着如同新世界般澎湃的果香，又不失法国葡萄酒平衡优雅的精髓。Fruity however you can also savour the elegance from French traditional wine.

瑰丽庄园（红）
Ch. Gravelier

¥

有丰富黑加仑子、香草以及熟透的红色浆果香气。口感圆柔厚实，回味绵长。Pretty currant nose. Vanilla laced red berry fruit flavours. The palate is round and thick with fruity aroma in mouth.

- 波尔多法定产区酒 Bordeaux AOC
- 14～17℃
- 活力派对，友人相聚 party, friends gathering
- 肉类，奶酪 meat, cheese
- 获奖无数，送礼首选。It's a great-honoured wine for gift.

美乐庄园（红）
Ch. Merlet

¥¥

入口浓郁大气，酒体平衡，有红色水果和樱桃的香味。Harmonious structure with a red fruit and cherry-stone flavours on the palate.

- 波尔多法定产区酒 Bordeaux AOC
- 14～17℃
- 温馨家宴，友人相聚 family gathering, friends gathering
- 牛扒，黑椒牛仔骨，叉烧 beef steak, rib with black pepper, sauce, barbeque pork
- 作为知名酒商歌迪雅旗下产品，酒质水平有保证。As joining the Club Cordier partnership, it meets Cordier's high-quality requirments.

小常识
Q & A

问：为什么葡萄酒中会含有二氧化硫（SO_2）？这对身体有影响吗？

答：如果没有SO_2，所有的葡萄酒都将会在短短的几个月之内变质。SO_2对葡萄酒的影响可谓是从内到外，主要有两种。第一，SO_2通常作为保护剂添加到葡萄酒中，有杀死葡萄皮表面的杂菌(SO_2几乎是酿酒师所能使用的唯一的细菌抑制剂)。第二，它又是一种抗氧化剂，在保护酒液的天然水果特性的同时防止酒液老化。

每个国家对酿酒过程中能加入的SO_2量都有专门的法律规定。欧盟规定红葡萄酒中SO_2的最高含量为160毫克/升，白葡萄酒和粉红葡萄酒为210毫克/升。其实绝大部分的葡萄酒在开瓶后摇杯的时间里，酒中有30%～40%的SO_2会跟氧气结合而消散了，剩下的含量非常少，对人体无任何伤害。而且一般进口优质的葡萄酒SO_2含量都没有达到160毫克/升。因此，大可放心饮用。

>波尔多其他流行法定产区
Other Popular Bordeaux Appellations

宝捷庄园（红）
Ch. Poujeaux

¥¥¥

单宁和果味之间平衡得很好，结构紧密。Well balanced between tannin and fruit, the structure and harmony of the wine contribute.

2003年美度区超级明星庄
Cru Bourgeois Exceptionnel

18～20℃

商务宴请，酒友交流 business dinner, wine appreciation

烧牛柳，粤式扣肉 roast tenderloin, cantonese double braised pork meat with fat

波尔多莫丽丝村之超级明星庄，曾在法国总统的宴会上被误认为是拉菲，其品质之优秀可见一斑。Was once mistaken as Lafite in the French president's dinner. Always reasonably priced, a wine whose quality can equal or even surpass that of Grand Cru.

阿旺庄园（红）
Ch. Moulin à Vent

¥¥¥

香气集中，酒体圆润，果香让人一试难忘。Round body, balanced, full of blackberry, wild fruit and oak aroma, it exhibits excellent concentration, depth, and length.

2003年美度区优质明星庄
Cru Bourgeois Supérieur

14～17℃

友人相聚，温馨家宴 friends gathering, family gathering

黑椒牛扒，烤肉，熏肉 black pepper steak, roast meat, bacon meat

上市后不需陈置便可欣赏到优质佳酿。Ready to drink sooner than other Médoc wines with a velvet structure.

宝捷庄园副牌（红）
La Salle de Ch. Poujeaux

¥¥¥

果香鲜美，单宁结构柔滑、成熟。散发出樱桃、黑加仑子的味道，香气馥郁，余味悠长。Showing cherry, blackberry aromas, long finish, the relatively low percentage of Cabernet lends the wine a slightly more supple texture.

宝捷庄园之副牌酒
2nd wine of Ch. Poujeaux

14～17℃

友人相聚，酒友交流 friends gathering, wine appreciation

牛扒，羊仔柳 beef steak, lamb

采用了园内较年轻的葡萄树果实酿造，酒性比其正牌酒更平易近人。Made mainly from fruit grown on young vines to display an easy access for joy in the palate.

力士将（红）
Ch. Listran

¥ ¥

酒中弥漫着咖啡香，酒体有力甘实，木香强。The wine offers an agreeably fruity bouquet, with fine tannins.

2003年美度区明星庄
Cru Bourgeois

18～20℃

活力派对，友人相聚 party, friends gathering

红肉，芝士 light red meat dishes, cheese platter

荣获明星庄评级，是性价比很高的佳酿。Dubbed as "Cru Bourgeois" with a very good value.

香宝庄（红）
Ch. Chambeau

¥ ¥

酒香柔软带果香和咖啡味。酒体柔滑，单宁成熟。This wine is its first indication of concentrated fruit. Well balanced between tannin and fruit, the structure and harmony of the wine contribute to a long velvety finish.

露莎-圣达美隆法定产区酒 Lussac-St. Emilion AOC

18～20℃

温馨家宴，友人相聚 family gathering, friends gathering

红肉，芝士 light red meat, cheese platter

产自波尔多名村露莎-圣达美隆，是优质的村庄级法定产区酒。A highly recommended village AOC wine.

碧朗庄园（红）
Ch. Blaignan

¥ ¥

淡淡的烟草清香，气味和谐诱人，口感平衡圆滑，单宁柔和。Restrained nose of smoky, savoury aromas. Harmonious with attractive. It is round and has moderate and soft tannins.

2003年美度区明星庄 Cru Bourgeois

18～20℃

酒友交流，温馨家宴 wine appreciation, family gathering

红肉 red meat

曾多次荣获法国葡萄酒品鉴赛的大奖，不容错过！You really can not miss such an awarded red in your life!

乐菲丝庄园（红）
Ch. Le Thys

¥ ¥

以红色浆果和香料味为主，果香宜人，温和优雅。Showing a crimson red colour, and with flavours of red fruits and spice. Elegant, fruity noses.

波尔多谷一级法定产区酒
1er Côtes de Bordeaux AOC

18～20℃

友人相聚，情侣约会 friends gathering, dating

牛扒，红肉类菜肴 beef steak, red meatdishes

拥有超过200年的酿酒历史，品质值得信赖。Has a history of wine-vinification for more than two centuries.

美雅（红）
Ch. Mayne-Vieil

¥¥

酒香优雅，酒体平衡，单宁细致，口感柔软。Well made, stylish smooth wine. Clean winemaking and firm structure. Full fruity finish.

佛朗莎法定产区酒 Fronsac AOC

18～20℃

友人相聚，情侣约会 friends gathering, dating

烧肉，烤海鲜 stew, barbeque fish

此酒是美国著名酒评家罗拔·派克非常推崇的物值酒。Highly recommended by Robert Parker.

浪都庄园（红）
Ch. Nardou

¥¥¥

酒体结构平衡，浓郁的黑色水果香味混合着淡淡的橡木味道，非常吸引人。It is full and fleshy, while the finish offers notes of red fruit compote, black pepper, as well as caramelized, roasted hints.

弗朗谷法定产区酒 Côtes de Francs AOC

18～20℃

温馨家宴，友人相聚 family gathering, friends gathering

猪扒，烤羊扒 pork, roast lamb

隶属波尔多著名酒商歌迪雅集团，如果想尝试波尔多主流产区以外的葡萄酒，该酒是不二之选。A property belongs to the famous negociant Cordier.

金武士庄园（红）
Ch. Combes Canon

¥¥¥

由橡木桶带出的淡烟草和烤面包味道，令酒体的气味更为复杂。酒香优雅，有紫罗兰花香和胡椒辛香。Ripe mature black fruit with some wood notes that add complexity. The harmony and charm of this wine cannot fail to stimulate your senses.

嘉朗佛朗莎法定产区酒 Canon-Fronsac AOC

18～20℃

温馨家宴，活力派对 family gathering, party

猪扒，烤羊扒 pork, roast lamb

隶属波尔多著名酒商歌迪雅集团，佐餐一流。A property belongs to the famous negociant Cordier. A friendly wine with seasoned meat.

情人庄园（红）
Ch. Valentin

¥ ¥

产自波尔多新兴产区贝尔谷，柔和的酒香中带有果香和花香，入口有成熟樱桃、玉桂、雪松香味。The palate shows ripe cheery and cedar. Fine and elegant tannins.

贝尔谷一级法定产区酒 1er Côtes de Blaye AOC

18～20℃

情侣约会，浪漫婚宴 dating, wedding

烧肉，烤海鲜 stew, barbeque fish

是一款适合与情人共饮的浪漫葡萄酒。It is good value for price. Gives valentines a romantic wine encounter.

乐图庄园（红）
Ch. Lardeau

¥ ¥

丰富浓郁的果味，使其有着柔顺平和又醇厚的个性。Dominates a rich fruity taste, and very soft, mellow.

贝吉拉法定产区酒 Bergerac AOC

18～20℃

活力派对，情侣约会 party, dating

红肉，芝士，烤鸭，乳鸽 light red meat dishes, cheese, roast goose, roast pigeon

口感良好，价格合理，是适合每天饮用的佳品。Suitable to everyday drinking by the good value and pleasance in the palate.

迪金庄园（红）
Domaine des CombesRouge

¥

中度酒体，优雅平衡易入口，果味足。This wine's spicy blackberry aromatics lead to a well-crafted core of flavourful dark fruits intermingled with garrigue and tar.

杜乐丝法定产区酒 Côtes de Duras AOC

14～17℃

友人相聚，活力派对 friends gathering, party

鸭肉，脆皮油封鹅，野味 fillet of duck, confit, game

比起其他波尔多酒更具热情，口感更甜美。Duras vineyards benefit from hotter, dryer weather than its Bordeaux neighbours, enabling the wines to mature in the best of conditions.

迪金庄园（白）
Domaine des Combes Blanc

¥ ¥

无论从酒色到口感都很诱人，香味超群、鲜活，又不失精致的果香。These seductive wines with their clear green-hued body are both distinguished and vigorous whilst remaining delicate and fruity.

杜乐丝法定产区酒 Côtes de Duras AOC

7～10℃

友人相聚，活力派对 friends gathering, party

鱼肉，贝类 fish, shellfish

一款体现度华谷传统酿酒技术和激情的佳酿。A wine carrying on traditional technique and a lot of passion.

布根地
Burgundy

布根地　位于法国中部略偏东，地形以丘陵为主，属大陆性气候，被称为“地球上最复杂难懂的葡萄酒产地”。布根地的红葡萄酒酒色偏浅，带有泥土和菌类气息；白葡萄酒清新雅致，带有矿物味和水果香气。得天独厚的土壤和气候孕育出味道独一无二的美酒，令世人留下深刻的印象。越资深的酒迷越知道这个地方，因为它出产全球最昂贵的红、白葡萄酒。

布根地葡萄业的特点可以归类为：1种土质，2个葡萄品种，3种产酒单位，4级葡萄酒，5个大产区。

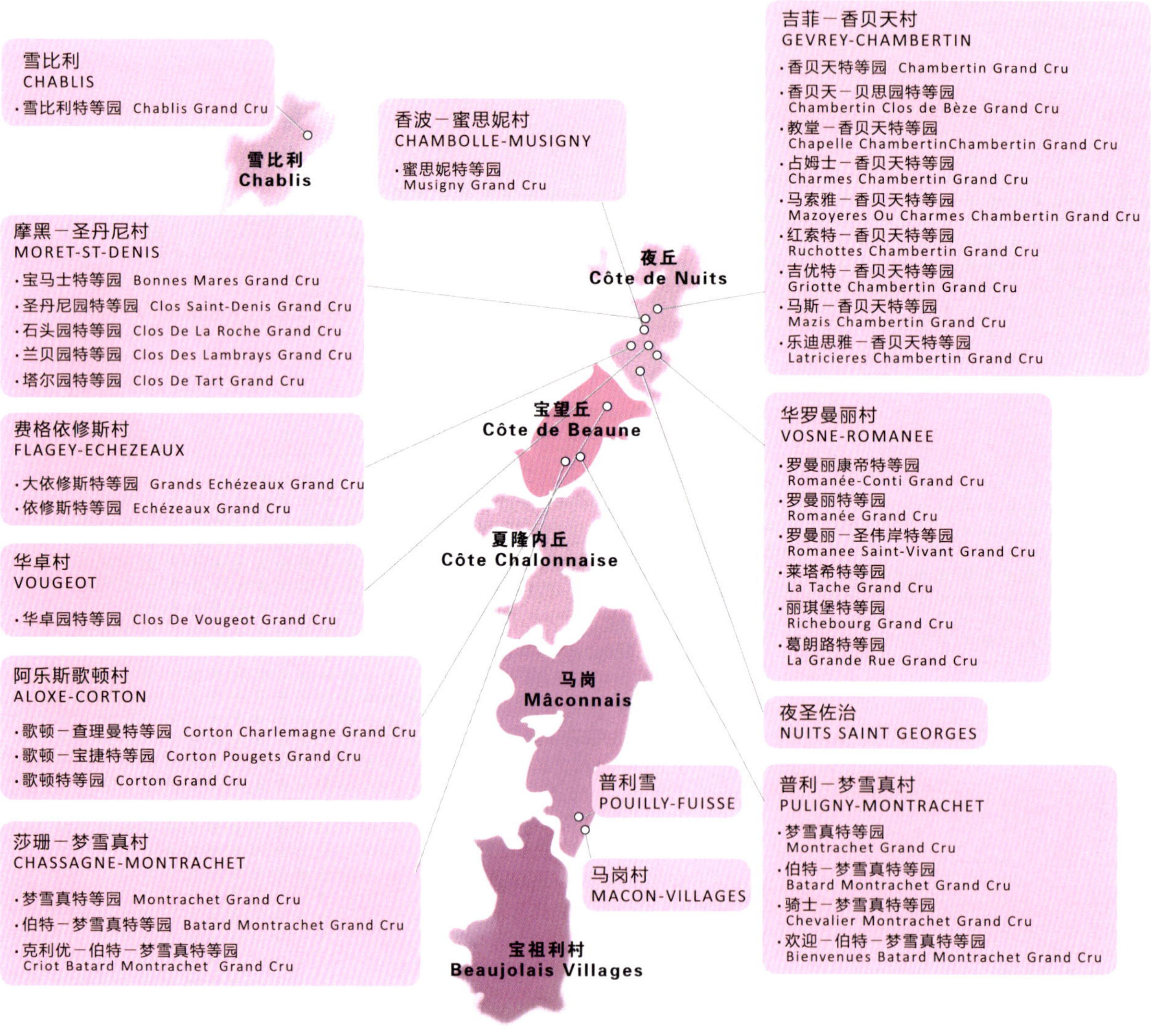

法国布根地葡萄酒产区示意图

{1种土质}

虽然布根地各区葡萄园的土质各异，但主要都由石灰质黏土（Calcareous Clay）构成。

石灰质黏土 Calcareous Clay

贝露娃 Pinot Noir

雪当利 Chardonnay

{2个葡萄品种}

布根地的葡萄酒大多数采用单一葡萄品种酿制，其主要的红葡萄是贝露娃，白葡萄是雪当利。在最南端的宝祖利村则盛产以佳美红葡萄为主的酒；此外，次要的白葡萄品种阿里高特（Aligoté）也比较常见。

3种产酒单位

1. 独立酒庄

只用自有葡萄园的葡萄酿酒，产量占布根地葡萄酒总量的15%，通常是经济实力雄厚的酒商，如生产世界最贵葡萄酒罗曼丽康帝（Romanée-Conti）的DRC集团、丽花酒园（Domaine Leroy）等。

2. 酒商

除了用自有葡萄园的葡萄，同时还从其他葡萄园收购葡萄进行酿酒，产量占布根地葡萄酒总量的60%，其中不乏顶级的葡萄酒，如法莱丽（Faiveley）、力高宝德（Nicolas Potel）和哥德利安（Claude Chonion）。

3. 酿酒合作社

自己并不种植葡萄，而是从无法自行酿酒的合约葡萄农那里收购葡萄进行统一酿造和销售，产量占布根地葡萄酒总量的25%，产量大且物美价廉。

4级葡萄酒

布根地的葡萄酒分为4个等级，这些分级其实就是产酒葡萄田的等级。精于分析土壤和总结经验的布根地人早已对自己土地的情况了如指掌。因此，对不同品质的葡萄田有不同的分级。

品质越高的葡萄田产量越少，仅有2%的葡萄园能列居塔尖的特等葡萄园，共33个；而大概一成的葡萄园被列入一级葡萄园，共562个。这些都是产量稀少，品质超群的典型布根地酒；而质量稍低的依次是村庄级法定产区及产量最大的地方性法定产区，后者生产布根地法定产区酒（Burgundy AOC）。

特等葡萄园
Grand Cru

▲

一级葡萄园
Premier Cru

▲

村庄级法定产区
AOC-Village

▲

地方性法定产区
AOC-Region

{5大产区}

布根地共分为5大产区，他们分别是雪比利（Chablis）、夜丘（Côte de Nuits）、宝望丘（Côte de Beaune）、夏隆内丘（Côte Chalonnaise）和马岗（Mâconnais）。夜丘（Côte de Nuits）和宝望丘（Côte de Beaune）又合称为金丘（Côte d' Or），是布根地葡萄酒产区的最精华的核心地带。

1. 雪比利

位于布根地的最北部，气候寒冷，只生产雪当利白葡萄酒，该酒酸度高，带有柠檬等清新果香及矿石类酒香，宜在浅龄时饮用，非常适合与各类海鲜搭配，做开胃酒也是不错的选择。唯一的特等葡萄园与产区一样名为雪比利（Chablis），法莱丽（Faiveley）是同时拥有雪比利特等葡萄园和雪比利一级葡萄园出品的酒庄。

2. 夜丘

是整个布根地红葡萄酒的精华区域，这里集合了布根地最多的特等葡萄园，一共有25个，包括法国国王拿破仑最爱的香贝天（Chambertin）特等园、世界上最昂贵的罗曼丽康帝（Romanée-Conti）特等园等。夜丘的华卓特等葡萄园（Vougeot）是整个布根地最大的特等园，其最大的地主拉图布根地（Château de la Tour），拥有最核心的一片葡萄田，在寸土尺金的布根地，能在葡萄园内酿酒和装瓶，酒标上可打上“Château”字眼的庄园酒少之又少。这里出产的贝露娃红葡萄酒，香气馥郁、酒质细腻，极具陈年天赋。另外，白葡萄酒产量虽小，但也堪称极品，带有迷人的矿物和坚果气息。

3. 宝望丘

盛产布根地最优质的白葡萄酒，也是布根地唯一一个同时拥有红、白葡萄酒特等园的产区（共有8个特等园，1红7白）。歌顿（Corton）是唯一的红葡萄酒特等园，以塞纳伯爵（Comte Senard）酒庄的出品最惹人眼球；白葡萄特等园个个都出身不凡，包括世界最昂贵的白葡萄酒园梦雪真（Montrachet）和查理曼大帝最爱的白葡萄酒园歌顿查理曼（Corton Charlemagne）。宝望丘出产的雪当利白葡萄酒芳香浓郁，有着与红酒媲美的复杂芬芳和耐久存的陈年潜力，冠绝全球。与夜丘相比，这里的红葡萄酒更为柔美，柔顺易入口。夜丘和宝望丘垄断了整个布根地的特等葡萄园，是优质葡萄酒的标志性产区。

4. 夏隆内丘

出产中低价的葡萄酒为主，酒体较为清雅。其中美格利村（Mercurey）的红葡萄酒以草莓香气闻名，精致柔顺，性价比高；布哲宏（Bouzeron）是阿里高特（Aligote）白葡萄酒的著名产区，果味芬芳，清爽怡人；路尼（Rully）则盛产起泡酒。

5. 马岗

靠近南部，气候炎热，所酿出来的酒也带有热带风情。马岗以出产价廉物美的雪当利白葡萄酒而闻名，其出品带有芒果、香蕉等热带水果的浓郁气息，口感丰厚可人；红葡萄酒多以佳美（Gamay）葡萄酿制，酒体淡雅，富有玫瑰、李子芳香。

此外，位于布根地最南部的宝祖利村（Beaujolais Village）面积约占布根地的一半，产量庞大，境内几乎全部种植佳美葡萄。其中最为人熟知的是宝祖利新酒（Beaujolais Nouveau）。

宝祖利新酒的酿造方法不同于一般红酒：将完整的一串葡萄放入注有CO_2的密封槽里进行发酵，使得发酵过程中的酒液不被氧化，最终酿造出来的葡萄酒酒色较浅，口感新鲜柔顺，一般在当年即可上市，因此得名为“新酒”。宝祖利新酒不耐久存，最好在3个月内饮用，在每年11月第三个星期四凌晨起于全球同步推出，售完即止。

罗曼丽康帝
Romanée-Conti

罗曼丽康帝酒庄，简称为DRC（Domaine de la Romanée-Conti），是布根地产区最具知名度的酒庄。单凭其显赫的声望，便能把布根地提升到世界级的地位。

DRC, short for Domaine de la Romanée-Conti, produces the purest, most aristocratic and most intense example of Pinot Noir you could possibly imagine in the world. Its wines exceed just the nectar but yardstick with which to judge all other Burgundies.

罗曼丽康帝（红）
Romanée-Conti

¥¥¥¥¥

花香和辛辣气息完美融合，优雅愉悦，口感和谐，带有红色水果和樱桃的味道，单宁丰富细腻。Combination of floral and spicy flavour, elegant and pleasant. Harmonious palate, red fruit and cherry taste with fine tannins.

- 罗曼丽康帝特等园法定产区酒 Romanée-Conti Grand Cru AOC
- 18～20℃
- 酒友交流，友人相聚 wine appreciation, friends gathering
- 黑椒牛扒，蜜汁烧鹅 black pepper steak, honey-stewed roast goose
- 在世界名酒中独占鳌头，曾被形容为谪仙飞返天际时“遗留在人间的东西”。Perhaps this is the most famous one among Burgundy's vineyards, in France, and bears grands crus status. Romanée-Conti wines are extremely highly sought out by collectors.

丽琪堡（红）
Richebourg

¥¥¥¥¥

带有浓郁的紫罗兰和松露的味道，让人回味无穷，齿颊留香。In the mouth, it is massive, sturdy and full of voilet and truffle nose.

- 丽琪堡特等园法定产区酒 Richebourg Grand Cru AOC
- 18～20℃
- 商务宴请，酒友交流 business dinner, wine appreciation
- 铁板类红肉 teppenyaki red meat
- 丽琪堡年产量仅为12 000瓶，许多酒评家对它的称赞不亚于罗曼丽康帝。Those 12, 000 bottles annual production as well as the dense but also harmonious nose make Richebourg nothing less than Romanée-Conti.

莱塔希（红）
La Tâche

¥¥¥¥¥

有浆果、樱桃以及泥土的芬芳，还带有一丝皮革和矿物质的气息。单宁紧密，酒体丰满、雄壮有力。Berry, cherry and earthy notes. Some leather and minerals. Firm, dry tannins, yet full-bodied and very masculine.

莱塔希特等园法定产区酒
La Tâche Grand Cru AOC

18～20℃

酒友交流，情侣约会 wine appreciation, dating

浓味红肉 red meat with rich sauce

莱塔希属康帝酒园所有，与罗曼丽康帝酿造方法、品质管理等也无差别，但比起罗曼丽康帝，此酒更强劲浓郁。Like Romanée-Conti, La Tâche is wholly owned by the Domaine de la Romanée-Conti. But La Tâche wines are richer, more intense, and more deeply colored than those from the Romanée-Conti vineyard.

大依修斯（红）
Grands Échézeaux

¥¥¥¥¥

这是一款强劲复杂的酒，带明显的樱桃香气。入口充满优雅的香草和红色水果气息，余味悠长。With a ripe cherry robe, Grands Échézeaux is a powerful and complex wine. Aromas of red fruits come to the forth, along with delicate vanilla notes. It has a great length on the palate.

大依修斯特等园法定产区酒
Grands Échézeaux Grand Cru AOC

18～20℃

友人相聚，酒友交流 friends gathering, wine appreciation

牛扒，羊扒 beef steak, lamb

本酒是康帝酒园中价格比较平易近人的一款，装瓶四五年后才会真正成熟。Typical of Grands Échézeaux palate reveals the DRC's mystery, mature after 4-5 years' aging. This is the best choice to experience DRC series at a relatively preferential price.

依修斯（红）
Échézeaux

¥¥¥¥¥

带有樱桃和香料的气息，橡木桶的培养使酒体结构圆熟。Aromas of spices and cherries. A silky structure with a mellow touch of oak.

依修斯特等园法定产区酒
Échézeaux Grand Cru AOC

18～20℃

酒友交流，温馨家宴 wine appreciation, family gathering

烤肉，熏肉 roast meat, bacon meat

同属顶级的依修斯品质不逊于大依修斯。口感紧实，品尝此美酒需要足够的耐心。Constantly high quality of DRC series. In the mouth, it is compact, rich "material" announcing a slow but promising evolution. It requires patience.

罗曼丽圣伟岸（红）
Romanée-St-Vivant

¥¥¥¥¥

红樱桃和黑莓的果香以及罗曼丽圣伟岸典型香料味。酸度怡人，是一款非常有力而不失优雅的美酒。Red and black cherry and berry on the nose with fantastic typical RSV spice. Great length on the palate with very nice acidity. A truly elegant wine with lots of power and grace.

圣伟岸特等园法定产区酒
Romanée-St-Vivant Grand Cru AOC

18～20℃

酒友交流，友人相聚 wine appreciation, friends gathering

牛扒，烧鸭 beef steak, roast duck

其味道就像舒曼的乐曲，细品之下，其中庸温和的特点和丰富的韵味着实令人难忘。It tastes like schumann's music, the mild flavour and rich characteristics really impresses.

枫丹甘露

Fontaine-Gagnard

“枫丹甘露”这个美丽的名字来源于两个历史悠久的酿酒家族的结合。“枫丹甘露”在出产最优质白葡萄酒村庄之一的莎珊梦雪真村庄拥有超过10公顷的优质葡萄园。

The name came from the marriage of two winemaking families. Over 10 hectares premier and grand crus in Chassagne-Montrachet where produce the best quality white wine of Burgundy owned by the family.

枫丹甘露（梦雪真）（白）
Fontaine-Gagnard
Le Montrachet Grand Cru

¥¥¥¥¥

此珍品产量稀少，风格更是像极其主人的气质：香气浓郁，而且结构良好，酒质稳定有保证。It's wonderfully delineated effort with a expressive nose.Sadly only microscopic quantities available of this treasure. It's well-structured, and rigorously authentic like it's owner.

- 梦雪真特等园法定产区酒 Montrachet Grand Cru AOC
- 12～14℃
- 酒友交流，友人相聚 wine appreciation, friends gathering
- 白肉，菌类酱汁菜肴 white meat, mushroom sauce dishes
- 此酒来自布根地顶级的白葡萄酒产区，产量极少，但独具风格，矿物味浓郁，酒质稳定耐久存。It came from the most top quality Burgundy white wine appellation. The wine is well-structured, clean and rigorously authentic which can be aged for long time.

枫丹甘露（伯特梦雪真）（白）
Fontaine-Gagnard Bâtard-Montrachet Grand Cru

¥¥¥¥

带有桃、梨、菠萝、芒果等水果的香气和一丝辛香的气息，风味浓郁，后味悠长。Exotic nose of peach, pear, pineapple, mango and hints of spice, powerful flavours, thick and concentrated, finish seems without end.

- 伯特梦雪真特等园法定产区酒 Bâtard-Montrachet Grand Cru AOC
- 12～14℃
- 友人相聚，温馨家宴 friends gathering, family gathering
- 中至浓味海鲜 medium to heavy seafood
- 庄主选用味美浓郁的葡萄做原料，在技术上保存了葡萄的原始风味，赋予它既精致又新鲜的口感。Domaine owner harvested a tiny crop of unusually small, but intensely concentrated fruit.

枫丹甘露（莎珊梦雪真）（白）
Fontaine-Gagnard Chassagne Montrachet 1er Cru Morgeot

¥¥¥¥

带有优雅而清凉的鲜水果香气，以及柠檬皮和草本植物的味道。中度酒体，风味浓郁，余味悠长。An elegant and cool nose with green fruit, lemon peel and an herbal character, solidly long finish.

- 莎珊梦雪真一级园法定产区酒 Chassagne-Montrachet 1er Cru Morgeot AOC
- 12～14℃
- 商务宴请，情侣约会 business dinner, dating
- 贝类，海鲜 seashell, seafood
- 庄主用最传统的酿造方法以及自己的无比热情所酿出的这款美酒，酒体丰满圆润，香气四溢。Being applied traditional methods both in the vineyard and the immaculate cellar. Body is full and round.

枫丹甘露（宝马一级园）（红）
Fontaine-Gagnard Pommard 1er Cru Les Rugiens

¥¥¥¥

贝露娃葡萄赋予此酒甘美醇香又典雅的清新香气，也不失果味和适度的酸味。Pinot noir gives it a concentrated and elegant flavour, nice acidity and also is fruity.

- 宝马一级园法定产区酒 Pommard 1er Cru Les Rugiens AOC
- 18～20℃
- 酒友交流，友人相聚 wine appreciation, friends gathering
- 牛扒，烧鸭 beef steak, roast duck
- 宝马只产红酒，且出品是全布根地最醇厚浓烈的。枫丹甘露将葡萄的原始风味表现得淋漓尽致。Red wines in Pommard are among the most tannic and robust wines in Burgundy. Fontaine Gagnard figures it to be intense, racy and deep.

法莱丽
Domaine Faiveley

自1825年创立至今，立足在圣佐治村庄的法莱丽家族在七代人的苦心经营下愈发壮大，现拥有超过120公顷的优质葡萄田，其中10公顷特等葡萄田，30公顷一级葡萄田。旗下85％产品均来自自有葡萄田，足见法莱丽的实力非凡。

Founded in 1825, Faiveley is a first and foremost domaine. Situated in the heart of Nuits-Saint-Georges, it has expanded strategically by seven Faiveley generations to include prestigious Crus from Côte d'Or and Côte Chalonnaise. Today, Domaine Faiveley totals more than 120 hectares, with 80% of Faiveley wines come from family-owned vineyards and the rest from select vineyards under long-term contracts with the family.

法莱丽（香贝天特等园）（红）
Domaine Faiveley
Chambertin-Clos de Bèze Grand Cru

¥¥¥¥

有黑色浆果香气，以及香料和糖渍水果的清香。口感强烈浓郁，不但优雅而且余味悠长。Black fruit, spice and fruit compote dominate the nose. The palate is dense, concentrated and energetic and on the beautiful clean, long finish, the class is there for all to see.

- 贝丝香贝天特等园法定产区酒 Chambertin-Clos de Bèze Grand Cru AOC
- 18～20℃
- 酒友交流，温馨家宴 wine appreciation, family gathering
- 铁板类红肉 teppenyaki red meat
- 产此酒的是以贝丝修道院而命名的贝丝香贝天特等园，也是吉菲香贝天村内历史最悠久、最闻名的葡萄园。The vineyard was named after the Abbey of Bèze. It's the most histrical and most famous vineyard in the Geverey-Chambertin Village.

亨利（占姆士香贝天特等园）（红）
Henri Rebourseau Charmes-Chambertin Grand Cru

¥¥¥¥

有浓郁的黑樱桃、黑醋栗的味道，伴有丝丝皮革、咖啡、湿土和烤橡木的香气。入口有樱桃、麝香和甘草的味道。This is a real Burgundy with a rich black cherry and currant fruit, spice, coffee, leather, wet earth, and plenty of toasty oak. This wine here is highly prized with flavours of musk and licorice.

- 占姆士香贝天特等园法定产区酒 Charmes-Chambertin Grand Cru AOC
- 18～20℃
- 商务宴请，酒友交流 business dinner, wine appreciation
- 牛扒，羊扒 beef steak, lamb
- 占姆士香贝天是吉菲香贝天内面积最大且较知名的特等名园，其酒颜色深浓，极具复杂性和层次感。Charmes-Chambertin is one of the better known grands crus of Gevery-Chambertin, wines here are highly prized with a real Burgundy with a "sauvage" nose.

亨利（吉菲香贝天）（红）
Henri Rebourseau Gevrey-Chambertin

¥¥¥

带有浓郁的矿物、草莓和酸莓的味道，单宁结构良好。Nice raspberry lucidity.On the palate, this one is full of aromas of minerals, strawberries and tart berries.

- 吉菲香贝天法定产区酒 Gevrey-Chambertin AOC
- 14～17℃
- 友人相聚，温馨家宴 friends gathering, family gathering
- 铁板类红肉 teppenyaki red meat
- 作为夜丘内最大的产酒区，吉菲香贝天只出产红葡萄酒，酒质因酿造工艺而异。Gevrey-Chambertin produce redwine only. As one of the biggest appellation in Côte de Nuits, the quality of wine ranging from just average to supreme.

丽朗碧奥
Laleure-Piot

丽朗碧奥现由碧奥家族第五代传人Frederic Laleure先生掌舵，产品涵盖了布根地的入门级别到特等园级别，满足不同酒迷的口味需求。

Now run by the fifth generation of Piot Family, current owner Frederic Laleure makes his wines vary from the simple village classification to the famous Grands Crus, offers a wide range of gourmet taste of Pernand-Vergelesses.

丽朗碧奥（宝卓雷丝一级园）（红）
Laleure-Piot Pernand-Vergelesses 1er Cru-Les Vergelesses

¥ ¥ ¥

此酒果香浓郁，悬钩子的味道异常突出，带有浓郁的红色浆果芬芳且口感复杂。It delineates a fruity and delicate raspberry aroma from the bouquet.It is good for value to indulge your palate by this intensely aromatic and concentrated 1er cru wine of Laleure-Piot.

- 宝卓雷丝一级园法定产区酒 Pernand-Vergelesses 1er Cru-Les Vergelesses AOC
- 14～17℃
- 友人相聚，商务宴请 friends gathering, business dinner
- 中至浓味菜肴 medium to heavy dishes
- 产自宝望丘北部鲜有人知的宝卓雷丝村一级园，酒客们用优惠的价格便可欣赏到其独特的风味。Les Vergelesses is one of the 1er crus in Pernand-Vergelesses, a lesser-known wine-producing village at the northern end of Côte de Beaune but generally of good quality and usually less expensive.

丽朗碧奥（宝卓雷丝一级园）（白）
Laleure-Piot Pernand-Vergelesses Blanc 1er Cru

¥¥¥

散发着宝望丘北部白葡萄酒特有的柚子和白花清香，以及新鲜苹果的芳香，又有些许辛香的口感。Wines all from Côte de Beaune have flavours of white flowers and grapefruit. It has a bouquet of fresh fruit (apple) and is slightly spiced, finally giving hints of honey and amber when mature.

- 宝卓雷丝一级园法定产区酒 Pernand-Vergelesses 1er Cru AOC
- 7～12℃
- 情侣约会，温馨家宴 dating, family gathering
- 中至淡味海鲜 light to medium seafood
- 能用实惠的价钱品尝到质量超卓的美酒，何乐而不为？White wine of a less-known 1er cru connotes preferential to this dry, lively and quite light nectar.

小常识 Q & A

问：有时候打开一瓶红酒，里面有一些沉淀物或者酒渣是怎么回事呢？

答：一般葡萄酒出现沉淀物或者酒渣的情形有两种：一种是葡萄酒经陈年变醇后，自然产生的沉淀物。一些名庄葡萄酒大概七八年后会开始出现沉淀，而不能久存的浅龄葡萄酒在一两年后就会出现沉淀。另一种是葡萄酒结晶石（wine crystals）。干净、澄透的葡萄酒也可能会出现沉淀物——葡萄酒结晶石。这种晶体主要构成物质是酒石酸（tartaric acid），就好像置放于家里橱柜中的酒石（cream of tartar）一样是完全无害的。白葡萄酒结晶石的外观看起来颇似白砂糖，而红葡萄酒结晶石则呈现出紫色的结晶体。形成结晶石的主要原因是曾经将酒瓶贮放于特别冷的环境当中，例如置放于温度特别低的冰箱里。酒石结晶体的形状没有一定的规律，有时还有点黏性，通常附着在瓶底、瓶肩，或者出现在软木塞之底端（平放或倒置酒瓶的缘故）。以上出现的这些沉淀物并不会影响葡萄酒的口感，对人体健康无任何损害，可以放心饮用。

力高宝德
Nicolas Potel

力高宝德（Nicolas Potel）在布根地是个颇为传奇的人物，他亲手酿制的第一款葡萄酒，于1997年一推出便击败了当地的众多名庄酒，使其一跃成为一颗耀眼的新星。他的实力与其被誉为“布根地葡萄酒教父”的父亲Gérard Potel先生不相上下。

Nicolas Potel, a name being famous by his laureate Chambertin Grand Cru, just launched his first wine until 1997 but already a dazzling stardom in Burgundy. It seems that like father, like son-that Nicolas' father Gérard Potel was one of the regionally influential men.

力高宝德（罗曼丽圣伟岸）（红）
Nicolas Potel
Romanée-Saint-Vivant Grand Cru

¥¥¥¥¥

复杂诱人，带有丰裕圆润的黑色水果味和怡人的单宁，酒香平衡但很有劲道，且散发着黑巧克力的味道。Full and deep nose of black cherries. Compexity and charm. Very rich and round attack of black fruits with present tannins, balanced by the richness of the wine. Notes of black chocolate on the length.

- 罗曼丽圣伟岸特等园法定产区酒 Romanée-Saint-Vivant Grand Cru AOC
- 18～20℃
- 酒友交流，友人相聚 wine appreciation, friends gathering
- 牛扒，羊扒 beef steak, lamb
- 罗曼丽康帝附近顶级产区的葡萄，配合优秀的酿酒技术，造就这款丰润甜美、酒香平衡的力高宝德美酒。Material from famous grand cru completing with unquestionable wine-making process by Nicolas Potel imprints good wine in a rich, sweet, impeccably well-balanced and harmonious taste.

力高宝德（宝乐梦雪真一级园）（白）
Nicolas Potel
Puligny-Montrachet 1er Cru

¥¥¥¥

此酒呈诱人的稻草金黄色，有牛油和太妃糖的味道。入口果香丰满浓郁，且结构丝滑圆润，让人爱不释手。A beautifully golden straw colour. Enticing butter and toffee aromas.On the palate the fruit is superbly rich.

- 宝乐梦雪真一级园法定产区酒 Puligny-Montrachet 1er Cru AOC
- 12～14℃
- 友人相聚，商务宴请 friends gathering, business dinner
- 中至浓味海鲜 medium to heavy seafood
- 宝乐梦雪真拥有出产顶级白葡萄酒的骑士梦雪真和欢迎伯特梦雪真葡萄田，此酒是最值得期待的佳作。A reputation based on the general consensus that the world's best dry white wines are produced in this village.

力高宝德（香贝天特等园）（红）
Nicolas Potel
Chambertin Grand Cru

¥¥¥¥¥

细闻下有些辛辣的野生红色水果、矿物、烟草和烟熏肉的味道，还有柔和的谷物香味未入口已让你感受到丝滑的感觉。香味悠长，余韵层次分明。Reduced, vinous nose hints at pungent wild red fruits, minerals, smoked meat and tobacco. Silky and fine-grained.

- 香贝天特等园法定产区酒 Chambertin Grand Cru AOC
- 18～20℃
- 酒友交流，商务宴请 wine appreciation, business dinner
- 中至浓味菜肴 medium to heavy dishes
- 香贝天虽被誉为“美酒之王”，但能像力高宝德般将此特等园葡萄的潜力发挥至极致的酒商并不多。Chambertin has been called "King of Wines", but only few vintners like Nicolas Potel could produces it silky and fine-grained.

力高宝德（宝马士特等园）（红）
Nicolas Potel
Bonnes Mares Grand Cru

¥¥¥¥

有柔顺的单宁和丰满的酒体，浓郁且优雅的黑樱桃配上红橙、野草莓和烤咖啡豆的香味，余味悠长。Elegant nose of black cherries, blood orange, wild strawberries with roasted coffee beans.

- 宝马士特等园法定产区酒 Bonnes Mares Grand Cru AOC
- 18～20℃
- 友人相聚，温馨家宴 friends gathering, family gathering
- 牛扒，烧鸭 beef steak, roast duck
- 许多酒评家都公认宝马士是能出产世上好酒的产区之一，樱桃、草莓味道浓郁。Most critics agree Bonnes Mares red wines can be some of the best in the world.

力高宝德（大依修斯特等园）（红）
Nicolas Potel Les Grands Échézeaux Grand Cru

¥¥¥¥¥

黑樱桃的浓郁香气加上黑醋栗、覆盆子的味道，让人回味。酒体丰满平衡，余韵紧密典雅。Generous and deep nose of black cherries, blackcurrant and raspberries. Full and complex attack on black fruits and raspberries.

- 大依修斯特等园法定产区酒 Les Grands Échézeaux Grand Cru AOC
- 18～20℃
- 酒友交流，商务宴请 wine appreciation, business dinner
- 黑椒牛扒，烤肉，熏肉 black pepper steak, roast meat, bacon meat
- 来自华罗曼丽村的顶级酒田，加上力高宝德的酿酒哲学——尊崇酒液的自我个性。One of famous grand cru from Vosne-Romanée village.

力高宝德（依修斯特等园）（红）
Nicolas Potel Échézeaux Grand Cru

¥¥¥¥

馥郁复杂但不失优雅的樱桃气息，让人心旷神怡，余味悠长诱人。Deep, complex and elegant nose of cherries. A ripe wine. Light toasted notes from ageing in barrels.

- 依修斯特等园法定产区酒 Échézeaux Grand Cru AOC
- 18～20℃
- 友人相聚，商务宴请 friends gathering, business dinner
- 牛扒，羊扒 beef steak, lamb
- 品尝此酒完全是一场味觉的享受盛宴：酒香馥郁，如同穿过古老的玫瑰园，浪漫典雅。A joy to drink such wine. It shows the full complexity of the exceptional Échézeaux vineyard.

力高宝德（石头园特等园）（红）
Nicolas Potel Clos de la Roche Grand Cru

¥¥¥¥

香味复杂，充满了浓郁的黑樱桃和黑加仑子以及矿物的气息。酒体幽雅细致，令人一再回味。Lovely complex nose, plenty of spicy black fruit. Mineral, supple and full attack of black cherries.

- 石头园特等园法定产区酒 Clos de la Roche Grand Cru AOC
- 18～20℃
- 酒友交流，友人相聚 wine appreciation, friends gathering
- 中至浓味菜肴 medium to heavy dishes
- 此酒产自石头园，一个位于夜丘内以出产优质贝露娃红酒而闻名的特等园。Clos de la Roche is a grand cru vineyard in the Côte de Nuits, well known for its Pinot Noir production.

力高宝德（圣丹尼特等园）（红）
Nicolas Potel Clos Saint-Denis Grand Cru

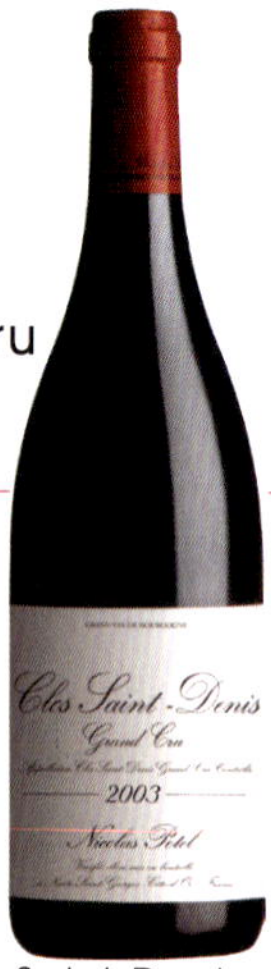

¥¥¥¥

此酒带有新鲜又复杂的黑樱桃、野草莓、丁香和优雅的烤可可豆味道。Fresh and complex nose of black cherries, spices (fine cloves) with elegant notes of roasted cacao beans.

- 圣丹尼特等园法定产区酒 Clos Saint-Denis Grand Cru AOC
- 18～20℃
- 友人相聚，商务宴请 friends gathering, business dinner
- 牛扒，烧鸭 beef steak, roast duck
- 此酒来自布根地赫赫有名的特等名园，红浆果果冻香气袭人，优雅中又带些许辛辣的野性。This wine comes from the famous Clos Saint-Denis Grand Cru AOC. Very fruity, a nuance of spice, and quite elegant.

拉图（布根地）庄园（红）
Ch. de La Tour Clos-Vougeot

深宝石红色的酒体尽显贝露娃葡萄的高贵和华丽，口感平衡雅致。The wines of Château de la Tour Clos Vougeot are balanced remarkable by their elegance and their deep ruby red colour which stems from the noblest variety: Pinot Noir.

- 华卓特等园法定产区酒 Clos Vougeot Grand Cru AOC
- 18～20℃
- 商务宴请，酒友交流 business dinner, wine appreciation
- 牛扒，羊扒 beef steak, lamb
- 酒香浓郁，让人感到悠然的花香扑鼻而来。如此佳酿岂能错过？The aroma is so concentrated and unforgetable, and the floral flavour is so strong on the nose. It's such a fine wine that you couldn't miss it.

小常识 Q & A

问：为什么同一个年份同一个酒庄出产的葡萄酒，在不同的时间喝会有不同的味道?

答：这个问题彰显了葡萄酒的复杂性。影响葡萄酒味道的因素有很多，其中最重要的一个是葡萄酒的发展。首先，葡萄酒是有生命的，酒在瓶子里会不断地变化，因此不同的时间饮用会感受到不同的风味；其次是喝酒时的温度，温度不同会影响葡萄酒的味道；再次是葡萄酒存放的地方，因为在不同地方存放的葡萄酒，对它们的发展是有影响的。因此，即便是同一年份同一酒庄的葡萄酒在同一时间喝，味道也有可能是不一样的。还有其他一些因素，如喝酒的环境、人物、配菜、心情等，都会对葡萄酒的味道产生影响。

莱宝酒园
Pierre Labet

由拉图（布根地）庄园主人François Labet建立，生产性价比极高的布根地好酒。

Share the same owner of Château de la Tour, Pierre Labet would be cared heartfully as well to have alike good quality wines.

莱宝酒园（布根地雪当利）（白）
Pierre Labet Bourgogne Chardonnay

¥¥¥

以有机方式种植出来的雪当利葡萄被打造成一款精致的美酒，带有丰满的矿物味道，酒香浓郁。Chardonnay from the organical winery was made in to a very delecate nice wine, with rich mineral taste on the nose and the aroma on the palate is so amazing.

- 布根地法定产区酒 Burgundy AOC
- 7～12℃
- 友人相聚，温馨家宴 friends gathering, family gathering
- 中至浓味海鲜 medium to heavy seafood
- 采用了出自有机葡萄田的雪当利，是一款物超所值的布根地白葡萄酒。Farmed organically, these are fabulous values from what is shaping up to be a fine vintage. Good minerality and plenty of stuffing.

莱宝酒园（布根地贝露娃）（红）
Pierre Labet Bourgogne Pinot Noir

¥¥¥

此酒拥有迷人的果香，如樱桃、洋李等，成熟后散发出复杂的巧克力、无花果和紫罗兰花香。The flavour of this Pinot Noir exhibits the simpler fruity characteristics of cherries, plums, raspberries, and strawberries.As being mature, it displays a variety of complex characteristics including chocolate, prunes, smokiness, truffles, and violets.

- 布根地法定产区酒 Burgundy AOC
- 14～17℃
- 商务宴请，友人相聚 business dinner, friends gathering
- 牛扒，羊扒 beef steak, lamb
- 莱宝酒园以极其优质的原料酿酒，务求酿造出适合任何场合享用的好酒。Made from that illustrious varietal which causes Burgundians to be envied by winegrowers throughout the entire world, this wine is perfectly suitable for all occasions.

菲利普

Philippe Leclerc

众多著名酒评家都对菲利普的酒极为推崇，并有人把它称为“布根地飞车党的酒”。而个性张扬的Leclerc先生更在酒塞上印上自己的模样，这也确实值得炫耀，因为他的酒品质确实优秀。Some wine critic once bantered, "Philippe Leclerc Burgundy's answer to a Hell's Angles gang member", and when you open one of his wine you find Mr. Leclerc printed on the cork-A winemaker who likes to show himself very much-but he can afford it, his wines mostly are excellent.

菲利普（吉菲香贝天一级园）（红）
Philippe Leclerc Gevrey-Chambertin 1er Cru les Champeaux

¥¥¥¥

此酒香气芬芳，尽显其精致的个性。既能在年轻时欣赏，随着岁月的积淀亦越发诱人。It is a wine that matures quite quickly, excellent for those who are impatient, and even better for those who will have been wise enough to wait. Several years are needed in order to appreciate its real value.

- 吉菲香贝天一级园法定产区酒 Gevrey-Chambertin 1er Cru les Champeaux AOC
- 18～20℃
- 酒友交流，友人相聚 wine appreciation, friends gathering
- 铁板类红肉 teppenyaki red meat
- 不仅在法国，菲利普的酒在美国亦有着很高的知名度，著名酒评家曾将其称为“布根地飞车党的酒”。Philippe Leclerc is principally known in the United States, surely also because Robert Parker has discussed his wines enthusiastically.

菲利普（吉菲香贝天）（红）
Philippe Leclerc Gevrey-Chambertin les Platières

¥¥¥

有浓烈的樱桃味道，还有来自甘草、麝香的诱惑，酒体丰满，酒质优秀。This is a wine that does not conceal its great finesse so far as its structure and aromas. Gevrey-Chambertin usually depicts an aromas of cherry, musk and licorice. Full-bodied, excellent quality thought just a Gevrey-Chambertin AOC.

- 吉菲香贝天法定产区酒 Gevrey-Chambertin les Platières AOC
- 14～17℃
- 温馨家宴，商务宴请 family gathering, business dinner
- 牛扒，烧鸭 beef steak, roast duck
- 除了酒质优秀，酒塞也很别具匠心，印着酒庄老板交叉双腿靠在葡萄榨汁机旁品酒的画面。When you open one of his ordinary Bourgogne you find Mr. Leclerc printed on the cork, leaning with crossed legs and a glass of wine in his hand against a wine press-a really cool guy.

哥德利安
Claude Chonion

哥德利安是布根地十大酒庄之一，它的园地和产品遍布几乎所有布根地最著名的法定产区。其产量大，品种丰富，且品质出众。
As one of the ten biggest Burgundian negocients, Claude Chonion has as many high classifications in Burgundy. A wide range of outstanding products can meet your various demand in taste.

哥德利安香贝天（红）
Claude Chonion Gevrey Chambertin

¥¥¥

有紫罗兰、鲜花、森林野果的香味，香气清新自然。散发着成熟的樱桃味以及一丝咖啡的清香，中度酒体，单宁平顺，后味清新干爽。This wine indicates ripen cheery, a hint of coffee. It is a medium body wine, smooth tannic and fresh in finish.

- 吉菲香贝天法定产区酒 Gevrey Chambertin AOC
- 14～17℃
- 友人相聚，情侣约会 friends gathering, dating
- 烤肉，熏肉 roast meat, bacon meat
- 此酒采用“御酒”产区香贝天邻居的葡萄酿造，想必也是一酒之下万酒之上了。Raw material from surrounding vineyards of Napoléon's favourite Chambertin, Claude Chonion molds it to be full of violet aromas, flower and wild fruit from forest, fresh and natural on the boquet.

哥德利安宝望庄（红）
Claude Chonion
Beaune 1er Cru

¥¥¥

有明显的花香及野果香，香气清新自然。中度酒体，酒体饱满而微带辛辣气息。Deliver fresh flower and fruit aroma. Medium body, powerful fruit favor with a hint of spicy.

- 宝望一级酒园法定产区酒 Beaune 1er Cru AOC
- 14～17℃
- 商务宴请，温馨家宴 business dinner, family gathering
- 牛扒，羊扒 beef steak, lamb
- 此酒来自布根地宝望丘之一级名庄，无论是品质还是声望皆属上品。This wine comes from the Beaune 1er Cru AOC, there is no doubt that it's quality and reputation are also high.

哥德利安普利雪（白）
Claude Chonion
Pouilly Fuissé

¥¥¥

此酒为高贵典雅的布根地白葡萄酒，香味和谐，有榛子和烤面包的香味，口感非常丰厚。The nature of the soil is conducive to the harmonious development of its fragrance, with a hint of hazelnuts and toasted almonds. A generous wine, full of flavour.

- 普利雪法定产区酒 Pouilly Fuissé AOC
- 7～12℃
- 情侣约会，商务宴请 dating, business dinner
- 中至浓味海鲜 medium to heavy seafood
- 布根地马岗区内Pouilly和Fuissé两条村并称为普利雪(Pouilly-Fuissé)，以出产高贵典雅的白酒而闻名。Pouilly and Fuissé are two distinct villages in the Mâconnais. A good white wine sold under the name of Pouilly Fuissé.

哥德利安雪比利（白）
Claude Chonion Chablis

¥¥¥

带有苹果、柠檬和白花香味，有时像浓郁的芝士。入口矿物味明显，酒体丰满。Apple scents, earthy note, a bit like ripe cheese. An obvious mineral taste and the body is quite rich.

- 雪比利法定产区酒 Chablis AOC
- 7～12℃
- 温馨家宴，友人相聚 family gathering, friends gathering
- 中至浓味海鲜 medium to heavy seafood
- 位于布根地的最北部，气候寒冷使得这里的雪当利葡萄酒口感清新爽脆，是最流行的布根地白酒。Showing lemon and floral noses and the lovely "stony" mineral and crisp, steely acidic structure that distinguishes Chablis by the extremely cold climate of northernmost Burgundy.

哥德利安风车（红）
Claude Chonion Moulin A Vent

￥￥

香气复杂优雅，有布根地的浆果香和一丝甘草香。酒体强劲而丰满，单宁结构扎实，伴有明显的浆果味道。Vinous complex aromas of Burgundy berry fruits with hint of liquorices. Heavy powerful round Beaujolais, generally with high tannin content, which marries well with deep fruit character especially raspberries.

- 风车法定产区酒 Moulin A Vent AOC
- 14～17℃
- 商务宴请，活力派对 business dinner, party
- 牛扒，羊扒 beef steak, lamb
- 此产区因其葡萄田中的风车而得名，其出品甚至被称作宝祖利村的酒王，知名度极高。It's name after the windmill that sits in the area's vineyards. Moulin-à-Vent is considered by many to be the best of the ten crus in Beaujolais region and is called the King of Beaujolais wines.

哥德利安宝祖利村（红）
Claude Chonion Beaujolais-Villages

￥￥

酒劲强烈，有新鲜的浆果和黑加仑子香味。圆润丰满，结构紧密，平衡好，果香丰盈。Very powerful with hints of raspberries and blackberries. Round and fat, firm, well balanced and deliciously fruity.

- 宝祖利村法定产区酒 Beaujolais AOC
- 14～17℃
- 商务宴请， 活力派对 business dinner, party
- 中至浓味菜肴 medium to heavy dishes
- 此酒是最流行的布根地葡萄酒，入口新鲜的典型宝祖利酒。It's one of the most popular Burgundy wine. Very characteristics of a Gamay wine.

哥德利安宝祖利新酒（红）
Claude Chonion Beaujolais Nouveau

￥￥

果香和花香十分突出。由于没有经过橡木桶培养，故拥有花果香醉人、入口新鲜的特点。Outstanding aroma of fruit and flowery.Excellent fruit and lovely flowery aroma, fresh palate because it do not ferment in the oak barrel at all.

- 宝祖利村法定产区酒 Beaujolais AOC
- 14～17℃
- 浪漫婚宴，友人相聚 wedding, friends gathering
- 牛扒，烧鸭 beef steak, roast duck
- 商家把每年11月第三个星期四冠以"宝祖利新酒节"，这款新酒从面世便受到热烈的欢迎。It is fermented for just a few weeks then officially released for sale on the third Thursday of November. The very short-time fermentation makes the wine particularly lightweight and fruity.

哥德利安马岗村（白）
Claude Chonion Mâcon-Villages Blanc

￥￥

充满果香和花香味，清新可人。口感清新，带有果香和矿物香。Full of fruit and flowery aroma, fresh and lovely.Easy to be appreciated. Fresh on the palate with fruit and mineral flavours.

- 马岗村法定产区酒 Mâcon-Villages AOC
- 14～17℃
- 情侣约会，温馨家宴 dating, family gathering
- 中至淡味海鲜 light to medium seafood
- 马岗村只产白酒，且现为布根地最大的白酒产地。价格实惠，可随时随意品尝。Only white wine in Mâcon-Villages. Nowadays, Mâcon is the largest producing area of white wine in Burgundy. It is typically an everyday wine, rather cheap and pleasant for everyday drinking.

Burgundy

隆河谷和朗克多—鲁西荣
Vale du Rhône & Languedoc-Roussillon

隆河谷 位于法国东南部，里昂（Lyan）和普罗旺斯（Provence）之间，这里是法国最早的葡萄酒产地，也是法国AOC制度的诞生地，目前是出口量仅次于波尔多的第二大产区。在法国出口的葡萄酒中，每4瓶就有1瓶是来自隆河谷。

这里整体气候较炎热，葡萄成熟度高，酿制的红葡萄酒仅经过短时间的橡木桶陈年，果香浓郁，略带辛辣，酒精浓度高，与川菜搭配效果非常不错。另外，隆河谷也生产白葡萄酒和粉红葡萄酒。隆河谷北部的主要AOC产区有丘隆河（Côtes du Rhône）、黄金坡（Côte Rôtie）和爱美迪（Hermitage），以穗乐仙葡萄酒为主；南部主要有新教皇城堡（Châteauneuf-du-Pape）和大福（Tavel），葡萄品种多样化，以调配型为主。

稀雅丝庄园
Ch. Rayas

独一无二的风土和四代传承的家族酿酒技术构筑了南法国的酒王集团。追求高品质，体现南法国美酒的独特个性是他们的经营理念。

The southern France wine king Château Rayas is created by unique terroir and passions of four-generation family. To make the wine with outstanding quality and express the terroir of southern France is the philosophy of the winery.

稀雅丝庄园（红）
Ch. Rayas
Châteauneuf-du-Pape Rouge

¥¥¥¥¥

富有香甜浓烈的荔枝味道，还有辛辣的胡椒味。酸度柔和，余韵适中，口感极好。Concentrated lichee aromas with some peppery flavours but elegant at the same time. A wonderful expression of the southern Rhône.

- 新教皇城堡法定产区酒 Châteauneuf-du-Pape AOC
- 18～20℃
- 商务宴请，酒友交流 business dinner, wine appreciation
- 扣辽参，鲍鱼 braised sea cucumber, abalone
- 被誉为法国南部的柏图斯。产量稀少，弥足珍贵。It's called the Southern Petrus in a limited production.

稀雅丝庄园（白）
Ch. Rayas
Châteauneuf-du-Pape Blanc

¥¥¥¥

富有桃子、芒果和甜瓜的气味。口感清爽，带有矿物、香料和核桃的余韵，留香持久。Creamy in texture, yet well-focused. Long, bright finish picks up hints of minerals, spice and peach pit.

- 新教皇城堡法定产区酒 Châteauneuf-du-Pape AOC
- 7～10℃
- 商务宴请，酒友交流 business dinner, wine appreciation
- 芝士焗龙虾 lobster with cheese sauce
- 新教皇城堡出产隆河谷地区最优质的葡萄酒，追求高品质，以歌海娜葡萄展现南法国美酒的独特个性。The most famous Côtes du Rhône wine displaying the unique southern Rhône character by such figure-flattering Grenache.

碧娜（新教皇城堡）（红）
Pignan Châteauneuf-du-Pape

¥¥¥¥

迷人的黑色樱桃与无花果的味道，口感香甜，中度酒体，富有深度和结实的单宁。Juicy, spicy and exotic, with enticing peppery lift. An elegant, tangy Châteauneuf with a silky texture and lovely inner-mouth energy. Finishes with very fine tannins.

- 新教皇城堡法定产区酒 Châteauneuf-du-Pape AOC
- 18～20℃
- 酒友交流，商务宴请 wine appreciation, business dinner
- 铁板类红肉 teppenyaki red meat
- 此酒是南法国酒王稀雅丝庄园的副牌酒，有稀雅丝的神韵。Second wine of Ch. Rayas to illustrate the temperament of southern Rhône wine king at a pleasant price.

芳莎丽庄园（红）
Ch. de Fonsalette Côtes du Rhône Syrah

¥¥¥¥

糅合着甜美的黑色水果、动物、烟熏和香料的香味。余味悠长而辛辣。Pure aromas of syrupy black fruits, game, smoke and spice. Finishes very long and peppery.

- 丘隆河法定产区酒 Côtes-du-Rhône AOC
- 18～20℃
- 友人相聚，酒友交流 friends gathering, wine appreciation
- 黑椒牛扒，烤肉，熏肉 black pepper steak, roast meat, bacon meat
- 与稀雅丝属同一老板的庄园，是隆河谷法定产区的精品酒。Owning by Ch. Rayas, this is a wonderful handpicked Syrah from the South.

芳莎丽庄园（白）
Ch. de Fonsalette Côtes du Rhône Blanc

¥¥¥

果香丰富，充满油桃和杏子的香气，入口感觉有矿物与桃子的韵味。It's mature, with nectarine and apricot notes followed by an edgy finish where hints of mineral and peach skitter underneath.

- 丘隆河法定产区酒 Côtes-du-Rhône AOC
- 7～10℃
- 情侣约会，浪漫婚宴 dating, wedding
- 芝士焗龙虾 lobster with cheese sauce
- 与稀雅丝属同一老板的庄园，是隆河谷法定产区的精品酒。This Côtes-du-Rhône AOC fine wine belongs to the owner of Ch. Rayas.

图尔斯庄园（华格士）（红）
Ch. des Tours Vacqueyras

¥¥¥

迷人的黑色樱桃味道突出，混合着山莓、黑醋栗与香料的气味，带有烟熏味和辛辣的成熟浆果香味。Spicy and exotic, with enticing peppery lift. Lots of ripe fruits. It is round and has moderate and soft tannins. A long and pleasant finish.

- 华格士法定产区酒 Vacqueyras AOC
- 18～20℃
- 酒友交流，友人相聚 wine appreciation, friends gathering
- 中至浓味菜肴 medium to heavy dishes
- 南法国酒王稀雅丝庄园旗下的一个附属品牌。歌海娜和穗乐仙的完美结合，是极具丘隆河特色的佳酿。Sub-brand of Ch. Rays. Consummate winemaking technique combines with Grenache and Syrah grapes to an accomplishment of typically regional character.

图尔斯庄园（丘隆河）（红）
Ch. des Tours Côtes-du-Rhône Rouge

¥¥¥

口感香甜，中度酒体，留香持久。Dense and silky, pure ripe fruit flavours, medium body, rich and long aftertaste.

- 丘隆河法定产区酒 Côtes-du-Rhône AOC
- 18～20℃
- 温馨家宴，友人相聚 family gathering, friends gathering
- 牛扒，烧鸭 beef steak, roast duck
- 南法国酒王稀雅丝的庄主艾玛努尔·海诺先生对附属品牌图尔斯同样爱护有加，让其酒质有目共睹。Care for Ch. des Tours series by owner of Ch. Rayas-Mr. Emmanuel Reynaud is obvious to guaranteened its superb quality.

图尔斯庄园（丘隆河）（白）
Ch. des Tours Côtes-du-Rhône Blanc

¥¥¥

入口感觉有矿物与桃子的韵味，口感丰富圆润，后味持久。Dry but rich, round in the mouth, hints of mineral and peach, long aftertaste.

- 丘隆河法定产区酒 Côtes-du-Rhône AOC
- 7～10℃
- 温馨家宴，浪漫婚宴 family gathering, wedding
- 白肉菜式 white meat dishes
- 南法国酒王稀雅丝庄园的附属品牌，品质极具保证。Brother of Southern wine king-Ch.Rayas, quality can be surely guaranteened.

威菲庄园
J. Vidal-Fleury

威菲酒业是一家历史悠久的酒厂，早在1781年就已经开始从事葡萄酒的酿造。其系列产量大，质量好，价格适中，说他是隆河谷里最好的酒厂，一点也不为过。

J.Vidal-Fleury is a well known and historic Rhône negociant, founded back in 1781. Wines of J. Vidal-Fleury are of good quality and high productivity at a preferential price.

威菲庄园黄金坡（红）
J. Vidal-Fleury Côte-Rôtie

¥¥¥¥

中度酒体。有红色水果、樱桃、黑加仑子、胡椒、孜然芹果的香味。酸度良好。Medium bodied. Red fruits, cherry, blackcurrant, spices (pepper, cumin). Very good acidity.

- 黄金坡法定产区酒 Côte-Rôtie AOC
- 18～20℃
- 商务宴请，酒友交流 business dinner, wine appreciation
- 黑椒牛扒，烤肉，熏肉 black pepper steak, roast meat, bacon meat
- 此地出产的葡萄酒成名于罗马帝国时期，而威菲庄园的黄金坡红葡萄酒更是盛名在外，曾于1787年在美国总统托马斯•杰弗逊访问法国时被选作其酒宴之用。Set up by the Romans, Côte-Rôtie is one of the oldest vineyards in France. This J. Vidal-Fleury one was even one of the state banquet wines in 1787, especially for President of America-Thomas Jefferson.

威菲庄园爱美迪（红）
J. Vidal-Fleury Hermitage

¥¥¥

有杨梅、黑加仑子、胡椒、孜然芹果的香气，余味更有动物性香。酒香浓郁悠长。Red plum, blackcurrant, spices (peppery, cumin), animal flavours on the finish. Good density and length.

爱美迪法定产区酒 Hermitage AOC

18～20℃

酒友交流，商务宴请 wine appreciation, business dinner

黑椒牛扒，烤肉，熏肉 black pepper steak, roast meat, bacon meat

17世纪时此产区的酒达到巅峰，在欧洲各皇室宫廷中的声望极高，尤其为俄国沙皇所挚爱。The first plantations date from the 10th century but it is under Louis the 17 that Hermitage obtains its credential letters. Hermitage was the favourite cru of the Tsar court in Russia.

威菲庄园新教皇城堡（红）
J. Vidal-Fleury Châteauneuf-du-Pape Rouge

¥¥¥

酒香复杂，带有黑色水果酱、黑醋栗、矮灌木、熏衣草和紫罗兰的香味。Black jam, blackberry, garrigue, lavender and violet touches.

新教皇城堡法定产区酒 Châteauneuf-du-Pape AOC

18～20℃

商务宴请，友人相聚 business dinner, friends gathering

禽鸟肉类菜肴 fowl

该葡萄园始建于12世纪，一直坚持以法定产区的法令法规为基准，严格控制其葡萄酒的优秀品质。The Popes used to have their summer residence there in Châteauneuf-du-Pape, then here came from such name! Wines are elaborated strictly with AOC rules.

威菲庄园爵士爱美迪（红）
J. Vidal-Fleury Crozes-Hermitage

¥¥¥

一入口即感单宁很新鲜，黑色水果的香甜和矿物的味道冲击着味蕾。余味丰满。It's straight and fresh tannin in the start, black fruit, mineral. Fatness in the finish.

爵士爱美迪法定产区酒 Crozes-Hermitage AOC

18～20℃

友人相聚，温馨家宴 friends gathering, family gathering

猪肉，禽类野味 pork, winged-game

爵士爱美迪的葡萄酒毫不逊色而且别树一帜，这里的酒比爱美迪产区的酒更具花香和果香，更重要的是价钱更实惠！Crozes-Hermitage wines are less robust then Hermitage. Nevertheless, they are very aromatic and fruity, still affordable and offers great value for your money and your palate.

威菲庄园（桃红）
J. Vidal-Fleury Tavel

此酒芳香浓郁，带有鲜花的芬芳与水果的香味，口感丰富，优雅而平衡。Extremely aromatic and fruity nose under a balanced structure.

- 大福法定产区酒 Tavel AOC
- 12～14℃
- 情侣约会，浪漫婚宴 dating, wedding
- 浓味鱼肉 fish with strong taste
- 最有名的法国玫瑰红葡萄酒，自文艺复兴时期已受到相当高的评价，曾被法王法兰索瓦一世（François 1）和路易十四所赞赏，也是众多伟人喜爱的佳酿。Tavel makes only rosé wines, which some believe are France's best. The rosé wines here have an international reputation ever since Renaissance.

威菲庄园丘隆河（红）
J. Vidal-Fleury Côtes du Rhône Rouge

有红浆果与香料的香韵，是一款端庄高雅的葡萄酒。The mouth reveals rounded tannins, a warm and full-bodied wine with an uncommon and lasting aromatic intensity.

- 丘隆河法定产区酒 Côtes-du-Rhône AOC
- 18～20℃
- 情侣约会，活力派对 dating, party
- 咖喱小羊肉，牛扒 lamb curry, beefsteak
- 此酒充分体现了丘隆河葡萄酒的优雅风格。It's a good proof that Côtes du Rhône can be a serious and elegant wine.

威菲庄园丘隆河（白）
J. Vidal-Fleury Côtes du Rhône Blanc

此酒带有非常浓郁的果香，散发着杏树与柑橘的味道。口感丰富圆润，后味持久，更带有一点蜂蜜的余韵。This J. Vidal Fleury one is dry but rich, round and powerful in the mouth, with lots of fruity flavours and a long sweet aftertaste.

- 丘隆河法定产区酒 Côtes-du-Rhône AOC
- 7～10℃
- 友人相聚，活力派对 friends gathering, party
- 小牛肉，鸡肉 veal, chicken
- 丘隆河区在2 000多年前还是罗马殖民地的时候已经以其极佳的葡萄酒而闻名。Since been Roman colony over 2,000 years ago, Côtes du Rhône was famous for its splendid wine.

威菲庄园伟道士（红）
J. Vidal-Fleury Ventoux

口感清新，中等至饱满的酒体，结构紧密，果味浓郁，且辛辣，余韵悠长。The mouth is fresh, structured, very fruity, peppery, and medium to full body with a rich and soft finish.

- 伟道士法定产区酒 Ventoux AOC
- 14～17℃
- 活力派对，友人相聚 party, friends gathering
- 鸡肉，禽类 fowl, chicken
- 伟道士因当地一闻名全国的伟道士山而得名，贫瘠的石灰石土质使得此地葡萄酒充满红色水果香气，容易欣赏且物值甚高。Mont Ventoux is one of the most famous mountains in France and the poor limestone soil of Côtes du Ventoux gives a fruity red wine, easy to drink and to appreciate. A good value wine.

朗克多—鲁西荣 位于法国南部从西班牙边界直到隆河三角洲之间的地中海沿岸，阳光充沛，葡萄酒年产量超过20亿瓶，是世界上最多产的葡萄酒产区。该产区以生产红葡萄酒为主，大部分为地区餐酒（VDP），口感较为厚实，十分适合日常饮用。此外，本产区也生产不错的甜酒，白葡萄酒则清爽而带有较突出的酸度。

雅奇侯爵堡（红）
Domaine de Baron'Arques

¥¥¥

酒色紫红，散发红色水果、咖啡、可可、雪茄的香气，中至厚度酒体，口感圆润，单宁结实，后味带有咖啡和莓果的香气。Purple color, opening aromas of red fruit, coffee, cocoa and cigar. A, mid full bodied wine with a round palate and firmed and fine tannin, bringing a long coffee and berry fruit finish.

利摩法定产区酒 Limoux AOC

18 ~ 20° C

商务宴请，酒友交流 business dinner, wine appreciation

野味，牛肉类，芝士 rich game, beef dishes, cheese platter

此酒由波尔多一级名庄武当王集团主理，位于法国南部的密内瓦生产朗克多区内顶级的红酒。The wine is made by Baron Philippe de Rothschild S.A. Minervois produces some of the best red wines in France's Languedoc-Roussilon region.

小常识 Q & A

问：喝不完的葡萄酒一般能放多久？

答：我们由于各种原因有时无法将打开的葡萄酒一次性饮用完毕。事实上，葡萄酒和其他新鲜蔬果、肉类食物一样，在常温下很快就会腐坏。如果将它们贮藏在冰箱或低温的环境里面，可延长腐坏的时间；不过至于保鲜，可能就没那么乐观了。所以喝不完的葡萄酒，假如贮藏于家用的冰箱，我们建议，一般的白葡萄酒24 ~ 36小时内应该喝完，红葡萄酒可维持约72小时。另外，放置葡萄酒时记得要直立瓶身，这样可以减少酒与氧气的接触面。

香槟区

Champagne

香槟区 是世界上最出名的起泡酒产区，只有按照法国政府有关法令规定，用香槟区的葡萄、按照传统工艺酿造的起泡葡萄酒，才有权称为香槟。香槟区位于法国北部，同时受大西洋海洋气候和大陆性气候的影响，年平均气温不超过10.5℃（这是保证葡萄成熟的最低气温），其土壤是独特的白垩土质，因此该区的葡萄单宁含量低，酸度恰到好处，最适合用来酿制优雅细致的香槟。

香槟因为采用独特的二次瓶中发酵法进行酿造而成就了细腻优雅的气泡，这生生不息的气泡也成了人们在庆典时刻或浪漫求爱的点缀。饮用香槟成为世界富豪和时尚人士们的一种习惯，从而构成欧美对香槟的巨大需求。世界各大奢侈品集团纷纷在香槟区购置庄园，而传统的酿酒家族也不断地推陈出新，令香槟永远都紧贴时代脉搏。

比较著名的香槟有卡地亚世家（Cattier）酿造的奢侈品香槟黑桃A（Champagne Armand de Brignac），不但荣获2009年世界头号香槟的称号，也是美国嘻哈音乐教父JAY-Z的挚爱香槟。而以品质著称的历史最悠久的香槟酒园菲丽宝娜（Philipponnat）被多家米其林三星餐厅选为店酒。香槟品牌与时尚元素结合的例子比比皆是。

{葡萄品种}

香槟的法定葡萄品种有3种：红葡萄贝露娃、贝露曼尼雅和白葡萄雪当利。3种葡萄各具特色，贝露娃为酒液提供骨架，贝露曼尼雅提供水果芳香，雪当利提供优雅酸度。

{香槟分类}

香槟是调配型的起泡酒，根据调配酒液的年份来源，可分为记年（Vintage）与不记年（Non-Vintage）两种，以不记年香槟较为常见。

（1）记年香槟：以单一年份的葡萄酿制，只在最好的年份生产。

（2）不记年香槟：以两个或两个以上年份的酒液混合，以单一年份的酒液为主体。

根据酿造工艺划分：

（1）白葡萄香槟（Blanc de Blancs）：用白葡萄酿制。

（2）红葡萄香槟（Blanc de Noirs）：用2个红葡萄品种或其中之一进行酿制。

（3）粉红香槟（Rosé）：一是用红葡萄酿制，在榨汁前进行短暂的浸皮得到红色素；一是在调配好的基酒（Cuvée）里加入一定比例的红葡萄酒，以获得颜色。

（4）优选香槟（Cuvée de Prestige）：用最好的酒液进行调配，是该香槟园质量顶级的系列。

根据含糖量划分：

类 型	含糖量（克/升）
不甜（Brut Nature/Zero Dosage）	0～2
超天然（Extra Brut）	0～6
天然（Brut）	0～15
特干（Extra Dry）	12～20
干（Sec）	17～35
半干（Demi Sec）	33～50
甜（Doux）	50以上

黑桃A

Armand de Brignac

2009年黑桃A香槟荣获香槟盲品大赛桂冠，成为世界头号香槟。由古老的香槟世家Cattier打造，是法国皇室的象征。它是世界上唯一一款纯人手制作的香槟，而且经由香槟区最深的地下酒窖陈年，由家传密法酿造而成。因品质超卓、外形精美而成为世界上最名贵的香槟，深受众多名人追捧。

In 2009 Champagne Armand de Brignac is rated No.1 Champagne amongst over 1,000 Champagnes in a blind tasting. It is created by the leading Champagne Cattier family and it owns the symbol of French monarchy. It is the world's only entirely handmade luxury Cuvée. Every bottle is matured in the deepest cellar in Champagne areas and made by a secret recipe. The shining golden bottles and the essense inside attacted lots of celebrities, making it the most expensive and famous Champange universally.

黑桃A白金香槟

Champagne Armand de Brignac
Blanc de Blancs

¥¥¥¥¥

淡雅清幽的香气，让你如同沐浴在清晨的花园中一般。再细闻更能发现有新鲜水果的香甜气息。雪当利香槟的特性发挥至极致，给味蕾十足的奢华享受。Bouquet is light and clear, with youthful fruit notes and floral accents. It's a genuine expression of the soul of the Chardonnay fruit and a true experience of luxury.

4～7℃

浪漫婚宴，商务宴请 wedding, business dinner

肉类，水果 meat, fruit

众多酒评家眼中的五星级香槟。有酒评家称："该款香槟，让人回想起20世纪八九十年代，还未被大公司染指的、未商业化的纯正香槟。" Five Star Champagne in the eyes of critics. Critics praised it as a ture art, reminding people the non-business Champange in the good old days.

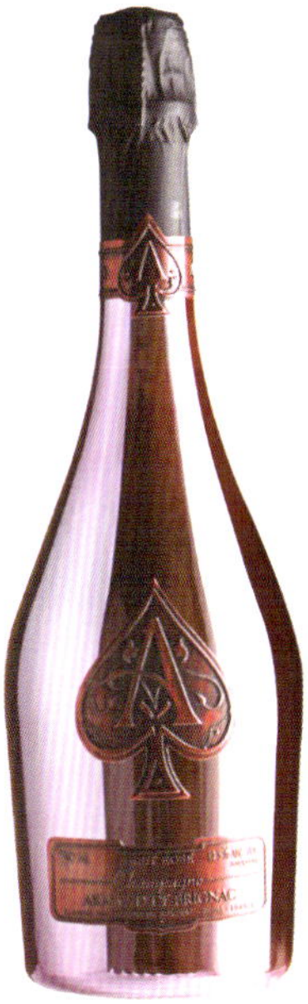

黑桃A粉金香槟
Champagne Armand de Brignac Brut Rosé

¥¥¥¥¥

口感新鲜圆润，充满草莓和黑醋栗的味道，清新醉人！余味悠长，入口丝滑。The Champagne is fresh and full-bodied on the palate with aromas of fresh strawberries and blackcurrant and Armand de Brignac's characteristic long, silky finish.

4～7℃

浪漫婚宴，商务宴请 wedding, business dinner

鱼肉，禽肉，上等蓝纹奶酪，果汁甜点 fish, poultry, blue cheese, fruity desserts

代表着粉红香槟的最高标准！夹杂着草莓和烟熏的丰满酒体，无论餐前、餐中和餐后饮用都是美妙体验。A highest level rosé Champagne. Beautiful salmon-hued wine with a rich, pure bouquet of red fruits up front and delicately smoky grilled notes behind. You could enjoy it before, during or after the meal.

黑桃A黄金香槟
Champagne Armand de Brignac Brut

¥¥¥¥¥

口感美妙之至，新鲜活泼的水果气息流淌于整个口腔之中，偶尔有奶油蛋卷的香甜作“调味”，令人一饮难忘。Has a sumptuous, racy fruit character that is perfectly integrated with the wine's subtle brioche accents.

4～7℃

浪漫婚宴，活力派对 wedding, party

龙虾，鸡肉 lobster, chicken

黑桃A的旗舰香槟，也是在盲品大赛中，一举夺魁的冠军酒。年产量只有5 000瓶。酒质如奶油般柔滑，口感复杂，后味良久，不可多得。The flagship Cuvée of Armand de Brignac. Also the winner in the blind-tasting. The production is only 5,000 bottles annually. Creamy texture with great depth and a long, silky finish.

菲丽宝娜
Philipponnat

作为世界上历史最悠久的香槟酒庄，菲丽宝娜自1522年起一直以他们传统的酿造工艺向世人诠释着香槟之美。
Champagne Philipponnat is the oldest Champagne house in the world and it has been keeping an enduring tradition since 1522 to commit excellent quality.

菲丽宝娜歌雪园香槟
Champagne Philipponnat Clos des Goisses

¥¥¥¥

混合了浓烈的烤咖啡豆、可可豆和若有若无的烤木香味。入口辛香，回味无穷。Powerful, complex aromas of toasted coffee bean, cocoa bean and toast with light woody hints. Surprising persistence on the palate.

- 4～7℃
- 商务宴请，酒友交流 business dinner, wine appreciation
- 龙虾，鸡肉 lobster, chicken
- 歌雪园优异的地理位置极优！酒液经酒窖陈放9年后才上市，入口辛香，充满活力。At the heart of Mareuil, Clos des Goisses is unique. It is a truly outstanding Champagne of both extreme intensity and minerality after 9 years aging in cellar.

菲丽宝娜白葡萄香槟
Champagne Philipponnat Grand Blanc

￥￥￥￥

混合了酒香与花香，还有精细的香茅气味。入口平衡优雅，后味持久而余韵悠长。Subtle citronella aromas, floral scents, and vinous notes. Elegant balance between power and finesse, good attack with long finish.

4～7℃

浪漫婚宴，商务宴请 wedding, business dinner

扇贝，龙虾 scallops, lobster

这款白葡萄香槟仅于最佳年份时酿造，顶级的酒质是毋庸置疑的。This Grand Blanc only made in the best vintage years and is a noteworthy exception in the otherwise Pinot Noir dominated range of Philipponnat wines.

菲丽宝娜甜魅香槟
Champagne Philipponnat Sublime Réserve

￥￥￥￥

有甜美的香梨、桃子味道，还有若隐若现的香料风味。雪当利赋予此酒蜜糖和奶油的优雅风味，且精致无比。Candied aromas of pears and peaches, hints of soft spices. Honeyed and buttery with the elegance and freshness of Chardonnay.

7～10℃

情侣约会，浪漫婚宴 dating, wedding

鹅肝，禽类 foie gras, poultry

甜魅香槟比干性香槟更适合和美食搭配。Specially created for gastronomical occasions when Brut Champagne proves too dry.

菲丽宝娜粉红香槟
Champagne Philipponna Réserve Rosée

￥￥￥

气泡持久，带有山莓和野生樱桃等红浆果的香味。酒体醇和平衡，玫瑰红色的光泽更添其高雅精致。Red fruits like raspberries and wild cherries with fine mousse. The white border enhances the exquisite delicacy of its rosy hue.

7～10℃

情侣约会，浪漫婚宴 dating, wedding

开胃酒，甜品 aperitif, dessert

酒液的光泽犹如她脸上那抹淡淡的红晕，娇羞又可爱。加上浓郁的果香便更让人讨喜，尤其为女士所爱。True to the tradition of style at the House of Philipponnat where taste takes precedence over the colour.

菲丽宝娜皇家珍藏香槟
Champagne Philipponnat Royale Réserve

￥￥￥

浓郁的酸橙味与红醋栗和黑莓的水果味道，口感平滑，结构良好，十分精致。Fruity with red currants and black berries, smooth, well-structured. A consistent composition, it is all freshness with a fruitiness of great delicacy.

7～10℃

活力派对，友人相聚 party, friends gathering

白肉菜肴，冷盘 white meat, cold cuts

新鲜的口感和优雅的酒质，传承了菲丽宝娜卓著的酿酒技艺。The Royale Réserve is the emblematic blend of the House of Philipponnat, combining freshness and vinosity.

法国起泡酒
French Sparkling Wine

法国起泡酒 无论是在喧哗热闹的欢庆聚会还是二人浪漫的烛光晚餐，都是您最好的选择。它容易欣赏的口感，丰富而清新的果香和不断升起的气泡，能马上营造出热烈而浪漫的气氛；其近乎百搭的特性，更能创造出与无限美食的完美搭配。

哥德利安粉红起泡葡萄酒
Claude Chonion Rosé Brut

¥ ¥

呈浪漫的浅玫瑰红色，伴有持续、轻快的气泡。带有新鲜的桃子香和花香，口感圆润。A light rose red colour with fine, lively bubbles. A nose of fresh fruit. Supple in the mouth with peach and flowery aromas.

- 7～12℃
- 浪漫婚宴，活力派对 wedding, party
- 清淡的红肉，白肉 light red, white meat
- 这是一款性价比超高的法国粉红玫瑰起泡酒，带有桃子香及花香。Extremely good for value.

哥德利安干白起泡葡萄酒
Claude Chonion Blanc de Blancs Brut

¥ ¥

浅黄中带点绿色，起着轻快的气泡。入口干爽，带苹果香。Yellow in colour, with greenish tints and lively bubbles. Dry on the palate with apple flavour.

7～10℃

活力派对，友人相聚 party, friends gathering

餐前开胃酒，椒盐虾 aperitif, pepper-salt shrimp

价廉物美的法国干型起泡酒，是开胃酒的不二之选。Aperitif, Pepper-salt shrimp. A really good appetizer.

哥德利安半干白起泡葡萄酒
Claude Chonion Blanc de Blancs Demi-Sec

¥ ¥

诱人的水果香味，口感稍甜。Lively bubbles. Slightly sweet on the palate with plenty of fruit flavours.

7～10℃

活力派对，浪漫婚宴 party, wedding

餐前开胃酒 aperitif

物超所值的法国半干白起泡葡萄酒。Good value with a guaranteed quality.

法国优良餐酒

Vin de France

法国优良餐酒 是朋友聚会或家庭聚餐的不二之选，这些酒价格平易近人，品质可靠，容易欣赏，有令人愉悦的果香和简单明了的口感，在入口的第一秒就能博得你的欢心。可与多种菜肴搭配，十分适合与亲朋好友一起开怀畅饮。

哥德利安古堡（红）
Claude Chonion Cabernet Sauvignon

¥

有多种果香，香气雅致。有新鲜浆果的香味，略带橡木和烟草香。Delicate noses with various fruity flavours. On the palate, the wine tastes of fresh berries with slight flavours of oak and tobacco.

- 法国优良餐酒 Vin de France
- 14～17℃
- 活力派对，温馨家宴 party, family gathering
- 烧鸡，烧鹅 fried chicken, roast goose
- 此款酒是非常优质的餐酒。It is a premium table wine.

花悦（红）
Lafleur Gloria Rouge

淡淡的烟草清香，气味宜人。酒体柔顺，带有樱桃的果味和橡木味。Delicious, rounded, soft wine possessing light cherry fruits, beautifully balanced oak and a lovely structure.

法国优良餐酒 Vin de France

14～17℃

情侣约会，活力派对 dating, party

烧鹅，乳鸽 roast goose, pigeon

是情侣小酌的极佳选择。Excellent choice for lovers no matter by its low price and good taste.

花悦（白）
Lafleur Gloria Blanc

淡淡的果香，气味宜人，酒体柔顺。Fruity nose with savoury aromas and a rounded, soft wine with fruit flavours

法国优良餐酒 Vin de France

7～10℃

温馨家宴，活力派对 family gathering, party

餐前开胃酒，椒盐虾 aperitif, pepper-salt shrimp

配食容易，且易饮易明。Match the white meat in a great way.

花悦古堡（红）
Les Héritiers Lafleur-Gloria Rouge

淡淡的烟草清香，气味宜人。酒体柔顺，带有樱桃的果味和橡木味。Delicious, rounded, soft wine possessing light cherry fruits, beautifully balanced oak and a lovely structure.

法国优良餐酒 Vin de France

14～17℃

情侣约会，活力派对 dating, party

烧鹅，乳鸽 roast goose, pigeon

是情侣小酌的极佳选择。Excellent choice for lovers no matter by its low price and good taste.

花悦古堡（白）
Les Héritiers Lafleur-Gloria Blanc

淡淡的果香，气味宜人，酒体柔顺。Fruity nose with savoury aromas and a rounded, soft wine with fruit flavours.

法国优良餐酒 Vin de France

7～10℃

温馨家宴，活力派对 family gathering, party

餐前开胃酒，椒盐虾 aperitif, pepper-salt shrimp

配食容易，且易饮易明。Match the white meat in a great way.

干邑区
Cognac

干邑区 位于法国西南部的夏朗德省（Charente），濒临大西洋，紧靠波尔多北部。这里无疑是世界上最好的白兰地产区，早在1909年法国政府就明文规定，只有产自干邑区、按照规定工艺酿制的白兰地才能称为“干邑”。这种对原产地的尊重，就像只有香槟区的起泡酒才能叫做“香槟”是一样的。

目前，人们最熟悉的干邑品牌当属人头马（Remy Martin）、轩尼诗（Hennessy）、拿破仑（Napoleon）和马爹利（Martell）。除了这四大品牌之外，轩尼诗和人头马等顶级干邑品牌的原酒供应商迪狮龙（Tesseron）也是备受关注的干邑品牌——世界上唯一一款被著名酒评家罗拔•派克评为100分的干邑品牌。

干邑是一种考验酿酒师调配功力的饮品，其原液被法国人称为“生命之水”（eaux-de-vie）。酿酒师使用的“生命之水”一般来自不同年份，因此干邑的酒标上一般不会标示年份。顶级干邑则要用到年份远久的“生命之水”，这原液是用少见少，而且不可再生。出于人们对“生命之水”稀缺性的宠爱，市面上顶级干邑的身价一直不菲，只升不跌。

{葡萄品种}

用于酿制干邑的葡萄原料需具有非常高的酸度，酒精度较低，介于8%～10%最佳。目前，法国允许采用的葡萄有7种，但干邑区的人们只采用白玉霓、白福尔和哥伦巴这3种白葡萄品种，其中以白玉霓为主。

白福尔 Folle Blanche

白玉霓 Ugni Blanc

哥伦巴 Colombard

{分级制度}

根据法国国家干邑酒行业管理局（Bureau National Interprofessionnel du Cognac，缩写为BNIC）的规定，干邑可以分为3个级别，如右图所示。

在X.O.的基础上，一些顶级干邑品牌会将一些酒龄更长的干邑划分为Paridis和Extreme级别。Paridis是用超过30年的“生命之水”来进行调配，而Extreme则用超过50年的“生命之水”。如人头马的路易十三、轩尼诗的李察、迪狮龙的传世典藏都是属于Extreme级别，用的是100年前的“生命之水”进行调配。

Extra Old，简称X.O.

用于调配最年轻的“生命之水”，在橡木桶陈年至少6年，平均年份一般都超过20年。

▲

Very Special Old Pale，简称VSOP

用于调配最年轻的“生命之水”，在橡木桶陈年至少4年。

▲

Very Special，简称VS

用于调配最年轻的“生命之水”，在橡木桶陈年至少2年。

迪狮龙
Tesseron

迪狮龙家族是法国显赫的酿酒世家，除了拥有顶级干邑，还拥有波尔多列级名庄宝德加纳庄园。家族历史超过100年，现由第三代人掌管。在品牌创建之初，是轩尼诗、人头马等顶级干邑的原酒供应商。家族拥有干邑区顶级的葡萄田，旗下所有产品均为X.O.等级；也同时拥有干邑区最古老的源自11世纪的地窖，是干邑区最后一批用濒临灭绝的贵族葡萄品种酿酒的酒庄。其干邑是世界上唯一一款被美国酒评家罗拔·派克评为100分的干邑品牌。

Tesseron family is a noted wine family that owns prestigious Château Pontet-Canet as well, a Pauillac classified growth in 1855. The century-old family is steered by the third generation now. It was the leading supplier to all majoy Cognac brands before creating its own brand. It's propertis are in the finest district of the Cognac region, its 11st century cellar is the oldest in Cognac. It is the one of the last winery to make Cognac from the endangered grape varieties. Tesseron is the only full-mark Cognac by Robert Parker in the world.

迪狮龙传世典藏干邑白兰地
Cognac Tesseron Extreme

¥¥¥¥¥

口腔中感觉到它的成熟、平衡，层次精彩，余味带有辛辣和坚果的气息，持续良久。Good depth on the palate, mature with a good balance, and a lot of complex flavours, nutty, spicy and very long finish.

X.O.

18～20℃

酒友交流，商务宴请 wine appreciation, business dinner

鲍鱼 abalone

这是家族三代人最古老的典藏。该款干邑透露出一种几欲失传的绝响的味道，创始人在世时亲自挑选出88坛家族的最优珍藏，将这些白兰地调配得浑然一体。One of those well kept secrets that only a few insiders ever have the opportunity of sharing. 88 of the finest "eaux-de-vie" from the brand's best "Grande Champagne" reserves have been drawn by the founder to mix this "Extreme".

迪狮龙百年珍藏X.O.干邑白兰地
Cognac Tesseron
Lot No.100 X.O. Paradis

¥¥¥¥¥

酒香持久，在口中久久不散。余味是浓郁的果酱味道。Complex palate with great length rich marmalade aftertaste.

X.O.

18～20℃

酒友交流，商务宴请 wine appreciation, business dinner

鲍鱼 abalone

蕴含了族人心目中最完美的100款白兰地的原液，它穿越时光被第三代传人装瓶。目前家族只剩下200瓶百年珍藏XO，因此市场上非常难觅得它的身影。饮之如同香气大观园，勾起对岁月的遐想。This was blended from 100 perfect reserves by the founder Mr. Abel Tesseron and bottled by the third generation. There are only 200 bottles left in the family, rare enough! The Cognac tastes like a puzzle in the palate. A true ageless art.

迪狮龙29至尊X.O.干邑白兰地
Cognac Tesseron
Lot No.29 X.O. Exception

¥¥¥¥¥

优雅的口感，浓烈的摩卡咖啡、可可豆和花朵的味道平衡得恰到好处。Elegant and endless with strong notes of mocha and cocoa, then floral notes extremely well balanced.

X.O.

18～20℃

酒友交流，商务宴请 wine appreciation, business dinner

鹅肝 foie gras

世界上唯一一款被权威酒评家罗拔·派克评为满分的干邑。The only full-mark Cognac rated by Robert Parker.

迪狮龙53完美X.O.干邑白兰地
Cognac Tesseron
Lot No.53 X.O. Perfection

¥¥¥¥¥

入口温顺柔滑不失活泼，有胡椒香料、巧克力、玉米的甜美和新鲜药草香味；酒香悠长，感觉纯净。A very gourmet Cognac tender but full of vivacity, peppers and spices then chocolate and fresh herbs, very good length on the palate, lovely smooth feeling exquisite Grande Champagne.

X.O.

18～20℃

酒友交流，商务宴请 wine appreciation, business dinner

菌类菜肴 fungus dishes

被权威酒评家评为98分。Its mark rates 98/100 by well-known critic.

迪狮龙65激情X.O.干邑白兰地
Cognac Tesseron
Lot No.65 X.O. Emotion

¥ ¥ ¥ ¥ ¥

气息交错复杂，微妙优雅，带着榛子、红糖、烟草、奶油杏仁糖、黑巧克力的香气。Very nice complexity on the nose, quiet light and elegant, yet it is profound with layers of aromas, hazelnuts, brown sugar, tobacco, nougat, dark chocolate and cedar wood.

X.O.

18 ~ 20℃

活力派对，商务宴请 party, business dinner

鲍鱼，龙虾 abalone, langouste

由1965年前后全来自一级产区大香槟区的酒液混合而成，2007年度最佳侍酒师安德烈斯·拉颂对该酒赞誉有加。A blend of 1960s "eaux-de-vie" which are all from Grande Champagne with applause even from Andreas Larsson-Best Sommelier of the World 2007.

迪狮龙76经典X.O.干邑白兰地
Cognac Tesseron
Lot No.76 X.O. Tradition

¥ ¥ ¥ ¥

核心气息是糖渍、蜂蜜混合着野性的皮革，而花香的融入使得整款酒优雅起来。口感辛辣热情，不失圆润。Exhibits a wealth of sugar, leather, almond and candied fruit aromas. This carries on magnificently through to the palate, with rich, delicate flavours of flowers.

X.O.

18 ~ 20℃

酒友交流，商务宴请 wine appreciation, business dinner

鲍鱼，龙虾 abalone, langouste

以1976年产的白兰地，混合了20世纪70年代的酒液而成。是权威杂志《葡萄酒爱好者》极力推荐的酒品。An exceptional blend of reserve stocks of 1970s of Grande Champagne Cognac, matured to perfection in old casks. A recommendation from *Wine Lover* magazine.

迪狮龙90卓越X.O.干邑白兰地
Cognac Tesseron
Lot No.90 X.O. Selection

¥ ¥ ¥ ¥

色泽金黄，风格亲切活泼，有着草药、坚果和果脯的味道。Very fresh pear and quince notes on attack, give way to herbaceous elements, dried fruits and nuts, fresh, with intriguing hints of almond.

X.O.

18 ~ 20℃

活力派对，友人相聚 party, friends gathering

鲍鱼，龙虾 abalone, langouste

由20世纪90年代的酒液混合调配而成的，是初尝干邑的人士的最佳选择，是年轻而卓越的干邑的典范。Typical of famous young cognacs, great quality of distillation being made from the blend of 1990s.

Cognac

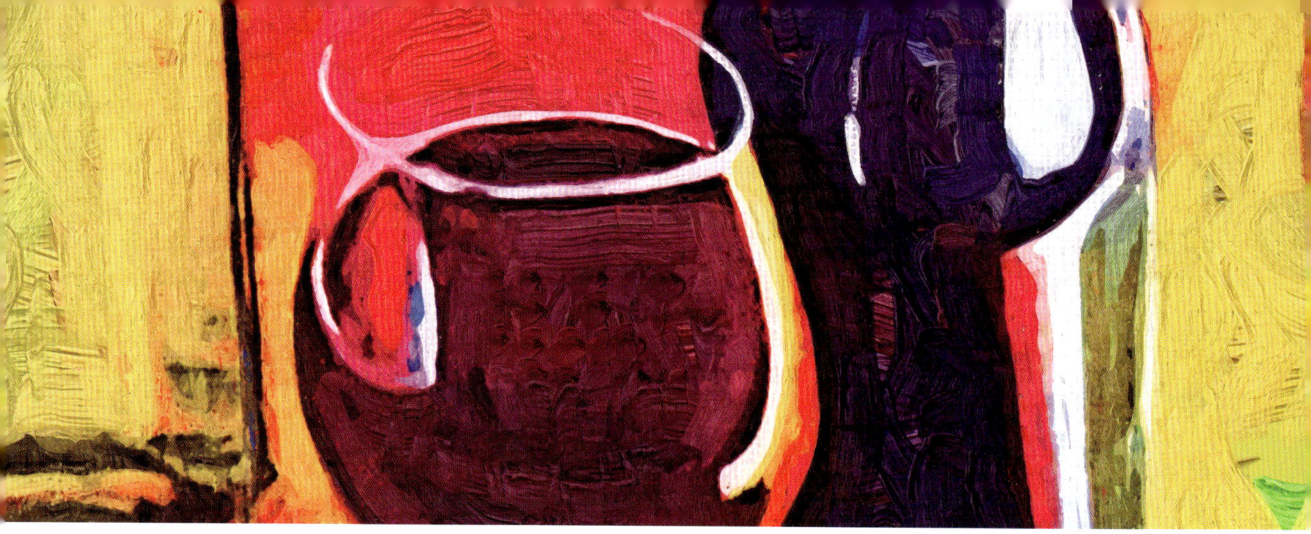

意大利

ITALY

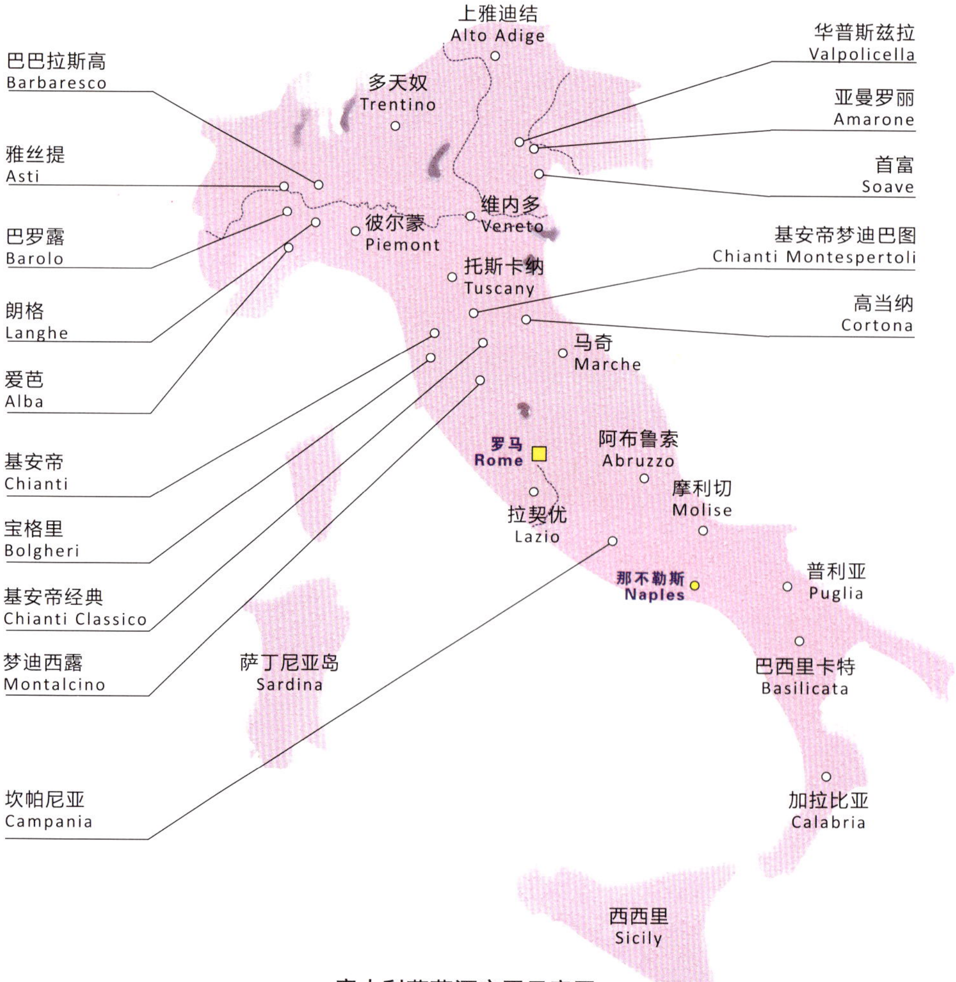

意大利葡萄酒产区示意图

意大利 拥有4 000多年的葡萄酒生产历史，是世界上最古老的葡萄酒产国之一。在很久以前，希腊人就已经在这片土地上种植葡萄，酿制美酒。在酿酒业发达的罗马帝国时代，规模化的葡萄种植和先进的酿酒与窖藏技术更是令这里的葡萄酒获得极高的赞誉。今天，意大利是世界上葡萄酒产量最大的国家，出产约全世界1/5的葡萄酒，人均葡萄酒饮用量也领先全世界。

意大利位于地中海地区，国土版图形似靴子，海岸线蜿蜒绵长，全国80%的土地是山峰和丘陵。由于地形变化较大，各地气候不同，加上葡萄品种繁多，意大利拥有许多风味不同、性格独特的葡萄酒。全国共有20个葡萄酒产区，主要的产区可分为四大区域：西北部、东北部、中部以及南部。

{葡萄品种}

据意大利农业局统计，意大利有超过350种法定葡萄品种，另外还有超过500种其他品种。近年来，酿酒师为了给葡萄酒增加与众不同的地域风味，挖掘出许多罕见的古老葡萄品种。常见的红葡萄品种包括圣祖维斯、纳比奥罗、巴比拉、多姿桃和梦特普西露；白葡萄品种包括扎比安奴、蜜思佳桃和灰贝露。

纳比奥罗 Nebbiolo

巴比拉 Babera

圣祖维斯 Sangiovese

多姿桃 Dolcetto

蜜思佳桃 Moscato

灰贝露 Pinot Grigio

{分级制度}

参照法国，意大利从1963年开始制定分级制度，到1966年正式实施，最初只有DOC和VDT两个等级，1980年增加了DOCG，在1992年又增加了IGT。等级由高到低如右图所示。

因为意大利的葡萄酒分级制度非常捍卫本土的葡萄品种，导致其分级制度相对法国比较暧昧，大家无法直接从等级上判断酒的质量和售价。1971年，未采用本土葡萄品种却被奉为新派“意大利酒王”的西施佳雅（Sassicaia）横空出世，当时仅能打上IGT等级。后因声誉日隆，1994年受当局“邀请”才打上DOC等级，再次证明了饮用意大利美酒，不必拘泥于其等级和出身。这也正是意大利葡萄酒引人入胜的一面。

高级法定产区酒
Denominazione di Origine Controllata e Garantita，简称DOCG

▲

法定产区酒
Denominazione di Origine Controllata，简称DOC

▲

地区餐酒
Indicazione Geografica Tipica，简称IGT

▲

日常餐酒
Vino da Tavola，简称VDT

{葡萄酒产区}

全国拥有20个产酒区，主要的葡萄酒产区分为四大区域：西北部、东北部、中部以及南部。

西北部的彼尔蒙（Piemont），囊括了人称“葡萄酒之王”的巴罗露（Barolo）和“葡萄酒王子”的巴巴拉斯高（Barbaresco）产区，以出产极具陈年天赋的纳比奥罗红酒著称。

东北部包括了多天奴—上雅迪结（Trentino－Alto Adige）和出产宝雪歌起泡酒（Prosecco）的维内多（Veneto）。

中部有以圣祖维斯葡萄为主的托斯卡纳（Tuscany），还有以红葡萄品种梦特普西露和白葡萄品种扎比安奴为主的阿布鲁索（Abruzzo）。

南部主要是西西里（Sicily），以气候炎热出产个性十足的葡萄酒。

彼尔蒙
Piemont

马佳连妮
Marcarini

一个酒性非常柔和的巴罗露名庄，位于巴罗露三大名村之一的拉梦罗村中。历经数个世纪的经营，坚持传统的酿酒工艺，带出最为地道的意大利佳酿风味，品质与波尔多列级名庄相似。

Situated in La Morra, one of famous villages in Barolo of Italy, Marcarini has been in wine business for centuries. Thanks to the traditional wine making process, their wines are full of local flavours, and feature as Bordeaux Grand Cru wines, especially for the varietals Barolo and Dolcetto.

马佳连妮（巴罗露）（红）
Marcarini Barolo Brunate

¥¥¥

口味复杂，单宁、酸度平衡感好，入口如天鹅绒般柔滑，余韵持久，陈年天赋可达40年甚至更长。This majestic wine fully reveals its complexity. Velvety, round and remarkable persistence. Ageing life can be 40 years or even more.

- 巴罗露优质法定产区酒 Barolo DOCG
- 18～22℃
- 温馨家宴，活力派对，浪漫婚宴 family gathering, party, wedding
- 意式香肠，烟熏肉类，披萨 salami and italian sausage, smoked meat, pizza
- 此酒是马佳连妮最具代表性的产品，产自意大利最早成名的优质法定产区。One of the most authentic Marcarini wines, produced from Italy's oldest DOCG appellation.

马佳连妮（巴比拉）（红）
Marcarini Barbera D'Alba

¥ ¥

香味丰富可人，酒体浑厚，单宁平衡柔滑，有陈年潜力。Pleasant rich aroma. Full-bodied, with smooth and balanced tannin. Potential for further ageing.

- 爱芭法定产区酒 Alba DOC
- 14～18℃
- 友人相聚，温馨家宴，活力派对 friends gathering, family gathering, party
- 小牛肉，小牛肝，羊腰 calf, veal liver, lamb kidneys
- 最受彼尔蒙地区当地人喜爱的红酒。One of the most popular red wines among Piemont's local people.

马佳连妮（多姿桃）（红）
Marcarini Dolcetto D'Alba

¥ ¥

呈深宝石红色，带紫罗兰光泽。酒香持久，有辛香和桂皮味；口感圆滑，带有一定酸度。Dark ruby color, with a violet highlight. The wine offers a persistent, peppery aroma, round on palate, with refreshing acidity.

- 爱芭法定产区酒 Alba DOC
- 14～18℃
- 友人相聚，温馨家宴，商务宴请 friends gathering, family gathering, business dinner
- 番茄肉酱的意大利面，浓味芝士，炖菜 pastas with red and meat sauce, strong cheeses, stews
- 彼尔蒙地区葡萄特色品种多姿桃的果味特性的完美体现。A perfect reflection of the fruity charm of Dolcetto varietal, which originates in the Piedmont region.

马佳连妮（雅丝提）（白）
Marcarini Moscato D'Asti

¥ ¥

呈浅金黄色，单宁柔和香浓，充满苹果、蜂蜜的水果香味。Pale gold in color. Intense aroma of fruits. Soft tannin with mouthwatering hints of apple, honey.

- 雅丝提优质法定产区酒 Asti DOCG
- 5～7℃
- 情侣约会，友人相聚，活力派对 dating, friends gathering, party
- 提拉米苏，法式芝士蛋糕，法式薄煎饼 Tiramisu, french cheese cake, french crepe suzette
- 浓郁热带水果气息伴随优雅小气泡升起，充满浪漫气质，颇受女士欢迎。Romantic bubbles rise up elegantly with rich tropical fruits aroma. This wine is particularly popular among ladies.

赛拉图
Ceretto

有意大利“巴罗露酒王”之称的赛拉图沿用传统的本土酿酒方法，经历了三代人的用心经营，有着70多年的历史，致力酿制出传统的佳酿，是意大利彼尔蒙酒的顶尖品牌。
The history of the Ceretto brand has all of this: three generations whose mission for more than seventy years has been excellence in wine, ambassador of Piedmont and Italy throughout the world.

百宝石头园（巴罗露）（红）
Barolo Bricco Rocche Prapo

深红色中略带砖红；成熟草莓、雪松的气息和花香明显；单宁结实，陈年天赋上佳。Deep red with a touch of brick. On nose there are clear ripened cherry, cedar and floral aroma. Solid tannin. Great ageing potential.

巴罗露优质法定产区酒 Barolo DOCG

18～22℃

浪漫婚宴，商务宴请，酒友交流 wedding, business dinner, wine appreciation

乳鸽配橄榄，白松露焗饭 pigeon with olives, white truffles risotto

反映出典型巴罗露酒的高超酿酒艺术和贵族气质，非常地道。It reflects the most typical style of Barolo wine's virtuosity and aristocracy. Very authentic.

碧高石头园（巴罗露）（红）
Barolo Bricco Rocche

丰富的花香味中藏有香料、巧克力和太妃糖的味道，酒体复杂而优雅，口感平衡，有宜人的甜美黑樱桃果味。Ethereal spices, chocolate and truffle in intense flowery aromas. On palate is a complicated, elegant and well-balanced body.

巴罗露优质法定产区酒 Barolo DOCG

14～18℃

友人相聚，浪漫婚宴，酒友交流 friends gathering, wedding, wine appreciation

烤野味，牛肉，牛扒，肉类炖菜 roast game, beef, beef steak, meaty stews

赛拉图的旗舰酒款，入选世界稀世珍酿，年产量仅7 000瓶。Named as "The Rarest Valuable Wine in the World", it has small annual production of just 7,000 bottles.

雅仙妮（巴巴拉斯高）（红）
Barbaresco Bricco Asili

¥¥¥¥

香味清甜而略带烟熏木头气息，温和的草药味混入成熟的果味之中，口感轻柔干爽。Sweet, smoky wood on the nose with some nice, gentle herbal undertones accenting the ripe fruit tones with its caressing, dry taste.

- 巴巴拉斯高优质法定产区酒 Babaresco DOCG
- 14～18℃
- 友人相聚，浪漫婚宴，酒友交流 friends gathering, wedding, wine appreciation
- 辛辣的意式肉类菜肴，蘑菇焗饭，陈年帕尔马芝士 spicy italian meats, mushroom risotto, well-aged parmesan cheese.
- 该款酒是巴巴拉斯高产区的经典代表作，典雅中显出柔美，口味更复杂，不像巴罗露酒那般强劲。A classic Barbaresco wine. Not as strong as Barolo wines, its elegance and mellowness are accompanied with complexity.

赛拉图（梦索多）（红）
Ceretto Monsordo

¥¥¥

深宝石红色中带微石榴红光泽，香味浓郁丰富，酒体结构饱满，单宁甜美柔滑，有陈年潜力。Deep ruby red, with slight garnet undertones. Rich, variformed nose. An opulent structure shows immediately on the mouth, with soft, sweet tannins that leave no doubts to its long life.

- 朗格法定产区酒 Langhe DOC
- 18～22℃
- 情侣约会，温馨家宴，商务宴请 dating, family gathering, business dinner
- 意大利面，焗饭类菜肴，轻度烹调的红肉或白肉 pastas, risotto, half-seasoned red meat or white meat
- 主要采用国际葡萄品种混合酿制而成，被誉为意式波尔多，收入日本著名漫画《神之水滴》。Made mainly with international varietals, Monsordo is an Italian fine wine in Bordeaux style. Featured in Japanese manga comics series *The Drops of God*.

赛拉图（布朗格）（白）
Ceretto
Langhe Arneis Blange

￥￥￥

果味十分突出，雪梨和苹果气息明显，发酵过程中保留的少量CO_2增强了果味与果香，酸度较低。A characteristically fruity nose, with pear and apple highlights. Its fragrance and flavour are further enhanced by the small quantity of CO_2 .

朗格法定产区酒 Langhe DOC

14～18℃

情侣约会，温馨家宴，活力派对 dating, family gathering, party

鱼类开胃菜 fish appetizers

用意大利特色白品种阿内斯酿制，带有独特的梨子、苹果的果香。Made of Arneis, a native Italian varietal.

赛拉图（多姿桃）（红）
Ceretto Dolcetto D'Alba

￥￥￥

呈宝石红色，有精致的花香与水果气息。口感干爽，单宁紧密，略带杏仁味，非常有层次。Ruby red, with a delicately vinous nose packed with flowery and fruity sensations. Its dry taste is highlighted by a slight almond streak.

爱芭法定产区酒 Alba DOC

14～18℃

友人相聚，温馨家宴，活力派对 friends gathering, family gathering, party

牛扒，烧烤红肉或白肉，各种地中海菜式 beef steak, grilled red meat or white meat, mediterranean food

由有“巴罗露酒王”之称的赛拉图选取著名优质产区所产多姿桃葡萄酿制的精品之作，极易配餐。Produced by "King of Barolo wine" with Dolcetto grape from a well-known DOCG region.

赛拉图（雅丝提）（白）
Ceretto Moscato D'Asti

￥￥￥

丰富的热带水果甜香，可圈可点的气泡，老少咸宜的口感，是热闹聚会的首选。Intensely fruity nose which is aromatic and very persistent. The sweet flavour is beautifully balanced with the low alcohol and the acidity.

雅丝提优质法定产区酒 Asti DOCG

5～7℃

友人相聚，温馨家宴，活力派对 friends gathering, family gathering, party

慕斯，芝士蛋糕 mousse, cheese cake

酒瓶设计独特，品味高雅，麝香葡萄的特殊香气令人愉悦，气泡更添浪漫气氛。Its very original bottle design embodies an ethereal taste of wine. The moscato grape and the lovely bubbles offer even more romantic and pleasant feel.

小常识
Q & A

问：没有专用冰桶，用冰箱冰镇葡萄酒是不是会降低酒的质量呢？

答：如果将葡萄酒长期存放在冰箱内，会使葡萄酒瓶塞干燥萎缩，所以不太好，但若是冰凉后马上饮用，就没有问题了。还要注意：别将红葡萄酒和芳香浓郁、酒体丰满的白葡萄酒等在过低温度下冰镇，以避免减低其香味和风味。葡萄酒冰桶，是可以感觉更专业、更正式，而且可以避免将葡萄酒在过低温度下冰镇，所以不妨准备一个吧！使用冰桶冰镇葡萄酒时，品尝中请留意在不同温度下的葡萄酒，风味都不一样喔！

内华城堡
Castello Di Neive

拥有5个世纪历史的意大利巴巴拉斯高名庄，传统与创新并重，精心酿制，屡获殊荣。

Mixing innovation with tradition of five centuries, Castello Di Neive has devoted scrupulously to their nectar no matter from presses, fermentation to bottling, contributing to the winery's successes as a producer of world class, award-winning wines of Barbaresco.

内华城堡山度园珍藏（红）
Castello Di Neive Santo Stefano Riserva

¥ ¥ ¥

有新鲜浆果、烟草气息，略带辛辣。酒体中度，单宁紧实，后味爽脆。
Fresh and slightly lean but some good berry, tobacco and light spice character. Medium-bodied, with firm tannins and a crisp finish.

- 巴巴拉斯高优质法定产区酒 Barbaresco DOCG
- 14～18℃
- 友人相聚，活力派对，商务宴请 friends gathering, party, business dinner
- 中至浓味菜肴，如黑椒牛扒、烤肉、熏肉等 medium to heavy dishes, such as black pepper steak, roast meat or bacon meat
- 该酒庄的顶级酒，葡萄精选自园内风土条件最好的田地，经层层筛选后严格按传统工艺酿制。As the top wine of the winery, this wine is made with top-quality grapes from the best fields in the vineyard after careful selection and traditional winemaking process.

内华城堡山度园（红）
Castello Di Neive Santo Stefano Barbaresco

¥¥¥

香味复杂，有草莓、雪松气息与淡淡的花香。中度酒体，单宁细腻。Strawberry, cedar and light floral character. Medium-bodied, with fine tannins and a long finish. Lovely refined wine.

- 巴巴拉斯高优质法定产区酒 Barbaresco DOCG
- 14～18℃
- 友人相聚，活力派对，商务宴请 friends gathering, party, business dinner
- 红肉，野味 red meat, game
- 每支内华城堡山度园都会在3 500升的大型橡木桶陈酿超过两年以上，因而拥有惊人的复杂层次。This wine is aged in large 3,500L oak for more than 24 months to obtain an impressive complexity.

内华城堡巴巴拉斯高（红）
Castello Di Neive Barbaresco

¥¥¥

巴巴拉斯高产区的入门级酒，有新鲜水果、皮革和花的香味。It displays a typical style of Barbaresco, bright color and featuring exuberant aromas of fresh fruits, leather and delicate flowers.

- 巴巴拉斯高优质法定产区酒 Barbaresco DOCG
- 14～18℃
- 友人相聚，温馨家宴，活力派对 friends gathering, family gathering, party
- 意大利面，烧烤牛肋排，菲力牛柳 pastas, grilled beef rib, beef fillet
- 领略传统意大利葡萄酒的入门首选。A best choice for beginners to experience the charm of traditional Italian wines.

内华城堡雅丝提（白）
Castello Di Neive Moscato D'Asti

¥¥

富有苹果和水蜜桃的香气，入口甜美清新，平衡度好。A traditional sparkling sweet white in Asti, with apple, juice peach nose and fresh, good balance in mouth.

- 雅丝提优质法定产区酒 Asti DOCG
- 5～7℃
- 情侣约会，温馨家宴，活力派对 dating, family gathering, party
- 海鲜，白肉 seafood, white meat
- 非常有特色的意大利微起泡葡萄酒，出自优质法定产区。A delightful Italian white wine with fruity aroma and lovely fine bubbles from the famous Asti DOCG.

多天奴和高里奥
Trention & Collio

胜利侯爵堡
San Leonardo

两个世纪的用心经营，Guerrieri Gonzaga家族在他们的酿酒事业上，以其一丝不苟的态度，遵循土壤的特点，并由酿酒师赋予其独特个性，使得胜利侯爵堡名气超卓，被誉为意大利东北部的西施佳雅，是不可多得的超级名庄。

Devoting scrupulous attention to every detail, the Guerrieri Gonzaga family is committed to an identical quest for quality. Like the wine producers of Bordeaux, the family strives to create wines that directly reflect the territory and the personality of the maker.

胜利侯爵堡（红）
San Leonardo

¥¥¥¥

风味独特，入口丰富而温和，酒香浓郁，混合着胡椒味和香草味，非常值得一试。Intense ruby red with garnet highlights. A wine of remarkable intensity on the nose. The palate is full, warm and impressively rounded, with intense aromatics that linger on the palate.

- 多天奴地区餐酒 Trentino IGT
- 18～22℃
- 商务宴请，酒友交流 business dinner, wine appreciation
- 黑椒牛扒，烤肉，熏肉 black pepper steak, roast meat, bacon meat
- 舍弃传统意大利葡萄品种而选取波尔多经典葡萄品种，该区域的独特风土造就出非同寻常的精品佳酿。Instead of adopting traditional Italian varietals this premium wine is made of classic Bordeaux grapes, characterized by unique local natural conditions.

胜利庄园（红）
Villa Gresti

¥¥¥

除了平衡柔滑的口感外，还增添了烟草、香草和可可粉的香味。Intense ruby red in color, it has a broad, pervasive nose with lingering notes of tobacco and hints of vanilla and cocoa powder.

- 多天奴地区餐酒 Trentino IGT
- 18～22℃
- 活力派对，商务宴请 party, business dinner
- 牛扒，羊扒 beef steak, lamb
- 大比例使用梅乐的调配，颇有波尔多右岸酒的风骨。Its blending features large percentage of Merlot, rendering a magnificent style similar to the produce from Bordeaux's right bank.

歌塔希
Cortaccia

以优质葡萄为原料，尊重土地环境所赋予葡萄酒的天然风味，再利用现代科技酿酒——Kellerei Kurtatsch将此酿酒理念贯穿至终，以致他们的酒品质上乘，深受人们的欢迎。

With a combination of traditional and modern processing techniques, through skill and devotion, constant research and the use of high-quality grapes, Kellerei Kurtatsch is able to produce precious and unique wines of superior quality.

歌塔希翠美纳（白）
Cortaccia Brenntal Gewurztraminer

¥¥¥

呈淡黄色，充满浓郁荔枝香，酒体丰满，成熟水果的味道在酒体中显得非常浓郁典雅，容易欣赏。Pale yellow in color. Intense lichee aroma. Full-bodied with ripe fruit hints. Highly drinkable.

上雅迪结法定产区酒
Alto Adige DOC

8～10℃

情侣约会，温馨家宴，活力派对 dating, family gathering, party

咖喱牛肉，烧烤猪排或野味，焖或烧烤牡蛎 beef with curry, barbecue pork ribs or game, poached or grilled oysters

此酒为该庄园三系列中最高级的白葡萄酒，只在最好的年份酿造，数量稀少，获奖无数。It is one of white wines in the premium line. Only the best vintages are used in the production. Its exceptional quality has won the estate numerous awards in Italy and abroad.

歌塔希白贝露（白）
Cortaccia WeiBburgunder Pinot Bianco

¥¥

十分容易欣赏，新鲜爽脆的口感又有苹果的香气，偶尔带有香料的辛香味道。Extremely drinkable and typical in its characteristics. Fresh, yeasty, appley aroma, sometimes with hints of spice.

上雅迪结法定产区酒
Alto Adige DOC

10～12℃

情侣约会，温馨家宴，活力派对 dating, family gathering, party

淡酱汁海鲜，白肉，淡味芝士 seafood with lite sausage, white meat, mild cheese

容易欣赏，充满意大利葡萄酒的特色，性价比高。A typical Italian white wine. Approachable, with excellent value for its price.

歌塔希白沙威浓（白）
Cortaccia Sauvignon Blanc

¥¥

有热带水果与接骨木的香气。口感清新爽脆，酸度怡人而平衡，带有矿物味的口感。Aroma of tropical fruits and elder. On palate it's fresh and mineral with vivacious acidity and fine structure.

上雅迪结法定产区酒
Alto Adige DOC

10～12℃

友人相聚，温馨家宴，活力派对 friends gathering, family gathering, party

奶油酱汁的肉类，淡味芝士，炖菜 meat with cream sauce, mild cheeses, stews

完美体现出白沙威浓葡萄的干爽、清新与酸度，容易配餐。This wine has fully expressed the dryness, acidity and refreshing character of Sauvignon Blanc. Very easy for food pairing.

维内多、多天奴、托斯卡纳和西西里
Veneto, Trention, Tuscany & Sicily

嘉迪堡
Ca' del Bosco

嘉迪堡——玛格丽集团最高端子品牌，历年来都是弗兰哥达地区生产优质起泡葡萄酒的领军酒庄。玛格丽集团对葡萄酒的热忱、纯熟的酿酒技术和独特的管理方式，令嘉迪堡当之无愧地成为意大利葡萄酒业中的一颗闪耀的明星。
As the top brand of Santa Margherita, Ca'del Bosco has always been the leading producer of refined and delicately sparkling wines that bear the name of the zone in which they are produced, Franciacorta.

嘉迪堡至尊起泡葡萄酒
Ca' del Bosco Cuvée Anna maria Clementi

¥¥¥¥

充满杏、桃和苹果的香气以及花香，带有香草和橡木味的果脯气息。优雅、平衡、细腻，酸度恰到妙处，香气味悠长。Rich, complex scents of apricot, peach and apple, flowers, then a pleasant scent of vanilla and oak. It marries structure and elegance, complexity and finesse, depth and grace. Perfect acidity with prolonged aroma.

- 弗兰哥达优质法定产区酒 Franciacorta DOCG
- 7℃
- 浪漫婚宴，商务宴请 wedding, business dinner
- 白肉，鱼肉，意大利面 white meat, fish, pastas
- 严格采取与经典香槟相同的葡萄品种和工艺，仅在最佳年份生产。发酵时间在7年以上。Made with the same varietals and crafts that contribute to classic champagne.

嘉迪堡珍藏起泡葡萄酒
Ca' del Bosco Cuvée Prestige

¥¥¥

口感复杂精致，结构平衡而优雅。水果、鲜花和香草的味道激活了整个味觉。后味是令人愉悦的香草和橡木的气息。It marries structure and elegance, complexity and finesse, depth and grace. Underlined by a pleasant scent of vanilla and oak.

- 弗兰哥达优质法定产区酒 Franciacorta DOCG
- 4～7℃
- 情侣约会，商务宴请 dating, business dinner
- 白肉，鱼肉，意大利面 white meat, fish, pastas
- 这款经典的弗兰哥达起泡酒适用于任何场合，从佳节晚宴到欢闹派对都可开怀畅饮。This classic Franciacorta sparkling wine is versatile for all occasions.

嘉迪堡粉红珍藏起泡葡萄酒
Ca' del Bosco Cuvée Prestige Rosè

¥¥¥

带有精致的红色水果香气。同时拥有白葡萄酒的曼妙香气与红葡萄酒的果感与骨架。Delicate fragrance of red fruits. It has the fragrance and delicacy of a white wine combined with the structure and fruit of a red wine.

- 弗兰哥达优质法定产区酒 Franciacorta DOCG
- 7℃
- 情侣约会，活力派对，浪漫婚宴 dating, party, wedding
- 白肉，鱼肉，意大利面，蓝纹芝士，鹅肝酱 white meat, fish, pastas, blue cheeses, foie gras
- 独具浪漫风情，适合重大庆典与浪漫场合。Ideal for momentous occasions, especially the most romantic ones.

嘉迪堡特别珍藏（红）
Ca' del Bosco Maurizio Zanella

¥¥¥

酒香中包含着新鲜苹果、梨和葡萄、橙子、柚子、菠萝和猕猴桃等水果香气。单宁有质感，后味持久。Fresh, rich and fragrant with notes of apple, pear and grape, as well as orange, grapefruit, pineapple and kiwi. The tannins are firm and round.

- 塞比诺地区餐酒 Sebino IGT
- 10～12℃
- 友人相聚，浪漫婚宴，酒友交流 friends gathering, wedding, wine appreciation
- 烟熏肉类，香肠 salami and Italian sausage, smoked meat
- 以庄园创始人名字命名的精品红酒，是嘉迪堡庄园红酒“最高水准之集大成者”。Named after the winery's founder, this fine wine embodies the highest red wine standard.

嘉迪堡加文拿（红）
Ca' del Bosco Carmenero

¥¥¥

充满浓郁复杂、有力且温暖的蓝莓果酱的味道。单宁紧密而结实，口感平衡且非常持久。Concentrated, complex and powerful nose. The palate is dry, intense, solid and incredibly persistent. The tannins are good and very well balanced.

- 弗兰哥达日常餐酒 Franciacorta VDT
- 12～14℃
- 友人相聚，酒友交流 friends gathering, wine appreciation
- 佛罗伦萨肉排，披萨 bistecca alla Fiorentina, pizza
- 加文拿葡萄引入意大利时曾被误为嘉本纳弗朗，酒标图案为披着羊皮的狼，即代表伪装下酒的卓越品质。The wolf on the label reflects the outstanding strength under disguise of this wine, as the Carmenere grape was mistaken for Cabernet Franc when being first introduced into Italy.

嘉迪堡贝露娃（红）
Ca' del Bosco Pinero

¥¥¥¥

丰满、细腻、柔和的特质都展现出少见的优雅。口感极致柔滑，有成熟水果的后味。It shows originality with well-combined richness, finesse and smoothness, matched with rare elegance. Extremely smooth to the taste, it leaves a lingering ripe fruit impression.

- 塞比诺地区餐酒 Sebino IGT
- 14～17℃
- 浪漫婚宴，酒友交流 wedding, wine appreciation
- 焗烤金枪鱼，三文鱼，禽类，猪肉 grilled tuna, salmon, poultry, pork
- 嘉迪堡于1983年起挑战贝露娃红葡萄酒的酿造巅峰，在国际葡萄酒盲品大赛中多次击败布根地名庄。Ca' del Bosco started its production of Pinot Noir red wine in 1983 and has defeated renowned Burgundy wineries in various international blind-tasting competitions.

玛格丽
Santa Margherita

玛格丽生产优质的新派意大利葡萄酒已超过半个世纪，其创新的酿酒哲学，时至今日还被人津津乐道。他们认为土壤决定葡萄的个性，所以会在不同的土壤种植与之相适应的品种。正因为对土壤特性的严格划分，这些表现优秀的单一葡萄品种足以成就一瓶美酒，展现不同的风味个性，不需要过多的修饰，有的只是纯粹和自然。

Santa Margherita has been producing modern, premium wines for over half a century. Its sensational new concept, which remains extremely topical even today, was that of producing a single varietal wine from a restricted production area that yields very specific characteristics.

玛格丽（灰贝露）（白）
Santa Margherita Pinot Grigio

¥¥

酒色呈明亮的稻草黄，芳香馥郁而清新，口感干爽，带有苹果等水果的复杂香气。This dry white wine has a straw yellow color. Its clean, intense aroma and bone dry taste make Santa Margherita's Pinot Grigio a wine of great personality and versatility.

- 瓦达迪杰法定产区酒 Valdadige DOC
- 12～14℃
- 情侣约会，活力派对 dating, party
- 海鲜，鱼类 seafood, fish
- 该酒是意大利灰贝露葡萄酒中的上佳之作，也是玛格丽酒庄在1961年的成名之作。It represents the top-of-the-line standard of Italian Pinot Gris wines. The winery earned its early fame with this wine in 1961.

玛格丽起泡葡萄酒
Santa Margherita Prosecco Brut 52

¥ ¥

酒体充满活力而不失优雅，复杂的果香和清爽的口感，令你在餐桌上食欲大增。A sparkling wine that is youthful and fresh, yet at the same time elegant and complex. It is well-structured, rounded and mouth-filling, with nice acidity and tanginess.

- 宝雪歌优质法定产区酒 Prosecco DOCG
- 4～7℃
- 情侣约会，活力派对 dating, party
- 慕斯，提拉米苏，芝士蛋糕 mousse, Tiramisu,cheese cake
- 酒标上的“52”是为了纪念酒庄1952年开始酿造汽酒，该款酒也成为酒庄经典的汽酒。The "52" on the label marks the year of 1952 when the winery began producing sparkling wine.

玛格丽（梅乐）（红）
Santa Margherita Merlot

¥ ¥

酒体饱满，单宁丝滑，带有成熟樱桃和洋李的香气，更有橡木桶赋予的香草味。Its bouquet is broad and persistent, with hints of ripe cherries and plums against a background of vanilla and violets, well-balanced, velvety and full-bodied.

- 维内多地区餐酒 Veneto IGT
- 14～17℃
- 友人相聚，温馨家宴 friends gathering, family gathering
- 浓郁酱汁烹调的肉类菜式 meat dishes with rich sauces
- 特色鲜明的梅乐葡萄酒，口感活跃。A distinctive Merlot wine among other Italian wines. Very active on palate.

玛格丽（圣祖维斯）（红）
Santa Margherita Sangiovese

¥ ¥

有明显的野浆果、黑樱桃的气味，果香浓郁，口感典雅，值得一试。It is clean and precise on the nose, with hints of morello cherries and wild berries, as well as a delicate spiciness. These sensations are echoed in a persistent manner on the palate.

- 蜜莲玛托斯卡纳地区餐酒 Maremma Tuscany IGT
- 14～17℃
- 友人相聚，活力派对 friends gathering, party
- 鸡肉，红肉，鱼，羊扒，猪肉，意大利面 chicken, red meat, fish, lamb, pork, pastas
- 新式的圣祖维斯葡萄酒，用最为现代的工艺，赋予传统葡萄品种另一番的风情。A stylish Sangiovese wine, hybrid of modern winemaking technology and Italy's traditional varietal.

蝶舞园

Lamole di Lamole

一个地道的意大利酒品牌。庄园至今保留着1480年所建的古堡，用其悠久的历史和丰富的文化底蕴，将基安帝经典产区标志性的葡萄品种——圣祖维斯，演绎出最为自然的风味。

Excellence, a quality of nature. Situated in the commune of Greve in Chianti, Lamole di Lamole Estate is a place that is rich in atmosphere and history. On this very spot stood the Castle, mentioned in documents of 1480. The estate try to bring out the full potential of the terroir and of the vintage.

蝶舞园珍藏（红）
Lamole di Lamole Riserva Chianti Classico

¥¥¥

有甜美的木香以及鸢尾草和香料的芬芳。单宁结构紧实，风味诱人，有很好的陈年潜质。On the nose, the initial sweetish woody sensations make way for the elegant perfumes that are typical of Chianti Classico, like hints of iris and spicy tones. On the palate, the tannic austerity of Sangiovese is truly traditional, and this is accompanied by the warm, savoury notes of a wine destined for long aging.

基安帝经典优质法定产区酒 Chianti Classico DOCG

14～17℃

情侣约会，友人相聚 dating, friends gathering

肉类菜肴，番茄肉酱意大利面，牛百叶 meat-based dishes, tomato and meat sauce pastas, tripe

此酒最能体现出酒庄对当地悠久酿酒传统的传承。This is the wine that mostly forms the winery's bond with the local heritage.

蝶舞园（红）
Lamole di Lamole Chianti Classico

¥¥

呈明亮的宝石红色，野生浆果的香气伴随微微樱桃和香料的气息。酒体饱满而复杂，橡木味明显。Its color is a bright, deep ruby red. Rich, precise nuances of wild berries, spices and cherries, along with a light hint of well-integrated oak.

基安帝经典优质法定产区酒 Chianti Classico DOCG

14～17℃

情侣约会，活力派对 dating, party

传统托斯卡纳美食，烤红肉 traditional Tuscany food, grilled red meat

历史悠久的庄园佳酿，以传统工艺充分展现出圣祖维斯葡萄品种的干爽与酸度。A fine product from the time-honored estate, this wine is made with traditional winemaking crafts to fully express the dryness and acidity of Sangiovese.

小常识
Q & A

问：为什么一些意大利酒瓶上会有粉红色的飘带？

答：有些意大利的酒瓶脖子上会有一些带颜色的飘带。其实这些飘带代表了这款意大利酒的级别。如果飘带是粉红色或粉绿色，表示这瓶酒是一瓶DOCG级别的高级法定产区酒，粉红色代表红葡萄酒，粉绿色代表白葡萄酒。如果飘带是黄色，表示这是一瓶DOC级别的法定产区酒。飘带上会带有一些序列号，表明该酒是经过官方认证的符合该等级标准的一个认证。所以消费者在选购葡萄酒的时候，如果对产区不太了解，可以直接通过这些简单的标志来选到高品质的意大利酒。一般情况下，带着粉红色飘带的意大利酒都是高品质美酒的象征。

丹凤园

Torresella

丹凤园是维内多产区经典美酒的代名词，只选该区内传统的白葡萄和红葡萄品种，糅合新旧世界的酿酒工艺，酿造出最为平衡的本土风味佳酿。旗下美酒更选用不同濒临绝种的珍稀鸟类作为酒标图案，提醒人们好酒源于好的土壤和气候，跟珍稀鸟类一样都需要大家的爱护。

Torresella has its headquarters in the heart of the Eastern Veneto. The company offers an excellent example of how typical grape and wine characteristics can go hand in hand with the most up-to-date technology. Every label on Cantine Torresalla is the images of birds that are rare or which belong to species that are in danger of extinction, offers further confirmation of Torresella's intimate attachment to its terroir.

丹凤园（粉红）
Torresella Pinot Grigio Rose

¥ ¥

果香型的粉红葡萄酒，带有柑橘、覆盆子、白桃等水果的气息，口感新鲜爽脆，余味悠长。This "copper" colored wine displays the variety's characteristic citrus-like notes, as well as suggestions of raspberries and white peaches that are also confirmed on the palate. The finish is long, intriguingly refreshing and unexpectedly rounded.

- 维内多地区餐酒 Veneto IGT
- 12～14℃
- 情侣约会，温馨家宴 dating, family gathering
- 鱼类，海鲜 fish, seafood
- 漂亮的色泽、清新易欣赏的口感，获得众多女士的青睐。Very popular among ladies with its graceful color and refreshing, easy-going taste.

丹凤园起泡葡萄酒
Torresella Prosecco Brut

¥ ¥

晶莹剔透的酒液不断有微小的气泡缓缓上升，果香四溢，酒体轻盈精致。This typical sparkling wine from the Veneto is fresh and delicately aromatic, exquisitely balanced and decidedly delicious.

- 宝雪歌法定产区酒 Prosecco DOC
- 4～7℃
- 情侣约会，浪漫婚宴 dating, wedding
- 海鲜，白肉做成的简单菜肴 seafood, white meat dishes
- 采用经典的起泡酒品种宝雪歌精心酿造而成，晶莹剔透，在意大利人心目中有着不输香槟的品质，只是名字不叫香槟罢了。Made with Italy's classic Prosecco variety, this delicate sparkling wine has a quality on par with premium champagne.

丹凤园（白）
Torresella Pinot Grigio

¥

果香充盈的意大利风格灰贝露，圆润柔滑，平衡巧妙。It represents the light fruity Italian style that has gained popularity. Characteristic mellow aroma. Smooth, delicate, fresh and well-balanced.

- 维内多地区餐酒 Veneto IGT
- 7～10℃
- 情侣约会，温馨家宴 dating, family gathering
- 鱼类，清汤 fish, light soup
- 所有葡萄采收由手工完成，尽力保留酒庄当地高海拔与寒凉气候带给这款酒的独特口感。All grapes are hand-picked to retain the special influence from the local high altitude and cool weather.

丹凤园（红）
Torresella Refosco

¥

充满野浆果等红色水果的香气，口感活跃，余味悠长，容易配餐。 It offers rich scents of wild berries and a long finish that is appealingly reminiscent of bitter cherries.

- 维内多地区餐酒 Veneto IGT
- 7～10℃
- 友人相聚，温馨家宴 friends gathering, family gathering
- 烤肉，口感浓郁的野味 roast meat, heavy-flavoured game
- 选用意大利北部特有葡萄品种莱弗斯科（Refosco）酿制，力度与单宁感都很强。Made with northern Italy's native grape Refosco, this wine shows greater strength. Very tannic.

飞度园
Feudo Zirtari

飞度园来自意大利家喻户晓的美丽西西里岛。这里的气候造就了绮丽的风光，亦是葡萄生长的乐园。充足的阳光，加上这里受到火山和风化而形成的土壤，令到所产的佳酿也充满了阳光般的活力，而又个性十足。

Feudo Zirtari, the vigor of Sicilyn Sunshine. Feudo Zirtari's products, which are designed to be paradigms of a special rapport with their area of origin. Here traditional winemaking practices and progress are perfectly combined. The result of these efforts is the exciting sensations that the Feudo Zirtari wines succeed in conveying.

飞度园（红）
Feudo Zirtari Rosso

¥¥

呈深红宝石色，充满香水的气息，在持续诱人的新鲜红色水果香味中，隐约透出一丝穗乐仙特有的辛辣气息，酒体饱满而不失优雅。Deep ruby red in color, it offers perfumes of fresh red fruits and a delicate but appealing spiciness. On the palate, it is elegant yet full-flavoured, with a supple and pleasantly refreshing texture.

- 西西里地区餐酒 Sicily IGT
- 14～17℃
- 友人相聚，活力派对 friend gathering, party
- 黑椒牛扒，烤肉 black pepper steak, roast meat
- 独特的本地品种与穗乐仙完美结合，典型的西西里风格，是户外烧烤享受烤肉时的最佳选择。A perfect blending of local varietals and Shiraz, this wine is of typical Sicilyn style. A hit when pairing with BBQ meat.

飞度园（白）
Feudo Zirtari Bianco

¥¥

该酒花香与果香充盈，带有杏仁香，入口后感觉更为明显，酒体饱满，酸甜度平衡。Deep straw yellow in color, it displays rich floral and fruity notes, with a faint hint of almonds. These sensations are echoed on the palate, along with an acidity that balances out the wine's alcoholic warmth.

- 西西里地区餐酒 Sicily IGT
- 7～10℃
- 情侣约会，温馨家宴 dating, family gathering
- 浇奶油酱汁的鸡肉或猪肉，淡味切达芝士 chicken or pork with cream sauce, mild Cheddar
- 西西里岛曾被评为意大利最佳白葡萄酒产地，此酒即西西里产区的经典白葡萄酒。It's a classic white wine from Sicily, which was once named "Best Appellation for Italian White Wines".

Sicily

西卓
Citra

一款价廉物美的意大利酒。2005年被世界上最有影响力的《葡萄酒观察家》杂志评为世界上20个最超值的品牌之一。受到众多名人如英国查尔斯王子、前首相梅杰等的喜爱。

As the Abruzzo region's most important wine producer, Citra attracts and international reputation on account of its well-made, affordably priced wines. Citra's wines have been served to such prominent figures as Britain's Prince Charles and former Prime Minister John Major.

西卓（红）
Citra Montepulciano

¥ ¥

有成熟的樱桃和草药气息。酒体中等偏浓，入口带香料及成熟浆果的味道。Ripe cherry and herbal aromas. Medium to full body, taste with spice and ripe berry flavour.

阿布鲁索法定产区酒 Abruzzo DOC

18～20℃

友人相聚，活力派对 friends gathering, party

烧烤肉类，意大利面，披萨 barbeque meat, pastas, pizza

意大利餐厅经典选酒，非常容易配餐。A classic house wine in many Italian Restaurants. Easy to find pairing food.

西卓（白）
Citra Trebbiano

¥ ¥

清新、明朗而典雅，容易欣赏，无论是餐前开胃，还是搭配美食，都一样的平易近人。Fresh, clean and refreshing! A delicious Italian white wine for all occasions, dry and zesty.

阿布鲁索法定产区酒 Abruzzo DOC

12～14℃

友人相聚，活力派对 friends gathering, party

作为开胃酒或搭配海鲜菜肴 served as aperitif or with seafood

意大利餐厅的畅销酒款，选用经典白葡萄品种扎比安奴酿制。A very popular wine in Italian restaurants, made with Italian classic Trebbiano white grapes.

西施佳雅
Sassicaia

大胆挑战传统意大利葡萄酒分级制度，选用优秀的外来葡萄品种，酿造出更胜DOCG的佳酿。其不拘传统、大胆革新的精神影响了众多生产现代型葡萄酒的酒庄，素有“新派意大利酒之父”的美誉，得到葡萄酒业界的一致推崇。
Sassicaia is a success story to challenge the old Italian wine classification and create a new style Italian wine. Dominated by foreign varietals, its wines expresse fruity and complex characters, totally different from the wines made by local varietals. For its great innovation, Saccicaia has a good reputation in the industry and gained a name as “Father of Italian modern wine”.

西施佳雅（红）
Tenuta San Guido Sassicaia

¥¥¥¥

酒香优雅，略显含蓄。口感丰富，单宁像丝般柔滑，较少浆果味而更多矿物味，体现出酒体的优雅平衡。Elegant, slightly closed on the nose. The structure is rich and resistant. Silky-smooth entry on the palate and compact tannins in the finish. Less berry fruit, more savoury mineral character but still lovely balance and good prospects for midterm.

- 宝格里法定产区酒 Bolgheri DOC
- 18～20℃
- 商务宴请，酒友交流 business dinner, wine appreciation
- 浇奶油酱汁的鸡肉或猪肉，鱼类，海鲜 chicken or pork with cream sauce, fish, seafood
- 位列意大利六十大“超级托斯卡纳”之首，有着“意大利的拉菲”、“托斯卡纳酒王”等美誉。荣获众多奖项，是不可错过的极品葡萄酒。A superb wine rated "Number One of Super Tuscan". A must-have for fine Italian wine lovers.

西施小教堂（红）
Tenuta San Guido Guidalberto

¥¥¥

香气浓郁而持久，酒体圆润温和，平衡良好，结构稳定。The nose is very long and persistent. On the palate is already evident a very well-balanced and persistent structure, with excellent fullness, gentleness and softness.

- 宝格里地区餐酒 Bolgheri IGT
- 14～17℃
- 浪漫婚宴，酒友交流 wedding, wine appreciation
- 肉类菜肴，意大利面，披萨 meat-based dishes, pastas, pizza
- 将本地传统葡萄品种圣祖维斯和外来品种梅乐、嘉本纳沙威浓精彩混酿。是一款不需太深度陈年就可饮用的优质名酒。A wonderful blending of local Sangiovese and introduced Merlot and Cabernet Sauvignon. It can be enjoyed without long time ageing.

雄狮城堡
Sonnino

从其酒标上的狮子就能感受到这款酒的霸气和王者风范。该庄园是意大利葡萄酒中的贵族，历史悠久，身世显赫。
The lion lable of this wine reveals its kingly manner and distinctive characters. This is a noble estate in Italy with a long history of brilliance.

雄狮王（红）
San Leone

¥¥¥

富有成熟的水果、香草、巧克力和烟草的味道。On the palate, it is full of aromas of chocolate and tobacco. Mature fruit, vanilla.

托斯卡纳法定产区酒 Tuscany DOC

14～17℃

商务宴请，酒友交流 business dinner, wine appreciation

红肉类菜肴，如牛肉、羊肉等 red meat dishes, e.g. beef, lamb

这是雄狮城堡的“旗舰”产品，备受行家青睐，正标上虽无DOCG字眼，但毫不影响其优秀品质，备受赞誉。It's San Leone's flagship product. It has earned the Gold Medal for the year 1998 at the "Brussels World Contest 2000" and various Grand Mentions at Viniltaly.

雄狮城堡（红）
Castello Sonnino

¥¥

酒体中度，口感结实而复杂，味道集中，是在任何时候、任何场合都可畅饮的美酒。The Castello Sonnino is a wine of medium substance yet pleasant and of a fruity taste. Savoury and medium body.

基安帝梦迪巴图优质法定产区酒 Chianti Montespertoli DOCG

14～17℃

温馨家宴，活力派对 family gathering, party

白肉，意大利面，新鲜芝士 white meat, pastas, fresh cheese

本款酒以4种最地道的意大利葡萄品种酿成，风格独特，底蕴深沉而有力。Made with four classic Chianti grapes, namely Sangiovese, Canaiolo, Malvasia and Trebbiano. Its strong structure displays power.

华姿山庄
Tenuta Di Valgiano

华姿山庄入选六十大“超级托斯卡纳”，被视为该区域的闪耀新星，更有“意大利酒中的一级庄”的美誉，其出品产量稀少，酒质超群。
Tenuta di Valgiano, a new super star in Colline Lucchesi, has been selected as "Super Tuscan". It has the good reputation of " First Grand Cru wine in Italy " for its complex personality fine wine.

华姿山庄（红）
Tenuta Di Valgiano

¥¥¥¥

深红宝石色的酒体强劲有力，浓烈而温暖，显示出酒的年轻，果香浓郁，口味丰富，单宁成熟平衡。Excellent concentration, which is already visible in its deep ruby color with crimson reflections, an indication of youth. Rich and full bodied on the palate with intense fruity aromas. Good content of mature, balanced tannins.

- 歌连露姬丝法定产区酒 Colline Lucchesi DOC
- 14～17℃
- 商务宴请，酒友交流 business dinner, wine appreciation
- 鸡肉，红肉，鱼，意大利面，炖菜，陈年芝士 chicken, red meat, fish, pastas, stews, well-aged cheeses
- 意大利一年一度葡萄酒界盛事“葡萄酒年度最佳评选”上的常胜将军，获得“三只酒杯”的最高殊荣。A constant winner of the annual "Wine of the Year" competition, this high-class wine has the good reputation of "First Grand Cru wine in Italy".

华姿山庄副牌（红）
Tenuta Di Valgiano Palistorti

¥¥¥

带有浓郁的香料和成熟浆果的香气，酒体饱满，口感丰富，带有浓郁的果香，单宁成熟平衡，余韵悠长。A nose that expresses elegance and aromatic refinement. The volume on the palate is delightful with the pleasant sweetness of the fruit, the structure develops with a dense texture of mature, soft tannins that ensure length and a pleasantly delicious aftertaste.

- 歌连露姬丝法定产区酒 Colline Lucchesi DOC
- 14～17℃
- 友人相聚，商务宴请 friends gathering, business dinner
- 浓郁酱汁烹调的肉类菜式 meat dishes with rich sauces
- 华姿山庄一款高性价比的副牌酒，香味浓郁，运用该产区最传统的酿酒工艺，传承意大利美酒的风骨，以品质取胜。A second wine with great value, Valgiano Palistorti is considered "very flavourful" with characteristic Italy style and premium quality.

美橡树庄园
Agricola Querciabella

托斯卡纳最有名的酒庄之一，入围六十大“超级托斯卡纳”，是世界上最环保的葡萄酒庄之一。
Through biodynamic viticulture, Agricola Querciabella celebrates the nature and history of their terroir, and respect and exalt the quality of its fruit. One of the sixty Super Tuscan.

巴特（白）
Agricola Querciabella Batàr

¥¥¥

口感丰满圆润，带明显的柠檬、香草及苹果香气。中度酒体，带有可爱的果香，回味悠长。"Perhaps the most ambitious Pinot Blanc on the planet." Jancis Robinson said. And this is the best Tuscan white for its attractive aromas of lemons, vanilla and apples. Medium-bodied, with lovely fruit, and apple on the long finish on the palate.

- 托斯卡纳地区餐酒 Tuscany IGT
- 12～14℃
- 浪漫婚宴，商务宴请 wedding, business dinner
- 鸡肉，火鸡，野味，猪肉，意大利熏火腿 chicken, turkey, game, pork, prosciutto
- 以托斯卡纳特有的浪漫风格酿制而成，是该区最好的白葡萄酒之一。Made with Tuscany's unique romantic style. One of the best white wines in the region.

巴拉芬奴（红）
Agricola Querciabella Palafreno

¥¥¥¥

充满贵族气息，又是一款具有强烈现代感，果味集中而又平衡的精品酒。The wine is deep yet silky, fruit driven yet with the perfect touch of toasty oak, enhancing rather than overwhelming. A modern, top-flight wine, at a reasonable price.

托斯卡纳地区餐酒 Tuscany IGT

14～17℃

浪漫婚宴，酒友交流 wedding, wine appreciation

牛扒，羊扒，中至浓味菜肴 beef steak, lamb, medium-flavour dishes

巴拉芬奴的原意是"贵族马"，所以酒标上面有一个贵族马头的标志。Palafreno means "noble horse". The image of a noble horse can be found on the label of the wine.

卡玛天娜（红）
Agricola Querciabella Camartina

¥¥¥¥

单宁柔和而持久，感觉极其完美。你能从中感受到波尔多酒的神韵。Camartina is made and released only if the vintage reaches a very good quality level, a majestic wine having the depth and elegance of a Bordeaux Cru Classe.

托斯卡纳地区餐酒 Tuscany IGT

18～20℃

商务宴请，酒友交流 business dinner, wine appreciation

精致肉类 delicately cooked meat

该庄园的极品佳作，也是意大利闻名全国的顶级红酒。This is the estate's iconic wine, also a top-quality wine well-known all through Italy.

嘉斯宝来（红）
Agricola Querciabella Querciabella

¥¥¥

该酒果香开放、酸度宜人，2～5年就成熟，适合年轻饮用。This model of a modern Chianti Classico producer serves up a gorgeously scented, rich-fruited Chianti Classico. Noses of leather, mineral and ripe plum on the palate.

基安帝经典优质法定产区酒 Chianti Classico DOCG

14～17℃

友人相聚，活力派对 friends gathering, party

烤肉、炖菜等浓味菜肴 heavy-flavoured dishes such as roast meat, stew

公认的基安帝经典区传统产品的领头羊，瓶帽上所贴的黑高卢鸡，已成为该产区美酒的经典标志。The black gaulcock image on the bottle cap has become an icon for the premium wines in this region.

德拉仙度

D'Alessandro

六十大“超级托斯卡纳”之一的德拉仙度，以出产优质穗乐仙葡萄酒而闻名全意大利，其酒多次登上权威葡萄酒杂志《葡萄酒观察家》的封面，足见其品质之高。

D'Alessandro, one of the sixty "Super Tuscan", is widely considered as the top Shiraz vintner in Italy. With exceptional premium quality, its wines have been repeatedly featured in the cover story of the acclaimed *Wine Spectator* magazine.

雅博斯高（红）

D'Alessandro IL Bosco Syrah

¥ ¥ ¥

该酒带成熟浆果及胡椒的香气，单宁丰富，层次感极强。Fifteen vintages of the estate wine, Il Bosco performs a recent history that has led to the greatest and super concentration of Syrah in Italy. Full-bodied, with lots of game, meat and ripe fruit and a long finish. Serious tannin structure.

- 高当纳法定产区酒 Cortona DOC
- 18 ~ 20℃
- 浪漫婚宴，商务宴请 wedding, business dinner
- 油性鱼类，牛扒，多脂菜式 oily fish, beef steak, fatty foods
- 德拉仙度酒庄顶级的红葡萄酒，雅博斯高是为了纪念该酒庄第一块种植穗乐仙的土地而得名。Named after the estate's first Shiraz field, this is the best red wine produced by D'Alessandro.

歌东娜（红）

D'Alessandro Cortona Syrah

¥ ¥

更为年轻有活力的穗乐仙美酒，酒体中度，高雅而果香丰富，有松树和皮革香，适合年轻饮用。Black currant, vanilla and incense aromas and flavours you can feel and it is medium-bodied, with good, simple fruit and a medium finish. This is a classified Bosco, this producer's top single-vineyard Syrah.

- 高当纳法定产区酒 Cortona DOC
- 14 ~ 17℃
- 活力派对，浪漫婚宴 party, wedding
- 手工制作的意大利面，肉类，野味，豆类，汤，沙拉 handmade pastas, meats, wild game, beans, soups, salads
- 百分百穗乐仙酿制，现代感十足。Made of 100% Shiraz, this is a rare fine wine in Tuscany with catering to modern.

乐姬丝
Le Chiuse

意大利葡萄酒中的贵胄，与托斯卡纳老酒王碧安仙帝（Biondi Santi）原属同一庄园。1990年分家独立成园。系出贵胄，品质自然优秀出众。

Established in 1990, Le Chiuse has very ancient origins. It was in fact part of the Biondi Santi family properties and was brought as a dowry by Maria Tamanti when she married Clemente Santi in 1840.

乐姬丝梦迪西露（红）
Le Chiuse Rosso Di Montalcino

有浓浓的樱桃果香。油腻感和单宁平衡得恰到好处，伴有鲜果香和很好的酸度。Very high toned cherry fruit on the nose, while the palate is reasonably fat and tannic with fresh fruit and good acidity. This is a very good "Rosso".

- 梦迪西露法定产区酒 Rosso di Montalcino DOC
- 14～17℃
- 友人相聚，温馨家宴 friends gathering, family gathering
- 肉类菜肴，番茄肉酱意大利面，牛百叶 meat-based dishes, tomato and meat sauce pastas, tripe
- 用乐姬丝上等工艺酿造，未经橡木桶陈年，年产量稀少，是上品之作。This premium wine of Le Chiuse has only a very small annual production. No oak ageing involved.

乐姬丝梦迪保罗（红）
Le Chiuse Brunello Di Montalcino

有浓浓的水果香，伴有淡巧克力味。单宁精致，酸度平衡，有不俗的深度，带有烘烤水果的浓香。High fruity tones and a little chocolate on the nose. Partly hidden, good tannins, nice acidity and concentrated, slightly cooked, fruit. Lots of depth.

- 梦迪保罗优质法定产区酒 Brunello di Montalcino DOCG
- 18～20℃
- 商务宴请，酒友交流 business dinner, wine appreciation
- 托斯卡纳香肠，意大利面，披萨 Italian sausage in Tuscany style, pastas, pizza
- 秉承意大利老酒王碧安仙帝传统酿酒工艺，果香浓郁，是能陈放几十至上百年的顶级佳酿。Following Biondi Santi 's winemaking tradition, this fruity wine has a marvelous ageing potential as high as 100 years.

碧安仙帝
Biondi-Santi

很多酒评家将碧安仙帝家族在意大利酿酒史上的地位同罗斯柴尔德家族在法国的地位相比，历史悠久、成就卓著，不仅培育出著名葡萄品种保罗，也成为意大利优质法定产区DOCG评级事实上的标准。

Biondi-Santi's winemaking legacy is to Italy what Rothchild's is to France. The winery is the birthplace of Brunello and the DOCG system is based mainly on standards developed on the estate starting in 1888.

碧安仙帝（梦迪保罗珍藏）（红）
Biondi-Santi Riserva, Brunello di Montalcino

¥¥¥¥¥

酒体圆滑，结构严谨，有纯净的果香与红色水果主导的气息，是一款难得的优雅而有力度的葡萄酒。A well-rounded Brunello with magnificent structure, purity of fruit and remarkable elegance for such a powerful wine.

- 梦迪保罗优质法定产区酒 Brunello di Montalcino DOCG
- 18～20℃
- 浪漫婚宴，酒友交流 wedding,wine appreciation
- 野味，烧烤类红肉，蓝纹芝士 game, grilled red meat, blue cheese
- 《葡萄酒观察家》评出“20世纪最伟大的葡萄酒”中唯一入选的意大利酒，只在最好年份生产，陈年天赋极佳，超过100年，价格昂贵。The only Italy wine that entered *Wine Spectator's* "Wine of the Century" list. More than 100 years of bottle life. Very sumptuous.

碧安仙帝（梦迪保罗）（红）
Biondi-Santi Annata, Brunello di Montalcino

¥¥¥¥

呈亮丽的宝石红色，带有迷人的成熟水果香气，酒体丰满，单宁圆熟，后味持久。Bright ruby red. Pleasant nose of ripe fruit. Full-bodied, with round matured tannin and a lingering aftertaste.

- 梦迪保罗优质法定产区酒 Brunello di Montalcino DOCG
- 18～20℃
- 商务宴请，酒友交流 business dinner, wine appreciation
- 野味，烧烤类红肉，浓味芝士 game, grilled red meat, heavy-seasoned cheese
- 碧安仙帝的DOCG系列都以无与伦比的陈年寿命著称，此款陈年天赋长达20～40年。Biondi Santi's DOCG are best-known for their incredible ability to age. This wine has an ageing potential as high as 20 to 40 years.

碧安仙帝（梦迪西露）（红）
Biondi-Santi, Rosso di Montalcino

¥¥¥

呈亮丽的宝石红色，有十分突出的果香，单宁轻盈。这款酒适于年轻时饮用，也可陈年15～20年。Bright ruby red, clean and outstanding fruity aroma, with gracefully light tannin. Drink young or after 15-20 years ageing.

- 梦迪西露法定产区酒 Rosso di Montalcino DOC
- 18～20℃
- 友人相聚，温馨家宴 friends gathering,family gathering
- 意大利面，浓郁型红肉菜式 pastas, rich red meat dishes
- 陈年天赋虽与DOCG系列相比略少，亦长达15～20年。Its ageing potential is lower than the winery's DOCGs but also can be as high as 15 to 20 years.

伯爵山庄

Villa Poggio Salvi

伯爵山庄是一座拥有悠久酿酒传统的酒庄，其出品早在公元1500年左右已经是意大利贵族餐桌上的常客。如今在碧安仙帝旗下，该酒庄将严格而科学的现代酿酒工艺与传统意大利美酒生产相结合，生产出一系列品质优异、兼具传统意大利风格和现代口感的葡萄酒，在意大利国内外都受到消费者的欢迎。

Villa Poggio Salvi is a winery company with a modern structure aimed to the future, where traditional wines are produced with modern technologies.

伯爵山庄（梦迪西露）（红）

Villa Poggio Salvi Rosso di Montalcino

¥¥¥

呈明亮的宝石红色。带有玫瑰花蕾和紫罗兰气息的花香。单宁和谐，平衡感好，温润细腻。Brilliant ruby red. On nose it's fruity with notes of rose buds and violets. On palate it has harmonic tannins. Well balanced and warm.

- 梦迪西露法定产区酒 Rosso di Montalcino DOC
- 14～17℃
- 情侣约会，友人相聚 dating, friends gathering
- 意大利面，烧烤类红肉，半烟熏芝士 pastas, grilled red meat, half-smoked cheese
- 100%圣祖维斯葡萄酿制，是旨在赢得新世界饮家欣赏的传统意大利酒，层次的打开比老派意大利酒更快。Made with 100% Sangiovese, this wine aims to be more more approachable to new world markets. It tends to open up sooner than traditional Brunellos.

伯爵山庄（白）

Poggio Salvi Bianco Vermentino

¥¥

呈明亮的稻草黄色。水果气息明显，带有清新的白色花香和异国果香。入口轻盈，甜度清晰，平衡感好。Brilliant, tending to a strawy yellow color. On nose it's fruity, fresh, with hints of white flowers and exotic fruit. On palate it's light and sweet, smooth and well balanced, very persistent.

- 托斯卡纳地区餐酒 Tuscany IGT
- 7～10℃
- 情侣约会，浪漫婚宴 dating, wedding
- 鸡蛋，茅屋芝士，海鲜 eggs, cottage cheese, sea-food
- 用古老的意大利白葡萄品种维蒙天奴酿制，葡萄采摘在拂晓时分进行，以最大限度保留其独特果味及甜度。Made with the old Italian Vermentino white grapes. Fruits are picked at dawn to maximize its fruity feature and sweetness.

伯爵山庄（梦迪保罗）（红）
Villa Poggio Salvi Brunello di Montalcino

¥ ¥

气息十分浓郁，细细品味可闻到樱桃、甘草、巧克力、咖啡等多重复杂香气。On the nose it has intense and complex aroma of cherry, liquorice, chocolate and coffee.

梦迪保罗优质法定产区酒 Brunello di Montalcino DOCG

18～20℃

温馨家宴，酒友交流 family gathering, wine appreciation

乳鸽配橄榄，白松露焗饭 pigeon with olives, white truffles risotto

葡萄采摘由全人手完成，上佳年份的陈年天赋可达40年，是美食珍品——松露的最佳搭配之一。Grapes are all hand-picked. Ageing life can be as long as 40 years. A wonderful companion for truffle dishes.

伯爵山庄（基安帝）（红）
Villa Poggio Salvi Caspagnolo, Chianti Colli Senesi

¥ ¥

散发出馥郁的果香以及黑加仑与紫罗兰的气息，平衡良好，单宁圆滑和谐。A well balanced, warm flavour, with harmonious roundness in tannins, a fruity fragrance with hints of black-currant and violet, bright ruby red color.

基安帝优质法定产区酒 Chianti Colli Senesi DOCG

14～17℃

友人相聚，温馨家宴 friends gathering, family gathering

中至浓味菜肴，如黑椒牛扒、烤肉、熏肉等 medium to heavy dishes, such as black pepper steak, roast meat or bacon meat

以圣祖维斯·格罗索及少量梅乐混合酿制的经典托斯卡纳红酒，果香是该酒的一大特色。A classic Tuscany red wine with a blending of Sangiovese Grosso and a small percentage of Merlot, renowned for its fruity nose.

葡萄牙

PORTUGAL

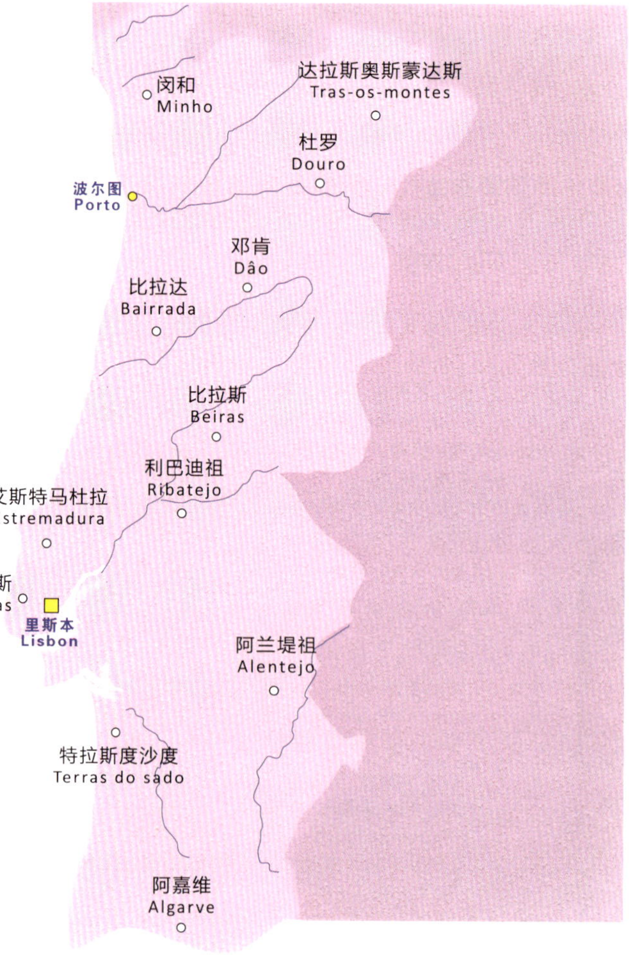

葡萄牙葡萄酒产区示意图

葡萄牙 毗邻西班牙，濒临大西洋，拥有典型的地中海气候。尽管葡萄田面积仅占国土面积8%，葡萄牙的人均年葡萄酒消费量却高达50升，仅次于法国和意大利，境内有约250种葡萄品种。1758年，波旁王朝把杜罗区（Douro）列为世界上第一个法定葡萄酒产区，奠定了杜罗区葡萄酒今日在葡萄牙乃至世界的霸主地位。

要想了解葡萄牙的葡萄酒，只需简单地把地图一分为二，划出一条1/3的界线。面积占1/3的北部有著名的杜罗（Douro）、邓肯（Dâo）、百乐达（Bairrada）和闵和（Minho），主要生产在国际上更具知名度的葡萄酒；占2/3的中南部有阿兰堤祖（Alentejo）、利巴迪祖（Ribatejo）、艾斯特马杜拉（Estremadura）和马德拉（Madeira）等，重点放在价廉物美的新世界形态葡萄酒，比较容易欣赏。令葡萄牙酒业引以为傲的是其驰名国际的加烈葡萄酒，其中以北部的钵酒（Port）和南部的马德拉酒（Madeira）为代表。

{葡萄品种}

葡萄牙的葡萄品种有数百种之多，大部分都是只在葡萄牙种植的富有地域特色的品种。其中用来酿制钵酒的葡萄主要有5种：红巴豪卡（Tinta Barroca）、红卡奥（Tinta Cão）、红好丽诗（Tinta Roriz，在西班牙称为Tempranillo）、法国杜丽丝（Touriga Francesa）和国产杜丽丝（Touriga Nacional）。法国杜丽丝是杜罗河种植最广泛的葡萄品种，它就像嘉本纳沙威浓那样赋予葡萄酒坚实的骨架和浓郁的酒体。国产杜丽丝则类似于贝露娃，果粒细小不易种植，令酒散发浆果的芳香。

国产杜丽丝 Touriga Nacional

红好丽诗 Tinta Roriz

红巴豪卡 Tinta Barroca

法国杜丽丝 Touriga Francesa

{分级制度}

跟欧洲许多生产国一样，葡萄牙很早就开始实行葡萄酒分级制度，甚至比著名的法国波尔多的1855年分级还早200年，以保护本土的葡萄酒文化和传承。这些等级主要根据葡萄品种、微型气候、土壤和酿酒技术等标准来划分，但由于种种原因，葡萄牙的葡萄酒分级制度仍在进一步完善，目前一共有八大级别。

法定产区酒
Denomination de Origem Controlada, 简称DOC

属最高级别，类似于法国的AOC或者意大利的DOC，目前有29个DOC。这一级别的名产区有Douro、Dâo、Bairrada、Vinho Verde、Bucelas、Golares、Gacravelos和Moscatel de Setuba等。

▲

推荐产区酒
Indicacao de Proveniencia Regulamentada, 简称IPR

即待定DOC，满5年考察期后政府就会决定其是否得到擢升，目前有4个IPR。

▲

准法定产区酒
Vinhos de Qualidade Produzidos em Regioses Determinadas, 简称VQPRD

有一部分已经升级为DOC或IPR的酒仍贴此标签，是一个惊喜倍出的级别。

▲

优质加烈葡萄酒
Vinhos Licorosos de Qualidade Produzidos em Regiao Determinadas, 简称VLQPRD

▲

优质起泡酒
Vinhos Espumantes de Qualidade Produzidos em Regiao Determinadas, 简称VEQPRD

▲

优质半干起泡酒
Vinhos Frisante de Qualidade Produzidos em Regiao Determinadas, 简称VFQPRD

▲

区域产区酒
Vinho Regional

相当于法国的Vin de Pays，目前有九大区域。不用按照法定酿酒要求，酿酒师可以自行决定葡萄品种、酿造工艺和陈年时间。虽然不是最高等级的酒，但却有不少富有地方特色的佳酿。

▲

日常餐酒
Vnho de Mesa

通常是没有列出生产年份、价格比较低的日常餐酒。

{葡萄酒产区}

北部 杜罗

Douro字面意思为“黄金”，因此杜罗河即黄金之河，产自此地的“葡萄牙国酒”钵酒（Port Wine）也被人们称为“黄金之酒”，而该河的确含有少量金矿沙。在杜罗河上游，是有着2 000多年的酿酒历史的名产酒区波尔图（Porto），2001年这里的葡萄园还被列入世界文化遗产名录。这里冬天寒冷，夏季炎热，所产的葡萄含糖量高，酿出的酒酒体圆润，通常带有肉汁的香气，因此盛产最著名的钵酒。除了钵酒，杜罗区也生产一般的红葡萄酒和白葡萄酒，同时拥有加烈葡萄酒“Porto”和静态葡萄酒“Douro”两种DOC，其中红葡萄酒占60％。由杜罗河的上游至下游又可划分成Douro Superior、Cima Corgo和Baixo Corgo三大部分。

钵酒 简单来说，钵酒是指葡萄牙北部杜罗河区域的加烈葡萄酒，在酒液发酵时加入白兰地强制终止发酵而成。酵母在高酒精条件下会被杀死而保持糖分，因此钵酒是甜的。通常，钵酒的酒精度达20%左右。我们通常说的钵酒指的是甜型的红葡萄酒。实际上钵酒除了甜型，也有干型、半干型，不管是红葡萄酒，还是白葡萄酒，一般都作为餐后酒。与钵酒形态类似的葡萄酒在澳大利亚、南非、加拿大等地也可找到，但根据欧盟的相关规定，只有产自葡萄牙才能打上“Port”的名号。

钵酒的种类 宝石红钵酒（Ruby）

年份钵酒（Vintage Port） 钵酒的顶级出品。只在好年份才会生产，一般平均三四年会生产一次。例如华莱仕酒庄2000年后目前只有2000、2003和2007年3个年份。生产商需经过钵酒协会评定合格才能在标签打上“年份”。通常，酒液先在橡木桶进行两年的陈酿，然后再进入瓶酿阶段。好的钵酒需经过15年甚至更长时间的瓶酿才完全成熟。由于年份钵酒在瓶中陈酿的时间比较长，需要先换瓶再进行品尝，其口感十分浓郁。

单一葡萄田年份钵酒（Single Quinta Vintage Port）

酿酒的葡萄来自单一的葡萄田，能更真实地反映风土的特性。这类钵酒的质量与年份钵酒比较接近，但价格更相宜。

迟装瓶年份钵酒（Late Bottled Vintage Port）

几乎每年都有生产。在橡木桶陈酿的时间比一般的年份钵酒长，4～6年才装瓶，酒液平衡圆润，也更容易欣赏，与微苦的黑巧克力搭配是绝配，被业内人士认为是最超值的钵酒。

陈年钵酒（Crusted） 混合不同年份的酒液而成，瓶酿至少要3年才可以上市，酒标标示的年份指的是装瓶时间。酒色深黑、结构紧密是其特点。只有少数酒商生产。

珍藏宝石红钵酒（Ruby Reserve） 不属于年份钵酒，混合平均年份为4年左右的酒液而成。酒色深紫，以成熟的莓果香气为主。

宝石红钵酒（Ruby Port） 酒体轻身、果香馥郁、容易欣赏的钵酒，是宝石红系列的入门类型，适合初次接触钵酒的人饮用。

钵酒的种类 茶色钵酒（Tawny）

单一年份茶色钵酒（Colheita） 用单一年份的葡萄酿造，与年份钵酒的区别在于它可以在橡木桶中陈酿多年再装瓶出售，是最少见、最独特的钵酒之一。

40年茶色钵酒（40 Year Old Tawny） 目前市面上最古老的茶色钵酒，是钵酒陈年天赋的最好诠释。酒色呈琥珀色，口感强劲但柔顺，后味回甘持久。

30年茶色钵酒（30 Year Old Tawny） 酒色比40年茶色钵酒深黑一些，也较新鲜，香气以坚果为主。

20年茶色钵酒（20 Year Old Tawny） 此类型以平衡取胜，与芝士搭配最佳。

10年茶色钵酒（10 Year Old Tawny） 陈年茶色钵酒中最年轻的类型，可开胃酒，也可餐后酒。以焦糖、蜂蜜和葡萄干的香气为主，与轻身芝士和布丁搭配最佳。

珍藏钵酒（Reserve） 在橡木桶陈年6~7年再装瓶。酒色深棕，以无花果和红色水果的香气为主。

茶色钵酒（Fine Tawny） 茶色钵酒中最年轻的类型，略带砖红色调，是茶色系列的入门类型，以樱桃、草莓和李子香味为主。

钵酒的种类 **白色钵酒（White）**

干型白色钵酒（Dry White） 唯一的干型钵酒，是极佳的开胃酒。温度较低时饮用最佳，以柠檬和薄荷香气为主。

白色钵酒（Fine White） 酒体中度的甜型白色钵酒。可做开胃酒，也可做餐后酒。

甜白钵酒（Lagrima） 钵酒中最甜的类型。用做餐后酒，香气馥郁，以蜂蜜和焦糖的气味为主。

邓肯 早在1390年当地政府就已经出台保护葡萄酒业的文件，生产高品质的红葡萄酒，也生产少量的白葡萄酒。

百乐达 是仅次于杜罗和邓肯的产区，红酒同样出色，但声名却来自Mateus Rosé这种葡萄品种，酿制中度酒体的碳酸甜酒，在世界各地的超市均有销售。

闵和 出产另外一种特产葡萄酒——绿酒（Vinho Verde）。取名绿酒，其实并不是指酒液鲜活的颜色，而是指其新鲜活跃的口感。事实上，除了用Alvarinho酿制的白绿酒（White Vinho Verde）外，还有用Espadeiro和Padeiro酿制的粉红绿酒（Rose Vinho Verde）以及用Vinhao和Amaral等酿制的红绿酒（Red Vinho Verde）。白绿酒通常带有微微的小气泡，可以说是世界上最让人喜爱的开胃酒之一，与烤青鱼、沙丁鱼等的搭配堪称绝妙。

南部

南部相对来说没有像北部那样引人瞩目的产区，但也不容小觑，特别是葡萄牙特产之一的马德拉酒。尽管葡萄牙南部气候过于炎热，不适宜葡萄生长，马德拉岛上的条件却比较温和，可进行葡萄种植。

马德拉葡萄酒产自马德拉岛（Madeira），字面意思为“木之岛”，源于岛上有茂密的森林。其属加烈葡萄酒，普遍运用Sercial, Verdelho, Bual和Malmsey这4种葡萄品种酿造，可用做开胃酒或饭后酒，也可在烹调过程加入为菜肴佐味。

马德拉酒的生产工艺与钵酒相似，都是在发酵后加入白兰地使发酵终止。不同的是，接下来要加热到30~50℃，然后再存放6个月左右，这样可以在高温下经过海运输往世界各地时仍保持新鲜度。早在17世纪人们就已经开始这样操作了。

马德拉酒的类型多样，从干型到甜型都有。值得一提的是，马德拉酒带有一种略呈氧化的特殊香味，在中世纪的时候，许多皇室或者贵族女性还会取一两滴马德拉酒洒在手帕上，当作香水使用。因此，有了这样一帮宣传能力一流的贵族铁杆酒迷，马德拉酒成了世界尤其是欧洲的高级社交场合的宠儿。

波尔图
Porto

华莱仕
Warre's

华莱仕始创于1670年，是葡萄牙第一家由英国人建立的钵酒品牌。其钵酒以结构扎实、劲道十足和香气醉人成为同类产品的佼佼者，在国际上更因质量卓越且在各大葡萄酒大赛中屡获奖项而拥有高知名度。

Warre's has been leading the Port trade since it was established as the first Britsh Port House in 1670 in Portugal. Its Ports are distinguished for their structure, power and softly perfumed nose and renowned the world over for their excellence and are consistently placed amongst the best in comparative tasting.

华莱仕特酿年份钵酒1985
Warre's Vintage Port 1985

¥¥¥¥

呈深宝石红色，散发华莱仕钵酒独有的花香气息，骨架感强劲，口感具有复杂的平衡度，单宁坚实，可长期陈放。Dark ruby colour. Characteristic Warre flowery nose, with tremendous backbone and a rich complexity of balanced fruit on the palate. Its solidity shows it to be a lasting Vintage.

- 名品级 Outstanding
- 14～17℃
- 商务宴请，酒友交流 business dinner, wine appreciation
- 芝士，各类甜点，单独享用 cheese, desserts or enjoyed alone
- 1985年是一款广受赞誉的佳酿，曾获得美国酒评家罗拔·派克90分（总分100）。A great classic single vineyard vintage port. Rated 90 out of 100 by Robert Parker.

华莱仕特酿年份钵酒1996
Warre's Vintage Port 1996

¥¥¥

充满复杂层次的香气中融合了多种成熟的红色水果气息。中度酒体，回味十分绵长。Packed with concentrated layers of ripe red fruits. Enormous mid-palate structure, and impressive length.

- 名品级 Outstanding
- 14～17℃
- 浪漫婚宴，酒友交流 wedding, wine appreciation
- 芝士，单独享用 cheese, enjoyed alone
- 1996年份钵酒获得2008年伦敦国际葡萄酒挑战赛银奖。Vintage 1996 has won the Silver Medal of London International Wine Challenge 2008.

华莱仕10年珍藏钵酒
Warre's Otima 10 Year Old Tawny Port

¥ ¥ ¥

呈现明亮的黄褐色，有浓郁的焦糖、蜂蜜和干果气息。酒体饱满，太妃糖一般甜蜜的口感，回味悠长。A ripe and rich tawny. Loads of caramel, honey and dried fruit. Full-bodied, sweet and very toffee like on the palate, long finish.

- 精品级 Excellent
- 12～14℃
- 浪漫婚宴，酒友交流 wedding, wine appreciation
- 开胃酒，餐后酒，单独享用 aperitif, digestif, enjoyed alone
- 一款经典明净的钵酒。获得伦敦国际葡萄酒挑战赛2001年金奖，《品醇客》世界葡萄酒大奖赛2009年金奖。A classic bright style port. Gold medal winner at 2001 International Wine Challenge, and gold medal at 2009's *Decanter* World Wine Awards.

华莱仕珍藏钵酒
Warre's Warrior Reserve Port

¥ ¥

酒体饱满丰盈、结构十分平衡的一款经典钵酒。A classic full-bodied wine with wonderful richness and balance.

- 优品级 Distinguished
- 12～14℃
- 情侣约会，温馨家宴 dating, family gathering
- 坚果类、巧克力类糕点，芝士 nutty desserts, chocolate cakes, cheeses
- “珍藏”是世界上最古老的钵酒系列，此酒在众多酒展获得荣誉，包括国际葡萄酒烈酒大赛，伦敦国际葡萄酒挑战赛与《品醇客》世界葡萄酒大赛等。Warrior is the oldest mark of Port in the world. This is a many-awarded wine, including International Wine & Spirit Competition and International Wine Challenge, *Decanter* World Wine Awards.

华莱仕宝石钵酒
Warre's Heritage Ruby Port

¥ ¥

此酒由在旧橡木桶平均陈年3年的不同年份的酒液混酿而成，是一款口感活跃、富有年轻气息的葡萄酒。A blend of young, vibrant wines from different vintages.

- 优品级 Distinguished
- 12～14℃
- 情侣约会，温馨家宴 dating, family gathering
- 芝士，巧克力甜点，黑巧克力 cheese, rich chocolate desserts, dark chocolate
- 这款“宝石”是经典风格的钵酒，与同类产品相比具有价格优势，是可以“畅饮”的钵酒。This is a full and fruity Ruby Port in the classic style. Excellent quality with good value. The perfect "pouring" Port.

匈牙利

HUNGARY

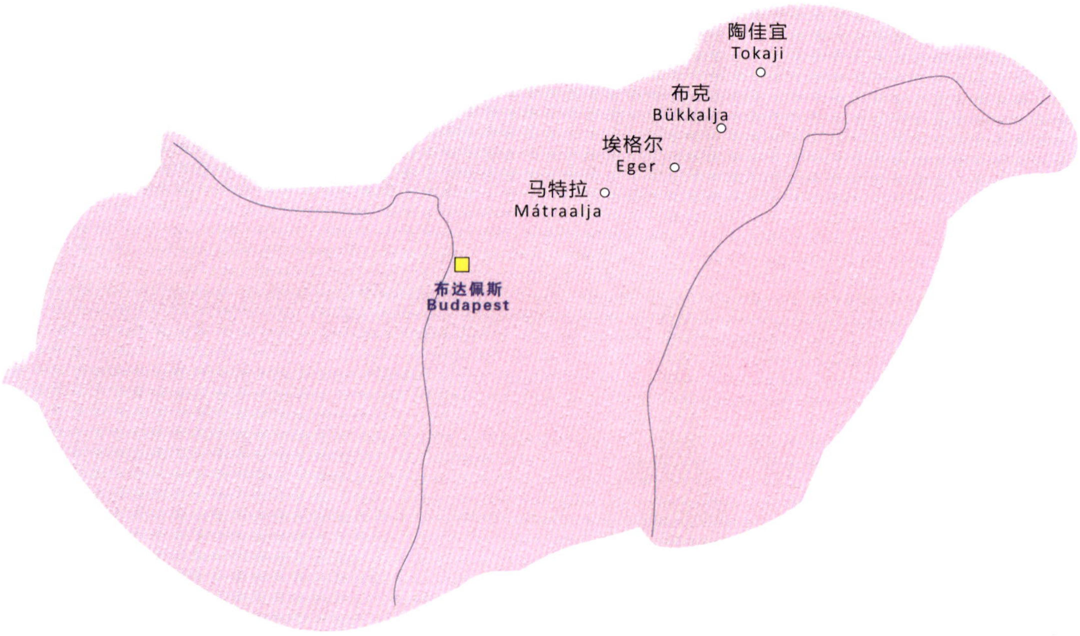

匈牙利葡萄酒产区示意图

匈牙利 在古罗马时就已是葡萄酒生产大国，著名的贵腐甜酒陶佳宜（Tokaji）曾经是欧洲皇室的御用酒，另外公牛血（Egri Bikaver）也是享誉世界的浓郁型红葡萄酒。现在，匈牙利每年都会举办丰富多彩的葡萄节、品酒会等活动，形成独具特色的葡萄酒旅游项目，充分展示了其葡萄酒生产的悠久历史和文化。

匈牙利四周环陆，是典型的大陆性气候，夏季酷热，冬天严寒，而在秋天葡萄采收时却经常阴霾笼罩，这种气候正是贵腐甜酒的天堂，因此这片土地上生产的贵腐酒总有着别处无法模仿的风味。匈牙利葡萄酒标签上，通常可以看到葡萄品种的名称。

陶佳宜
Tokaji

皇家园
Hétszőlő

皇家园（陶佳宜）是匈牙利最具历史的酒庄之一，声名显赫。从1502年1月建园到现在，已经有500多年历史。第一个将圣经翻译成匈牙利语的著名教徒和特兰西瓦尼亚王子都曾管理过庄园，令这里的佳酿充满了贵族气息，让饮家难舍难离。

The estate was created in January 1502 by the Garay family. Several renowned owners have headed the estate over the years, including Gaspar Karolyi, the famous Calvinist over the preacher, the first personto translate the bible into Hungarian, and Gabor Bethlen, Prince of Transylvania.The wine is very elegant and attractive.

皇家园（陶佳宜）特级甜白
Hétszőlő Tokaji AszÚ 5 Puttonyos

¥ ¥ ¥

复杂的花香中有杏子、洋李、蜜桃和香橙的味道以及丝丝蜂蜜与坚果的芬芳。入口后味蕾犹如沐浴在花海中。On the nose, the aromas are elegant, fine and complex with hints of fruit (apricot, plum, peach, orange) or honey, nuts. On the palate, this wine is sumptuous and incomparable.

- 名品级 Outstanding
- 12～14℃
- 商务宴请，酒友交流 business dinner, wine appreciation
- 餐后甜点，水果 dessert, fruit
- 陶佳宜所产的甜酒举世闻名，历史上欧洲众多皇室更设有长驻人员专事采购，路易十四称之为“王者之酒，酒中王者”。Renowned wine with premium quality. Considered "king of wines, wine of kings" by Louis XⅣ.

皇家园（陶佳宜）甜白
Hétszőlő Tokaji Aszú 3 Puttonyos

¥¥¥

酒液散发出阵阵的成熟水果味，以及杏仁和蜂蜜的味道。口感温和圆润，但不失爽脆，后味悠长。To the nose, the wine exudes delicious ripe fruit (dried apricots and prunes) and honey. To the palate, the wine is relatively soft but full-bodied. Fairly rich (though crisp) and has a long finish.

优品级 Distinguished

12～14℃

温馨家宴，浪漫婚宴 family gathering, wedding

餐后甜点，水果 dessert, fruit

陶佳宜地区的甜酒早已为欧洲的医书所记载，对于养生有非常好的功用，陶佳宜甚至出现在匈牙利的国歌中。Well-known for the health-enhancing effects of its wine, Tokaji was even proudly cited in Hungary's national anthem.

小常识
Q & A

问：甜酒需要醒酒吗？如果要醒酒，应该注意些什么？

答：一般人的观念里需要醒酒的不外乎陈年红酒以及陈年钵酒（Port），几乎很少有人提及白葡萄酒，尤其是甜白葡萄酒。因为甜白酒产量少，陈年的甜葡萄酒就更不多见，而且在国内饮用甜白葡萄酒的人也不多，所以一般都比较少提到甜白酒的醒酒问题。

其实并不是每一种甜白葡萄酒都需要醒酒，质量一般或浅龄的甜白酒是不需要醒酒的，只有品质特别优异，又具有数十年陈年潜质的甜白酒才需要醒酒。上好的法国苏玳（Sauternes）出产的甜白酒，一般具有50年以上的陈年潜力，当经过20～30年的陈放之后，会产生些许残渣，在这种情况下就需要醒酒，其主要是滗酒的程序，以便于分离酒瓶内的沉淀（Sediment）。

甜白酒的醒酒过程与一般陈年红酒不同。甜白酒适饮温度比红酒要低许多，因此，甜白酒醒酒时要确保酒和醒酒器都已处于冰镇状态，如果醒酒器处于常温，则酒倒入醒酒器中，短时间内便会回温，酒质因而大打折扣。甜白葡萄酒完成滗酒后，应马上开始饮用而无须等待醒酒，否则越醒越热，若按照红酒30～60分钟的醒酒时间来醒甜酒，到时候喝到的也就是温热的糖酒，而非沁凉可口的甜白葡萄酒。如果非要醒酒的话，那么请将盛着酒的醒酒器浸在冰水之中，或放置于冰箱内，等数十分钟再饮用。

西班牙

SPAIN

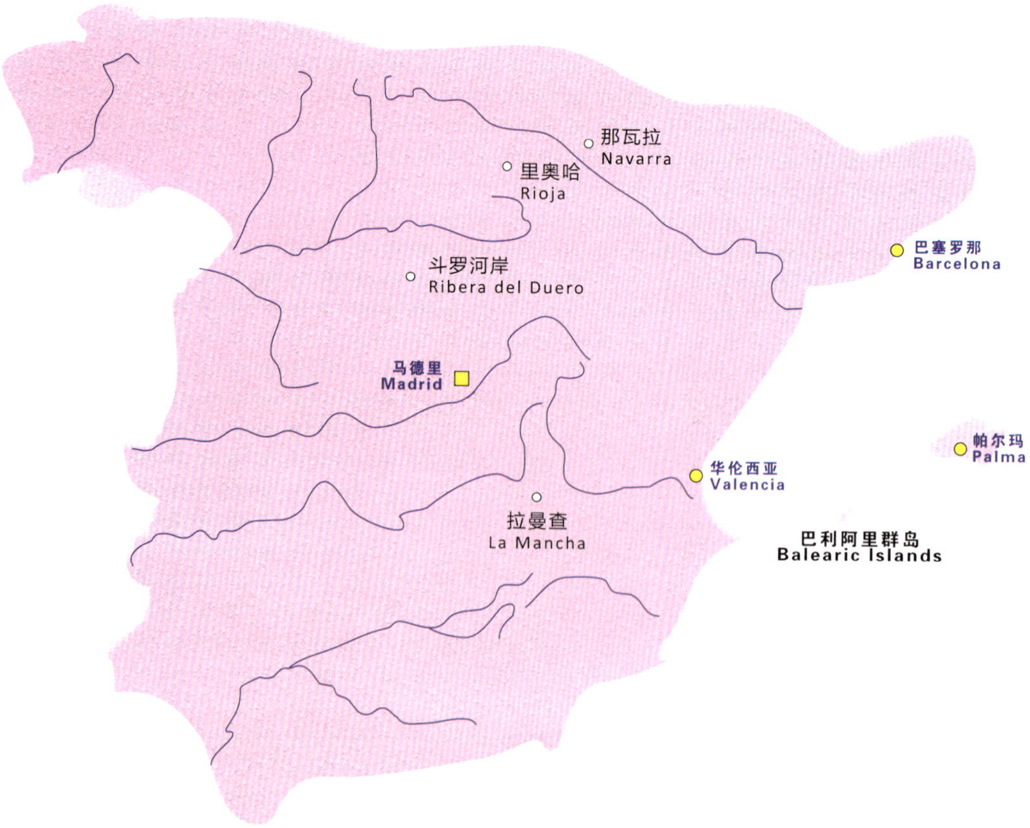

西班牙葡萄酒产区示意图

西班牙 是世界上葡萄种植面积最大的产酒国，总产量仅次于意大利和法国，位居第三，出产众多质量上乘的葡萄酒。西班牙拥有地中海充足的阳光和温暖的气候，所产红葡萄酒都以浓郁风格为主，另外还生产著名的起泡酒加瓦（Cava）以及加烈酒雪莉（Sherry）。

目前，西班牙酒并不像法国酒那样受世人关注，对消费者来说或者也是一件好事，可以用实惠的价格觅得更多高性价比的好酒。此外，西班牙酒最大的特点是，法律规定葡萄酒装瓶后一定要在酒窖里存放到成熟后才能上市，某些优质的葡萄酒存放的时间长达七八年，所以市面上很容易找到旧年份但价格却不贵的西班牙好酒，对比起法国波尔多昂贵的名酒预售，实在是广大酒迷之福。

{葡萄品种}

西班牙拥有600个以上的葡萄品种，但经常使用的大约有20种，白葡萄品种爱人（Airén）的种植最为广泛，用来酿制雪莉酒（Sherry）；最主要的红葡萄品种是添帕尼优，大部分的红葡萄酒都是用它来酿制的。

爱人 Airén

{分级制度}

西班牙葡萄酒有5个等级，级别由低到高分别是：

优质法定产区酒
Denomination de Origen Calificada，简称DOC

相当于意大利的DOCG，严格规定产区和葡萄酒酿造过程。目前西班牙共有3个DOC产区，里奥哈Rioja在1991年成为第一个划分为此等级的产区，继其之后，普利奥拉（Priorat）和斗罗河岸（Ribera del Duero）分别在2003年和2008年成为DOC产区。

▲

法定产区酒
Denomination de Origen，简称DO

相当于法国的AOC。

▲

准法定产区
Vino de La Tierra，简称VDT

相当于法国的VDQS。

▲

优良餐酒
Vino Comarcal，简称VC

相当于法国的Vin de Pays。

▲

日常餐酒
Vino de Mesa，简称VDM

相当于法国的Vin de Table，也有一部分酒相当于意大利的IGT，使用非法定葡萄品种或者指定方法酿酒。

{葡萄酒的陈年规定}

西班牙葡萄酒有着严格的陈年规定，需成熟再上市，是不需等待的美酒，可以从酒标上了解葡萄酒的陈年时间段。

新酒（Joven/Sin Crianza）

几乎不需经过橡木桶陈年，或者只在橡木桶陈酿很短时间，上市后最好在一两年内饮用。

年份酒（Vino de Cosecha）

要求用85%以上该年份的葡萄酿造。

陈酿（Crianza）

在葡萄收获年份后的第三年才能够上市的酒，红葡萄酒需要在橡木桶陈年最少 6个月和在瓶中陈酿2年，在里奥哈和斗罗河岸地区则要求在橡木桶陈年最少1年和在瓶中陈酿1年；白葡萄酒则需在橡木桶陈年最少 6个月和在瓶中陈酿1年。

珍藏（Reserva）

红葡萄酒最少需陈酿3年，其中最少要在橡木桶陈酿1年。白葡萄酒要求最少陈酿2年，其中最少要在橡木桶陈酿6个月。

特级珍藏（Gran Reserva）

只有少数极好的年份才会酿造，而且要得到当地政府的许可，红葡萄酒要求最少陈酿5年，其中最少要在橡木桶陈酿1年半。特级珍藏级别的白葡萄酒比较罕见，要求最少陈酿4年，其中最少要在小橡木桶内陈酿6个月。

{葡萄酒产区}

西班牙著名的葡萄酒产区主要有斗罗河岸（Ribera del Duero）、里奥哈（Rioja）和那瓦拉（Navarra）。

斗罗河岸 的产量不是很大，但有不少精品和极品酒庄。西班牙葡萄酒的四大天王全部产自这里，它们分别是有“西班牙拉菲”之称的维加西西利亚（Vega Sicily）、百斯嘉乐（Pesguera）、拉美达（L'Ermita）和有“西班牙的柏图斯”之称的彭高斯（Pingus）。

里奥哈 是西班牙红葡萄酒产量最大的产区，是西班牙最早成名的优质酒产区，也是无可争议的西班牙红葡萄之王。该区有很多西班牙精品至极品的酒庄，同时它还出产一大批质量稳定但价格不太贵的中价位酒。红葡萄酒的特点是陈年时间长，深沉而柔顺。白葡萄酒由于经过橡木桶的陈年，带有独特的坚果香气和干爽的后味。

那瓦拉 位于西班牙北部，和前两者相比，算是一个较新的产区，出产性价比非常高的中价位西班牙好酒。它因歌海娜葡萄酒而出名，同时也启用流行品种嘉本纳沙威浓、梅乐、雪当利等。

另外，杰里（Jerez）是雪莉酒的家乡，而西南部加利西亚（Galicia）的下海湾（Rias Baixas）是阿尔巴力诺（Albarino）白葡萄酒和加瓦起泡酒的著名产地。

里奥哈、斗罗河岸和下海湾
Rioja, Ribera del Duero & Rias Baixas

喜悦酒庄
C.V.N.E

C.V.N.E是西班牙的知名品牌，拥有超过120年的历史，所产的葡萄酒具有很高的性价比。旗下有7个不同系列，包括皇家田园（Imperial）和喜悦（Cune）等。皇家田园是里奥哈葡萄酒的经典代表作，是西班牙家喻户晓的品牌。喜悦更被誉为“西班牙优质葡萄酒的必选系列”之一，是非常地道的西班牙佳酿。

C.V.N.E is a national prestige brand in Spain with a history of more than 120 years. It produces high quality wine of affordable price. There are seven wine series under the brand, including Imperial and Cune. Imperial is one of the big brands of Spain. It is a true classic in Rioja and was first produced in the twenties, while Cune is present ranged among all of Spanish highest regarded wine lists.

皇家田园（至尊珍藏）（红）
Imperial Gran Reserva

¥¥¥

呈深宝石红色，有馥郁的浆果和甘草气息，散发烤橡木和多种树脂的香味。酒体饱满，口感丰盈。Intense ruby red resulting from the long maceration. Deep berry nose and liquorice predominating in the powerful structure. There are fine hints of toasty oak with fine balsamic nuances. On the palate it is full, generous and rich.

- 里奥哈法定产区酒 Rioja DOC
- 14～17℃
- 浪漫婚宴，商务宴请 wedding, business dinner
- 羊肉，牛肉，各种炖菜 lamb, beef, stew
- 皇家田园系列是该酒庄的高端品牌，更是西班牙皇室婚宴的指定用酒，只选用超过20年树龄的葡萄酿制，只在非常优秀的年份才出产。下分Reserva和Gran Reserva两级，其中Gran Reserva品质最高。The Imperial range includes a "Reserva" and a "Gran Reserva" and is only produced in exceptional vintages. The Gran Reserva is produced from grapes that have been hand-harvested from bush-pruned, low yielding, old vine vineyards.

皇家田园（珍藏）（红）
Imperial Reserva

¥ ¥ ¥

呈亮丽的宝石红色，红色和黑色浆果的香味丰富而浓郁。酒体圆润而平衡。Stylish, bright ruby red and very intense in colour. Highly aromatic on the nose with hints of red and black autumn fruit aromas with some toasty and spices (coming from the American oak).

里奥哈法定产区酒 Rioja DOC

14～17℃

浪漫婚宴，酒友交流 wedding, wine appreciation

牛扒，烧烤红肉或白肉，各种地中海菜式 beef steak, grilled red meat and white meat, Mediterranean food

这款屡获殊荣的葡萄酒由80%的添帕尼优、10%嘉西诺和10%马士罗酿制而成，在橡木桶中陈年24个月，品质出众。This award-winning wine is made from 80% Tempranillo, 10% Graciano and 10% Mazuelo and aged for 24 months in oak.

喜悦（珍藏）（红）
Cune Reserva

¥ ¥ ¥

浓郁的果香中带有莓子和红色水果的味道，单宁平衡，精致复杂，而后味持久。Intense ruby red, bright and deep in colour. Rich, deep aromas of bramble, red autumn fruit with a hint of balsamic and warm spices from fine oak. The palate is fine, complex and long, with balanced tannins and an excellent bright finish.

里奥哈法定产区酒 Rioja DOC

14～17℃

情侣约会，浪漫婚宴 dating, wedding

羊排，炖肉 short ribs, kale stew

陈酿系列的成功催生了珍藏系列。葡萄均是从特选葡萄园中手工采收，控温发酵，罐瓶后陈放1年方才发售。The success of the Cune Crianza motivated the Cune Reserva creation. The grapes were hand picked from selected vineyards. After bottling it was cellared for a year before release.

喜悦（陈酿）（红）
Cune Crianza

¥ ¥

红色浆果的香气伴随着丝丝的橡木香扑鼻而来，酒体既优雅又充满活力。Bright cherry colour with some violet nuances. In the nose, red berries aromas remain over the oaky and balsamic notes from its aging in wood. It shows an elegant mouth pass, yet very lively, with some spice back notes and a balanced acidity.

里奥哈法定产区酒 Rioja DOC

14～17℃

情侣约会，浪漫婚宴 dating, wedding

沙拉，禽类，鱼类，意大利面 salads, birds, fish, pastas

来自里奥哈、阿拉维沙地区富含白垩的土壤，令酒具有更强劲的结构，体积感明显。A wine of excellent quality from Rioja Alavesa, which has more chalky soils and makes wines with greater structure.

喜悦（白）
Cune Blanco

¥ ¥

口感新鲜，清新而爽脆，酸度平衡，果味丰富，余味悠长。Pale yellow with steely notes and tinges of green. A vibrant colour. Fresh, fragrant fruity aromas, typical of Viura. Bright and fresh in the palate, with good balancing clean acidity and a lingering rounded finish.

里奥哈法定产区酒 Rioja DOC

12～14℃

情侣约会，浪漫婚宴 dating, wedding

味道丰富的亚洲菜肴 flavourful Asian dishes

以经典的西班牙白葡萄品种维奥娜酿制而成，酸度清新爽口，具有很高的性价比。Made from the classic Spanish white grape variety Viura, this crisp wine has very refreshing, pleasant acidity. Very good value for money.

橡树河畔
La Rioja Alta S.A.

橡树河畔是西班牙的精品酒庄。旗下所酿制的葡萄酒系列众多，有很高的性价比。其卓越的水准得到了各类酒展和酒评大赛的认可，跃升为西班牙里奥哈的顶级佳酿，同时也是国际上享有盛誉的几个西班牙葡萄酒品牌之一。 La Rioja Alta S.A. is the fine wine brand in Spain. It has a large selection of fine wine series at affordable price. The achievements in different international wine competitions have proved the quality of wine, superior and elegant. Meanwhile, it is also one of the most renowned brands in Spain.

橡树河畔特级珍藏890（红）
La Rioja Alta Gran Reserva 890

¥¥¥¥

果酱香味混合着烤面包、皮革和焦糖的味道，酒体强劲而有力。柔滑的单宁加上微酸度，令酒体平衡雅致。The initial aroma is both complex and powerful. On opening, the aromas of toast, leather and caramel mix with tones of dried prunes and fruit compote. In the mouth the wine is powerful and balanced with smooth and silky tannins coupled with a noteworthy light acidity. The aftertaste is full and very complex leaving the flavours full on the palate.

- 里奥哈法定产区酒 Rioja DOC
- 14～17℃
- 商务宴请，酒友交流 business dinner, wine appreciation
- 烤肉 roast meat
- 该酒庄的顶级酒，只在最好年份生产。为了纪念酒庄创立之年1890而得名890。Gran Reserva 890 is named after the year of the creation of La Rioja Alta (1890). This is the winery's top quality wine, produced only in exceptional years.

橡树河畔特级珍藏904（红）
La Rioja Alta
Gran Reserva 904

¥¥¥

成熟水果香气丰富，带有香料和皮革的气息。入口强劲，不失圆润和丝滑的口感。An intense, penetrating and complex aroma with overtones of spices, leather and ripe fruit. In the mouth, strong flavoured yet round and silky with good balance between fruit and acidity.

- 里奥哈法定产区酒 Rioja DOC
- 14～17℃
- 商务宴请，酒友交流 business dinner, wine appreciation
- 红肉，面包，芝士 red meat, bread, cheese
- 为了纪念1904年两个庄园的合并，而且当年是里奥哈有史以来葡萄收成最好的一年而特别推出。This wine is named after the year of 1904 when the La Rioja Alta and Bodegas Ardanza merge into one.

橡树河畔雅丹莎（红）
La Rioja Alta
Reserva Vina Ardanza

¥¥¥

红色水果香味突出，同时混合着椰子、肉桂、烟草和皮革的味道。酒体醇厚而结构平衡。Intense and complex to the nose. Wild berry aromas predominate, blended with hints of coconut, cinnamon, tobacco and leather. Full-bodied and well structured to the palate, with silky and enveloping tannins. Long after-taste.

- 里奥哈法定产区酒 Rioja DOC
- 14～17℃
- 友人相聚，商务宴请 friends gathering, business dinner
- 浓味红肉 red meat with rich sauce
- 1942年以创始人Alfredo Ardanza的名字来命名的一款酒。First released in 1942 the wine was named after winery founder Alfredo Ardanza.

橡树河畔雅芭迪（红）
La Rioja Alta
Reserva Vina Alberdi

¥¥¥

香气明显而愉悦，充满成熟水果的香味，酒体结构平衡，后味持久和充满水果香。Remarkable bouquet, reminiscent of ripe fruit with gentle hints of cinnamon, caramel and coconut. Pleasant and well-structured to the palate, very well-balanced with a pleasing final acidity.

- 里奥哈法定产区酒 Rioja DOC
- 14～17℃
- 情侣约会，友人相聚 dating, friends gathering
- 浓味红肉 red meat with rich sauce
- 这款酒在瓶中陈放时间越长，带果香的复杂后味表现得越有层次。Long, fruity after-taste, which will become more complex the longer it remains in bottle.

橡树河畔雅拉娜（红）
La Rioja Alta
Reserva Vina Arana

¥¥¥

香气复杂而典雅，同时带有甘草和太妃糖的味道。细滑的单宁，令酒体的结构平衡而圆润。Of high aromatic intensity, complex and elegant, with notes of mature fruit, caramel and toffee. In the mouth, good body, very round, with silky tannins.

- 里奥哈法定产区酒 Rioja DOC
- 14～17℃
- 友人相聚，浪漫婚宴 friends gathering, wedding
- 野味，烧烤类红肉，蓝纹芝士 grilled, red meat, blue cheese
- 入口时令人联想到典雅精致的布根地红葡萄酒，十分顺滑，有细腻的果香。On first sip you may think of Red Burgundy. This is the smoothest, silkiest, most fluid of Riojas.

爵士园
Barón de Oña

爵士园最初由热爱葡萄酒的古巴人Leandro Vázquez创立，但最终因经营不善而被迫出让。当时，西班牙的老牌酒王橡树河畔酒厂正有意收购各个名产区的优质葡萄园，两者不谋而合。1995年1月橡树河畔酒厂正式买入该葡萄园，增添了更丰富的产品结构。

Baron de Ona was originally owned by Leandro Vázquez, a Cuban and citizen of the world. For business reasons, Leandro Vázquez decided to leave the wine industry. This situation coincided with the desire of La Rioja Alta, S.A. to complement its traditional style with a new wine. Some changes were made after the purchase in January, 1995. It put more focuses on improving and enhancing what was already there than on changing the château philosophy and the modern and powerful wine initially produced by Baron de Ona, S.A.

爵士园（红）
Barón de Oña

¥¥¥

成熟的浆果香中混合中皮革、甘草和香料的味道。酒体圆润，单宁柔美，口感优雅。Aromatically intense with a mixture of leather, licorice and spices over a background of forest fruits (dark berries). The palate is round, with soft tannins and an elegant mouthfeel, perfectly bred.

- 里奥哈法定产区酒 Rioja DOC
- 14~17℃
- 温馨家宴，酒友交流 family gathering, wine appreciation
- 烤肉，辣味炖菜 roast meat, grilled meat and spicy stews
- 具有陈年潜力，同时由于在推出前已在瓶中陈放2年，因而也完全可以即时享用。This wine will age well but is also ready to drink on release as it has spent two years in the bottle.

雅斯特园
Áster

雅斯特是用智慧、热诚和足够的耐心酿造而成的结晶。雅斯特园由橡树河庄投资建立，是一块位于西班牙新兴精品葡萄酒产区斗罗河岸的葡萄园，该区是近几十年来西班牙发展迅速的一个明星产区，出品相当不凡，声名远播的维嘉西西里亚就产自于此。拥有95公顷的雅斯特园是这里的明星酒园之一。

Áster was created with wisdom, enthusiasm and great patience. It was invested by La Rioja Alta, S.A., and locates in Ribera del Duero, which is a new star appellation of Spain wine industry in recent years. Vega Sicily, one of the best wines in Spain, is also from this appellation. Áster is one of the star wineries in Ribera del Duero, whose winery represents a perfect combination of cutting-edge wine-making technology with a timeless and elegant design.

雅斯特园（红）
Áster

¥¥¥

黑莓和醋栗味十分突出，隐约透出一丝丝甘草和肉桂的味道。酒体结实而平衡，非常诱人。Intense aroma, strongly reminiscent of ripe fruit (blackberries and gooseberries).Well-structured to the palate, harmonious and tasty.

- 斗罗河岸法定产区酒 Ribera del Duero DO
- 14～17℃
- 温馨家宴，活力派对 family gathering, party
- 烤肉（烤羊、烤乳猪等），辣味炖菜，烟熏芝士 roast meat (lamb, suckling pig, etc.), peppered spicy stews and smoked and cured strong cheese
- 在法国新橡木桶和两年陈的美国橡木桶中发酵2年，使得这款酒的单宁细腻柔滑，后味格外悠长。It was aged for 24 months in new French and two-year old American oak casks.

施乐华
Lagar de Cervera

1988年，为了推出高品质的白葡萄酒，橡树河庄四处寻找最适合的土地，最后他们在西班牙最有名气的白葡萄酒产区下海湾找到了施乐华。施华乐的酒芳香怡人、清爽、精致而优雅。此酒还入选2004年《葡萄酒观察家》评选的“世界百大葡萄酒”，品质备受肯定。

In 1988, La Rioja Alta, S.A. was looking for somewhere to branch out into white wine-making. After great effort, it found Lagar de Cervera in Rias Baixas, the most famous white wine appellation in Spain. The region's good weather and the nearby river give this wine its subtlety. This elegant white wine has won "Top 100 worldwide wines" of 2004 by *Wine Spectator*, from which you perceive its charm.

施乐华（白）
Lagar de Cervera

¥¥¥

带有该葡萄品种非常典型的柠檬柑橘味。酒精度和酸度非常平衡，酒体饱满，呈现黄油的质感，清新爽脆，回味悠长。The variety's typical bouquet combined with hints of very ripe stone and citric fruit. Good balance between alcohol content and acidity; well-structures to the palate.

- 下海湾法定产区酒 Rias Baixas DO
- 14～17℃
- 友人相聚，温馨家宴 friends gathering, family gathering
- 海鲜，鱼类，沙拉，谷物，芝士 seafood, fish, salads, rice dishes, cheese
- 在贫瘠的土壤、充足的降水和海洋性气候的共同造就下，施乐华出产西班牙最好的白葡萄酒之一。Lagar de Cervera produces some of the finest dry white Albarino in Spain thanks to poor soils, adequate rainfall and a cool maritime climate.

德 国

GERMANY

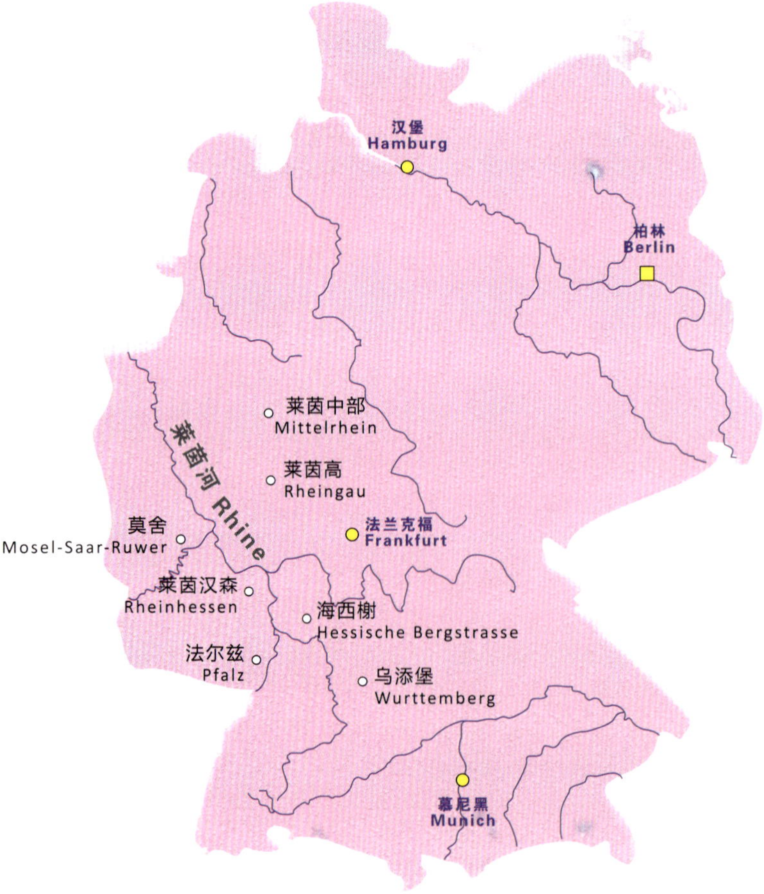

德国葡萄酒产区示意图

德国 的葡萄酒产区是全世界葡萄酒产区的最北限，分布在北纬47°～52°，由于气候寒冷，为了让葡萄达到充分成熟，德国的葡萄采摘时间较迟，因此酿出酒精浓度较低，果香芬芳清爽的顶级葡萄酒，是寒冷地区葡萄酒的典范。德国以出产白葡萄酒为主，从一般的干白到甜白到不多见的贵腐葡萄酒，几乎占葡萄酒产量的85%。此外，德国还是全世界闻名的冰酒的故乡，生产清甜爽口、甜而不腻、性价比甚高的冰酒。

{葡萄品种}

德国葡萄酒多数使用单一品种酿造，主要的白葡萄品种有威士莲和慕勒（Müller-Thurgau），红葡萄品种有贝露娃（Pinot Noir，在德国称为Spätburgunder）和丹菲特。

威士莲 Riesling

{分级制度}

德国葡萄酒的分级制度分为4个级别，越高级别的葡萄成熟度越高，级别由低到高如下：

优质法定产区酒
Qualitätswein mit Pradikat，简称QmP，原名为Prädikatswein

德国分级的最高级别。根据葡萄采摘时间和含糖量的不同，QmP又分为6个级别，级别越高，含糖量越高，酒的口感越浓郁，价格也越高。级别由高到低如下：

（1）精选干颗粒贵腐葡萄酒（Trockenbeerenauslese/Dry Berries Selection）
只选用干萎的受贵腐霉菌感染的葡萄酿制而成。因为葡萄已失去了大部分水分，所以酒的甜度非常高。

（2）冰葡萄酒（Eiswein/Icewine）
选用在自然条件下非常成熟的结冰葡萄酿制而成，葡萄采摘需在-8℃进行，并在葡萄颗粒结冰的状态下进行榨汁。生产条件非常苛刻，只有在气候适当的年份才生产。

（3）精选颗粒贵腐葡萄酒（Beerenauslese/Berry Selection）
只选用受贵腐霉菌感染的葡萄酿制而成。葡萄需经人手一颗颗筛选。

（4）串选葡萄酒（Auslese/Select Harvest）
用成熟度更高的葡萄酿制而成，大多数是甜型，也有少数是干型。这一级别的葡萄采摘时间更晚一些，部分葡萄会有轻微的贵腐霉菌感染。

（5）晚摘葡萄酒（Spatlese/Late Harvest）
葡萄采摘在Kabinet级别葡萄采收后的12～14天进行。

（6）一般葡萄酒（Kabinet）
采用成熟初期的葡萄酿造，口感清盈平淡。

▲

法定产区酒
Qualitätswein bestimmter Anbaugebiete，简称QbA

德国二等葡萄酒，占全国总产量的70%以上。产于德国政府指定的法定葡萄酒产区，并以当地栽种的优质葡萄为原料，必须经官方的质量管理和控制中心鉴定，合格后下达检测标准号码才能销售。

▲

乡土葡萄酒
Landwein

德国普通佐餐酒。等同于法国 VDP 级别。

▲

日常餐酒
Tafelwein

德国最低等级的葡萄酒。可在德国内各地生产，酒精浓度不得低于8.5%，也可用各地同类品质葡萄酒勾兑而成。

{葡萄酒产区}

德国一共有13个葡萄酒产区，葡萄大都种植在河谷地区。北部地区生产的葡萄酒一般清淡可口，果香四溢，并有新鲜果酸味。而南部生产的葡萄酒则圆满充实，果味诱人，有时带有更刚烈的味道而不失温和适中的酸性。最常见到的德国酒主要集中在莱茵河岸（Rhein）和莫舍河岸（Mosel）的4个产区：莫舍（Mosel-Saar-Ruwer）、莱茵高（Rheingau）、莱茵汉森（Rheinhessen）和法尔兹（Pfalz）。

莫舍 是世界公认的德国最好的白葡萄酒产区之一，境内有莫舍河以及两条支流河萨尔河（Saar）和卢温河（Ruwer）三大河流，能对寒冷季节起到调节温度的作用。土壤以板岩为主，几乎所有的葡萄园都位于陡峭的河岸上。该区主要出产酒体轻盈、口感爽脆、酸度高、带有特殊矿物味的威士莲葡萄酒。

莱茵高 位于莱茵河的转角处，葡萄种植面积只有莫舍的1/4，只有一个子产区约翰山（Johannisberg），被认为是威士莲的真正老家，许多顶级德国酒的生产阵营都位于此地，如著名的威士莲起泡酒生产商欧洲王子（Fürst von Metternich）。该区的威士莲葡萄酒与莫舍区的相比酒体略重，芳香更为细腻。另外该区也产酒香优雅、柔顺如丝的贝露娃红葡萄酒。

莱茵汉森 是德国最大的葡萄酒产区，气候温和，所产葡萄酒的类型多样化，质量较为普通。该区的特色葡萄是西尔瓦娜（Silvaner），用来酿制著名的莱茵干白葡萄酒，又称圣母的乳汁（Liebfraumilch）。

法尔兹 在拉丁语意为“宫殿”，因古罗马皇帝奥古斯都曾在此建行宫得名，是德国第二大葡萄酒产区，产量却位居德国第一。目前红葡萄酒在近年产量有攀升的趋势，但白葡萄酒仍是该区主要的酒款，以威士莲和慕勒白葡萄酒出名，还是德国最著名的冰酒及贵腐甜酒产区，出产的冰酒甜而不腻，清纯冰爽，带有丰富的鲜果香、干果味、花香和蜂蜜香。

{冰酒的故乡}

德国是世界上最早酿制冰酒的国家。在1765年，德国下了一场大的早雪，加上天气冷得早，雪结冰积在葡萄串上。酒农们以为该年的收成全都完了。结果到了11月，葡萄串还好好地挂在树上。因为收割晚了，葡萄比正常情况成熟了很多，含糖量也随之增高。在寒冷的气候影响下，葡萄里的水分大部分结成了冰，而糖分却不容易结冰，所以在榨汁后，葡萄汁的糖度很高，酒体却爽脆清新，因此意外地酿出了举世闻名的冰酒。

冰酒适合与很多中餐菜式搭配，从甜品和水果，到川菜和湘菜等辣味菜肴都可搭配，是目前中国越来越流行的葡萄甜酒。

由于对自然环境的要求甚高，到目前为止，全世界仅有德国、奥地利和加拿大生产冰酒。而全球环境日益暖化，也造成冰酒的产量逐渐减少而越来越珍贵。

莱茵高

Rheingau

欧洲王子

Fürst von Metternich

欧洲王子是由Metternich家族拥有的德国起泡酒品牌，主人是奥地利贵族最高等级的亲王家族，世袭罔替。从开始生产葡萄酒到现在，其每年都要将总量的1/10上贡给奥地利皇族。

Fürst von Metternich is a German sparkling brand owned by Metternich family, who was raised to the highest rank of Austrian peerage Fürst and passed the hereditary title from one generation to the next. Then as now one tenth of each year's wine harvest had to be handed over to the Austrian imperial family.

欧洲王子起泡葡萄酒
Fürst von Metternich
Riesling Sekt Trocken

¥ ¥

这是一款给人愉悦口感的起泡酒，呈现淡淡的金黄色调，带有明显的橘子和桃子香气，口感温柔清雅。It owes its unique taste and character to the carefully selected German Riesling grapes. It shows a pleasant, pale gold colour and boasts a subtle bouquet that hints soft, clear and distinct fruit aromas of tangerine and peach.

- 优品级 Distinguished
- 7~10℃
- 情侣约会，浪漫婚宴 dating, wedding
- 海鲜，时蔬 seafood, appetizer
- 此酒的葡萄来自被誉为"威士莲的正宗家乡"的约翰山，是德国顶级白葡萄酒的招牌产区。Fürst von Metternich is a German sparkling brand owned by Metternich family, who was raised to the highest rank of Austrian peerage Fürst and passed the hereditary title from one generation to the next. Then as now one tenth of each year's wine harvest had to be handed over to the Austrian imperial family.

欧洲王子粉红起泡葡萄酒
Fürst von Metternich Rosé Sekt Trocken

¥ ¥

粉红色调浪漫迷人，缓缓升起的气泡灵动优雅，口感温婉细腻，不愧是一款供懂酒之人欣赏的佳酿。Its tingling sensation, full-bodied elegance, and sparkling gracefulness have created a modern brand appreciated and demanded by discriminating consumers.

优品级 Distinguished

7~10℃

浪漫婚宴，酒友交流 wedding, wine appreciation

海鲜，时蔬 seafood, appetizer

这是一款珍贵的贝露娃起泡酒，具有极为优异的质量。As a remarkable quality sparkling wine with a unique character from white-pressed Pinot Noir grapes, Fürst von Metternich Rosé meets the highest expectations.

小常识
Q & A

问：贵腐霉这一名字的来源?

答：贵腐霉(botrytis cinerea)也称为贵族霉，是一种天然的霉菌。由于受气候的制约，全世界能符合其生长条件的葡萄酒产区屈指可数，而且每年的气候状况都不一样，并不是每年都可以生产出这种酒，所以这种长在葡萄上如此珍贵的霉菌又被称为"noble rot"，“贵腐”一词由此而来。由于贵腐霉附在成熟的葡萄上，霉菌的菌丝会穿透葡萄皮，吸取葡萄颗粒的水分，因此葡萄会干缩，而使葡萄内的糖分和其他成分浓缩，并产生特殊的香味。法国波尔多苏玳区的滴金庄，德国金冰王、德国冰白、贵族冰甜等都是在国内享有高知名度的贵腐葡萄酒。

法尔兹
Pfalz

威特驰
Weltachs

威特驰是已经营了五代人的德国法尔兹优质酒庄，以产果香、花香丰富的甜葡萄酒而闻名。
Founded in 1987 as a new company within Weltachs family, the winery itself was originally founded in 1920. The wine making tradition is now in its fifth generation guaranteeing a traditional high standard of quality.

德国至尊冰甜（白）
Weltachs Pinot Noir Eiswein

¥¥¥

香味胜似芒果、草莓和蜂蜜。入口有成熟蜜瓜和热带水果的香味，酸度适中，让口感活跃无比。The taste of ripe honey melon and tropical fruits is well combined with the lively acidity.

- 优质法定产区酒 QmP
- 4~7℃
- 温馨家宴，商务宴请 family gathering, business dinner
- 甜品，开胃菜 dessert, appetizer
- 这款以红葡萄品种酿造而成的白色冰酒极其罕有，是威特驰的顶级产品。This premium ice wine is a rare white dessert wine made with red grapes.

德国金冰王（白）
Weltachs Trockenbeerenauslese

¥ ¥ ¥

该酒采用符合糖度要求的葡萄颗粒酿造而成。采摘时需要逐粒葡萄精挑细选，才能酿出带有独特的蜂蜜芳香和浓郁花果香的甜美甘露。It is made by selected grapes with highly concentrated sugar. So the wine has honey and flower nose with sweet and complicated taste.

优质法定产区酒 QmP

4~7℃

活力派对，浪漫婚宴 party, wedding

海鲜，白肉 seafood, white meat

这款酒采用单一葡萄园中手工采摘的高度感染贵腐霉菌的单一葡萄品种精制而成，品质超群。The wine is made from hand selected, highly botrytis effected single grapes (similar to raisons) from a single estate.

德国蓝冰王甜（白）
Weltachs Eiswein

¥ ¥ ¥

采用已经结冰的成熟葡萄颗粒压榨而出的浓缩汁液。酒液散发着蜂蜜、桃子和草莓的芳香，口感酸甜适中，清新爽脆。It is a quality icewine produced in Germany. Pressed the ripe grapes when they frozen and obtained the fresh concentrated juice. That's why the wine brings honey and flower aromas and sweet but crispy taste.

优质法定产区酒 QmP

4~7℃

活力派对，商务宴请 party, business dinner

淡酱汁海鲜，白肉，淡味芝士 seafood with lite sausage, white meat, mild cheese

这是一款正宗的德国冰酒，具有十分典型的冰酒的果香和清新口感，非常值得一试。A genuine German ice wine with typical fruity aroma and refreshing taste.

德国冰红（红）
Weltachs
Red October Rotwein

¥ ¥

此款色泽诱人的红色冰酒，果味芳香，甜度和酸度相当平衡，酒精度较低。No tannic acidity. Very comfortable mouth feeling, very mild fruity.

法定产区酒 QbA

4~7℃

情侣约会，活力派对 dating, party

餐后甜点 a very nice dessert wine

这款是威特驰针对中国市场的需求以创新的酿造技术推出的精品冰酒。A premium Weltachs ice wine specially made for Chinese market with art-of-the-state winemaking technology.

德国冰白（白）
Weltachs Beerenauslese

¥ ¥

一款玫瑰香型葡萄酒。贵腐霉的作用让颗粒榨出的汁液浓稠芬芳无比，如香料和香草一般浓烈芳香。Single selected, hand picked and overripe bunches are harvested to make such a very complex wine.

优质法定产区酒 QmP

4~7℃

友人相聚，酒友交流 friends gathering, wine appreciation

沙拉，海鲜意大利面，偏辛辣的亚洲菜式 salads, sea-food pastas, spicy foods such as Chinese and Thai dishes

酒香十分迷人：强烈的香料和草药气息以及浓郁的麝香。Strong flavour such as spice and herbs. Intense aromatic and muscatel flavour.

德国贵族冰甜（白）
Weltachs Auslese

¥ ¥

采用部分感染贵族霉的葡萄颗粒酿造此酒。带柠檬、樱桃、芒果香味，甜美而容易入口，酸度配合得恰到好处。Weltachs selects partly-Botrytis-affected grapes to make this Auslese to be fruity, like lemon, cherries and mango on the smell. Mild and crisp, at the same time is well balanced between sweetness and acidity.

优质法定产区酒 QmP

7~10℃

友人相聚，活力派对 friends gathering, party

菠萝，柑橘，甜品 pineapple, citrus, other sweets

白葡萄果实采自最成熟的枝条，带来柔和圆润的口感，几乎可以与所有食物搭配。This wine is made with white grape types from the the ripest brunches. Matches almost all kind of food.

威特驰威士莲（白）
Weltachs Riesling, QbA Pfalz

¥ ¥

这款威士莲葡萄酒以平衡的酸度和甜度搭配制胜。果香味道浓郁，口感爽脆。This Weltachs Riesling is well balanced between alcohol, sweetness and acidity. The taste is fruity and crisp with a hint of sweetness.

- 法定产区酒 QbA
- 7~10℃
- 情侣约会，浪漫婚宴 dating, wedding
- 淡味肉类，沙拉，海鲜 light meat, salad, seafood
- 是非常典型的德国白葡萄酒。餐前或餐后饮用均可。A very typical German white wine for enjoyment before or after dinner.

德国晚秋清甜（白）
Weltachs Spatlese

¥ ¥

此酒微甜，果香和花香突出，入口则清爽怡人。It is a late harvest style, resulting in a agreeably sweet palate. Easy drinking wine is fruity, like apple, grape, banana.

- 优质法定产区酒 QmP
- 7~10℃
- 情侣约会，友人相聚 dating, friends gathering
- 鱼类开胃菜 fish appetizers
- 采用晚收琼瑶浆和白贝露葡萄酿制，风味独特。Made with late harvest Gewürztraminer and Weißer Burgunder (Pinot Blanc). Very unique.

丹菲红（红）
Weltachs Dornfelder Rotwein

¥

充满成熟樱桃与黑莓的浓郁气息。口感温和圆润，单宁柔软，清淡而迷人。No fermentation on the skin. Heat treated to extract the colour and minimise the extraction bitter aromas so as to have very intense like fully ripe cherries and blackberries.

- 法定产区酒 QbA
- 4~7℃
- 温馨家宴，活力派对 family gathering, party
- 海鲜，汤，各种小吃 seafood, soup, assorted snacks
- 采用高于法定要求的优质丹菲红葡萄，去皮后用热处理技术获取葡萄的美丽色泽。High quality Dornfelder grapes are picked at a certain level above the legal requirements. Heat treated to extract the colour and minimise the extraction bitter aromas.

邓肯博士

Dr. Deinhard

邓肯博士是德国最高级别的VDP酒庄，也是最早加入VDP的几个酒庄之一，可见其酒的品质早已得到极高的认同，相当于法国波尔多的列级名庄。数十年来优异的品质，让邓肯博士酒厂的出品在国内外获奖无数，深受葡萄酒爱好者的欢迎。

For decades, the outstanding quality of Weingut Dr. Deinhard wines has been recognized again and again with numerous national and international honors.

邓肯博士冰（白）

Dr.Deinhard Riesling Eiswein

¥ ¥ ¥ ¥ ¥

柠檬奶酪和酸橙的香气浓郁，口感圆润，酸度怡人。
Excellent concentration with intriguing lemon-cream and lime aromas. It's warm and round on the palate, but no hint of botrytis and enough acidity to keep it aloft.

优质法定产区酒 QmP

4~7℃

温馨家宴，商务宴请 family gathering, business dinner

慕斯，提拉米苏，芝士蛋糕 mousse, cheese cake, Tiramisu

从19世纪晚期开始，邓肯博士庄园就开始酿造质量卓越的威士莲冰酒，这款酒即其所产佳酿的最佳代表之一。 Since the late half of 19th century Weingut Dr. Deinhard has been producing premium quality Riesling ice wine and this is one of its most iconic products.

邓肯博士晚秋威士莲（白）
Dr.Deinhard Riesling Spatlese Trocken

¥¥¥

有芬芳的柑橘、蜜桃等水果香气，入口充满酸橙和油桃果香。Fragrantly perfumed aromas of citrus and nectarine. Round and full - bodied, showing a supple taste.

- 优质法定产区酒 QmP
- 12~14℃
- 商务宴请，酒友交流 business dinner, wine appreciation
- 海鲜，白肉 seafood, white meat
- 曾荣获优质精品葡萄酒挑战赛中最高级别金奖，这款晚秋威士莲的酒质不容置疑。Gold award winner at the Premium Select Wine Challenge, this outstanding Deidesheimer Langenmorgen Riesling has unquestionable quality.

邓肯博士威士莲（白）
Dr.Deinhard Riesling Kabinett Halbtrocken

¥¥

这款半干白酒留香非常持久，酸度清新，花香更会在口中久久不散，余味悠长。This semi-dry Riesling will be with us for the palate journey through its concentrated flavours and aromas of the world Pfalz Riesling.

- 优质法定产区酒 QmP
- 12~14℃
- 友人相聚，活力派对 friends gathering, party
- 烤干果，黑橄榄 roast salty nuts, black olive
- 来自法尔兹闻名遐迩的代德斯海姆村庄的威士莲，风味超卓。A premium wine from the renowned Deidesheim region in Pfalz.

巴莎曼博士

Dr. von Bassermann

两个世纪以来，巴莎曼博士以其优秀的酿酒技术和超卓的酒质赢得众多的美誉，当之无愧成为法尔兹地区最优秀的酒厂之一。For two centuries, Dr. von Bassermann-Jordan has been one of the leading producers of fine Pfalz wines with superb quality and state-of-the-art winemaking technology.

巴莎曼博士威士莲（白）
Dr. von Bassermann
Jordan Riesling Kabinett

¥¥¥

口感温暖悠长，散发出雪梨蜜饯和成熟蜜桃的气息，果香持久。Warm and expansive, this shows rich aromas of pear compote and ripe peach, complicated by a sweetly herbal note like shiso. The fragrant, bold fruit flavours last.

优质法定产区酒 QmP

12~14℃

情侣约会，友人相聚 dating, friends gathering

鹅肝酱，鸡肝酱，辣味的泰国及亚洲其他国家菜式 foie gras, chicken liver parfait, Thai and Asian cuisine

风格平衡，口感丰富，是非常容易配餐的一款酒。A well balanced wine with versatile capability to pair with different kinds of food.

巴莎曼博士晚秋威士莲（白）
Dr. von Bassermann Jordan Riesling Spatlese

¥¥¥

活泼的酸橙、苹果和蜜桃气息带有一丝二氧化碳气泡。入口后逐渐变得坚实直至后味消失。Racy, with lime, apple and peach notes and a hint of carbonic gas. Turns firm midpalate through the finish, yet seems to have all the elements to develop well.

- 优质法定产区酒 QmP
- 12～14℃
- 情侣约会，温馨家宴 dating, family gathering
- 腌渍水果，水果馅饼 fruits that are poached, baked or caramelized
- 微甜的口感和清新的酸度令人愉悦，非常适合在佳节与好友、亲人共同分享。Its ethereal sweetness and pleasant acidity make it an ideal wine to enjoy with your loved ones at holidays and festivals.

巴莎曼博士贵族清甜（白）
Dr. von Bassermann Jordan Riesling Auslese

¥¥¥

有成熟的热带水果香气，菠萝、杏、柑橘和矿物的气息是这款优雅的威士莲的特点。Ripe, tropical fruit notes of pineapple and apricot, along with quince and mineral, highlight this bright, delicate Riesling.

- 优质法定产区酒 QmP
- 12～14℃
- 活力派对，浪漫婚宴 party, wedding
- 提拉米苏，法式芝士蛋糕，法式薄煎饼 Tiramisu, french cheese cake, french crepe suzette
- 品质极高，2005年获得《葡萄酒观察家》94分的高分。Premium quality. Vintage 2005 was rated 94 points by *Wine Spectator* in 2007.

附录一 全国葡萄酒专卖店列表

APPENDIX 1 NATIONAL WINE STORE DIRECTORY

- 富隆酒窖 Aussino Cellar
- 富隆酒屋 Aussino Wine shop
- 富隆酒坊 Aussino Wine Corner
- 富隆酒膳 Aussino Wine & Dine
- 富隆酒库 Aussino Wine House

{华南地区}
Southern China

>>广东 Guangdong

广州 / Guangzhou

珠江新城华夏路39号（星汇园首层商铺）
Ground Floor, No.39, Zhujiang New Town, Huaxia Road （Galaxy Garden）
Tel: 020-3862 1613 / 3883 9233

天河北路439号首层A铺（阿一鲍鱼旁）
A, Ground Floor, No.439, Tianhe Bei Road
Tel: 020-3881 1612 / 3881 2603

天河东路信诚南街9号
No.9, Xincheng Nan Street, Tianhe Dong Road
Tel: 020-3880 0474

天河路天河城百货吉之岛
Jusco, TeeMall, Tianhe Road

天河路正佳广场友谊商店三楼
F3, Friendship Store, Grand View Mall, Tianhe Road

林和中路154号东方宝泰购物广场吉之岛
Jusco, Popark, No.154, Linhe Zhong Road

天河区冼村路2号裙楼五层
F5, Skirt Building of No.2, Xiancun Road, Tianhe District

天河区员村湖景金阁酒家
Hujingjinge Restaurant, Yuancun, Tianhe District

汇景新城亚太盛汇C2C3街区负一层16-21号商铺
Shop 16-21, B1, Zone 2-3, Favorview Palace
Tel: 020-8550 2259

广州大道北路1811-1813号太阳城广场负一层
B1, Sun City Mall, No.1811-1813, Guangzhou Dadao Bei Road

北京路广百百货新翼五楼
F5, Grandbuy Department Store, Beijing Road

农林下路王府井百货二楼
F2, Guangzhou Wangfujing Department Store, Nonglin Xia Road

先烈路东山百货广场首层食品超市
F1, Dongshan Department Store, Xianlie Road

海珠区滨江东路479-481号
No.479-481, Binjiang Dong Road, Haizhu District
Tel: 020-3432 0648

花都区新华街公益路47号金宏利大厦首层
Ground Floor, Goldvole Building, No.47, Gongyi Road, Xinhua Street, Huadu District
Tel: 020-3691 3386

增城文化会馆
Culture Guild Hall, Zengcheng, Guangzhou
Tel: 020-8266 9998

增城新塘镇现代城103号商铺
Shop 103, Modern City, Xintang Town, Zengcheng
Tel: 020-3286 6018

增城市荔城街岗前路11号首层
Ground Floor, No.11, Gangqian Road, Licheng Street, Zengcheng
Tel: 020-8261 2688

增城市新塘镇荔新十二路99号03号铺
Shop 3, No.99, Lixin 12 Road, Xintang, Zengcheng
Tel: 020-8288 1028

从化街口青云路 381 号
No.381, Qingyun Road, Conghua District
Tel: 020-3790 0008

珠海 / Zhuhai

凤凰路1088号扬名广场二层吉之岛
Jusco, F2, Yangming Plaza, No.1088, Fenghuang Road

拱北情侣南路288号之113号
Suite 113, No.288, Qinglü Nan Road, Gongbei, Zhuhai
Tel: 0756-3868 999

中山 / Zhongshan

古镇灯都华庭商业街C19
C19, Commercial Street, Dengdu Huating, Gu Zhen
Tel: 0760-2238 3663

火炬开发区中山港大道中山港商业大厦
Zhongshan Port Business Building, Zhongshan Port Street, Torch Development District
Tel: 0760-8828 7333

石岐区中山二路8号君悦广场二期一层
F1, Phase 2, Junyue Plaza, No.8, Zhongshan 2 Road, Shiqi District

富湾东路2号之1、2卡富豪轩悠闲驿站
Shop 1-2, No.2, Fuwan Dong Road, Kafuhaoxuan Regal Court Inn
Tel: 0760-8861 8868

三乡镇金涌大道雅居乐花园H35幢12号铺
Shop 12, Building H35, Agile, Jinchong Avenue, Sanxiang

小榄镇新华中路28号
No.28, Xinhua Zhong Road, Xiaolan
Tel: 0760-2255 0888

小榄镇民安中路顺昌广场二楼
F2, Shunchang Plaza, Min An Zhong Road, Xiaolan
Tel: 0760-8782 0183

深圳 / Shenzhen

宝安区新安四路旭士达名苑一楼
F1, Xushidaming Court, Xin'an 4 Road, Bao'an District
Tel: 0755-8884 1555 / 8884 2111

罗湖区太宁路百仕达花园吉之岛
Jusco, Baishida Garden, Taining Road, Luohu District

福田区福华路星河国际COCO PARK购物公园吉之岛
Jusco, COCO PARK Shopping Mall, Fuhua Road, Futian District

南山区海岸城吉之岛
Jusco,Hai'an City, Nanshan District

南山区蛇口龟山路1号美伦会所一楼
F1, Maillen Club, No.1, Guishan Road, Shekou, Nanshan District
Tel: 0755-2668 7777

汕头 / Shantou

龙湖区华山路8号金东海大厦首层
Ground Floor, Jindonghai Building, No.8, Huashan Road, Longhu District
Tel: 0754-8848 8333

龙湖区长平路星湖清华城2栋107
No.107, Building 2, Noblest Territory, Changping Road, Longhu District
Tel: 0754-8881 9929

清远 / Qingyuan

清城区沿江路一号（未开业）
No.1, Yanjiang Road, Qingcheng District

梅州/Meizhou

江南团结路1号
No.1, Jiangnan Tuanjie Road
Tel: 0753-2302 812 / 2302 813

开平 / Kaiping

长沙区幕桥东路29号紫荆花园4栋首层101-102号
No.101-102, Ground Floor, Building 4, Zijing Garden, No.29, Muqiao Dong Road, Changsha District

江门 / Jiangmen

蓬江区东华二路2号益源商业广场二楼之二
Suite 2, F2, Yiyuan Commercial Plaza, No.2, Donghua 2 Road, Pengjiang District
Tel: 0750-3378088

新会区中心南路6号-101
Shop 101, No.6, Zhongxin Nan Road, Xinhui District
Tel: 0750-6677 128

江华一路 135 号首层
Ground Floor, No.135, Jianghua 1 Road
Tel: 0750-3127 066

中天国际花园嘉华苑7栋116号
No.116, Building 7, Jiahua Court, Zhongtian International Garden

迎宾大道中路118号逸豪酒店3楼11-12铺
Shop 11-12, F3, Yucca Hotel, No.118, Yingbin Dadao Zhong Road

惠州 / Huizhou

江北金裕碧水湾三景园B栋4-5号铺
No.4-5, Building B, Sanjing Yuan, Jinyubishui Wan, Jiangbei District
Tel: 0752-2060 022

河源 / Heyuan

建设大道东路5号华达凯旋城101栋03号
No.3, Building 101, Victory City, No.5, Jianshe Dadao Dong Road

佛山 / Foshan

顺德区大良新桂路明日广场二座首层5号
No.5, F1, Building 2, Future Edifice, Xingui Road, Daliang, Shunde District
Tel: 0757-2268 9338

顺德大良云桂路82号
No.82, Yungui Road, Daliang, Shunde District
Tel: 0757-2613 6633

顺德区容桂镇中华路华厦新城13号铺
No.13, Huaxia New Town, Zhonghua Road, Ronggui Town, Shunde District
Tel: 0757-2327 6307

顺德大良南国东路永旺购物中心吉之岛
Jusco, Yongwang Shopping Center, Nanguo Dong Road, Daliang, Shunde District

佛山东方广场吉之岛
Jusco, Dongfang Plaza, Foshan

南海区桂城街道海六路与千灯湖东路交界处，保利水城购物中心首层
Ground Floor, Poly Canal Plaza, the cross of Hailiu Road and Qiandenghu Dong Road, Guicheng, Nanhai District

禅城区湖景路8号（天湖郦都）1区38座P5-P6铺
Suite P5-P6, Building 38, Zone1, No.8, Hujing Road(Tianhu Lidu), Chancheng Disrtict
Tel: 0757-8378 4077

禅城区祖庙路佛山宾馆5号铺
Shop 5, Foshan Hotel, Zumiao Road, Chancheng District
Tel: 0757-8312 6536

东莞 / Dongguan

东城区东城大道金月湾广场A8、A9号铺
Shop A8-A9, Jinyuewan Plaza, Dongcheng Avenue, Dongcheng District
Tel: 0769-8138 1998

厚街镇体育东路盛和花园地铺10号
No.10, Shenghe Garden, Tiyu Dong Road, Houjie
Tel: 0769-8227 3555

虎门金龙南路88号俪城商场地铺A11-A16
Shop A11-A16, Licheng Mall,No.88, Jinlong Nan Road, Humen
Tel: 0769-8161 2000

塘厦镇花园街北二巷5号
No.5, Bei 2 Lane, Garden Street, Tangxia Town
Tel: 0769-8203 3888 / 8203 3633

东城区花园贸易广场吉之岛
Jusco, Garden Trade Center, Dongcheng District

>> 广西 Guangxi

南宁 / Nanning

金湖南路37号（马可波罗假日酒店）一楼
F1, No.37, Jinhu Nan Road
Tel: 0771-5803 511

青秀区金湖路58号建兴苑A座109号1层
Ground Floor, No.109, Building A, Jianxing Court, No.58, Jinhu Road, Qingxiu District

柳州 / Liuzhou

东环路101号华林君邸3-1-12,3-1-13号
No.3-1-12,3-1-13, Hualin, No.101, Donghuan Road
Tel: 0772-2607 198

桂林 / Guilin

翊武路桂湖景苑C栋1-18号
No.1-18, Building C, Guihujing Court, Yiwu Road
Tel: 0773-2899 696

防城港 / Fangchenggang

东兴市新华路
Xinhua Road, Dongxing

>> 海南 Hainan

海口 / Haikou

蓝天路28号名门广场首层
Ground Floor, Main Plaza, No.28, Lantian Road
Tel: 0898-6530 8828 / 6530 8898

>> 香港特别行政区 Hong Kong

香港 / Hong Kong

新界荃湾海盛路9号有线电视大楼27楼9号室
Unit 9, 27/F., Cabel TV Tower, No.9 Hoi Shing Road, Tsuen Wan, New Territories, Hong Kong
Tel: 00852-2498 2390 / 2498 2391

{华东地区} Eastern China

>> 浙江 Zhejiang

杭州 / Hangzhou

求是路48号
No.48, Qiushi Road
Tel: 0571-8893 9899

余杭区临平水景公园云水轩
Shuijing Park, Linping, Yuhang District

武林广场1号杭州大厦商场C座裙楼地下一层
B1, Skirt Building of Building C, Hangzhou Mansion, No.1, Wulin Square
Tel: 0571-8893 9899

慈溪 / Cixi

三北西大街354-356号
No.354-356, Sanbei Xi Avenue
Tel: 0574-6381 3999

湖州 / Huzhou

众鑫广场一期一楼B区021号
Shop 021, Zone B, F1, Phase 1, Zhongxin Plaza
Tel: 0572-2020 277

市南街延伸段86号
No.86, Shinan Street

金华 / Jinhua

中山路26号
No.26, Zhongshan Road
Tel: 0579-8231 9577

武义县俞源街51号
No.51, Yuyuan Street, Wuyi County
Tel: 0579-8766 4567

宁波 / Ningbo

江北区中马路145号
No.145, Zhongma Road, Jiangbei District
Tel: 0574-8738 4779 / 8796 5523

象山县丹城靖南路655号
No.655, Jingnan Road, Dancheng, Xiangshan County
Tel: 0574-6500 1881 / 6500 2279

宁海县气象北路247号
No.247, Qixiang Bei Road, Ninghai County

台州 / Taizhou

温岭县万昌中路1099-1109号
No.1099-1109, Wanchang Zhong Road, Wenling
Tel: 0576-8699 8999

玉环县玉环客运中心
Yuhuan Coach Terminal, Yuhuan County
Tel: 0576-8071 0999

路桥区玉宏半岛花园108号商铺
Shop 108, Young Peninsula Garden, Luqiao District

义乌 / Yiwu

丹溪路33号
No.33, Danxi Road

丹溪路167-169号
No.167-169, Danxi Road
Tel: 0579-8581 0055

舟山 / Zhoushan

普陀区沈家门兴建路463、465号
No.463, 465, Xingjian Road, Shenjia Men, Putuo District

>> 福建 Fujian

福安 / Fuan

漫洪路华兴苑3号店
No.3, Huaxing Court, Manhong Road

晋江 / Jinjiang

竹园东路福隆花园
Fulong Garden, Zhuyuan Dong Road
Tel: 0595-8200 6788

龙岩 / Longyan

九州一南路天马湾大厦8号店
Shop 8, Tianmawan Mansion, Jiuzhouyi Nan Road
Tel: 0597-2265 899

泉州 Quanzhou

丰泽区田安南路金帝商厦7号店
Shop 7, Jindi Business House, Tian'an Nan Road, Fengze District
Tel: 0595-2810 0899

厦门 Xiamen

海湾新城一期25#-109号店面
25#-109, Phase 1, Haiwan New Town, Xiamen
Tel: 0592-5369 188

>> 江苏 Jiangsu

常州 / Changzhou

新北区通江大道398号富都商贸饭店（香格里拉酒店集团成员）夹层
Mezzanine, Traders Fudu Hotel by Shangri-la, No.398, Tongjiang Avenue, Xinbei District
Tel: 0519-8516 8255

江阴 / Jiangyin

朝阳路101号
No.101,Chaoyang Road
Tel: 0510-8680 2777

昆山 / Kunshan

桃花江路东方华庭5号商铺（浦发银行对面）
No.5, Dongfang Garden, Taohuajiang Road
Tel: 0512-5790 8868

南京 / Nanjing

中山东路198号109室
Shop109, No.198, Zhongshan Dong Road
Tel: 025-8467 9799

玄武区北京东路4号江苏广电城主楼一楼大厅西南角
Ground Floor, Jiangsu Broadcasting Building, No.4, Beijing Dong Road, Xuanwu District

苏州 / Suzhou

苏州工业园区金鸡湖商业广场D区
Zone D, Jinjihu Business Plaza, Suzhou Industrial Estate
Tel: 0512-6280 5998

金阊区金门路945号
No.945, Jinmen Road，Jinchang District
Tel: 0512-6533 9799

无锡 / Wuxi

梁青路一号无锡大饭店西楼
West Building of Wuxi Restaurant, No.1, Liangqing Road

学前街35号
No.35, Xueqian Avenue
Tel: 0510-8017 7788

>> 山东 Shandong

东营 / Dongying

西四路616号东胜大厦一楼
Ground Floor, Dongsheng Building, No.616, Xi 4 Road

济南 / Jinan

二环东路3379号百花公园商业楼
Business Building, No.3379, 2 Huan Dong Road

临沂 / Linyi

罗庄区湖北路华盛江泉城大酒店内
Huasheng Jiangquancheng Hotel, Hubei Road, Luozhuang District
Tel: 0539-3118 118

沂蒙十路与三和二街交汇处（澜泊湾国宾馆）
(Lanbowan Hotel) the cross of Qimeng 10 Road and Sanhe 2 Street

青岛 / Qingdao

即墨市万科四季花城
Vanke Wonderland, Jimo

淄博 / Zibo

联通路26号东方之珠
Pearl of the Orient, No.26, Liantong Road
Tel: 0533-3167 099

张店区柳泉路银座商城
Silver Plaza, Liuquan Road, Zhangdian District

>> 上海 Shanghai

上海 / Shanghai

闵行区金汇路463弄28号B栋1楼
Ground Floor, Building B, No.28, Lane 463, Jinhui Road,Minhang District
Tel: 021-6091 3179 / 6126 3559

{华北地区}
Northern China

>> 北京 Beijing

北京 / Beijing

东城区工体北路66号瑞士公寓一层
Ground Floor, Regent Land Apartment, No.66, Gongti Bei Road, Dongcheng District
Tel: 010-6552 0133

朝阳区新源南路甲2号昆仑汇地下一层B101
Shop B101, No.2(Jia), Kunlun Hui, Xinyuan Nan Road, Chaoyang District
Tel: 010-6508 9008

朝阳区光华路国贸商城烟酒屋
Tabacco & Liquor House, China World Shopping Mall, Guanghua Road, Chaoyang District

朝阳区东大桥北京蓝岛商场超市
Supermarket of Blue Island Shopping Center, Dongdaqiao Chaoyang District

朝阳区西大望路华贸中心地下一层烟酒屋
Tabacco & Liquor House, B1,China Central Place, Xidawang Road, Chaoyang District

朝阳区东四环中路189号百盛购物中心
Parkson Shopping Center, No.189, Dong 4 Huan Zhong Road, Chaoyang District

朝阳区安贞西里五区四号楼北京安贞华联烟酒屋
Tobacco & Liquor Department of Hualian Anzhen Store, Building 4, District 5, Anzhen Xili, Chaoyang District

海淀区西三环花园桥北路89号中国外文大厦B座首层
F1，Building B, China Foreign Language Mansion, No.89, Xi 3 huan Bei Road (Huayuan Bridge), Haidian District
Tel: 010-8882 0332

海淀区中关村大街40号当代商城地下一层烟酒部
Tobacco & Liquor Department, B1, Modern Plaza, No.40, Zhongguancun Avenue, Haidian District
Tel: 010-6269 6046

海淀区金源燕莎购物中心北侧一层
Ground Floor, Youyi Shopping City, Haidian District

东城区王府井大街88号乐天银泰地下一层烟酒屋
Tobacco & Liquor Department, B1, Intime Lotte, No.88, Wangfujing Street, Dongcheng District

西城区金融街（临太平桥大街）首层商铺
F1, Financial Street(near the Taiping Bridge Street), Xicheng District
Tel: 010-6629 0265

西城区复兴门外大街长安商场超市
Supermarket of Chang'an Shopping Center, Fuxingmen Wai Street, Xicheng District

丰台区右安门外大街56号2号楼一层
F1, Building 2, No.56, You'an Men Wai Street, Fengtai District
Tel: 010-8397 4579

宣武区广安门外大街168号天虹商场B1层超市
B1, Supermarket of Rainbow Shopping Mall, No.168, Guang'anmen Wai Street, Xuanwu District

顺义区北京首都国际机场三号候机楼
No.3 Terminal Building, Beijing Capital International Airport

>> 河北 Hebei

秦皇岛 / Qinhuangdao

迎宾路99号
No.99, Yingbin Road

唐山市 / Tangshanshi

新华西道商业步行街（唐人街）3-10号
No.3-10, Bussiness Street (Chinatown), Xinhua Xi Road
Tel: 0315-5265 988 / 3898 989

>> 山西 Shanxi

太原 / Taiyuan

府西街 69 号山西国际贸易中心首层
Ground Floor, Shanxi International Trade Center, No.69, Fuxi Street
Tel: 0351-8689 282

>> 黑龙江 Heilongjiang

大庆 / Daqing

让胡路区伟恒时代商务中心08-09
No.08-09, Weiheng Times Business Center, Ranghulu District
Tel: 0459-5906 788

开发区巨鹰国际公寓1-1-7
Shop 1-1-7, Lucky Roc, Development District
Tel: 0459-6692 888

哈尔滨 / Haerbin

香坊区丽顺街10号
No.10, Lishun Road, Xiangfang District
Tel: 0451-8226 7383

>>辽宁 Liaoning

大连 / Dalian

西岗区万达华府276号
No.276,Wanda Huafu, Xigang District
Tel: 0411-8689 7851

沈阳 / Shenyang

沈河区青年大街55号百联购物中心一层
F1, Bailian Shopping Mall, No.55,Qingnian Street, Shenhe District
Tel: 024-8297 7299

沈河区沈阳华府天地购物中心一层19号
No.19, F1, Shopping Mall of Shenyang Rich Gate, Shenhe District
Tel: 024-2259 5519

>>天津 Tianjin

天津 / Tianjin

和平区解放南路188号海信广场地下一层
B1, Hisense Plaza, No.188, Jiefang Nan Road, Heping District
Tel: 022-2319 8902

和平区马场道162号
No.162, Machang Road, Heping District

塘沽区金元宝商厦地下一层
B1, Jinyuanbao Commercial Building, Tanggu District
Tel: 022-2586 6868

塘沽开发区二大街御景园F3号 狄拉西餐厅
F3, Yujing Yuan, 2 Da Street, Tanggu Development District
Tel: 022-6620 9874

{华中地区} Central China

>>湖南 Hunan

长沙 / Changsha

芙蓉区迎宾路82号
No. 82, Yingbin Road, Furong District
Tel: 0731-8890 2879

五一广场新世界百货负一楼
B1, Xinshijie Store, Wuyi Plaza

娄底 / Loudi

娄星区乐坪东街26号(广成大厦)
No.26, Guangcheng Building, Leping Dong Street, Louxing District
Tel: 0738-8271 919

张家界 / Zhangjiajie

金海岸首层
Ground Floor, Golden Coast

>>江西 Jiangxi

赣州 / Ganzhou

章江北大道36号景江德威园A5店
Shop A5, Jingjiangdewei Yuan, No.36, Zhangjiang Bei Avenue
Tel: 0797-8356 557

九江 / Jiujiang

柴桑春天一区8-9栋167-169号
No.167-169, Building 8-9, Zone 1, Chaisang Spring

>>湖北 Hubei

武汉 / Wuhan

武昌区新民主路768号
No.768, Xinminzhu Road,Wuchang District
Tel: 027-8771 2988

江汉区西北湖路3-85号万豪国际大厦A-111-112
A-111-112, Wanhao International Mansion, No.3-85, Northwest Lake Road, Jianghan District
Tel: 027-8549 1268

江汉区武汉国际广场负一楼超级生活馆
Super Living Shop, B1, Wuhan International Plaza, Jianghan District
Tel: 027-8548 3467

江岸区香港路武商量贩店超级生活馆1楼
Ground Floor, Super Living Shop, Wushang Bulksale Chain Company, Hong Kong Road, Jiang'an District

武昌区丁字桥路渔人码头餐厅
Ding Bridge, Wuchang District

襄樊 / Xiangfan

樊城区汉江大道特1号闽发·汉江国际1栋
Building 1, Min Fa Top International, No.1, Hanjiang Avenue, Fancheng District
Tel: 0710-3433 366

>>河南 Henan

洛阳 / Luoyang

南昌路25号
No.25, Nanchang Road

濮阳 / Puyang

中源路273号
No.273, Zhongyuan Road

{华西地区} Western China

>>重庆 Chongqing

重庆 / Chongqing

渝北区新南路160号晶郦馆1-1-2号
Shop 1-1-2, Jing Li Guan, No.160, Xinnan Road, Yubei District
Tel: 13368092134 / 023-6739 6600

江北区观音桥塔坪120号同创国际L113
L113, Topsom World Building, No.120, Guanyinqiao Taping, Jiangbei District
Tel: 023-6786 2776

>>贵州 Guizhou

贵阳 / Guiyang

文昌北路368号
No.368, Wenchang Bei Road
Tel: 0851-5609 979

箭道街149号
No.149, Jiandao Road

遵义 / Zunyi

上海路鹭岛花园1楼2号
No.2, Ground Floor, Ludao Graden, Shanghai Road

>>四川 Sichuan

成都 Chengdu

人民南路4段38号，紫檀1号楼1-1
No.1, Ground Floor, Zitan Building 1, No.38, 4 Duan, Renmin Nan Road
Tel: 028-8592 1899

长寿路8号负4号
(4)No.8, Changshou Road
Tel: 028-8523 6862

红星路三段大科甲巷8号伊藤洋华堂
Ito Yokado, No.8, Kejia Street, Hongxing Road
Tel: 028-8671 5111

建设路2号伊藤洋华堂
Ito Yokado, No.2, Jianshe Road

二环西路一段逸都路6号伊藤洋华堂
Ito Yokado, No.6, Yi Du Road, Western Second Crossroads
Tel: 028-8705 1203

二环路东五段29号万达广场伊藤洋华堂
Ito Yokado, Wanda Square, No.29, Eastern Second Crossroads
Tel: 028-8419 2000

>>陕西 Shanxi

西安 Xi'an

南大街9号塞纳河酒店一楼
F1, La Seine Restaurant Francais,No.9, South Street
Tel: 029-8726 5558

西大街桥梓口208号唐人街A座世纪金花美居生活家一层
Ground Floor, Century Jinhua, Building A, China Town, No.208, Qiaozikou, West Street
Tel: 029-8740 0756

西大街1号钟鼓楼广场金花商场
Ginwa Shopping Center, Bell & Drum Tower Plaza, No.1, West Street
Tel: 029-8721 3610

>>云南 Yunnan

昆明 / Kunming

西山区日新中路319号
No.319, Rixin Zhong Road, Xishan District

五华区翠湖北路太龙公馆-103
No.130, Tailong Gongguan, Cuihu Bei Road, Wuhua District
Tel: 0871-5515 099

丽江 / Lijiang

古城区长水路丽军酒店对面
Opposite the Lijun Hotel, Changshui Road, Gucheng District
Tel: 0888-5173 355

附录二 世界著名葡萄酒产国年份表

APPENDIX 2 WORLD WINES VINTAGE CHART

极差：1=very poor
最好：10=outstanding
资料来源：富隆国际酒业
Reference from: Aussino World Wine

年份Vintage	81	82	83	85	86	87	88	89	90	91	92	93	94	95	96	97	98	99	00	01	02	03	04	05	06	07	08
区域 Appellation	**旧世界 Old World**																										
法国 France																											
波尔多 Bordeaux																											
宝物隆Pomerol	7	10	7	8	8	6	8	10	10	4	4	7	7	9	9	7	10	7	10	8	8	8	9	10	9	7	9
圣达美隆St.Emilion	6	9	7	8	8	4	8	9	10	4	4	6	7	9	9	7	9	7	10	8	8	8	9	10	9	7	9
圣达使提芬St.Estephe	7	10	7	8	8	5	8	9	10	5	4	6	7	9	10	6	9	7	10	8	8	9	9	9	9	7	9
菩依乐Pauillac	7	10	7	8	8	5	8	9	10	5	4	6	7	9	10	6	8	7	10	8	8	9	9	9	9	7	9
圣祖利安St.Julien	7	10	7	8	8	5	8	9	10	5	4	6	7	9	10	6	8	7	10	8	8	9	9	9	9	7	9
玛歌Margaux	6	9	9	8	8	5	8	9	9	4	4	6	7	9	9	6	8	7	9	8	8	8	9	10	9	7	9
格拉芙Graves	6	9	7	8	8	5	8	9	9	4	4	6	6	9	9	6	9	7	10	8	8	8	9	10	9	7	9
苏玳Sauternes	9	8	9	8	9	8	10	9	10	7	7	7	8	8	9	9	9	9	9	10	8	9	8	9	9	9	8
布根地 Burgundy 红 Red	6	5	7	9	7	7	8	9	10	8	6	9	7	9	9	7	8	9	9	8	9	8	7	10	7	6	9
布根地 Burgundy 白White	4	7	8	8	8	6	7	8	9	6	8	8	7	9	10	9	7	8	9	8	9	8	9	9	9	7	9
卢瓦雨河谷Loire Valley	6	7	7	8	8	6	8	9	10	4	5	7	6	9	8	9	7	7	9	8	9	7	8	9	8	8	8
隆河谷Rhone	5	8	9	9	8	5	8	9	10	7	6	5	7	9	8	7	8	9	8	9	7	10	9	9	9	10	8
阿尔萨斯Alsace	7	5	9	8	7	5	8	10	10	5	7	8	6	9	8	9	8	7	7	8	9	7	7	8	7	7	9
香槟Champagne	7	8	7	9	6	4	8	9	10	6	7	6	5	8	9	8	9	8	8	8	9	8	8	8			9
意大利 Italy																											
托斯卡纳Tuscana	5	8	7	9	8	7	9	7	9	7	6	7	8	8	8	10	7	9	8	8	7	8	9	8	9	9	9
彼尔蒙Piemont	5	8	7	9	8	9	9	8	10	6	6	7	7	8	10	9	7	9	8	8	7	8	8	8	9	9	9
德国 Germany	6	4	8	8	7	5	8	9	10	7	8	7	8	8	7	10	7	8	7	10	9	9	8	9	8	9	9
西班牙 Spain	9	9	7	8	8	8	9	9	9	8	9	9	9	9	9	9	8	9	9	9	8	9	9	8	9	7	8
葡萄牙 Portugal	5	10	9	8	6	5	8	7	7	7	5	4	7	8	6	6	7	6	9	9	8	8	8	9	7	7	8
区域 Appellation	**新世界 New World**																										
澳大利亚 Australia																											
南澳省South Australia	6	9	6	8	9	8	7	6	8	8	7	6	7	8	9	7	9	8	9	8	9	9	9	10	9	7	8
西澳省Western Australia	5	9	6	9	8	8	7	5	8	7	7	7	8	9	9	7	7	9	9	9	8	8	9	9	9	7	9
维多利亚省Victoria	5	9	7	8	9	8	6	6	7	8	6	6	7	9	8	7	8	8	9	8	9	8	8	7	8	8	8
美国 U.S.A	6	7	7	9	7	8	8	7	8	9	8	7	8	8	7	10	7	9	9	8	9	9	7	8	8	8	9
新西兰 New Zealand	6	6	9	8	7	6	7	9	7	8	7	6	8	7	9	7	9	8	8	8	7	8	7	8	10	8	8
智利 Chile															7	8	8	9	8	9	7	8	8	9	9	9	9
阿根廷 Argentina															7	9	6	9	8	8	7	8	8	7	9	9	9
南非 South Africa	6	7	5	7	7	7	8	7	6	8	9	8	7	9	7	8	8	7	7	8	8	8	8	9	9	8	7

1. 本医院免费建档，禁止外带
2. 病历保存 5 年，最终解释权归本院所有
3. 本医院不允许重复建病历

病　历　号

病 历 袋

动物种类＿＿＿＿＿＿＿＿ 宠物名＿＿＿＿＿＿＿＿

动物品种＿＿＿＿＿＿＿＿ 性别＿＿＿＿＿＿＿＿

动物出生＿＿＿＿＿＿＿＿ 年＿＿＿＿ 月＿＿＿＿ 日＿＿＿＿

主人姓名＿＿＿＿＿＿＿＿＿＿＿＿＿＿＿＿

住址＿＿＿＿＿＿＿＿＿＿＿＿ 联系电话＿＿＿＿＿＿

×××动物医院

年　　月　　日

病历档案

年　　月　　日　　　　　　　　病历号

主　　人		住　　址		联系方式	
宠物呼名		品　　种		性　　别	
颜　　色		年　　龄		体　　重	
特　　征		免疫情况		其　　他	

主诉及病史：
检查所见：　体温（　　℃）　脉搏（　　次/min）　呼吸（　　次/min）

月　　日	主　要　症　状　及　处　置	兽医师签名

病历档案

年　　月　　日　　　　　病历号

主　　人		住　　址		联系方式	
宠物呼名		品　　种		性　　别	
颜　　色		年　　龄		体　　重	
特　　征		免疫情况		其　　他	

主诉及病史：
检查所见：　体温（　　℃）　脉搏（　　次/min）　呼吸（　　次/min）

月　日	主　要　症　状　及　处　置	兽医师签名

病历档案

年　　月　　日　　　　　　病历号

主　　人		住　　址		联系方式	
宠物呼名		品　　种		性　　别	
颜　　色		年　　龄		体　　重	
特　　征		免疫情况		其　　他	

主诉及病史：
检查所见：　体温（　　℃）　脉搏（　　次/min）　呼吸（　　次/min）

月　日	主　要　症　状　及　处　置	兽医师签名

病历档案

年　　月　　日　　　　　　病历号

主　　人		住　　址		联系方式	
宠物呼名		品　　种		性　　别	
颜　　色		年　　龄		体　　重	
特　　征		免疫情况		其　　他	

主诉及病史：
检查所见：　体温（　　℃）　脉搏（　　次/min）　呼吸（　　次/min）

月　　日	主　要　症　状　及　处　置	兽医师签名

病历档案

年　　月　　日　　　　　　　病历号

主　　人		住　　址		联系方式	
宠物呼名		品　　种		性　　别	
颜　　色		年　　龄		体　　重	
特　　征		免疫情况		其　　他	

主诉及病史：
检查所见：　体温（　　℃）　脉搏（　　次/min）　呼吸（　　次/min）

月　　日	主　要　症　状　及　处　置	兽医师签名

病历档案

年　　月　　日　　　　　　　　病历号

主　　人		住　　址		联系方式	
宠物呼名		品　　种		性　　别	
颜　　色		年　　龄		体　　重	
特　　征		免疫情况		其　　他	

主诉及病史：
检查所见：　体温（　　℃）　脉搏（　　次/min）　呼吸（　　次/min）

月　　日	主　要　症　状　及　处　置	兽医师签名

病历档案

年　　月　　日　　　　　　病历号

主　　人		住　　址		联系方式	
宠物呼名		品　　种		性　　别	
颜　　色		年　　龄		体　　重	
特　　征		免疫情况		其　　他	
主诉及病史：					
检查所见：　体温(　　℃)　脉搏(　　次/min)　呼吸(　　次/min)					

月　日	主 要 症 状 及 处 置	兽医师签名

病历档案

年　　月　　日　　　　　　病历号

主　　人		住　　址		联系方式	
宠物呼名		品　　种		性　　别	
颜　　色		年　　龄		体　　重	
特　　征		免疫情况		其　　他	

主诉及病史：
检查所见：　体温（　　℃）　脉搏（　　次/min）　呼吸（　　次/min）

月　日	主　要　症　状　及　处　置	兽医师签名

病历档案

年　　月　　日　　　　　　病历号

主　　人		住　　址		联系方式	
宠物呼名		品　　种		性　　别	
颜　　色		年　　龄		体　　重	
特　　征		免疫情况		其　　他	

主诉及病史：
检查所见：　体温（　　℃）　脉搏（　　次/min）　呼吸（　　次/min）

月　日	主 要 症 状 及 处 置	兽医师签名

病历档案

年　　月　　日　　　　　　病历号

主　　人		住　　址		联系方式	
宠物呼名		品　　种		性　　别	
颜　　色		年　　龄		体　　重	
特　　征		免疫情况		其　　他	

主诉及病史：
检查所见：　体温（　　℃）　脉搏（　　次/min）　呼吸（　　次/min）

月　日	主　要　症　状　及　处　置	兽医师签名

病历档案

年　　月　　日　　　　　　病历号

主　　人		住　　址		联系方式	
宠物呼名		品　　种		性　　别	
颜　　色		年　　龄		体　　重	
特　　征		免疫情况		其　　他	

主诉及病史：

检查所见：　体温（　　℃）　脉搏（　　次/min）　呼吸（　　次/min）

月　日	主　要　症　状　及　处　置	兽医师签名

病历档案

年　　月　　日　　　　　　　　病历号

主　　人		住　　址		联系方式	
宠物呼名		品　　种		性　　别	
颜　　色		年　　龄		体　　重	
特　　征		免疫情况		其　　他	

主诉及病史：
检查所见：　体温（　　℃）　脉搏（　　次/min）　呼吸（　　次/min）

月　日	主　要　症　状　及　处　置	兽医师签名

病历档案

年　　月　　日　　　　　　病历号

主　　人		住　　址		联系方式	
宠物呼名		品　　种		性　　别	
颜　　色		年　　龄		体　　重	
特　　征		免疫情况		其　　他	
主诉及病史：					
检查所见：　体温（　　℃）　脉搏（　　次/min）　呼吸（　　次/min）					

月　日	主　要　症　状　及　处　置	兽医师签名

病历档案

年　　月　　日　　　　　　病历号

主　　人		住　　址		联系方式	
宠物呼名		品　　种		性　　别	
颜　　色		年　　龄		体　　重	
特　　征		免疫情况		其　　他	

主诉及病史：
检查所见：　体温(　　℃)　脉搏(　　次/min)　呼吸(　　次/min)

月　日	主 要 症 状 及 处 置	兽医师签名

病历档案

年　　月　　日　　　　　　　病历号

主　　人		住　　址		联系方式	
宠物呼名		品　　种		性　　别	
颜　　色		年　　龄		体　　重	
特　　征		免疫情况		其　　他	

主诉及病史：

检查所见：　体温（　　℃）　脉搏（　　次/min）　呼吸（　　次/min）

月　日	主　要　症　状　及　处　置	兽医师签名

病历档案

年　　月　　日　　　　　　　　病历号

主　　人		住　　址		联系方式	
宠物呼名		品　　种		性　　别	
颜　　色		年　　龄		体　　重	
特　　征		免疫情况		其　　他	

主诉及病史：
检查所见：　体温（　　℃）　脉搏（　　次/min）　呼吸（　　次/min）

月　日	主　要　症　状　及　处　置	兽医师签名

病历档案

年　　月　　日　　　　　　病历号

主　　人		住　　址		联系方式	
宠物呼名		品　　种		性　　别	
颜　　色		年　　龄		体　　重	
特　　征		免疫情况		其　　他	

主诉及病史：
检查所见：　体温(　　℃)　　脉搏(　　次/min)　　呼吸(　　次/min)

月　　日	主　要　症　状　及　处　置	兽医师签名

病历档案

年　　月　　日　　　　　　　病历号

主　　人		住　　址		联系方式	
宠物呼名		品　　种		性　　别	
颜　　色		年　　龄		体　　重	
特　　征		免疫情况		其　　他	

主诉及病史：
检查所见：　体温(　　℃)　脉搏(　　次/min)　呼吸(　　次/min)

月　日	主　要　症　状　及　处　置	兽医师签名

病历档案

年　　月　　日　　　　　　病历号

主　　人		住　　址		联系方式	
宠物呼名		品　　种		性　　别	
颜　　色		年　　龄		体　　重	
特　　征		免疫情况		其　　他	

主诉及病史：

检查所见：　体温（　　℃）　脉搏（　　次/min）　呼吸（　　次/min）

月　日	主　要　症　状　及　处　置	兽医师签名

病历档案

年　　月　　日　　　　　　病历号

主　　人		住　　址		联系方式	
宠物呼名		品　　种		性　　别	
颜　　色		年　　龄		体　　重	
特　　征		免疫情况		其　　他	

主诉及病史：
检查所见：　体温(　　℃)　脉搏(　　次/min)　呼吸(　　次/min)

月　日	主要症状及处置	兽医师签名

病历档案

年　　月　　日　　　　　　病历号

主　　人		住　　址		联系方式	
宠物呼名		品　　种		性　　别	
颜　　色		年　　龄		体　　重	
特　　征		免疫情况		其　　他	

主诉及病史：
检查所见：　体温（　　℃）　脉搏（　　次/min）　呼吸（　　次/min）

月　日	主　要　症　状　及　处　置	兽医师签名

病历档案

年　　月　　日　　　　　　病历号

主　人		住　址		联系方式	
宠物呼名		品　种		性　别	
颜　色		年　龄		体　重	
特　征		免疫情况		其　他	

主诉及病史：
检查所见：　体温（　　℃）　脉搏（　　次/min）　呼吸（　　次/min）

月　日	主　要　症　状　及　处　置	兽医师签名

病历档案

年　　月　　日　　　　　　病历号

主　　人		住　　址		联系方式	
宠物呼名		品　　种		性　　别	
颜　　色		年　　龄		体　　重	
特　　征		免疫情况		其　　他	

主诉及病史：

检查所见：　体温（　　℃）　脉搏（　　次/min）　呼吸（　　次/min）

月　日	主要症状及处置	兽医师签名

病历档案

年　　月　　日　　　　　病历号

主　人		住　址		联系方式	
宠物呼名		品　种		性　别	
颜　色		年　龄		体　重	
特　征		免疫情况		其　他	
主诉及病史：					
检查所见：　体温（　　℃）　脉搏（　　次/min）　呼吸（　　次/min）					

月　日	主　要　症　状　及　处　置	兽医师签名

病历档案

年　　月　　日　　　　病历号

主　　人		住　　址		联系方式	
宠物呼名		品　　种		性　　别	
颜　　色		年　　龄		体　　重	
特　　征		免疫情况		其　　他	
主诉及病史：					
检查所见：　体温（　　℃）　脉搏（　　次/min）　呼吸（　　次/min）					

月　日	主　要　症　状　及　处　置	兽医师签名

病历档案

年　　月　　日　　　　　　病历号

主　　人		住　　址		联系方式	
宠物呼名		品　　种		性　　别	
颜　　色		年　　龄		体　　重	
特　　征		免疫情况		其　　他	

主诉及病史：

检查所见：　体温（　　℃）　脉搏（　　次/min）　呼吸（　　次/min）

月　　日	主　要　症　状　及　处　置	兽医师签名

病历档案

年　　月　　日　　　　　　病历号

主　　人		住　　址		联系方式	
宠物呼名		品　　种		性　　别	
颜　　色		年　　龄		体　　重	
特　　征		免疫情况		其　　他	

主诉及病史：

检查所见：　体温(　　℃)　脉搏(　　次/min)　呼吸(　　次/min)

月　日	主　要　症　状　及　处　置	兽医师签名

病历档案

年　　月　　日　　　　　　病历号

主　　人		住　　址		联系方式	
宠物呼名		品　　种		性　　别	
颜　　色		年　　龄		体　　重	
特　　征		免疫情况		其　　他	

主诉及病史：

检查所见：　体温（　　℃）　脉搏（　　次/min）　呼吸（　　次/min）

月　日	主　要　症　状　及　处　置	兽医师签名

病历档案

年　　月　　日　　　　　　病历号

主　　人		住　　址		联系方式	
宠物呼名		品　　种		性　　别	
颜　　色		年　　龄		体　　重	
特　　征		免疫情况		其　　他	

主诉及病史：
检查所见：　体温（　　℃）　脉搏（　　次/min）　呼吸（　　次/min）

月　　日	主　要　症　状　及　处　置	兽医师签名

病历档案

年　　月　　日　　　　　　病历号

主　　人		住　　址		联系方式	
宠物呼名		品　　种		性　　别	
颜　　色		年　　龄		体　　重	
特　　征		免疫情况		其　　他	

主诉及病史：
检查所见：　体温（　　℃）　脉搏（　　次/min）　呼吸（　　次/min）

月　日	主 要 症 状 及 处 置	兽医师签名